D0024688

THE PETRASHEVTSY

A STUDY OF THE RUSSIAN REVOLUTIONARIES OF 1848

The Petrashevtsy were the first large group of socialists in Russia. The name derives from the political meetings which Mikhail Petrashevskii held on Fridays on his Petersburg flat, during the 1840s, but as many as ten separate circles were involved. The Petrashevtsy took ideas from the French socialists of the day, especially Charles Fourier, and modified them through the prism of the Russian temperament, people and reality to form a specifically Russian socialism. Their discussions culminated, in 1848, in the formation of a revolutionary conspiracy. It was Dostoevskii's involvement in this conspiracy which, as he said, 'broke my life in two' and led him to prison and Siberia. Dostoevskii and other leading Petrashevtsy were arrested in April 1849, just as they were on the point of putting their ideas into practice.

In the West, the Petrashevtsy affair has traditionally been treated as an insignificant and slightly comic episode. In the Soviet Union, their ideas have been subjected to the same ideological distortion which has befallen all pre-marxian socialists, they are treated as 'Leninists before Lenin'. This book is based on two years' research in Soviet archives. During this time, the author was able to examine more material on the subject than any previous scholar, including some important and previously undiscovered sources. The result is the first detailed study of the Petrashevtsy in the English language. It shows that the Petrashevtsy have been wrongly neglected. They were Russia's first revolutionary socialists. Their ideas contain, in germ, all the main features of later populist theory. In particular, they were among the very first to suggest that the peasant commune might enable Russia to pass straight to socialism, avoiding the horrors of capitalist development. The Petrashevtsy deserve to be placed alongside the radical democrats Herzen and Belinskii and represent an important early stage in the development of the Russian revolutionary movement. This is a book that should appeal both to specialists in the period and to everyone interested in the origins of the Russian revolution.

THE
PETRASHEVTSY

A STUDY OF THE RUSSIAN
REVOLUTIONARIES OF 1848

J. H. SEDDON

Manchester
University Press

© J.H. Seddon 1985

Published by
Manchester University Press   Oxford Road, Manchester M13 9PL, UK
and 51 Washington Street, Dover, New Hampshire 03820, USA

British Library cataloguing in publication data
Seddon, J.H.
  The Petrashevtsy: a study of the Russian revolutionaries of 1848.
  1. Revolutionists—Soviet Union—History—19th century
  2. Soviet Union—Politics and government—1825–1855
  I. Title
  322.4'2'0947   DK210

Library of Congress cataloging in publication data
Applied for

ISBN 0-7190-1727-0 *cased*

Printed in Great Britain
at the Alden Press, Oxford

TABLE OF CONTENTS

ACKNOWLEDGEMENTS

This book grew out of my doctoral thesis, the work on which began at Oxford in 1975 and was finally completed in 1981, after long periods of study at Leningrad and Moscow Universities and in Paris. I am grateful to the British Council and Department of Education and Science, whose grants made this research possible.

Many people helped me in the course of my research on the Petrashevtsy. I would like to thank three of them above all: Harry Willetts, who guided me in the work from start to finish and without whom it would never have got anywhere; Isaiah Berlin, who gave me inspiration when I really needed it; and Stepan Stepanovich Volk, whose enthusiasm and help were indispensable to my work on all of my visits to the Soviet Union. I'd also like to express my appreciation for the unstinting help I received from *sotrudniki* in many Soviet archives. I'm particularly grateful for the kindness shown me by Bella Ulanovskaia, in introducing me to the Speshnev letters, and Professor Alekseev, in pointing me towards new sources in Pushkinskii Dom. Finally, without the patience and forebearance of Alex Callinicos, this project would never have been brought to a conclusion.

Joanna Seddon
London, June 1985

GLOSSARY OF RUSSIAN WORDS AND PHRASES

barshchina — labour service. Along with *obrok*, one of the two main categories of service performed by serfs for their owners.

chinovnik — Tsarist bureaucrat. Derived from *chin'* rank, referring to the table of 14 bureaucratic ranks drawn up by Peter the Great. Attainment of the ninth rank conferred personal nobility, the fifth hereditary nobility. *Chinovniki* is the plural; *chinovnichestvo* the collective noun.

Chukhonets — member of a minor ethnic group in N. Russia.

deistvitel'nost' — reality, actuality.

dolshchina — a profit-sharing scheme invented by Valerian Maikov.

fel'd-sherbel — a military punishment in which the soldier had to run a gauntlet of knotted whips.

gubernia — Russian province.

gymnaziia — Tsarist secondary school.

ispravnik — chief county police officer.

meshchanin — member of the free town population (shopkeepers, artisans, white-collar workers).

kruzhki — small, tightly knit circles of like-minded people who met for discussion and relaxation.

lishnyi chelovek — the romantic superfluous man.

mir/obshchina — the peasant village commune.

muzhik — Russian peasant.

narod — the common people.

narodniki — the Russian Populists (derived from the idea that they were going 'to the people', *v narod*).

narodnost' — national spirit.

obrok — money in lieu of labour service.

obshchestvo — educated society.

ocherk — a sketch or short story, with a democratic theme.

pochetnyi grazhdanin — 'honorary citizen', a member of the town population exempted from conscription, poll-tax and corporal punishment through service in the lower ranks of the bureaucracy.

rashkol'niki — the schismatics or Old Believers, who broke away from the official (state-controlled) church in the seventeenth century but continued to have a substantial following among the peasants.

raznochinets/tsy—person of indeterminate rank. Used to refer to sons of non-noble free men (clergy, merchants, soldiers) who had risen in society by acquiring an education and entering bureaucratic service.

sobornost'—communal spirit (in the sense of the Russian village commune).

uezd—district within a province.

I — INTRODUCTION

The Russian revolutionary movement has been much studied by scholars, both Western and Soviet. Interest in the subject has been prompted by the desire to understand the antecedents of 1917 and, above all, to explain the origins of Bolshevism. This has led attention to be concentrated on the late nineteenth and early twentieth centuries. It is about this period that the majority of modern studies have been written.

Detailed treatment of the revolutionary movement as a whole begins from the late 1850s and early 1860s. Its earlier history has been examined less systematically, even by such exhaustive scholars as Franco Venturi. The tendency has been to spotlight a few dramatic events and outstanding individuals — the Decembrist rising, Aleksandr Herzen, Vissarion Belinskii, Mikhail Bakunin. In particular, the period between the suppression of the Decembrist revolt in 1825 and the 'thaw' on the accession of Alexander II in 1855 has been treated as a gap, in which isolated individuals operated but no revolutionary movement or group existed. The severity of Nicholas I's absolutism has been regarded as such as to prevent the appearance of any serious radical activity during his reign.

The one outburst of trouble under Nicholas — the affair of the Petrashevtsy — arrested in April 1849 for attending political meetings as Mikhail Petrashevskii's St. Petersburg flat, has traditionally been seen in the West as an insignificant and slightly comic episode. The Petrashevtsy's lack of revolutionary achievement before their arrest has led them to be credited with a lack of revolutionary intention; their admiration for French socialism has caused their ideas to be dismissed as derivative. Their activities have been regarded as not related in either a practical or a theoretical manner to the development of the Russian revolutionary movement. As a result, they have, until recently, been largely ignored by scholars.

The objective of this study is a reappraisal of the nature of radicalism under Nicholas I, through a reassessment of the significance of the Petrashevtsy affair. This will be done by examining the Petrashevtsy themselves, their background, occupations and numbers; by looking in detail at their circles, meetings, publishing and other ventures; and by a thorough analysis of the ideas contained in their speeches, articles, stories and other writings. The aim is to ascertain the nature of the Petrashevtsy's activities, to assess the seriousness of their intentions and to determine the extent to which they were merely passive 'receivers' of Western ideas, the extent to which they contributed to moulding these ideas into a specifically Russian socialism. It is hoped that this will help to shed new light on the development of the Russian revolutionary movement and the place of the Petrashevtsy within it.

The ideas and activities of the Petrashevtsy can only be understood if viewed in the context of the constraints within which they had to operate – those of the Russia of Nicholas I. On Nicholas's accession, Russia was particularly out of step with Western Europe. The political system was still that of the eighteenth century. Russia had been untouched by revolution. It had no hint of a constitution. The country was ruled by an autocratic monarch, from whom all power flowed. He had Ministers, a Senate, a Council of State to advise him and laws to guide him, but all of these could be overturned by his will. The state over which he thus held sway was far too vast for effective control by one man – stretching from the Pacific Ocean to the Caspian, containing approximately sixty million people of over a hundred different nationalities. The Tsar attempted to assert his rule over his domains through an immense, sprawling bureaucracy. Its officials (*chinovniki*), especially at lower and provincial levels, were ignorant, corrupt and inefficient, types immortalised by Nikolai Gogol in *The Government Inspector*. Herzen called them, 'an artificial, uneducated, voracious class, totally incompetent, ... wholly ignorant of all except official forms, a sort of lay priesthood ... sucking the people's blood with thousands of thirsty and dirty mouths'.[1]

The Tsar could only get this system to work at all by virtue of a partnership with the gentry or 'hereditary nobility', who formed approximately one per cent of the population. The principle was: the gentry served the state; in return they received privileges. This meant that, as service nobility (in some cases having shed all ties with the land), they supplied incumbents for all higher positions in the armed services and bureaucracy; as landowners, they acted as the Tsar's 'policemen' (Nicholas' phrase) in the countryside. In exchange for these services, they were exempted from taxes, from corporal punishment, from conscription and granted almost unlimited powers over the rest of the population.

Ninety per cent of the population were peasants, either serfs, who had to work or pay dues on the landowner's estate (according to either the *barshchina* or *obrok* system), who could be flogged, married off, or sent to Siberia at his whim; or state peasants, whose conditions were slightly (but only slightly) better. The peasants bore the state on their backs. They were liable to conscription (twenty-five years service under extremely harsh conditions), paid all the taxes and deprived of virtually all opportunity of education. They had their own form of dress (beards, long hair and smocks), lived in their own contained social world (the wooden huts of the collective village system, known as the *obshchina* or *mir*), had their own oral literature, traditions and superstitions.

In social terms, Russia was thus divided sharply into two camps: the monarchy and the gentry (*obshchestvo* or educated society) on the one hand; and the peasants (the *narod* or people) on the other, two worlds which faced each other with almost total mutual incomprehension. There was almost nothing to link them. The intermediary layers of the population were meagre in numbers, devoid of power and rights. There were some poor gentry, owners of a handful of serfs, but they were almost indistinguishable from the peasants. The combination of appalling communications and serfdom not only kept agriculture backward, but, by restricting the flow of labour, hindered the development of industry. As a result, the towns were underdeveloped, merchants a small and inferior caste, in no way comparable to the European bourgeoisie. The Church, kept under tight control by the state (via the Holy Synod), was not adequate as a uniting force. Its rigidity and dogmatism alienated much of educated society. Though the lower classes were in general religious, the Church's close links with authority had turned an influential section of them (especially the merchants) away from it, towards the *raskol'niki* (sectarians or Old Believers). There was very little social mobility and even less social cohesion in Russia.

Nicholas was not the man to change this system. Reared for the parade ground, not for rule, he came to power unexpectedly in the aftermath of the Decembrist rising. This was the first real attempt at challenging the autocracy. It was very much a challenge from within the ruling order, in the tradition of the nobles' *putsch*. Its perpetrators were members of the aristocracy, mostly army officers, who had become imbued with liberal and constitutional ideas as a result of Russia's involvement with Western Europe during the French Revolutionary and Napoleonic wars. They tried to take advantage of the confusion arising on Alexander I's death in 1825 with an extremely badly-planned and half-hearted insurrection on Senate Square. Five of the leaders were hung, the rest exiled to Siberia.

Nicholas made it his permanent concern to ensure that nothing like this ever happened again. He saw it as his mission to save Russia from the horrors of liberalism and revolution, to impose order, stability and reaction. To this end, he began his reign by introducing a much severer and more arbitary system of censorship. Censors were exhorted to 'search for double meanings', editors were held personally liable for anything which appeared in their publications, only the subservient *Syn otechestva* was allowed a political section. Aleksandr Nikitenko, a censor himself, wrote, 'Minister Uvarov is oppressing the journals terribly ... of course, this may be done for important state reasons, in this country we are extremely rich in state reasons. If we were forbidden ... to brush a fly from our noses, this would be for state reasons.'[2] In the first known instance of the use of psychiatry for political purposes, the writer Peter Chaadaev was confined as a lunatic for suggesting that Russia had no history. At the same time, Nicholas created the Third Department of His Majesty's Chancery. This was the first modern political police, reporting directly to the Tsar and responsible for gathering information on subversive activity of all kinds, in every corner of the Empire. Count Sergei Uvarov, Minister of Education, developed an ideology to express the intentions of Nicholas's regime. Its motto was, 'Orthodoxy, Autocracy, Nationality', a reactionary retort to the revolutionary slogan, 'Liberty, Equality, Fraternity'. Nationality (*narodnost*) meant an extreme Russian nationalism and chauvinism. Its essence was spelled out by Count Aleksandr Benkendorf, first head of the Third Department, Russia's past is admirable; her present more than magnificent; as to her future, it is beyond the grasp of the most daring imagination'.[3] Nicholas' intentions were thus to freeze Russian society in its eighteenth century mould, to resist all pressures for change and reform. To do this he mobilised all the forces at his disposal. It was a regime of systematic repression. These are the reasons that led Herzen to declare, 'it is oppressive and vile to live in Russia'[4] and which have caused Nicholas' reign often to be regarded as a period of unrelieved gloom in Russian history.

It is true that the twenties and thirties were dark years – Nicholas seemed wholly to have succeeded in his aims. But, by the mid 1840s, Russia had experienced twenty years of peace and stability. The natural, unavoidable result of this was that even Nicholas' despotism mellowed, the regime relaxed its grip a little. The effects of small changes, ac-cumulating over the years, began to make themselves felt. The govern-ment hesitantly began to contemplate small steps towards reform and modernisation. The vigilance against subversives slackened and life began to open up. Change could be seen to be taking place and a new atmosphere prevailed in the social, economic and intellectual spheres.

Educational reform inaugurated social change. The impulse to reform came from Nicholas's wish to impose his authority more effectively by increasing the efficiency of his bureaucracy. This meant both enlarging it and raising the calibre of its staff. This led him to sanction an expansion of higher education and improvement of the quality of its teaching, under the auspices of Count Uvarov. By the 1840s, the gymnasia and univer- sities were turning out not just a larger number of educated Russians, but a larger number of those who could properly be called intelligentsia, i.e. people in whom an enlightened education had aroused a critical attitude to the regime and a predeliction for the discussion of alternative ideas. Previously, the intelligentsia had been few in number and had come almost exclusively from the richer levels of the gentry class. Uvarov's reforms, in spite of a large number of restrictions, led to the opening up of the educational system to poorer gentry and a section of the non-noble classes (especially priests' sons). Education began to form a bridge from the lower to the upper caste. The result was the emergence of the first examples of a new type of intelligentsia, whose members (known as *raznochintsy*) were poor, *declassé*, and, in general, far more disaffected from the regime than the intelligentsia of the preceeding generation.

In the economic realm, Russia was still extraordinarily backward compared to Western Europe. But, the population was growing fast, the pace of industrial development quickening. The larger towns, and especially St. Petersburg, began to manifest the rapid growth and appalling artisan conditions typical of the first phases of industrial- isation; a sizeable textile industry grew up around Moscow. In 1842, Nicholas belatedly authorised the construction of the first railway line inside Russia; steamships began to run on the Volga. All this contributed to a sense of movement in Russian society, creating new problems, destabilising and exposing the inadequacies of the traditional order.

The most glaring problems, however, were in agriculture, based on the inhumane and wretchedly inefficient system of serfdom. A drive to commercialise grain production was spurred on by increasing demand from the industrialising countries of Western Europe, particularly England, after the repeal of the Corn Laws, and Russia's grain exports doubled in the years 1835–45. This made the limitations imposed by serfdom painfully evident. Nicholas (who was no fool), found the problem impossible to ignore. In the late 1830s he authorised Pavel Kiselev to take measures to improve the condition of the state peasants. He set up a series of very secret committees to examine the state of the landowners' serfs and in 1842 went as far as to admit, 'It is necessary at least to pave the way for a very gradual transition to another order of things'.[5] Nicholas seems to have been aware of the economic necessity of abolishing serfdom, but to have felt it impossibly dangerous to attempt. Though he did nothing, his remarks and committees helped to make emancipation a major issue of the day.

But it was in the intellectual sphere that relaxation was the most pronounced. The mid-1840s were marked by an explosion of new literary talent; the appearance of a new 'natural' style of literature; a new freedom and liveliness of intellectual discussion and debate, partly inspired by a new ease of availability of Western ideas, and channelled to an increasingly large educated public through the medium of the journal.

In literature, the 1820s and 1830s had been the age of poetry and of two great writers, Aleksandr Pushkin and Mikhail Lermontov. In the 1840s the short story took over. Although the only great work to appear in the decade was Gogol's *Dead Souls*, the period was remarkable for the number of new and talented writers who burst onto the scene. Many of those later to become great novelists produced their first youthful works: Fedor Dostoevskii, *Poor Folk* and *The Double*; Ivan Turgenev, the first parts of his *Sketches from a Hunter's Album*; Ivan Goncharov, *A Common Tale*; Mikhail Saltykov, *A Tangled Affair*; Dmitrii Grigorovich, *The Village* and *Poor Anton*. Lev Tolstoi, Nikolai Leskov and Aleksei Pisemskii also made their literary debuts. Much of this writing was immature, naive and poorly constructed, but there was an extraordinary richness and freshness of talent and excitement in literary life. It was the beginning of the age of the novel in Russia.

The new literature adopted a new tone − down to earth, critical and realistic, a great contrast to the lofty romanticism of the preceeding decade. It became known as the natural school. The inspiration for this derived from Gogol (though younger writers preferred more straightforward realism to his satire); the theory was worked out by Belinskii, a professional literary critic and one of the most influential figures of his time. Belinskii's keyword was *deistvitel'nost* (reality). Art had no existence of its own. It found justification and merit according, first, to the faithfulness with which it depicted real life, and secondly, to the artist's attitude to his subject. For his work to be successful, the artist had to be inspired by a conscious goal — the search for truth and social justice. Belinskii was thus advocating a committed art. But it was not yet a completely utilitarian one, far less so than that which Chernyshevskii was to argue for in the sixties. Belinskii believed that man and nature, art and reality, were closely intertwined. So, the truer art's depiction of reality, the higher its aesthetic merit was likely to be. Truth was defined not as the preaching of a doctrine, but as the artist's instinctive reaction to a particular subject.

The change of atmosphere between the thirties and forties was most obvious in the arena of philosophical and political debate. The years after the suppression of the Decembrist revolt had been years of intro-spection, self-absorption and gloom. Intellectuals felt impotent and alienated from Russian life. There was absolutely no public outlet for their activities. So, they sought refuge in German philosophy and, in particular, in the romantic idealism of Schelling. This taught that real life, the particular, was unimportant and called on the individual to plunge himself into the universal, the ideal life of the spirit, which was all that mattered, and in which everything, self, humanity and the world, (but especially the self) was subsumed. Towards the end of the decade, the vogue for Schelling gave way to adulation of Hegel. Hegel shared Schelling's desire to absorb the particular into the universal, but com-bined it with a belief in the omnipotence of reason. His system allowed endless (and abstruse) debate about the way in which reason was realised in history, and about the role of individuals and of nations in this process, and was the natural culmination of the absorption in speculative philosophy. The centre of idealist philosophy in Russia was the circle formed around Nikolai Stankevich in Moscow. Stankevich himself died of consumption in 1840, but his circle included many of the leading writers and thinkers of the next decade: Belinskii, Bakunin, Konstantin Aksakov, Iuri Samarin, Timofei Granovskii, Mikhail Katkov. These men were largely responsible for the diffusion and lasting influence of Hegel in Russia. The circle broke up on its founder's death. Already, by this time, its members had carried their Hegelianism to its farthest limits and had begun to seek in Hegel's writings a way of reintegrating the individual into the real world. This took the form, first of a recon-ciliation with autocracy, through a very literal interpretation of the formula 'what is rational is real'; then of a rebellion against Hegel and a drift in other directions.

The 1840s saw a more political orientation of thought and a differen-tiation of intellectual trends. The clearest intellectual divide was between the supporters of the government and the rest of educated society. The official doctrine was that of Official Nationality, as developed by Uvarov. Outside immediate government circles, the most notorious proponents of these ideas were Faddei Bulgarin and Nikolai Grech, joint editors of two major newspapers, *Syn otechestva* and *Severnaia pchela*. These two were zealous informers on their fellow writers and editors and sent a constant stream of denunciations to the Third Department. The chief theoreticians of the doctrine were the historians Mikhail Pogodin and Stepan Shevyrev. Its chief manifestation was a strident, often crude Russian nationalism, derived from a distinction between the nature of the state in Russia and Western Europe. The Western states were said to have originated by conquest; the Russian state by an 'invitation to rule'. The Western states represented the Roman principle − reason; Russia, the Eastern principle − faith. The Western states had from their origin been divided and conflict-ridden; Russia, on the other hand, had evolved peacefully and harmoniously under the creative hand of a beneficent autocracy. Russian civilisation was qualitatively superior and all attempts to import the Western 'malady' had to be resisted.[6]

The rest of educated society was oppositional, in one way or another. The major split was that between 'Slavophiles' and 'Westerners'. These terms originated in friendly discussions between former members of the Stankevich circle, but soon came to stand for two distinct and opposed schools of thought. The leading representatives of the Slavophiles were Aleksei Khomiakov, Ivan Kireevski, Konstantin Aksakov and Samarin; of the Westerners, Belinskii, Herzen, Granovskii and Aleksandr Kavelin. Disagreement centred on the definition of individual freedom and the interpretation of Russian history.

The Slavophiles were believers in the organic society. This was a society in which individuals achieved complete harmony with the community and did not see themselves as separate from it. Freedom was defined as spontaneous identification with the community, or *sobornost'*. The social solidarity of *sobornost'* grew up on the basis of tradition, custom and faith. The Orthodox religion was a very important part of this social bond. The Slavophiles believed that all the elements of the organic society had existed in the peasant villages of pre-Petrine Russia. They pointed to the village commune or *mir* as surviving proof of this. They were opponents of the autocracy. The organic nature of Russian society had been destroyed by the state. The reforms of Peter the Great, based on divisive Western principles, had played the major role in disrupting the original harmony.

For the Westerners, the rebellion against Hegel had taken the left-Hegelian form of the assertion of the primacy of the individual over the absolute. The autonomy of the individual became for them the greatest existing principle. They believed that history had a goal — the emancipation of the individual from external constraints and the maximising of his conscious freedom of choice. Progress took place through the destruction of all traditional and irrational bonds and their replacement by rational legal and political norms. The state played an important historical role in establishing the rule of law and thus paving the way for the emancipation of the individual. The Westerners admired Peter the Great, in spite of the autocratic nature of his regime, because he had at least made a start at rousing the Russian people from their instinctual slumbers and raising them to the level of self-consciousness and reason.

The Slavophiles thus looked to traditional Russian values; the Westerners to European ones, to the principles of the Enlightenment, the French Revolution and liberalism. Both sides were utopians in their way. The Slavophiles looked backwards to an idealised version of Russia's medieval past; the Westerners looked forwards to an artificially constructed rational society in which individual freedom would be maximised. The differences between them, however, should not be exaggerated. The views of neither side were clear cut. They were all opposed to autocracy (even though some parts of Slavophile theory were directly inspired by Pogodin), almost all in favour of emancipation and some sort of democratic reforms. They all believed that Russia had some kind of mission and would be able to solve problems that the West had been unable to deal with. They all (eventually) came to see the village commune as having a particular role to play in this process. As Herzen said, 'Yes we were their opponents, but very strange ones. We had the same love, but not the same way of loving ... Like Janus or the two-headed eagle they and we looked in different directions, while one heart throbbed within us.'[7]

There were relatively few Slavophiles and their ideas were comparatively coherent. The Westerners formed a broader body with a less homogeneous world view. They were united in their opposition to Official Nationality and Slavophilism. They were all in favour of individual freedom, seen as guaranteed by representative government, democratic liberties and emancipation of the serfs. But, by the mid 1840s a rough distinction between liberals and radicals had appeared. The leading liberals were Granovskii, Turgenev, Kavelin and Boris Chicherin; the leading radicals Herzen and Belinskii. The two groupings differed in their attitude to art, religion, the French Revolution and the 'capitalist' society of Western Europe (by which the Russians really meant France). The liberals were supporters of 'art for art's sake'; the radicals believed in art's social mission. The liberals were in general religious; the radicals had, under the influence of left Hegelianism and, in particular, Ludwig Feuerbach, become more or less atheists. In French revolutionary history, the liberals were admirers of the Girondins, of moderate revolutionism, reasonableness and legal norms; the radicals preferred the Jacobins and accepted the necessity, in some circumstances, of violence, bloodshed and dictatorship. The liberals were mostly uncritical of Western society; the radicals (above all Herzen) were sickened by the vulgarity, complacency and corruption of Louis-Philippe's 'bourgeois monarchy'. The similarities between the two groups were much stronger than the differences, which amounted, as much as anything, to a question of tone. Radicals and liberals had not yet separated into the two hostile camps they were to become in the sixties.

However, in the 1840's, it was the more radical figures among the Westerners who won the allegiance of Russia's educated youth. Herzen and, above all, Belinskii were the most popular writers of the day, exerting an enormous influence on the younger generation.

Belinskii stood out among the established writers of the older generation as one of the first examples of the *raznochinnyi intelligent* in Russia, i.e. of those who depended on their literary work for a living. Literature was for him a life and death affair. He was nervous, irritable, unstable and incapable of moderation. He leapt from one extreme idea to another. As a member of the Stankevich circle in the thirties, he, together with Bakunin, had carried the Hegelian idea of 'reconciliation with reality' to almost ludicrous lengths, descending to panegyrics to the Russian autocracy. Then, in 1840, after an intense intellectual struggle, he threw off his Hegelianism and espoused 'the social idea', the human personality' and 'dignity and sanctity of the individual'.[8] Belinskii's strength and influence flowed from his passionate moralism, his complete sincerity and total adhesion to any cause he espoused. It was this that made his torrents of hastily written, often clumsy prose eagerly devoured all over Russia. It was this that led him, as literary critic first for *Otechestvennye zapiski* (1839—45) and then *Sovremennik* (from 1845 to his early death, mainly from overworking, in 1848), to become the 'literary dictator' of the age.[9]

Literature was for Belinskii the centre of life. But, the essence of art was for him bound up with its social and political content and he used his literary criticism to argue for social and political change. His views were most strikingly expressed in his *Letter to Gogol*, a reply to Gogol's 'betrayal' of the democratic cause, by the publication of his reactionary *Selected Passages from Correspondence with Friends*. In an intense outpouring of feeling, Belinskii denounced Gogol as 'preacher of the whip, apostle of ignorance, champion of obscurantism and black reaction'; the Orthodox Church as 'the prop of the knout and the toady of despotism'; Russia as a country which 'offers the terrible spectacle of a land where men buy and sell other men without even the cant of the Americans, who say negroes are not men'. He called for 'the awakening in the people of a feeling of human dignity', declaring 'Russia sees her salvation not in mysticism, or aestheticism, or piety, but in the achievements of education, civilisation and humane culture.'[10]

Herzen, the leisured son of a wealthy landowner, was in social terms a more typical representative of the intelligentsia of his generation. The illegitimacy of his birth, however, helped to foster a natural rebelliousness and carry him intellectually to a position far more radical than his contemporaries in the 1830s and 40s. He had a piercing brain, a burning independence of outlook, the gift of wit and conversation, and a broad human sympathy and understanding. All this contributed to his becoming one of the outstanding political writers of the nineteenth century. His radicalism can be traced back to the oath to avenge the Decembrists which he and his friend Nikolai Ogarev took at the age of sixteen.

The early evolution of his ideas was romantic, but romantic in the more political sense of the French Saint-Simonians and Schiller, rather than Schelling. Throughout the 1830s he remained more political, less absorbed in philosophy than others of his contemporaries. He first read Hegel in the early 1840s, later than the members of the Stankevich circle, quickly progressing through Feuerbach to his own very particular version of left-Hegelianism. His principles veered between historicism (a slightly more materialist version of Hegel's theories) and an anarchistic rejection of everything outside the individual ego (this was most clearly expressed in *Letters from the Other Shore*, written in the aftermath of 1848). His writings in the 1840s fall into two categories, philosophical and literary. His two major philosophical articles, *Dilettantism in Science* and *Letters on the Study of Nature*, did more than anything else at this time to popularise left-Hegelian ideas in Russia. His short stories, especially *Who is to Blame?* were more conspicuous for their didacticism than their literary merit. The main theme was the right to free love, but they included attacks on serfdom and all constraints in Russian society which hindered the free development of the individual. Herzen went to Europe in 1847, and there became caught up in the events of 1848, thus accidentally beginning his career as Russia's first political emigré in the sense of a force in Russian politics, operating from outside Russia. In the 1840s his career was very much at its first stage. It was only under Alexander II that he began publication of *Kolokol* and developed his theory of a Russian socialism based on the peasant commune.

The ideas of Herzen and Belinskii were propagated through the medium of the journal, which, in the absence of public life, became the forum in which theoretical discussion was concentrated and ideological battles fought. The number of periodicals in Russia rose from 47 in 1826 to 130 in 1850. There were two major anti-government journals: *Otechestvennye zapiski* edited by Andrei Kraevskii; and *Sovremennik*, Pushkin's old journal, revived in 1847 by Nikolai Nekrasov and Ivan Panaev. A third, less successful, but often more radical journal was *Finskii vestnik* (1845–50), run by Fedor Dershau. The old-established reactionary journals – *Syn otechestva, Severnaia pchela* and *Biblioteka dlia chteniia* run by the notorious triumvirate of Grech, Bulgarin and Osip Senkovskii, were badly hit by the new competition. New, more lively right wing journals, *Moskvitianin* (edited by Pogodin) and *Maiak*, failed to attract a wide readership. The circulation of *Biblioteka dlia chteniia*, the most popular pro-government publication shrank from 5 to 7,000 in the 1830s to 3,000 by 1847: In contrast, *Otechestvennye zapiski* had a circulation of 4,000 by 1847; that of *Sovremennik* rose under its new ownership from 233 in 1846 to over 3,000 in 1848. The actual readership was many times greater – subscriptions were high, so copies were passed from hand to hand and were available in public reading rooms and cafes, such as Izler, Vol'f, Passazh and Ivanov's, where they were often read aloud.

Through *Otechestvennye zapiski, Sovremennik* and *Finskii vestnik*, the ideas of Herzen and Belinskii became known to educated youth all over Russia. Numerous contemporaries testify to the crucial role played by Herzen and Belinskii in the intellectual formation of a generation. Vladimir Stasov remembered how, at the Law School in the early forties:

> Belinskii was definitely our real teacher. No classes, courses, essay writing, exams and so on did as much for our education and development as Belinskii on his own with his monthly articles. In this we were no different

from the rest of Russia of that time. Of course, Belinskii's enormous importance wasn't just due to the literary aspects of his work: he purified everything for us, he formed our characters, he felled, with his strong man's hand, the patriarchal predujices by which the whole of Russia had lived until then ... We are all his direct pupils.

According to Petr Pekarskii, the students of Kazan University learned Belinskii's articles off by heart. As Ivan Asksakov (Konstantin's brother) regretfully wrote, 'the name of Belinskii is known to every thinking young man, to everyone who is hungry for a breath of fresh air in the stinking bog of provincial life'.[11]

The success of Belinskii, Herzen and other radicals in getting their ideas across in the journals was partly due to their slipping political and social criticism into their articles in such a way that the censors didn't notice it, but the public could read between the lines. This art had been developed to a high degree in Russia – even *Sovremennik*'s fashion section was noted for its radical opinions; Belinskii in particular excelled at it. However, the main reason why criticism of the regime got into print in the 1840s was a more indulgent attitude on the part of the censors, many of whom (such as Nikitenko) were closet liberals. The reduction of the censorship's rigour applied not only to works appearing in Russia, but also to the importation of foreign books. An astonishing quantity of forbidden works, especially those of the French socialists, flooded into Russia during the decade.

The views of Herzen and Belinskii were thus widely disseminated among the younger members of educated society. However, a significant section of this young intelligentsia also took advantage of the opportunities to get hold of Western socialist literature and were greatly influenced by it, in many cases becoming convinced socialists. The outcome was the formation of socialist and revolutionary circles in different parts of Russia, but, especially, around Petrashevskii in St. Petersburg.

The Petrashevtsy were united by an avid interest in Western and especially French socialist ideas. They drew together around the reading of foreign literature, in particular, banned socialist writers, whose works were housed in a collective library kept at Petrashevskii's. These young radicals met on appointed days for earnest discussion of a radical approach to philosophical, economic, political and literary questions. They spread their views beyond the confines of the circles through their literary and journalistic activity (the young Dostoevskii was one of the most prominent of the Petrashevtsy) and especially through the *Pocket Dictionary of Foreign Words*, a mini-encyclopedia of socialist propaganda. After the outbreak of revolution in France in 1848, the tone of the circles became increasingly dangerous and subversive. A section of the Petrashevtsy came to accept not only that revolution was necessary in Russia but that they should organise to promote it. By March 1849 a revolutionary conspiracy had been formed, a printing press purchased.

Petrashevskii's extreme views and extrovert behaviour had attracted the attention of the Third Department as early as 1844. In spring 1848 his circulation of a letter on emancipation led the Tsar to order a police watch to be put on his movements. Responsibility for this was placed with Ivan Liprandi, an agent of the Ministry of Internal Affairs. He recruited three spies, Petr Antonelli, Nikolai Naumov and Vasilii Shaposhnikov. Antonelli was given a job in Petrashevskii's department of the Foreign Ministry and managed to infiltrate the circle, attending the last seven Friday meetings, 11 March to 22 March 1849. Beginning from 23 March 1849 over two hundred people were arrested, 122 seriously investigated by a special Commission of Inquiry headed by General Ivan Nabokov. On 22 December 1849, twenty-one people were sentenced to hard labour or exile in Siberia or army service in the Caucasus, for their 'criminal intentions of overthrowing the existing state order in Russia'.

In their adoption of socialism, these young radicals went further than Herzen or Belinskii, both of whom, though they leaned towards socialism in the 1840s, could not be called socialists in any definite sense. Belinskii was a humanist, a radical democrat and a bitter enemy, in the theoretical sphere, of theology and metaphysics, in the practical, of serfdom, absolutism, the Orthodox Church, of every sort of injustice and oppression, but there was no socialist doctrine in his writings − they would not have converted anybody to socialism. Herzen was quite certainly a socialist and influential in the development of a specifically Russian, populist socialism. But he formulated his ideas later, in the 1850s and 1860s. Also, he always regarded individual liberty as more important than socialist theory. Intellectually, therefore, the Petrashevtsy stood close to Herzen and Belinskii and were very much part of the Western tradition.[12] But, their interest in and adoption of socialist and revolutionary ideas placed them on the extreme left-wing of this movement.

The Petrashevtsy circles were thus part of the general intellectual movement of the time. Their appearance must be seen in the context of a radicalisation of the younger members of the intelligentsia in the years before 1848. This occurred as a result of a relaxation in the political atmosphere (though Nicholas's regime could still not be called anything but oppressive). The Petrashevtsy were the first large group of socialists and revolutionaries in Russia, the first to enjoy a widespread measure of sympathy in educated society. They were also the first group of Russian radicals not to come primarily from the upper layers of Russian society. In their social origins, in their ideas, their materialism and atheism, their views on art, their advocacy of popular and revolutionary methods of action, and above all in their emphasis on the socialist possibilities of the peasant commune, the Petrashevtsy were the direct forerunners of the populists of the 1860s and 1870s. Many of the Petrashevtsy were indeed later to become involved in the populist movement.

The study of the Petrashevtsy has suffered more than most subjects from the vicissitudes of Russian history and historiography. The intimate connection between the ideas of the Petrashevtsy and the general intellectual trends of their time was long ignored; their numbers were underestimated; doubts were cast on the genuinely socialist, let alone revolutionary nature of their convictions; they were seen as trivial and irrelevant to the history of the Russian radical movement.

The underestimation the Petrashevtsy occurred because the importance of the affair was deliberately played down, first by the government, later by its liberal opponents. After the arrest of the Petrashevtsy in 1849, the government of Nicholas I, terrified at the thought of socialist and revolutionary ideas spreading among the Russian youth, labelled the case a mere 'conspiracy of ideas' which was 'far from having either the importance or the widespread nature which the town gossip at first attributed to it'.[13] Then, the emergence of the populists in the 1860s helped to throw their immediate predecessors into shadow. The populists began to act directly against the government, whereas the Petrashevtsy had been arrested when they were just on the point of putting their ideas into practice. And, though former Petrashevtsy were later active in the populist movement, they tended to lie low and leave the leadership to others. The result was that, except for material published in Herzen's *Kolokol*, nothing of significance was written about the Petrashevtsy until the end of the nineteenth century. The serious study of the Petrashevtsy was begun in the pre-revolutionary and revolutionary period by a group of liberal historians headed by Vasilii Semevskii who, as the Petrashevets Dmitrii Akhsharumov said, went to work, 'like an archaeologist, digging us Petrashevtsy, forgotten by everyone, out of the ground',[14] and published voluminous concoctions of quotations from the archives. But, in the interests of those Petrashevtsy who survived Siberia (the last of them, Nikolai Kashkin, died as late as 1901), the liberal historians continued the government's policy of concealing the size and revolutionary nature of the circle. They successfully established the opinion that the Petrashevtsy were a small group of moderate liberals, harmless disciples of the peaceful theories of Charles Fourier, who had nothing in common with the revolutionaries of later years. Aleksandr Pypin, for example, maintained that the Petrashevtsy's socialism was 'completely harmless in a political sense', just a manifestation of 'platonic idealism';[15] Nikolai Rusanov called Petrashevskii 'a martyr of Fourierist apoliticism'.[16]

After the revolution, this view was accepted by the Soviet historians of the Pokrovskii school. They denounced the Petrashevtsy for their 'bourgeois tendency' just as vehemently as the liberal historians had defended them for it. Pokrovskii believed the Petrashevtsy belonged, 'not even to the history of democratic thought in Russia, but simply to the history of Russian liberalism'.[17] His followers went further. According to G. Beshkin, the Petrashevtsy had not an idea of their own, but 'took their ideology from their 'elder' Western brothers'.[18] Leonid Raiskii called them 'bourgeois-capitalist ideologues', and summed up their ideas as, 'to contribute with all means to the flourishing and development of capitalism in Russia'.[19] It was not until the 1940s that the wind began to change. The hitherto suppressed information about Speshnev's conspiracy came to light. Historians such as Aleksandr Nifontov, Izrail Bliumin, Vasilii Evgrafov and Vera Leikina-Svirskaia began to argue that it was not a 'conspiracy of ideas' but 'a worked-out plan for a large political organisation to move towards the overthrow of the autocratic system'.[20]

Today the Petrashevtsy are regarded as the socialists and revolutionaries they undoubtedly were. The former view of them has been turned on its head, but the dogmatism remains. The Petrashevtsy have been incorporated into the ideological apparatus invoked for the historical legitimisation of the Soviet regime. Their ideas are taken out of context and subjected to the distortion that has befallen those of Belinskii, Herzen and other pre-Marxian Russian socialists. The writings about them now have a nationalist tint. Evgrafov writes, 'Soviet people today commemorate with patriotic pride the names of Petrashevskii, Speshnev, Mombelli, Khanykov, L'vov, Pleshcheev, Balasoglo, Tol' and many other Petrashevtsy who raised high the flag of revolution against Tsarism in Russia a hundred years ago.'[21] Their ideas are presented as being of Russian inspiration and the view that the Western socialists had a 'decisive influence' on their formation is said to be 'completely un-founded'.[22] In addition, some aspects of the Petrashevtsy's ideas are ignored, others exaggerated, to make them seem, as nearly as possible, Marxist. We are told, for example, that only the backwardness of Russian industry 'prevented them from understanding the importance of the working class' and from 'arriving at the theory of historical materialism'.[23] The ideological restrictions imposed on writing about the Petrashevtsy have made them a subject many Soviet scholars prefer to avoid. Though the Petrashevtsy are a compulsory part of every Soviet history course, in school and university, the only serious Soviet work devoted to them is Leikina-Svirskaia's unpublished doctoral thesis, which bears the obvious marks of having been written in Stalin's last years.

If the study of the Petrashevtsy in the Soviet Union has been one-sided, very little attention has, until recently, been paid to them elsewhere. Today, although their importance in the history of the Russian intelligentsia is no longer contested and the group has become a subject of interest in the West (see, for example, Joseph Frank's recent book on Dostoevskii), a thorough study of them has yet to be written in any language.[24]

The aim of this work is to take a fresh look at the Petrashevtsy and to clear away some of the misconceptions which have crept into the analysis of their circles. This reappraisal is based on a more comprehensive collection of material than previously available to scholars. The main published source on the Petrashevtsy is the volumes of the *Delo petrashevtsev*, which contain material relating to their trial. Also relevant are the memoirs, collected works etc. of individual Petrashevtsy and their contemporaries; and the radical journals of the 1840s, to which many Petrashevtsy contributed. Among these published materials, particularly interesting are the Petrashevtsy's writings in *Finskii vestnik*, the importance of which has generally been ignored. In addition, a great deal of valuable material remains unpublished, including 111 out of 136 parts of the *Delo petrashevtsev* in the Central State Military History Archive (TsGVIA); the reports of police spies in The Central State Archive of the October Revolution (TsGAOR); and the Balasoglo *fond* in the Central State Historical Archive in Leningrad (TsGIAL). A number of new discoveries have recently been made, notably the Petrashevtsy's version of *Paroles d'un croyant* in TsGAOR, and the letters of Nikolai Speshnev in the Archive of Irkutsk Oblast', a major collection, which I was fortunate enough to be the first scholar to use.

II — THE PETRASHEVTSY CIRCLES

The name Petrashevtsy is usually taken to refer to the twenty-one young men sentenced as a result of the affair, almost all of whom were regular visitors to the political meetings which Mikhail Butashevich-Petrashevskii held on Fridays at his St. Petersburg flat from 1845 to 1849. In fact, these men were only the tip of the iceberg. It is possible to identify ten distinct groupings, apart from that of Petrashevskii, whose composition overlapped with Petrashevskii's and at which the same subjects were discussed and it is probable that there were many more (a lot of material, diaries etc. is known to have been destroyed in 1849[1]). These included, in St. Petersburg, the circles around the Beketov brothers, Valerian Maikov, Aleksandr Maderski, Irinakh Vvedenskii, the famous translator of Dickens, the young guards officer Nikolai Mombelli, and the hot-headed students grouped around Petr Shaposhnikov, as well as the two groups very closely associated with Petrashevskii – those of Nikolai Kashkin and Sergei Durov. There were sympathetic circles in other towns, the most important at Kazan University, which the Petrashevtsy set on the path to becoming a major centre of student unrest, but also in Rostov (around Nikolai and Vladimir Kaidanov), Reval, Tambov, Kostroma and Moscow. As Ivan Liprandi, the officer in charge of the investigation, said, the Petrashevskii affair had a 'broad and substantial base' which went far beyond the meetings at Petrashevskii's. Over two hundred were arrested in connection with it and released for lack of evidence, many more were never arrested at all. Members of Petrashevskii's circle estimated their known sympathisers at between five and eight hundred.[2]

The circles linked with Petrashevskii deserve to be treated as a single group. Their members were united by strong social, generational and ideological ties. The similarities in their outlook and origins were far greater than any differences which existed between them. They were such as to enable the Petrashevtsy clearly to be distinguished from other circles of Westerners and radicals active in the 1840s. Significantly, the

Petrashevtsy thought of themselves as separate and as a group. They had an *esprit de corps*. They were able easily to differentiate between those whose convictions and circumstances did and did not entitle them to be considered one of their number. The Petrashevtsy's *esprit de corps* was derived partly from their social origins and circumstances, partly from their ideological sympathies. They were young, younger by over ten years than Herzen, Belinskii and their friends, and mostly graduated from school and university in the 1840s. Some were still studying, one or two were still at school, the majority had recently begun their careers. Of the core group, most were in their early twenties. Part of the reason for the authority exercised by Petrashevskii and Speshnev was that, at about thirty, they were slightly older.

The Petrashevtsy were the first representatives of the new intelligentsia created by Nicholas I's educational reforms. In contrast to the intelligentsia of preceeding years, only a few belonged to the wealthy upper classes. The majority came from the impovershed gentry, a few from the non-noble classes. The Petrashevtsy thus represented the first stage in the democratisation of the radical movement, intermediary between the upper class intelligentsia such as Herzen and Bakunin and the truly *raznochinnaia* intelligentsia of the 1860s and 1870s. They were distinguished from the previous intelligentsia in that they had to earn their own living. The majority had low-ranking jobs in government service − as petty civil servants, junior army officers or teachers. A few (including Durov, Dostoevskii and Aleksei Pleshcheev) managed to gain a precarious independence from the state and support themselves as writers. They were united by the common nature of their occupations and by a common dissatisfaction with their circumstances. Their radicalism arose in large part from disillusionment arising from the gulf between the expectations aroused in them by their education and by the miserable nature (and miserable pay) of the jobs they received.

Ideologically, the Petrashevtsy were linked, and distinguished from other contemporaries, by the degree of their interest in Western socialist ideas, above all in those of the utopian thinker Charles Fourier, and by a common agreement about the type of radical changes which needed to be introduced in Russia. There were clear general lines of thought to be found in their circles. The leading elements among the Petrashevtsy were humanists and materialists, anticapitalists, democrats, the first advocates of a Russian socialism based on the *mir*, champions of a utilitarian theory of art, of the emancipation of women and, finally, supporters of revolution.

Previous historians have made much of the ideological disagreements within the Petrashevtsy circles.[3] It is true that differences did exist. It would have been very odd if the Petrashevtsy had been homogeneous in their outlook. This was a very early stage of the revolutionary movement in Russia. Western socialist and revolutionary ideas were new and were becoming the subject of serious discussion among the Russian intelligentsia for the first time. It was the beginning of a long process of absorption and digestion of Western socialism, its re-evaluation and adaption to suit the Russian temperament and reality. Because a Russian socialist ideology was only beginning to evolve, it was necessarily incoherent, and as a large number of people were involved, there were inevitably different groups and tendencies among them, with different interpretations of and placing different emphases on, Western ideas. The main split was that between the moderate revolutionaries, headed by Petrashevskii, and the extremists, led by Nikolai Speshnev. But there were also Petrashevtsy, such as Nikolai Danilevskii, Aleksandr Beklemishev, who were purely liberals; others, among them Dostoevskii, Maikov and Aleksandr Miliukov, who were Christian socialists; others, including both the leisure-time Fourierists of Kashkin's circle and the students grouped around Aleksei Tolstov, the seriousness of whose socialist convictions was open to question. Though its clear that these different tendencies existed within the Petrashevtsy, the exact lines are very difficult to draw, especially as, under the impact of 1848, almost all of them moved sharply to the left. The most clearly separate group was the Maikov circle, whose members were more interested in academic socialism than action, who preferred Saint-Simon to Fourier. Yet, even here, the differences were not what they seemed − Vladimir Miliutin, to all appearances serious, scholarly and prudent, turns out to have been a member of Speshnev's revolutionary conspiracy. In spite of their diversity, (and, in some cases, immaturity), the Petrashevtsy were something new in Russia, socially a new and more democratic layer of the intelligentsia, ideologically socialists and revolutionaries, a new extreme wing of the radical movement.

The origins of dissidence: the social background

The way in which the Petrashevtsy reflected a change in the social composition of the Russian intelligentsia can be seen from the personal details collected in 1849 by the government's Commission of Inquiry from over two hundred people arrested and interrogated in connection with the affair.[4] The few who came from wealthy gentry families tended to play an important part in the circles — they had greater social confidence and they could afford to entertain others at their homes — but there were only a few of them. The most notable examples were Speshnev, Kashkin and Petrashevskii himself. And of them, Speshnev was outstanding. Owner of an estate of five hundred souls in Kursk province, sole heir to his mother's much larger property, he could afford to leave the Lycée in 1839 without finishing his course, though this meant that he was not qualified for government service. He could afford a European trip which lasted several years and a house of his own in Shestilevochnaia Street when he came back. When a thief in Dresden stole the 2,100 talers he kept lying about in his desk, all he had to do was write to his mother for more.[5] His foreign friends included the aristocratic Polish Cechanowiecki family. He was the only one of the Petrashevtsy to lead the life of a leisured gentleman and the only one who had been abroad. The twenty-year-old Kashkin, a relative of the Decembrist of the same name, also came from a superior and well-off family — his parents had an estate of 2,500 souls in Kaluga. He could afford to entertain his friends once a week and he looked down on the other Petrashevtsy as people of a lower social tone. Petrashevskii was also wealthy, he had an estate of several hundred souls and two houses in St. Petersburg, but he lacked the social standing of the other two. He was a newcomer — the family fortune had been made by his father who, starting out as a humble medical assistant, had worked his way up during the Napoleonic wars to the post of Chief Inspector of the medical services of the armed forces and of the hospitals of the St. Petersburg district, and the elevated rank of Acting State Councillor.[6] Miliutin and Maikov also came from well-off and well-established families.

But the majority of the Petrashevtsy (over 150 of those interrogated) were from the impoverished gentry. Some had a little land and a handful of serfs, like Nikolai Serebriakov who owned an estate of twenty-four souls, or Dmitrii Kropotov, who owned fifteen. Others, for example the Kaidanovs, Roman Shtrandman, Aleksandr Pal'm, Aleksandr Balasoglo, Konstantin and Ipollit Debu, had severed their ties with the land completely and belonged to families of hereditary *chinovniki*. The Petrashevtsy also included a fair sprinkling of people from the non-noble classes, though the proportion was not as high as in the later revolutionary movement. Seven merchants and three *meshchane* (town citizens), one of whom, Petr Shaposhnikov, had organised a circle of his own, were arrested for their connections with Petrashevskii. Vasilii Katenev, one of the noisiest revolutionaries among the Petrashevtsy, was the son of a *pochetnyi grazhdanin* (an honorary citizen); Aleksandr Maderski,[7] Petrashevskii's flatmate, was the son of a peasant, Chernyshevskii, who associated with the circles, the son of a priest.

All the Petrashevtsy were products of the improved and expanded higher education system, directed by Uvarov (1832−49). The changes were a direct result of Nicholas's passion for bureaucracy. Properly organised and enlarged, Nicholas believed, bureaucracy would cure all the ills of the country. But for this he desperately needed more intelligent and efficient bureaucrats. His quest for these resulted in the doubling of the number of institutions of higher education in Russia and their opening up to new layers of the population.

The most privileged schools in St. Petersburg remained restricted to people of the gentry class. But the number of such institutions grew and the increase in the number of state subsidised places opened them up to the sons of the poorer gentry and *chinovnichestvo* (the bureaucratic caste). These included the Tsarsko-sel'skoe Lycée (in 1844 moved to St. Petersburg and renamed the Aleksandrovskii) the most elitist school in the capital (it was attended by the more upper class Petrashevtsy, thirteen of those arrested, including Petrashevskii, Speshnev and Kashkin); the Law School and the military training corps, of which there were in the 1840s ten in St. Petersburg and twelve (all new) in the provinces. Other special schools − the Medical and Surgical Academy, the Mining Institute, the Institute of Communications and the Pedagogical Institute were less exclusive and accepted people of a lower class origin.

But it was the expansion of the ordinary secondary schools, the *gymnasia*, which really opened secondary education to the sons both of the impoverished gentry and to *raznochintsy*. In 1828 there was one gymnasium in St. Petersburg. In 1832 two more, the First and Second Gymnasia, were added; in 1836 a Fourth, named after the merchant Larin; and a Fifth in 1845. Only the First Gymnasium (formerly the Nobles' Pension) was reserved for the gentry; the Second accepted the children of *raznochintsy* and merchants; the Third children of the classes who paid poll-tax and the Fourth was especially for merchants' sons. By 1849 Russia as a whole had seventy-seven gymnasia with almost 20,000 pupils. In some areas, such as Nizhni-Novgorod, the proportion of *raznochintsy* among the pupils was as high as two thirds.[8] It was in the gymnasia that the majority of the Petrashevtsy received their basic education.

The appointment of Uvarov as Minister of Education marked the beginning of a new era in university education. The number of students at Russia's five universities − Moscow, Kazan, Kharkov (founded 1803), St. Petersburg (1819) and Kiev (1834) shot up from 2,002 in 1836 to 4,016 in 1848.[9] Over thirty of the sixty-three people sentenced in connection with the Petrashevsky affair had studied at St. Petersburg University The percentage of *raznochintsy* at the universities varied from 30 per cent in St. Petersburg to as high as 56 per cent in Kazan.[10] In addition there was a high proportion of non-nobles among the *free listeners*, part-time students, of whom there were over seven hundred at St. Petersburg University by 1847. The Petrashevets Maderski, son of a state peasant, was one of these. A. Chulinikov, a merchant's son, describes the growing friction between the new type of poor *raznochinnii* student and the aristocratic ones, who (like Herzen) came in carriages, 'communicated with each other only in French' and 'appropriated the right to sit on the benches in the faculty nearest the professors'.[11]

Under Nicholas I the syllabuses of all Russian educational institutions became directed towards training boys for various branches of government service. The Military training corps produced 500 officers a year for the army and navy; the Lycée, bureaucrats for the Ministry of Internal Affairs; the Law School, personnel for the Ministry of Justice. The aim of a university education was also to produce civil servants. This can be seen from the emphasis on law, the subject required for entry into government departments. St. Petersburg University had only two faculties − the Law Faculty, to which two thirds of the students belonged; and the Philosophy Faculty, which embraced all other branches of knowledge. The new generation of poor students to whom fate had not, as Boris Utin said, 'given several hundred souls', looked on education 'as a trade which would later enable them to earn a yearly crust of bread'.[12] The vast majority of them went straight into government service. In the civil service, as a contemporary testified, 'people of the *meshchanin*, the merchant, and the clerical class and from the gentry' lost 'the sharp and distinctive features of these classes' and merged to form a new hereditary caste of *chinovniki* and intelligentsia.[13]

This new caste was naturally concentrated in the capital, the centre of the bureaucracy. The number of civil servants in St. Petersburg grew from 5,416 to 13,528 between 1804−32.[14] As Belinskii wrote, 'the *chinovnik* is the native, the true citizen of Petersburg'. The *chinovniki* may not have predominated in absolute numbers, but they set the tone of the city. To Tolstov, arriving from Moscow, it seemed, 'a sort of military camp, everywhere there were soldiers, everything felt fettered, constrained, oppressed. Before my eyes there passed only a *chinovnik* in a torn uniform, battered, pitiful, with a work-worn face, running to his office, or a soldier, or a wretched *chukhonets*, or a foreigner.'[15]

The overwhelming majority of the Petrashevtsy belonged to this new caste. Some of them, for example, Pavel Filippov, Aleksandr Khanykov, Katenev, Tolstov, Aleksandr Evropeus, were still students. Some, Miliutin, Aleksandr Mikhailov, Petr Latkin, were taking higher degrees. The rest worked either as civil servants, army officers, teachers or doctors. The largest number worked in one or another of the twelve government departments in the capital. There was a particularly important group of them in the Asiatic Department of the Ministry of Foreign Affairs, where Petrashevskii, Balasoglo, Kashkin and the Debu brothers worked as translators. The Petrashevtsy were low-grade civil servants – *gubernia* secretaries, college secretaries, titular councillors and college assessors (the twelfth – eighteenth ranks of the bureaucratic hierarchy). Among the army officers were Nikolai Mombelli, Nikolai Grigor'ev, Fedor L'vov, and Pavel Kuz'min, all again occupying junior ranks, ensign, second lieutenant, lieutenant, captain. Many other Petrashevtsy, including Balasoglo, Rafail Chernosvitov, Fedor and Mikhail Dostoevskii, had been educated in military schools and had spent some time in the army or navy. Others, for example, Feliks Tol', Petr Beletskii, Jan-Ferdinand Jastrzebski and Miliukov, worked as teachers, in various military and civilian institutions. Dmitrii Aksharumov was the only one of the Petrashevtsy to become a doctor, though the medical profession was one of the easiest for the *raznochintsy* to enter, but several of the Petrashevtsy came from medical families. Typical was Dostoevskii's father, the son of a priest, who ended up (1821) as the doctor of the Marinskii Hospital in Moscow and bequeathed his children property and hereditary nobility.

For a very few of the new intelligentsia, there was an alternative to the service. By 1837 there were about seventy people in St. Petersburg earning their living as writers and artists. Literature was almost the only way in which the poor man could, as Vvedenskii said, while working, 'escape the clutches of the state'.[16] Thirty years before, as Durov says, literature had been regarded with scorn, a matter for idlers and parasites, or for people who had already obtained a reputation in society and could afford to indulge themselves. It was just starting to become respectable, a profession with a salary, like any other.[17] Professional writers and artists among the Petrashevtsy included the critic Maikov, the poet Pleshcheev, writers Durov, Vasilii Tolbin, Fedor

and Mikhail Dostoevskii, the artists Evstafii Bernadskii and Aleksei
Berestov. Others, including Pal'm and Saltykov, combined literature and
the civil service.

Nicholas I had certainly succeeded, at least in the capital, in educating
the bureaucrats he needed. But, for his purposes, he had over-educated
them. The special schools, and above all the universities, had become
too civilised, too European. When he came to the throne, the standard
of teaching had been abysmal. Most of the professors were foreigners
and were forced to lecture in Latin. In 1827 the government decided to
send twenty of its best students to train as professors abroad. They
returned in the late thirties, imbued with enlightened principles and began
to impart these to their students and, above all, to teach them to think.
In 1845, for example, the arrival of Dmitrii Meier, fresh from
Heidelburg, caused a revolution in the Law Faculty of Kazan University.
Previously the practice had been that a professor, 'on taking up his post
once and for all drew up the course for the subject and gave his notes
to his students'. When they had learned them by heart and passed their
exams, they handed them on to the next generation. When Meier gave
his first lecture, the students undetstood very little of what he said, but
were enthralled by his 'zeal, his unprecedented enthusiasm' and he
quickly became the object of hero-worship. In St. Petersburg, Mikhail
Kutorga ignored the official ban and gave his students a short sketch
of the French Revolution, which he praised as 'in the fullest sense of
the word social[18] and Viktor Poroshin managed to introduce Fourier
into his lectures on political economy; in Moscow, Granovskii used
an analysis of the Greek and Roman republics to preach political
democracy.

Such an education was a bad preparation for life and work in
nineteenth-century Russia. After it, the service was a nasty shock. In
the civil administration, the eager, sensitive young members of the new
intelligentsia discovered that they were required to act as petty clerks.
Jobs often proved to be nothing more than the copying of documents,
'over and over again'. The young men hated it. Akhsharumov began
an account of 'the circumstances that oppress me' with the fact that his
lack of property forced him to serve. Those who could, like Petr Semenov
T'ian-Shanskii, who decided that the service was 'a completely fruitless
waste of time', got out of it and got jobs as librarians or secretaries
instead. Dostoevskii summed up their general feeling about it. 'The
service is as boring as potatoes'.[19]

The Petrashevtsy, as little men, without wealth or connections, found it difficult to get into a decent job in the bureaucracy, let alone get on within it. In Nicholas's Russia, nothing could be done without influence, without protection. Tolstov explained 'When you finish your (university) course, you leave, you have no protection and no money, all the decent posts are already filled and no-one pays any attention to your abilities.' The literature of the time abounds with descriptions of this predicament. In his short story *Protection*, Pleshcheev shows Semen Snezhov, a handsome, talented but poor young man of twenty-three, eaten up with rage at the sight of 'a fat, red-cheeked gentleman', he passes in the street 'I can definitely say he's no better (than me), but he's got a good post.' Nekrasov's *Makar Osipovich*, Iakov Butkov's *A Good Post* and Saltykov's *A Tangled Affair* all deal with the same theme. Those who did get jobs felt their initiative stifled, their intellect dulled by the monotony of the labour and were tyrannised and held back by jealous superiors, whom they could not afford to bribe. Durov concluded, 'The fate of the poor *chinovnik* is more deserving of pity that the fate of a serf.'[20]

The alternatives to the civil service were little better. In the army, the savage beatings inflicted on the common soldier were enough to turn the stomach of any delicately brought-up young man. Lieutenant Mombelli kept a diary of these atrocities and recorded how the army was destroying his health, stultifying his brain and exhausting his pocket. Even the officers were treated 'despotically'.[21] Teachers were poorly paid and poorly regarded. As Konstantin Arsen'ev wrote, 'Prejudices are ingrained against the teaching profession, alienating it from society.' The life of the poor student, forced to become a tutor in some household of the provincial gentry, and treated by them little better than the serfs, was a favourite subject of fiction – a good example is Krutsiferskii's experiences with the Negrov family in Herzen's *Who is to Blame?* The fate of the intelligent doctor, isolated in the provinces, deprived of intellectual stimulation, is described by Herzen in the person of Doctor Krupov, who becomes more and more bitter and cynical. Those who became professional writers escaped the clutches of the state only to fall into the hands of rapacious publicists and booksellers. Kraevskii's treatment of Belinskii, for instance, is notorious. The publisher of *Otechestvennye zapiski* exploited his chief editor's precarious financial position, piled work onto him, held him captive by advancing money to him. Kraevskii gave other, less well-known, writers an even harder time. He, for example, gained complete control of the literary output of Butkov, (a *meshchanin* by birth) by buying his exemption from military service. As Durov said, 'Talent is in the hands of, or rather trampled underfoot by publicists, who look on literature as if it were leather or tallow.'[22]

Not only did the jobs available fail to match up to the intellectual expectations education had raised in the minds of the Petrashevtsy, they also failed to meet their material requirements. As educated men, they felt entitled to the standards and lifestyles of the comfortably-off gentry classes. And yet, in many cases, their families were impoverished, their salaries meagre, (on average about 1,500 paper roubles p.a.). They were, if not compared with the peasants, at least in their own terms, horribly poor. But, even when they were out of work, they had to keep up an appearance of their class. An article in *Sovremennik* in 1847, written by the Petrashevets Shtrandman, describes this problem:

> Who doesn't know how often a man makes great sacrifices to conventional ideas of propriety and the gentry class? He cannot overturn these concepts, they are the consequences of his education. He is tormented by his poverty, he would gladly go and chop wood or stick up posters to pay for the repair of his uniform which has gone white at the seams and perhaps also feed and educate his hungry, freezing family, but the thought of his origin sits heavy upon him.[23]

Mombelli describes how, in order to buy the clothes etc. necessary to preserve his dignity, he often had to go without dinner for several days and even think up ways of hiding this from his own servant. Balasoglo, while fruitlessly seeking a bureaucratic job, 'lived for whole months on macaroni' with his wife and five children; Pal'm, left in his early twenties with his mother and two young brothers to support, also suffered great poverty.[24]

The hopes raised by their education, the unsatisfactory nature of their jobs and their financial worries combined to make the new intelligentsia feel out of place, unwanted in Russian society and frequently induced psychological depression. Shtrandman relates how the struggle to keep up appearances causes a man 'to wither in body and mind, he becomes gloomy, frightened'. Mombelli explained how his troubles made him hour by hour more bilious and sarcastic. Finally, he became a hypochondriac, unable to tolerate the presence of any other person for days on end. The student Tolstov fell into a similar state of gloom soon after his arrival in St. Petersburg:

> I was obsessed by the questions: What am I living for? ... Do I have a future? ... Is living worth the effort? ... I succumbed to despair, not the

sort of despair that can be cured by a bullet, but a cold impotent despair.
I began to drink and drank heavily, drinking cheap wine by the tumblerful
… My friends called me Hamlet as a joke.

The new knowledge

According to Akhsharumov, the whole of the intelligentsia suffered from
this 'moral illness' to a greater or lesser degree. Its cause was, 'the
depraved order of things in our society'. He himself was 'constantly ill,
psychologically destroyed by life'. This sense of their pointlessness, as
educated men in a country that had no use for educated men led many
(including Mombelli, Tolstov, Vladimir Engel'son and Petrashevskii
himself) to thoughts of suicide. Petrashevskii described how, 'For three
months in a row I was obsessed with the idea of suicide … for three
months a loaded pistol lay beside me … life and death were indifferent
to me.'[25]

The Petrashevtsy eventually found an escape from their depression
through an intellectual rebellion against their situation. They turned
to the new left-wing philosophical and socialist ideas coming from
Germany, and in particular from France and found in them an explanation of their situation and a focus for this dissatisfaction. Engel'son
threw away his loaded pistol and abandoned thoughts of suicide on
reading Herzen's Feuerbachian *Dilettantism in Science*. Petrashevskii's
psychological crisis ended with his recognising, also *à la* Feuerbach, his
unity with the whole of nature, his obligation not to destroy its harmony
but to concern himself with his own and his neighbour's welfare.[26] The
intelligentsia turned from introspection and gloom and began to search
eagerly in books for answers to the questions confronting it. Tolstov
explained how, 'Science began to reveal its treasures (to me), my
questions were gradually answered.' Balasoglo describes the feeling of
'an inescapable need for knowledge' which possessed the soul of the poor
raznochinets, 'Alas! Alas! It seemed to it that all it had to do was to
get into these ten thousand volume libraries which are usually so firmly
locked, in order to get to know everything!' When at last he succeeds
in gaining entrance to one, 'The soul is in its element for the first time
in its life … time goes unheeded … the soul is lost in the joys of the
mind.'[27]

The source of the new knowledge was Europe and especially France.
The *raznochinnaia* intelligentsia dreamed with Balasoglo, 'Europe!

Europe! Paris!' Books imported from Europe (and especially France) were in theory subjected to strict censorship. *The Alphabetic List of Forbidden French Books* included works by 119 left-wing writers. Also banned were many works of the new German philosophers – Feuerbach, David Strauss, Bruno Bauer. But in practice, the censorship was slow and inefficient. Extremely revolutionary works like Pierre-Joseph Proudhon's *Qu'est-ce que la propriété?* escaped the censor's eye by accident. Others they missed through ignorance – the works of many of Fourier's French disciples – Mathieu Briancourt, Victor Considerant, Francois Cantagrel, Zoe Gatti de Gamond, Jean Czyinski, – were banned, but not the more difficult writings of Fourier himself. And some were banned only after a long delay – Etienne Cabet's *Voyage en Icarie*, for example, not until 1848, eight years after it was first published. Books were not subject to censorship until *after* they had been imported into Russia and their pages cut. It was left to the booksellers to submit their stock to the censors, which much of the time they failed to do. And then there were the exemptions – universities and university lecturers (though not students) and some other teachers were allowed to possess forbidden books. According to the official (and very incomplete) figures 863,000 volumes were imported into Russia from Europe in 1847 alone.[28] A large proportion of these were banned. When the government clamped down in 1849 it was horrified at what it found. Officials sent to investigate a report that forbidden books were being sold by post from Riga and Derpt to people as far away as Penza, unearthed 2,024 books in the shops and libraries of Riga and 1,124 in Derpt, not approved by the censor. In St. Petersburg, Moscow, Mitau, Libau, Kiev, Kharkhov, Vilna and Odessa, the booksellers were also found to 'trade in forbidden books'. Lurie, Petrashevskii's bookseller in St. Petersburg, was caught with 2,581 illegal volumes.[29]

It was thus easy to get hold of forbidden literature. The whole of the educated public read banned books, and above all French ones. How widespread they were can be seen from the fact that when a young guards officer Smirnov, went to a bookseller on Nevskii Prospekt, and asked him to recommend some books that someone like him might like, the bookseller automatically suggested works by Alphonse de Lamartine, Pierre-Jean Béranger, Fourier's *Le Nouveau monde industriel et sociétaire* and *Essai sur les harmonies physiologiques* by Alexandre Baudet-Dulary, one of Fourier's disciples.[30] The officials sent to confiscate forbidden books in Riga and Derpt said in mitigation that 'all the works concerned are known to the whole reading public'.

A student at the Lycée admitted 'There was not one forbidden book which could not be found at the Lycée in the possession of children of fourteen and fifteen'. It was possible for the poor *raznochinets* to acquire quite a respectable library of the new literature. Mombelli, for example, had 135 Russian books (79 of them banned) and 454 foreign ones (195 banned). Their needs were catered for by a new trader – the *bouquiniste* or second-hand bookdealer, who visited his clients regularly, offering them books at half the normal prices. Evgenii Lamanskii tells us how each Lycéen 'had his own *bouquiniste*' and that 'we read the books they procured us secretly, at night'.[31]

These books included the works of the German left-Hegelians, but the overwhelming majority of them were French. When Pavel Annenkov arrived in St. Petersburg from Europe in autumn 1843:

> I was far from having finished with Paris, but on the contrary, immediately came across the reflection of many aspects of the intellectual fervour of its life at this time: Proudhon's work *De la propriéte*, almost passé; Cabet's *Icarie*, little read in France itself, with the exception of a small circle of dreamers, poor men and workers; Fourier's system was more widespread and popular, but all these served as subjects of ardent discussion, questions and expectations of every kind ... the theories of Proudhon, Fourier, to which was joined later Louis Blanc, with his famous treatise *Organisation du travail* had here a special school where all these teachings were jumbled up together and preached over and over again by their adepts ... the books of the above-mentioned authors were in everyone's hands at that period.[32]

The new ideas could not be discussed openly in Russia. The new intelligentsia had to create its own atmosphere, one in which it felt safe. They drew together in small, tightly-knit circles of likeminded people (*khruzhki*). Miliukov described how:

> Here in St. Petersburg there gradually began to form small circles of people close in their way of thought ... at first with the sole aim of meeting at a friends, sharing news and gossip, exchanging ideas, talking freely without fearing a stranger's immodest ear ... in such friendly circles new acquaintances were made, friendly ties were strengthened.[33]

They were, as a rule, quiet and modest groups of serious and idealistic young men, who met for earnest discussions about the problems of the world and earnest appraisals of each other's literary efforts. The circles acted as a surrogate family for young men who had come from the provinces to make their way in Petersburg without relatives or protectors.

The members of a circle might meet as often as three or four times a week. Though the atmosphere was sometimes stifling (they got to know each other too well), the friendships formed were extremely important to them. They would often club together to share the expenses of their entertainment or to help one of their number in need.

Such circles were rather different from the literary salons of the day, the most famour being those of Vasilii Botkin in Moscow (frequented by Herzen and Ogarev) and of Ivan and Avdot'ia Panaev in St. Petersburg (whose star was Belinskii). Here the guests were more glamourous, the atmosphere was more competitive. The discomfiture of the highly-strung, socially insecure young *raznochinets* in these surroundings is illustrated by Dostoevskii's experience at the Panaev's. They took him up, after the publication of *Poor Folk* and 'trumpeted him about'. He was at first too shy to speak, bowled over by the beautiful and witty Avdot'ia. Then, he took to hysterically boasting about his talents (behaving quite insufferably). The members of the circle, especially Turgenev, revised their original opinion about him, 'picked him to pieces', laughed in his face and finally drove him out of their group with a poem which called him 'a pimple on the face of Russian literature'. Balasoglo, another *raznochinets* who ventured into literary society, also felt out of place. He decided to throw over 'these respectable people with their white gloves and complacent frock-coats .. and seek other people, younger and simpler, fresher and stronger of spirit'. To his 'indescribable delight', he found whole groups of such people, 'people complete and simple and noble, who not only talked but believed in their ideas', among the circles of the Petrashevtsy.[34]

Circles in St. Petersburg and the Provinces

Among the forerunners of Petrashevskii's circle were the Beketovs, formed by Aleksei Beketov and his two younger brothers, Nikolai and Andrei, who were at this time still students, but who went on to become professors (of chemistry and botany respectively) at St. Petersburg University. Their most important visitor was Valerian Maikov, a precocious and brilliant young man from a talented intelligentsia family (his father, Nikolai, was a well-known painter; his brother, Apollon, a notable poet). Valerian had an encyclopaedic range of knowledge — from

literature and political economy to chemistry − and in 1846 replaced
Belinskii as chief critic of *Otechestvennye zapiski* at the age of twenty-
three. Other guests included Fedor Dostoevskii and Dmitrii Grigorovich,
both of whom has been with Aleksei at the School of Engineers and were
now just beginning their careers as writers; Aleksandr Khanykov, a
rebellious student, twice thrown out of St. Petersburg University for
riotous behaviour and then taken back again, one of the leading figures
in the Petrashevskii circle; and Aleksei Pleshcheev, the poet of the
Petrashevtsy, who, in spite of the fiery nature of some of his verse,
appears to have been a charming and gentle young man. In this company,
Dostoevskii says he was 'cured' of his experiences in literary society.[35]
The members of Beketov's circle were not only honourable and sincere,
they were socialists. Grigorovich hints carefully at the circle's political
nature, 'But whoever spoke and whatever was spoken about, whether
we talked about events in Petersburg, in Russia or abroad, or whether
we discussed literature or aesthetic questions ... everywhere one could
hear indignant, noble outbursts against oppression and injustice'.[36]
Under the influence of the discussions at the Beketov's, Grigorovich
began work on his first major story, *The Village*, a vivid description of
the consequences of serfdom.

The Beketov circle began to disintegrate with the departure of the two
younger brothers for Kazan in 1845. In 1846, Maikov founded his own
circle, mainly composed of other young writers, like him just starting
to write for the radical journals. The main figure after Valerian was
Miliutin. He also came from distinguished family − his mother was the
daughter of the statesman Kiselev; his brother Dmitrii became War
Minister under Alexander II; his brother Nikolai played a leading part
in the emancipation of the serfs.

Vladimir, while working for his doctorate on the history of Russian
law, began to publish an extremely well-received series of left-wing
articles on economic themes (*Otechestvennye zapiski* 1847). Other
members included Mikhail Saltykov, the future satirist, who, while
working as a civil servant during the day, was writing his first stories,
Contradictions and *A Tangled Affair*, (published in 1847 and 1848);
Shtrandman, who had just started to write the 'Domestic news' section
of *Sovremennik* and Evgenii Esakov, a civil servant, educated at the
Lycée. The circle met at Maikov's, Miliutin's and Shtrandman's in turn.
They discussed, according to Apollon, 'literature, aesthetics and political
economy'. This is the typical circle that Saltykov describes in *Brusin*,
a small group of people who soon came to know each other inside out:

It was known, for example, that on such and such a day M-n would reproach M-ov for his systematic, childish spontaneousness, for his reckless, pointless and rather Scythian boldness, and, what is even worse, it was even known what M-ov would retort to such accusations. In a word, we were terribly bored because we knew each other by heart. On Monday we would talk about the latest number of our favourite journal; on Tuesday M-*** would develop some economic question; on Thursday we talked about what was going on abroad and whether it was a good thing etc.

Maikov had collaborated with Petrashevskii over the first part of the later notorious *Pocket Dictionary of Foreign Words*, and most of his circle had previously visited Petrashevskii's but had broken off with him after quarrels over the dictionary and the nature of the meetings at Petrashevskii's. There was rivalry, but no great ideological disagreement between Maikov's circle and Petrashevskii's. They were all socialists. Petrashevskii said 'Although a *quid pro quo* sometimes takes place between the two societies, they both aspire to a single aim.' The circle came to an unfortunate end in summer 1847 when Maikov died from sunstroke after swimming near Moscow. Saltykov was arrested and exiled soon afterwards.[37]

Another circle met at the house of Irinakh Vvedenskii in the late forties and early fifties. Vvedenskii, the son of a poor priest, graduated with flying colours from St. Petersburg University, but (perhaps for class reasons) failed to get a lectureship and ended up teaching literature in the Noblemen's Regiment. He supplemented this income by his translations and articles on the theory of literature and became famous as the first Russian translator of Dickens and Cooper. His visitors included Aleksandr Miliukov, who also combined teaching and writing; the writers Dmitrii Minaev, Vasilii Iakovlev, Vladimir Riiumin; civil servants V. V. Deriker, Petr Biliarskii, Aleksandr Chumnikov and the students Khanykov, Grigorii Blagotsvetlov and Nikolai Chernyshevskii. Many of them were socialists – Chernyshevskii rejoiced that he found there 'more of such men than one could suppose'. They discussed literature and politics and from 1847–8 events in Europe became, 'almost the exclusive topic of conversation ... the works of Proudhon, Louis Blanc and Pierre Leroux in turn gave rise to discussion and quarrels'. Some of Vvedenskii's guests, including Khanykov, Minaev and Miliukov, also visited Petrashevskii's. The tone of the circle was particularly close to Petrashevskii's and its members were very shaken by the arrests in 1849 – in October they discussed the possibility of a rising to free Petrashevskii and his friends from gaol and in September 1850, Minaev talked about Nicholas' 'cruelty and despotism' and suggested that they should try to assassinate him. Pogodin later accused Vvedenskii of being 'the father of the Nihilists'.[38]

One circle whose existence was discovered quite accidentally on the arrest of the Petrashevtsy, was that which met at Nikolai Mombelli's flat in the barracks of the Light Guards of the Moscow Regiment in autumn and winter 1846–8. Mombelli was a bold and idealistic young man with a 'passion for knowledge' and particularly elevated ideas about friendship. His circle was devised as a sort of 'literary experiment'. 'We agreed to meet once a week to write, to translate and to compose articles and to read them, without being embarrassed and after the reading of each article to discuss it, without sparing one another.' According to Mombelli, there were twenty-three gatherings and forty-five visitors, both civilian and military. The nucleus of the group was the officers Mombelli, Fedor L'vov, Aleksei Maksheev, Nikolai Karmalin, Aleksandr Nikitin, Nikolai Iazykov, who all took up their pens and wrote articles. The political nature of these can be gathered from their titles – *The Contemporary Battle of Opinion, Why the Russians have no Literature, The Present State of Germany, A Contemporary Conversation in the Spirit of Otechestvennye zapiski*. They also made and read translations from Voltaire, Volney and other Encyclopaedists, excerpts from Petr Dolgorukov's banned life of Catherine I, articles on the Polish rising of 1830 and poems – from Byron's *Don Juan* to *The Marseillaise*. 'Finally we discovered that they were talking about our evenings in the town, about the fact that we read translations from Voltaire and Diderot.' In 1848 the government stepped in and stopped the meetings. Mombelli and his inseparable friend Staff Captain L'vov started visiting Petrashevskii's instead.[39]

Two circles verly closely connected with Petrashevskii's and to a certain extent formed as rivals to it were Kashkin's and the Pal'm–Durov circle. The circle of the rich and fashionable Nikolai Kashkin met at his house every Tuesday (from October 1848) and had a slightly superior tone to it. Its members were wealthier and more aristocratic, 'young people of good *ton*' as Speshnev put it; many of them had been educated at the Lycée. At Kashkin's they said, 'everything had a respectable air' in contrast to Petrashevskii's where 'people met as if in a tavern.' The investigating Commission noticed that they did not encourage the approaches of people of less education and a lower social standing, so that even Petrashevskii did not have free access to their gatherings. The most important member of this circle was probably Konstantin Debu.

He was older than the others (forty), and more experienced, a man of quiet but strong character. He and his younger brother Ippolit appear to have been responsible for introducing many of the others to socialism. Most of the other members were young civil servants: Aleksandr and Pavel Evropeus, Dmitri Dmitrievich and Dmitrii Ivanovich Akhsharumov, Erast Vashchenko, Petr Trubetskoi, Semen Cherkasskii, Evgenii Esakov, Sergei Penskii, Ivan Nikolaev, Vasilii Iakovlev, Nikolai Rakhmaninov and Oskar Ott, at whose flat about eight of the Tuesdays were held. The circle was also visited by two of the most radical and influential members of Petrashevskii's circle, Khanykov and Speshnev. Many of the features of the evenings were copied from Petrashevskii's. They were more organised than many other groups − they had a bell and a president; they made speeches (Kashkin on philosophy, Aleksandr Evropeus on morality; Ipollit Debu on political economy); they started a collective library (with 120 roubles). However, their discussion of socialist ideas was more moderate and abstract than in some of the other circles. On the whole they were, as they later claimed, 'really pure Fourieriests and thought and preached nothing political'. The 'sole aim' of the circle was 'the study of Fourier's system as a universal truth'.[40] Their boldest action was the organisation of a dinner to celebrate Fourier's birthday (7 April 1849).

The second circle, Pal'm and Durov's, was formed at the beginning of 1849 and almost all its members had previously visited Petrashevskii's. The idea of the circle was conceived by a group of writers, Pleshcheev, Durov, Pal'm, Miliukov and the Dostoevskii brothers, who disliked the exclusively political tone of Petrashevskii's evenings and wanted somewhere where they could discuss literary questions, read their own works and listen to music.[41] The circle originated from a highly successful series of evenings held at Pleshcheev's at the end of 1848. In 1849 they were regularised and transferred to the flat shared by Pal'm, Durov and Aleksei Shchelkov. Pal'm and Durov had lived together for several years and were deeply attached to each other, in what was probably a homosexual relationship. Durov, who was six years older than Pal'm (thirty-two in 1849) had the dominant, if not the more stable character. His nature, according to Pal'm was 'noble and poetic', he was an ardent lover of truth, justice and humanity. Unfortunately in combined this with an almost compulsive habit of carrying arguments to extremes and a tendency to fly off the handle, though he was always very quick to apologise after his outbursts.[42] Both he and Pal'm published short stories and poems. Durov had thrown up his job in the Naval Ministry to concentrate on literature; Pal'm was still in the army. In addition to the writers mentioned above, their regular guests included their flatmate Shchelkov (a civil servant), who played the violoncello, Nikolai Kaszewski (a music teacher) who played the piano which they hired jointly, and the young civil servants, the brothers Evgenii and Porfirii Lamanskii. All these, (with the possible exception of Fedor Dostoevskii) were more interested in art than in politics and at first the evenings did have a refreshing literary and musical tone. But, from the start, there was another element in the circle, formed from a group of the most revolutionary of Petrashevskii's visitors — Speshnev, Mombelli, Vasilii Golovinskii, a young graduate of the law school, Nikolai Grigor'ev, a lieutenant in the Mounted Grenadiers and Nikolai Mordvinov, who worked in the Ministry of Internal Affairs. They were dissatisfied with Petrashevskii's evenings for quite other reasons. Little by little foreign politics, recent events in Russia and French socialism crept into the conversation. They discussed Robert Owen's *New Lanark*, Cabet's *Icaria*, Proudhon's theory of progressive taxation and, in particular, Fourier's phalanstery.[43] In the end, this circle became the most political of all and the cover for a secret society.

Petrashevskii himself was admitted to neither of these circles, though many of their members visited him. There were however, two circles close to his own, which he did visit.

The first and most important was a disorganised circle of hot-headed and immature young men, headed by the students Aleksei Tolstov and Vasilii Katenev, and grouped around the tobacco shop owned by the eccentric and effervescent Petr Shaposhnikov. The composition of this group was much more democratic socially than many of the others — Katenev was the son of a *pochetnyi grazhdanin*; Shaposhnikov and his assistant Vasilii Vostrov, *meshchane*. Their friends included the students Grigorii Danilevskii, Boris Utin, Erast Zalebedskii, Fonvizin, the merchants Stein and Mazurin, the painter Frolov, the architect Aleksandr Tverskoi and a number of army cadets. Unfortunately for them, their steps were dogged from early 1849 by two active if ignorant police spies, Vasilii Shaposhnikov (not to be confused with Petr) and Nikolai Naumov. All these people met several times a week and Katenev and Tolstov in particular ardently preached atheism and republicanism.[44]

The second circle was much quieter and more inoffensive. It was formed by Aleksandr Maderski, the peasant's son, who rented a room in Petrashevskii's house. As well as pouring out the tea at Petrashevskii's evenings, he held literary parties of his own for his university friends – Vladimir Blagoveshchenskii, Miliukov, Konstantin Polianskii, Grenkov, the Bibikov brothers and Matroshennikov. Here they read Miliukov's translations of children's stories from the English; and an introduction to *Don Quixote*, written by Petrashevskii; and Maderski gave his friends Cabet and forbidden books about Russia to read, including Custine's *Lettres de Russie* and *Mystères de Russie* by Lacroix.[45]

In the provinces, circles were founded on the model of those in St. Petersburg. The most important was formed by professors and students of Kazan, already the most democratic of Russia's universities. Vasilii Bervi-Flerovskii, later a prominent populist, recalls how, in 1845, when he was a student at Kazan, 'Three men came to us from the St. Petersburg circles founded by Petrashevskii.' These were Nikolai and Andrei Beketov and Nikolai Blagoveshchenskii. They were soon joined by Vladimir Blagoveshchenskii and Nikolai Ratovskii. Ratovskii and the Blagoveshchenskii brothers had all been at Petrashevskii's.[46] Nikolai Beketov and Vladimir Blagoveshchenskii were still post-graduate students, the rest held teaching posts at the University. They recruited other lecturers to their circle, including Dmitrii Meier, Professor of Civil Law and Evgraf Osokin, Professor of Financial Law. All of them used their lectures to propagate radical and socialist ideas. In the words of one student, 'They acted in the same way as Petrashevskii: they spread the teaching of Fourier and here the results were the same as in Petersburg. In a very short time they obtained a great influence in the university.'[47]

Osokin was particularly successful in introducing the French socialists into his lectures on political economy; Meier in turning his law lectures into denunciations of bureaucratic corruption and serfdom. Some students associated directly with the Beketov's new circle, including Vasilii Bervi-Flerovskii and Petr Pekarskii. Others formed socialist study circles of their own. One group sat in the cramped flat belonging to Mikhail Chulkov 'for nights on end' rapturously listening to their host reading Fourier.[48] The Petrashevtsy thus set Kazan on the path to becoming what it was to be in the sixties – one of the main centres of student disturbance. Though less is known about them, we know from the testimony of the Petrashevtsy about the existence of similar circles in various educational institutions in St. Petersburg – including the Lycée, the Law School and the University – and among the students of Moscow University.[49]

Other circles in non-university towns included Vladimir Kaidanov's circle in Rostov (in Yaroslav *gubernia*). Kaidanov was an attractive young official in the Ministry of State Properties with an active, independent mind. He met Petrashevskii through his brother Nikolai in 1844, visited his Fridays and was introduced by him to Fourierism. When in April 1845 the Ministry sent him to Rostov he made every effort to keep in touch with the new ideas, ordering socialist literature through his brother: 'Most of all I should like to read the Fourierists, but I will be very glad if you can get me somehow the works of the other socialists, for example, Proudhon, Louis Blanc, and I wouldn't mind reading Saint-Simon'. He urges Nikolai, 'Don't spare money. I would rather go without boots than do without the books of one of the apostles of Fourier'. The books were not only for himself but for the 'small local flock' he had formed — mainly of local civil servants — Bersen'ev, Mirizhanov, Rubakov, Leont'ev, Temkin, Savin, Stratasoev and others. When they found Fourier difficult he began to translate from the German for them Karl Biederman's *Vorlesungen Über Sozialismus und soziale Fragen*, because, as he said, in it 'all the social theories are analysed'.[50]

At attempt was made to found socialist circles in Reval by Konstantin Timkovskii and Aleksandr Beklemishev, both of whom worked in the local department of the Ministry of Internal Affairs and had visited Petrashevskii in St. Petersburg. They were an ill-matched pair. Timkovskii was erratic, unreliable and poor, a very revolutionary Fourierist who made the most passionate speech to be uttered at Petrashevskii's. Beklemishev was cautious, solid and came from a landowning family, a conservative Fourierist, author of the *Correspondence of Two Landowners*, which preached a sort of paternalistic socialism. Timkovskii claimed in a letter to Speshnev 'J'ai organisé deux cercles ou l'étude prospéra' and named three of the members — his brother, General Baranov and Father John.[51] However Timkovskii was prone to exaggeration and it is difficult to say how far they ever got off the ground. There is also mention of other circles connected with Petrashevskii's in Tambov (under the auspices of Lieutenant Pavel Kuz'min) and Kostroma (Katenev and Ivan Aristov).[52]

The Petrashevskii circle

The most notorious circle in St. Petersburg, and the largest, was that of Mikhail Vasil'evich Butashevich-Petrashevskii. Petrashevskii's father, who came originally from the impoverished Ukrainian gentry, had distinguished himself sufficiently in his career as a doctor to be able to afford to send his eleven-year-old son to the Lycée (1832). From the evidence we have, Petrashevskii seems to have been one of those naturally refractory characters who seem to have something in their make-up which makes it almost physically impossible for them to obey rules or to submit to authority in any way. From his earliest years, he instinctively made fun of and disobeyed his superiors, and played elaborate practical jokes on them. From the beginning he was too unconventional, too intense in his jokes – his contemporaries felt there was something eccentric, almost mad about him. As his class mate Engel'son said 'He would accept the golden mean in nothing'. He carried his pranks further than was tasteful, or acceptable either to his teachers or his class-mates. By the time he was fifteen the Lycée authorities had him labelled 'an extremely obstinate character with a liberal mode of thought', his class-mates, though they sometimes followed his leadership, were in general frightened of him and avoided him.[53] Although he did brilliantly at his lessons, Petrashevskii got such bad marks for behaviour that he left in 1839 with the lowest grade (the fourteenth service rank). He went on to study part-time for a postgraduate degree at the University (Lycée students were allowed to do this without taking a first degree), while working during the day as a translator in the Ministry of Foreign Affairs. There he continued to make his scorn of authorities felt in unconventional ways. In the University, he quarrelled with his professor, whom he regarded as stupid, and, not because he was lazy (far from it) but in order to show his contempt for the educational system, he paid a friend a hundred roubles to write his thesis for him. When this was rejected, he wrote one himself, in which he carefully made up all the references (this was accepted). He also refused to conform at work. He went about in a long black cloak and four-cornered hat and grew his hair and beard long (which was strictly forbidden). When he was ordered to cut his hair, according to one story, he shaved it all off and came to work in a long black wig and false beard.

After leaving school, like so many of his contemporaries, he went through a bout of black depression. Then, at the University he discovered an organised channel for his wilful disobedience – in socialism, and especially Fourierism, which he first encountered in Professor Poroshin's lectures on political economy and statistics. From then on, with a passion, determination and single-mindedness rarely equalled, he 'vowed (himself) to the service of humanity'. In all his actions he was disinterested and completely dedicated, 'a man of strong spirit and firm will'. Not a minute of his time would he waste on something that wasn't useful to the cause. He refused to marry, and became an indefatigable, almost twenty-four hour a day propagandist. He rarely slept, he could only be found at home on Friday nights. He was always out and about, acting, preaching, trying to convert people to socialism. At work his main job was dealing with foreigners' complaints. He took their interests to heart and enthusiastically defended them against the arbitrary actions of the police. He set up a law office with Aleksandr Baranovskii and offered 'to act free of charge in court cases for all poor people who cannot afford to hire a lawyer'. Out of work he 'worked hard at his self-education' and buried himself fanatically in the reading of socialist books. At the same time he carried his outbursts against authority into the streets in an attempt to rouse the masses. Above all he rushed around talking to people, meeting people, in their homes, in the clubs, in the Nobles' Assembly, at masquerades. As a result he was soon 'acquainted with the whole of Petersburg'. He joined the *meshchane* dancing class, (where no member of the gentry would normally be seen), he forced himself to drink wine (which he hated) and to play cards (which he disapproved of) 'with the sole aim of making acquaintances, of getting to know and choosing people' to invite to the evenings he held at his house on Friday nights.[54] These evenings started more or less accidentally. In autumn 1845 Petrashevskii, left by his father's death independent and in possession of a considerable fortune, began to ask his acquaintances to drop in.[55] Then he set aside regular days – Fridays. The guests came in the period from October to April, in summer Petrashevskii went away to his dacha. For the first two years of its existence, the winter of 1845–6 and 1846–7, the core of the circle was formed by Maikov and his friends – Miliutin, Shtrandman, Saltykov and Esakov. The most notable of his other visitors was Nikolai Danilevskii, the future Panslavist and author of *Russia and Europe*. At this time he was studying for his master's degree in botany in St. Petersburg University. He had a brilliant mind and quickly became the circle's expert on Fourierism. He was, however, always one of the most right-wing of Petrashevskii's visitors, attracted to Fourierism because it could be interpreted in a peaceful, apolitical sense. Danilevskii was a regular visitor at Petrashevskii's right up to 1849. Other early guests who stayed to form the backbone of the circle included the omnipresent and talkative student Khanykov, the poet Pleshcheev, the writer Miliukov and a host of minor figures – civil servants Baranovskii, Nikolai Serebriakov, P.V. Berevkin, students Maderski and Petr Latkin. Passing guests included Ratovskii, assistant professor at Kazan and the poet Apollon Grigor'ev, at this time close to Petrashevskii and interested in Fourierism, although his ideas were already developing in an opposite direction.[56]

In the winter of 1846–7, Petrashevskii's visitors were joined by others who were to play a prominent part throughout the circle's history – Dostoevskii, Durov, Aleksandr Balasoglo and Feliks Tol'. Balasoglo and Tol', unlike Dostoevskii and Durov were staunch supporters of Petrashevskii and didn't visit any other circle. Balasoglo was one of the more original of the Petrashevtsy. The son of a major-general of Turkish origin, he was born with an unquenchable enthusiasm for life and developed a passion for travel. His dream was always to go to the East. He began by joining the Black Sea Fleet as a cabin boy in 1826 when he was thirteen. In 1829 he was promoted to midshipman and transferred to Kronstadt. Devoured by a passion for knowledge, he began to attend lectures on Eastern languages at St. Petersburg University and to search for a civilian post which would enable him to visit, or at least study, the East. Finally after long periods of unemployment, when he tried unsuccessfully to support himself and his family by various literary enterprises, he found a job in the Eastern archives of the Ministry of Foreign Affairs.[57] Balasoglo was self-educated but highly intelligent and had an extraordinary capacity for the direct expression of ideas and feelings. His writings are an uncontrolled, but vivid jumble of ideas and images. Tol', a German by birth, a teacher by trade, was a more sober character. His knowledge of the language led him to take a particular interest in the ideas of the German left-Hegelians, especially on religion. Other new members at this point included the ex-Lycéen Vladimir Engel'son, Speshnev's and later Herzen's friend, Maikov's brother Apollon, Nikolai Semenov, the future peasant reformer and also the officer L. N. Khovrin, the teachers Vladimir Kuznetsov, V. A. Geler, Petr Egorov; the economist Ivan Vernadskii; Nikolai Blagoveshchenskii; civil servants Petr Mal'te, Mikhail Chirikov, Evstafii Marcinowski, Ignatii Poniatowski, Karl Ol'dekop; students A. G. Begurnii, Platon Deev, Erast Zalebedskii and Vladislav Sipko.[58]

The main emphasis of the circle in the first two years was on self-education; the main event the organisation of a collective library (Spring 1846). According to Baranovskii, Petrashevskii was, 'always saying that our education was far from finished and that it needed to be completed'. The way to achieve this was through the study of the works of the French utopian socialists. They discussed Fourier most of all, but also the French eighteenth-century *philosophes*, Cabet, Pierre Leroux and the new Russian journals. As Danilevskii said, 'Petrashevskii dragged us all into literature and politics.' Apart from the fact that they had a library, the circle was really no different from other groups of high-minded, idealistic young men. Saltykov describes the Petrashevskii circle as typical, 'I remember long winter evenings and our friendly modest conversation, lasting long after midnight. How easy it was to live in that time, what a deep faith in the future, what various hopes and ideas inspired us ... a new life blew over our souls.'[59]

But at the beginning of 1847, Baranovskii says, the circle began to fall apart. Maikov, Shtrandman, Miliutin, Saltykov and Esakov stopped coming to it. This was partly because, as happened with so many small circles, its members had got to know each other too well and had exhausted their topics of conversation. It had become insipid and boring. Petrashevskii and Pleshcheev told 'the most pitiful and tedious anecdotes about their professors'. But the defectors were also influenced by their dislike of Petrashevskii and his 'wild and inappropriate outbursts' (i.e. his habit of making public scenes). Dostoevskii several times saw Maikov pretending not to be in when Petrashevskii called. They also disapproved of the turn the Fridays were taking. In the winter of 1846–7 Petrashevskii invited lots of new people without consulting the others and instead of a circle of close friends, it was becoming more like a club.[60]

This tendency became more pronounced when Petrashevskii revived his Fridays in the autumn of 1847. In Russia, as in Europe, 1847 was the year in which, intellectually, things really began to happen. As Evgenii Lamanskii said, 'In 1847 a social movement began in Petersburg.'[61] It was the year of Belinskii's *Letter to Gogol*, the year of the foundation of *Sovremennik*, Herzen's *Letters from the Avenue Marigny*, about life in Paris, Miliutin's economic articles, the first instalments of Turgenev's *Sketches from a Hunter's Album*, and Saltykov's first story. Petrashevskii rushed round St. Petersburg recruiting people wherever he went and was 'extremely undiscriminating in his choice of guests'. They flocked to his little wooden house at the end of Bolshaia Sadovaia Ulitsa, usually fifteen to twenty on a Friday and as many as sixty on his birthday. They were no longer his friends, or even people he really knew at all. There was a rapid turnover – every Friday new faces appeared. Members of different circles met each other for almost public discussions and a whole cross-section of radical society could be seen. The circle soon became famous. V. Petrov, a university friend of Mikhailov, for example, wrote to him in Novocherkassk about the sights of the capital, 'We've got the opera, the circus, the Mikhailovskii theatre ... we've got the sermons of Nil'sen and the propaganda of Petrashevskii, we've got the public lectures and the *feuilletons* of Pleshcheev.' The liberal economist Konstantin Veselovskii agreed, 'the whole town knew about Petrashevskii's evenings', though according to him, 'they only spoke of them to laugh'.[62]

Among the new visitors was Nikolai Speshnev, the only person to exercise in Petrashevskii's circle an influence comparable to Petrashevskii's own. Speshnev was, from the start, 'someone out of the ordinary'. He was rich, clever and handsome, with long flowing curls, 'outstanding masculine beauty' and 'could well have served as a model for sketches of the head and type of the Saviour'.[63] He was one of the few Petrashevtsy who did not have to work for a living, and the only one who had been abroad. He was cold, silent and withdrawn but he possessed an extraordinary charisma. He'd been expelled from the Lycée in 1829 largely because the authorities were frightened of his power over his friends. He promptly ran off to Helsinki, then Europe, with Anna Cechanowiecki, his neighbour's young and beautiful wife (he was nineteen). He remained abroad for almost seven years (1840–7), visited Germany, Austria, Switzerland and France and plunged himself into the ferment of the latest ideas, writing to his mother, 'All that matters is whether life, life will be long enough to swallow everything that's written.'[64] His calm logic carried him further and further to the left. He had no prejudices, no moral scruples, so there was no obstacle to his proceedings to where reason logically carried him. His study of the German philosophers ended up with the unlimited egoism of Max Stirner, his study of the French socialists with the materialist communism of Theodore Dézamy – the most *outré* theories of the day. In Petrashevskii's circle he represented the revolutionary extreme and he used his power and influence to push it dramatically to the left. Other new arrivals in winter 1847–8 included *chinovniki* Ippolit Debu, Porfirii Lamanskii and Aleksei Shchelkov.

The most prominent newcomers in autumn-winter 1848 were Konstantin Debu, the army officers Mombelli, L'vov and Grigor'ev, the student Pavel Filippov, Dmitrii Akhsharumov, a civil servant, and Jan-Ferdinand Jastrzebski, a teacher. Filippov, reckless and left-wing, soon became associated with Speshnev. Akhsharumov, another official from the Asiatic Department of the Ministry of Foreign Affairs, later wrote some of the fullest and most balanced descriptions of Petrashevskii and his friends. But, in spite of his perspicacity and the revolutionary nature of some of his writings, he comes across as a colourless, pedantic character. Jastrzebski (known affectionately as *Pan* among the Petrashevtsy) was a Pole from Minsk, an expert on and teacher of

political economy and the probable author of articles on the subject in
Finskii vestnik. He was a great wit, always the centre of attention and
loved by everyone. Pal'm described him as 'a man not in his first youth
(he was thirty-five), extremely intelligent, with the most charming
eccentricities and also a terrible ladies' man'.[65]

More people appeared in Spring 1849 – Konstantin Timkovskii,
Vasilii Golovinskii, a lawyer, the naval officer Pavel Kuz'min; the artists
Aleksei Berestov, Evstafii Bernadskii and others. The most interesting
of these were Timkovskii, whose revolutionary fervour has already been
mentioned and Golovinskii, who had developed independently to a
position on the far left of the Petrashevtsy (especially on the question
of serfdom). Other people, new to St. Petersburg, came by hearsay –
including the Siberian gold prospector, Raphael Chernosvitov, and
Aleksandr Beklemishev from Reval. Even older men, members of more
exalted circles, like Ogarev, considered going out of curiosity.[66]

The circle represented 'an extraordinary kaleidoscope of the most
varied opinions about contemporary events, the actions of the government, the newest works of literature in the different branches of
knowledge and town news was discussed – everyone talked loudly about
everything without any constraint'. According to Dostoevskii, nobody
at Petrashevskii's ever agreed with anyone else about anything. But this
did not matter. The point of going to Petrashevskii's was to argue, and
without the quarrels, the evenings would have been extremely boring.[67]
People argued in small groups, all over the room, all talking at once.
The first step towards bringing some order into the evenings was made
in winter 1847, on Speshnev's suggestion, when they introduced a bell
(with a figure of Liberty on top) and elected a president (usually
Chirikov) to ring it. Conversation, however, still only became general
occasionally when a quarrel on some question of general interest flared
up. The circle only became properly organised as a debating club in 1848
when the February Revolution in France imparted a sense of urgency
and a unity of purpose to the discussions. They began with tea, poured
out by Maderski, who lived at a nominal rent in Petrashevskii's house
on condition that he performed this duty. Then someone made a speech
and they discussed it. Then, between nine and ten, they had a break for
a free supper (after this some of the more unscrupulous, like the spiteful
Serebriakov, 'rushed into the hall, put on their galoshes and went home').
Then, once 'rum, cognac and wine had warmed the voices and imparted
an involuntary freedom to the conversation' the debates became much
rowdier – sometimes there was another speech, sometimes a continuation

of the first discussion. The guests stayed until one, two, sometimes three in the morning. In June 1848, for example, the Russian situation was talked about before supper, Danilevskii lectured on Fourierism after it. Jastrzebski spoke on political economy, Tol' on religion and Dostoevskii read Belinskii's *Letter to Gogol*.[68] Anton Rubinstein, the pianist, just back from Berlin, described how a new acquaintance led him unsuspecting:

> beyond Pokrovskii Church ... to some flat and there we found a large gathering of men, young and middle-aged, military and civilian ... But I did not see our host. I asked about him, they replied: 'Wait, you will see, we will be called in'. At last a bell rang, the doors were opened, and we went into a large room where in front of a platform stood a row of chairs as at a concert. Onto the stage there came a handsome man with a beard and he began to read some sort of socialist and communist tract – as far as I remember, printed. All this surprised me exceedingly and I did not hide by surprise from my neighbours: 'I never expected to meet anything like this here in Russia!' I said.[69]

As the police chief Liprandi notes, it was 'the full procedure of organised Western clubs'. People coming to Petrashevskii's for the first time in 1848–49, like Chernosvitov and Timkovskii, refused to believe it was just a circle, were sure it was a secret society and demanded to know its aim.[70]

III — THE PETRASHEVTSY AND FRENCH SOCIALISM

The Petrashevtsy were set apart from other radical contemporaries by their open adherence to socialist doctrines. These doctrines all derived in the first place from France. In the 1840s, France (or rather Paris) was still very much the centre of socialism in Europe. The word socialism meant French socialism. Elsewhere only a few men had developed similar ideas: in England, Robert Owen; in Switzerland, Wilhelm Weitling; in Germany Karl Marx was only just beginning to formulate his theories.

The decade saw the great flowering of utopian socialism in France. The ideas which came to be known as socialist go back to two highly individual and very isolated thinkers — Comte Henri de Saint-Simon and Charles Fourier, both of whom developed their theories during and as a reaction to, the French revolution and Napoleonic wars. By the 1830s, two schools had emerged, basing themselves on the writings of these two men. The followers of Saint-Simon were initially much more influential; the Fourierists few in number and mediocre in calibre, their activities hampered by the continued presence and irascible behaviour of their ageing mentor. By the 1840s, the position had been roughly reversed and Fourierism had become the more popular doctrine.

French socialist doctrine

In the 1840s, there appeared a multitude of other socialist leaders, each with his own group of followers; his own publications, his own meetings, clubs, protests and quarrels — and his own blueprint for the perfect society. There was an extraordinary number of ideologists and an extraordinary diversity among them. There were socialists and communists, Christians and atheists, pacifists and revolutionaries. However they were united by their hatred of capitalism, their belief in progress, their conviction of the need to reform society on the principle of association and their faith in the creative power of the people. They made social and economic questions the order of the day. These were discussed everywhere − from the workshop to the academic hall. Republicans and socialists alike poured abuse on the head of Louis-Philippe and Paris hummed with the schemes and schisms of the different socialist and communist sects.

The main lines in this ferment of ideas were Fourierist, Saint-Simonian, socialist *à la* Blanc and *à la* Proudhon, Christian socialist and utopian communist. Fourierism, which preached a socialism based on unlimited freedom for human nature and the peaceful reform of society through the establishment of socialist communities (*phalansteries*), simplified and clarified under the leadership of Victor Considerant, was probably the most important socialist school.[1] Saint-Simon's idea of an elitist, technocratic and governmental socialism, radicalised by his disciples (through, for example, the idea of abolishing inheritance) continued to have a great influence in France. However the Saint-Simonians' religious and mystical extravangances (culminating in the famous trial in 1832 and subsequent exodus to the East), had discredited them as a movement. In the 1840s their theories were developed in a more egalitarian direction − their mysticism and ideas on history by Pierre Leroux and his disciple the novelist George Sand,[2] and their ideas on association and government intervention by Louis Blanc. Other famous ex-Saint-Simonians included Auguste Comte, Saint-Simon's secretary, who abandoned socialism to become the father of positivist philosophy. Proudhon represented popular anarchism, or, as he called it at this stage, mutualism. His was a contradictory socialism, full of excessively radical statements − 'Property is theft!' 'God is dead!' -but moderate in essence, in favour of the golden mean, a balancing between contradictions, and the transformation of France into a land run by independent peasant farmers. Among the Christian socialists were Philippe Buchez, Alphonse Esquiros, L'Abbé Constant and, above all, Felicité Robert de Lamennais, the leading Catholic theologian who broke with the Church to write *Paroles d'un croyant*, a passionate denunciation of tyranny. The utopian communists were bitterly divided between the religious and moral theories of Cabet and the atheism and materialism of Dézamy. Both the socialism and the communism of the 1840s were predominantly peaceful in nature. But, by their side, there subsisted another, older current of French radicalism − the tradition of revolutionary conspiracy deriving from Gracchus Babeuf. Its chief representatives in the thirties and forties were Armand Barbès and Auguste Blanqui.

The Petrashevtsy were influenced by all these theories, though it was

for Fourier they expressed the greatest enthusiasm. They refused to subscribe totally to any one socialist system and studied and borrowed from
them all. They adopted an eclectic attitude, picking out ideas here and
there from the theories of different French socialists and radicals, which
for some reason or other seemed appropriate to their own situation in
Russia. Chief among these was the Fourierist idea of a socialism based on
unlimited freedom for human nature. Other ideas they adopted were: the
Saint-Simonian philosophy of history; the emphasis on science, evident
in the writings of Saint-Simon and Comte; a virulent anti-capitalism,
derived from Fourier, Louis Blanc and others; the notion of the organisation of production and of basing socialism on association, common
to all the French socialists, but most pronounced among the Fourierists;
the Saint-Simonian theory of art as propaganda; and an emphasis on
the emancipation of women. Other aspects of utopian socialist theory
were either ignored or rejected outright by the Petrashevtsy. They had
little patience with the more bizarre elements — the extravagant romanticism of the Saint-Simonians or the fantastic cosmogony and sexual
theories of Fourier. They differed most strikingly from the majority of
French socialists in their attitude to religion and to revolution, on the
latter tending to side with the radical conspirators.

The most valuable idea in French socialism, was, in the Petrashevtsy's
opinion, the Fourierist notion of basing socialism on unlimited freedom
for human nature. They were attracted to Fourierism more than to any
other doctrine, because, in theory at least, it appeared to offer a greater
freedom to man.

Fourier drew heavily on the mechanistic ideas of the eighteenth
century *philosophes* about a fixed human nature, and even more so, on
Rousseau's theory of a natural man. He argued that all man's instincts
(or as he called them *passions*) had been planted in him once and for
all. Man's nature could not be changed by society; it was society that
had to be changed to fit man's nature. All man's instincts and impulses,
even the wildest, were given him by God. They were therefore basically
good and would produce good if society was organised according to
them. He poured abuse on the present organisation of society (*Civilisation*) which was based on a flagrant disregard for human nature, in
which the passions were repressed, men miserable, and on the
philosophers and moralists who taught men that it was right to repress
their passions. Instead, Fourier advocated *Harmony*, a social system
which would free and legitimise the passions. If they were correctly
combined, unlimited freedom for the passions would, he believed,

produce order and concord and allow each individual to achieve the aim of his existence – a full development of his nature and an abundance of pleasure.[3]

Fourier's utopian community, the phalanstery, is an an illustration of how the passions can be correctly combined. It is based on a detailed and imaginative analysis of human nature, the main outlines of which the Petrashevtsy adopted.

Fourier said that man had twelve chief passions. These included five material or sensual passions, which corresponded to the five senses and inspired man to desire *luxury*; four affective passions, friendship, love, ambition and family feeling, which inspired men to combine with one another in *groups*; and three distributive or motor passions, Fourier's most interesting and original conception. These were the most important and brought all the others into play. There was the *cabaliste*, 'the passion for intrigue', which inspired man to emulate and compete with others; the *papillone*, the butterfly passion, which inspired the need for a constant variety of occupation; and the *composite*, a feeling of ecstacy, which arose from the simultaneous satisfaction of more than one passion. These different passions were present in different degrees of intensity and different combinations in different individuals.[4]

Fourier called this the theory of passionate attraction, the law of social bodies, and declared it to be a discovery as great as Newton's theory of gravitation – the law of material bodies.[5] In his discussion of the organisation of life in the phalanstery, he developed it in several interesting directions: into a theory of 'attractive labour', a theory of vocational education, a theory of crime and a theory of sexuality. The Petrashevtsy had a particular admiration for the first three.

The theory of attractive labour was the means by which Fourier solved the unpleasant problem of the need to work in utopia. Fourier was the first thinker seriously to put forward the idea that work might become pleasure.[6] The secret was to relate it to the twelve passions. In the phalanstery, people would be free to choose only those jobs which wholly appealed to them; they would work at a variety of occupations and change their jobs every few hours (to satisfy the *papillone*) they would compete in *groups* and *series* of different branches of labour (to satisfy the *cabaliste*); they would be involved in their labour by the payment of a dividend rather than a wage; everyone would be guaranteed a comfortable minimum of existence.[7] There would be no problem in finding people attracted to even the most repulsive and dirtiest jobs, Fourier believed – these would be done by children, especially little boys, organised in *little hordes*, since they had 'a natural penchant for filth'.[8]

Education occupies a particularly important place in Fourier's system and many of his ideas have been incorporated into the tenets of modern educational theory. He banned all coercion in the upbringing of children. From the age of two-and-a-half children's instincts and curiosity would be aroused by giving them miniature tools and instruments. They would at once begin imitating their elders, through trial and error discover the occupations to which they were attracted and thus gradually become involved in the production process. By the age of four they would be earning their own living. Involvement in production would arouse in them a desire for knowledge which sooner or later would cause them to ask to be taught how to read and write. Fourier also laid great stress on the education of the senses (children's sense of hearing and sight would be developed by opera; of taste and smell, by *cuisine*).[9]

Fourier also advanced the bold theory that all crimes were the result of the unnatural organisation of society, rather than any evil inherent in human nature. Crimes were the direct result of Civilisation's denial of expression to the passions, which 'driven out of the door come back through the window', taking on pernicious new forms. They became warped and perverted and developed 'recurrences of the subversive genre' i.e. corrupt versions, which produced a double evil instead of the double good which would have been born of their free development.[10] Gambling, for example, arose from a denial of the passion for intrigue; snobbery from the denial of the passion for unity. All of these forms would disappear automatically if society was organised correctly and all passions were freely satisfied. Meanwhile no-one should be held responsible for his crimes. This theory was developed by the novelist Eugène Sue in his *Mystères de Paris* and had a particularly strong influence on the Petrashevtsy.

In his argument that freedom of development for the passions meant legitimisation of love in all its manifestations, that everyone should be free to enjoy the amount and the type of sexual freedom that appealed to them, Fourier was far ahead of his time. Though not quite as priggish as Fourier's French disciples, who edited the 'panerogenous customs' out of his book *Le Nouveau monde industriel et sociétaire*, and refused to publish his *Le Nouveau monde amoureux*,[11] most of the Petrashevtsy were little influenced by his sexual theories.

The Petrashevtsy's second chief debt to the French socialists was to

Saint-Simon and his followers, from whom they derived both their
philosophy of history and their respect for science.

Their ideas on history came partly from Saint-Simon, partly from his
disciple Saint-Amand Bazard. Saint-Simon's whole theory rests on his
interpretation of history as a process of social change. All social institutions, including property, the political system and religion, had only
a relative historical importance. They were changed through the class
struggle.[12] This was to some extent a material process. Saint-Simon held
that the property relations sustained by any social order confer upon
it its essential character and that a shift of the balance of property and
productive relations in favour of the oppressed class contributed to its
victory over its oppressors.[13] For Saint-Simon, the increase in the
economic weight of the oppressed class was the outcome of its superiority
to the oppressing class in the field of scientific invention. 'The prisoners
are always cleverer than the gaolers and oppression stimulates inventions
which overthrow repression'. Ideas were the moving force in history.
History was the process of the self-transformation of man through his
own intellectual progress.[14] New ideas, originated by the representatives
of new social classes, mature within an old society, undermine it and
finally destroy it. This leads to a creative era in which the new ideas
develop, flourish and hold undisputed sway, uniting the whole of
mankind. According to Saint-Simon there had been two great creative
eras in the West so far − Graeco-Roman civilisation and the Middle
Ages (the Petrashevtsy, however, were little interested in Saint-Simon's
analysis of these). The institutions of the Middle Ages had been
disintegrating since the fifteenth century. The work of destruction had
been completed by the French Revolution and it was now time for a new
and superior period of unity and order to begin.[15] Saint-Simon saw
history as an uninterrupted chain of progress, determined and inevitable,
even though historical changes were the result of human inspiration. The
aim of the study of history was to allow mankind to predict its future.
Saint-Simon had his eye obstinately fixed on the future − 'The golden
age of the human race lies not behind but ahead of us.'[16]

The idea of alternative creative and destructive epochs was amplified
by Bazard in his theory of critical and organic epochs. In organic epochs
individuals were linked by a common social bond and common social
values. However, mankind progressed, the ideas and institutions of these
epochs became obsolete, and disintegrated, giving way to critical epochs,
in which, 'all communication of thought, all action of the whole, all co-
ordination ceases'. Saint-Simon had seen critical epochs as periods in

which the oppressed freed themselves and therefore greeted them with enthusiasm. For the Saint-Simonians, however, they were the most terrible periods of history, periods of emptiness, isolation, egoism, loneliness and longing. (The difference in attitude was largely explained by the Saint-Simonians' religious fervour — organic epochs were religious, successively fetishism, polytheism and monotheism, critical epochs were atheistic.) Bazard also added to Saint-Simonism the idea of history as the gradual lessening of antagonisms and increasing association between men.[17]

The Petrashevtsy were also interested in Pierre Leroux's development of Saint-Simon's concept of the continuity of history into a mystical theory of humanity as a great collective being, stretching from the beginning to the end of time, absorbing all the men who had ever lived and all those who were yet to live. As parts of an immortal whole, men lived eternally, died and were reborn.[18] His ideas were illustrated in George Sand's novel *La Comtesse de Rudolstadt*, whose hero, Albert, is a reincarnation of John Hus with a visionary insight into his previous existence.

In spite of this, the Petrashevtsy laid a great emphasis on science, which they derived from Saint-Simon and especially from Comte, and which distinguished them sharply from the more impractical French utopians. In his early works, Saint-Simon said that the great unifying principle which was to replace that of the Middle Ages (religion) was to be science; the new leaders of society, the scientists. In 1803 he called on his fellow men to end the prevailing moral and social crisis by appointing a *Council of Newton*, composed of scientists and artists, to the spiritual leadership of mankind. Its task was to prepare a new encyclopedia, which would synthesise the dreadfully fragmented branches of the sciences, uniting them around a single principle, Newton's law of gravity, and replacing Diderot's purely destructive encyclopedia.[19]

Comte broke with Saint-Simon because Saint-Simon turned to practical social problems before creating the new encyclopedia, which Comte regarded as the essential preliminary. In the six volumes of his *Cours de philosophie positive*, (1830—42) he made a systematic study of the sciences with the aim of determining the boundaries and the essence of each and creating a synthesis of knowledge. It is also a history of science, based on the law of three states in the human intelligence. These were the theological (with its three subdivisions — fetishism, polytheism and monotheism), the metaphysical and the positive. They corresponded to three phases of development:

Man began by seeing phenomena of all sorts as due to the direct and continuous influence of supernatural agents; he considered them next as produced by various abstract forces inherent in bodies but distinct and heterogeneous; finally, he limited himself to envisaging them as subordinated to a certain number of invariable natural laws, abandoning the search for higher causes.[20]

Comte traced the development of the various sciences from one state to another — the natural sciences had already reached the exact or positive stage, the social sciences, however had been left behind and were still at the theological or metaphysical stage — and tried to show how positive truth could be introduced into the social sciences. His idea was that the world was governed by two principles — order and progress. Under a correct state of affairs, these would always be found in indissoluble connection. This connection had to be reflected in the method of the social sciences, which would combine a static, i.e. descriptive and a dynamic, i.e. historical approach to society.[21] The Petrashevtsy were among the first men in Russia to study Comte, and Maikov, in particular, was very heavily influenced by his ideas.

The Petrashevtsy were much less interested in the religious aspects of French socialism. Neither of the great utopians, Fourier or Saint-Simon, had been strongly religious. Fourier had included God in his system, but as a distant, impartial being, just the force which sets the world in motion.[22] Religion is largely replaced in his teaching by the strange science of analogy and the even more fantastic cosmogony. According to these, animals and plants were the offspring of the planets, produced by copulation between them. Everything in the universe was linked, everything from plants and animals to geometrical shapes, mirrored the same twelve passions to be found in man. When the passions were organised harmoniously, there would be new creations of animals — anti-lions, anti-sharks, etc., as peaceful and useful to man as their predecessors had been harmful; a new Aurora Borealis would warm the earth.[23] At the end of his life, Saint-Simon had second thoughts about the efficacy of science as a unifying theory and in 1825 published *Le Nouveau Christianisme* invoking an improved version of the Christian moral principle: 'All men should behave to one another as brothers', adding that, 'The whole of society should work towards the moral and physical amelioration of the poorest and most numerous class', to back it up.[24] However, his remained essentially a secular doctrine.

The romantic socialists of he 1830s and 1840s were much more under

the influence of religion. The Fourierists abandoned Fourier's cosmogony and attempted to reconcile their master's principles with those
of Christianity. Some of them, for example Zoé Gatti de Gamond, leader
of a dissident group of Fourierists, were extremely devout, others
combined Fourierism with the religious mysticism of Swedenborg.[25]
The Saint-Simonians were much more extravagantly religious. They took
up and developed the ideas of *Le Nouveau Christianisme*, speaking of
Saint-Simon as an inspired prophet, almost a god; proclaiming Saint-
Simonism to the world as a religion; and, finally, organising themselves
into a Church. The central doctrine of the Saint-Simonian religion, the
rehabilitation of the flesh, however was a sort of neopaganism, which
merely added a religious varnish to Saint-Simon's industrial theory.[26]

There were some socialists in the 1840s who were religious in the
conventional sense and definitely believed in God — Lamennais, Buchez,
the Abbé Constant and others. There were also a few who definitely did
not believe in God — including Dézamy (a materialist) and Proudhon
(who rejected God as he did every authority over man). The majority
— the Fourierists, the Saint-Simonians, Leroux (with his Religion of
Humanity), Cabet (who identified communism with Christianity) and
Louis Blanc — came somewhere in between. They shared the Saint-
Simonian reaction against the critical, atheist philosophy of the eighteenth century. There was a common feeling that socialism would need
new moral principles to unite mankind, that these principles should be
a purified version of the principles of Christianity. As well, the identification of socialism with the teaching of Christ and the communalism
and egalitarianism of the early Christians helped to legitimise it historically. Almost all the socialists filled their writings with Christian imagery.
The revolution of 1848, unlike that of 1789, did not attack religion but
exalted Christ 'the holy, the sublime republican, the republican of all
times and all countries'.[27]

The Petrashevtsy also drew from the French socialists, and from
Fourier above all, a strong dislike of capitalism. Fourier's critique of
capitalism is the most powerful part of his theory. It was erratic, but
wonderfully violent and contained prophetic flashes of insight into the
workings of the system. Echoing Rousseau's contempt for society,
Fourier applied to the whole of Civilisation his principle of 'absolute
doubt'. Civilisation was 'a world upside-down', a 'social hell'. It made
men each other's natural enemies, one man's meat was another man's
poison — doctors made their living from other people's illnesses; lawyers
from their quarrels; architects from the fires which burned down their

houses; glaziers from the hailstorms which broke their windows. More than this, most people were parasites, engaged on work which would be completely unnecessary in a sane world, including almost all women, children and servants, all employees of the state, nine-tenths of merchants. Fourier was also horrified by the waste and inefficiency of civilised society, by the squandering of natural resources which could have been used to increase the sum of pleasures in the world — the 300 women in 300 little houses cooking 300 little dinners over 300 little fires for 300 men coming home from work, while three or four women with one big fire, using one-thirtieth of the fuel, could have done the job better. The greatest evil of all, 'the vampire which sucks the blood out of the social body', was commerce. Fourier was bitterly hostile to it and greatly exaggerated its importance, partly because he had been unsuccessful in various business dealings, partly because it was the most visible feature of early capitalism. All these vices of Civilisation, Fourier felt, were concentrated in the squalid, teeming cities, where men were heaped up in units far too big for their own good (Fourier was one of the first to point to bigness as the curse of modern society).[28] Fourier's critique of competition was taken up and amplified by Louis Blanc. Louis Blanc's view of economics was very simple — unrestricted competition was the cause of all evils. His *Organisation du travail* passionately denounced competition as 'a system of extermination' for the people; for the bourgeoisie, 'an active cause of impoverishment and ruin' — no-one benefited from it.[29]

The Petrashevtsy added to this a more sophisticated analysis of capitalism's workings and critique of the political economists, inspired partly by Sismondi, partly by Proudhon and partly by their own study of political economy. Sismondi was the first economist to voice doubts about capitalism and to disturb the complacency of his colleagues. In his *Nouveaux principes de l'économie politique*, (1819), he rejected Say's Law, according to which supply created its own demand and with it the central notion of classical political economy — that the unregulated expansion of industrial production would necessarily increase the welfare of the whole human race. According to Sismondi, the discovery of new mechanical methods of production would lead to over-production and the markets would be flooded with goods. Cut-throat competition between capitalists would force them to cut wages and increase working hours. There would thus be no purchasers for their goods because the mass of the population, the workers would have no money. The glut could only be cleared and the system survive by means of repeated crises, in which the weakest capitalists would go to the wall and thousands of workers be thrown out of their jobs. Sismondi's view of capitalism offered the prospect of ever-increasing social chaos — of capitalists fighting each other for markets, of workers fighting each other for jobs and uniting to fight the capitalists. The only solution, in Sismondi's opinion, was government intervention and the rational organisation of industry, which would henceforth have as its aim not the increase of wealth, but the happiness of man.[30]

Proudhon based his socialism on the principle of justice, defined as 'the respect spontaneously felt and reciprocally guaranteed of human dignity'.[31] In his *Système des contradictions économiques*, a book which both influenced and irritated the Petrashevtsy, he combined Sismondi's idea that every economic phenomenon had both a bad and a good side, produced misery as well as wealth, with his own particular version of Hegel's dialectic, and tried to show that social justice rests on the reconciliation of extremes. According to Proudhon, the principles of justice and equality which existed externally in the realm of intelligence, lost their original coherence on their embodiment in the chaotic sphere of space and time.[32] He tried to show how this had happened through an exposition of economic history, which he treats as an ahistorical series of antitheses. Each phenomenon arises in contradiction and antagonism to another, for example machines to the division of labour, monopoly to competition, protection to free trade, etc., and each is itself a contradiction, with a warring good and bad side. The battle of contradictions gives rise to a perpetual conflict of interest and uncontrolled competition between individuals, groups, social classes. In this competition the selfish, unscrupulous few always triumph over the mass of the people and over reason and justice. But Proudhon did not believe in resolving the contradictions in any synthesis or system, or in ending competition, (this would only lead to some sort of communist despotism). All that was needed was to establish a balance between the contradictions, 'the mutual interaction of antagonistic elements or reciprocity'.[33] This would ensure the independence and security of the individual, while allowing him freedom of action.

In addition, the evils of pauperism in the West were brought home to the Petrashevtsy by the studies of Eugène Buret, Louis Villermé, le Vicomte de Villeneuve-Bargemont and other writers sympathetic to socialism, which were full of illustrations of the terrible living and working conditions of the lower classes.

The Petrashevtsy accepted wholeheartedly the central socialist idea that the solution to the problems of capitalism was a reorganisation of society on the basis of a redistribution of wealth and the association of worker and capitalist.

Work, all the socialists agreed, should be the chief criterion in the division of wealth. The fundamental principle was established by Saint-Simon when he divided society into the *industriels*, who performed useful labour and the *oisifs*, who lived idly off incomes from landed property or government service. His view of the relative importance of these classes was set out with revolutionary clarity in his *Parabole*, in which he claimed that if France were to lose her, 'three thousand leading scholars, artists and industrialists', it would be a national catastrophe which it would take a generation to repair, while the loss of the thirty thousand leading nobles, ministers, clergy, lawyers and landowners would only benefit the country.[34] The Petrashevtsy had less sympathy, however, for the Saint-Simonian idea of rewarding people for their work, according to the elitist principle of talent, 'from each according to his capacities, to each according to his works'. Their sympathy was divided between the solutions of Fourier − the division of the product in the ratio: three parts in twelve to talent, four to capital, five to labour − and of the more democratic socialist thinkers of the forties − above all Louis Blanc, inventor of the famous formula, 'from each according to his capacities, to each according to his needs'.[35]

Association was the great remedy, the antidote to capitalism. The rift between worker and capitalist in France had grown wide enough to be noticeable, but not wide enough to seem impossible to bridge. The utopian socialists of the 1840s all believed that it was possible to associate the two classes and eliminate the differences between them. The great apostle of association was Fourier, who designed the phalanstery as the nucleus of the future society. This was a small unit, of 1,620 people, and would occupy one square mile of land. All the phalansterians would live in one huge building, bigger than Versailles, its wings connected by covered street-galleries heated in winter, ventilated in summer. It would contain collective dining rooms, nurseries, meeting rooms, ballrooms and, on the outer wings, workshops. The phalanstery was intended to associate men without destroying their freedom and individuality. It preserved a large element of choice − in the matter of living accommodation, dress, meals, etc., as well as occupation. There would still be rich and poor, − Fourier believed, 'all equality is political poison' − but all workers could become capitalists by saving up and buying shares in the phalanstery, and this, Fourier hoped, would cause class hatreds to evaporate.[36] Work would be mainly agricultural and would be made attractive by being organised in series, each dealing with a different sort of job — for example, rose-growing or cattle-farming; each series would be subdivided into groups, for example, that of pear-growers into growers of citron pears, butter pears etc. The groups and series would compete against each other in a friendly fashion, and people would change their job every one or two hours. People from different phalansteries would work together in huge industrial armies, which would replace Civilisation's harmful armies and transform the surface of the globe, by, for example, irrigating the Sahara.[37] The more economical organisation of labour, and in particular, the abolition of the family unit, would, Fourier believed, give rise to an unbelievable increase in wealth. The poorest man in Harmony would be richer than the richest man today. Life would become a succession of different pleasures. Fourier's phalanstery was taken as a model by a large number of socialists and communists, including both Cabet and Dézamy.

Louis Blanc and Proudhon, however, suggested slightly different and more down-to-earth forms of association. Blanc recommended 'social workshops', the association of workers in state-sponsored, profit-sharing productive cooperatives. Competition would be forever ended as the social workshops peacefully absorbed the old type of enterprise. Proudhon's solution was just a new organisation of credit, based on a series of free contracts, and designed to guarantee the independence of the individual producer. In 1848 he published his project for a *People's Bank*. All income from capital, 'this despot which oppresses labour' was to be suppressed, and with it money. A central bank would make free credit available to all producers and a new system would be introduced for the direct exchange of all goods according to the amount of labour put into them.[38]

The Petrashevtsy tended to be swayed by opposing views on the question of the state — those of the statist socialists, the Saint-Simonians and Louis Blanc, and those of the anarchists — Fourier and Proudhon. Saint-Simon envisaged a great increase in the powers of the state. He was the first to put forward the idea that the state should take over the direction of industry and organise production, consumption and exchange according to a rational 'plan'. However, the government would also change in nature — the unruly government of man by man would give way to an impartial 'administration of things'. Saint-Simon's followers developed his theory into a complete system of state socialism by abolishing the right of inheritance and making the state not just the organiser of industry, but also the sole owner of property. Louis Blanc also wanted to take over, rather than abolish, the state. However, his state was to be subject to democratic control and its powers would be more limited than those of the Saint-Simonian state. The state would become the sole owner of capital and set up the social workshops. But, after the first year, it would hand the enterprises over to the workers.[39]

Fourier and Proudhon were the chief exponents of anti-government socialism. They both hated every sort of authority, every power over the individual man. Fourier's phalansteries were entirely self-contained self-governing units, each with its own elected council, though he hoped there would be cooperation between them. Proudhon declared 'Whoever lays his hands on me to govern me is a usurper and a tyrant and I declare him my enemy!' The state had become the instrument of the upper classes and was used by them to oppress the poor. Like Fourier, Proudhon envisaged the replacement of the state by small units − small craftsmen and peasants associated in loose federations, linked together by a system of free contracts.[40]

One aspect of French socialism which appealed particularly to the Petrashevtsy was the fact that all the socialists, statist and non-statist, united in seeing socialism as a world system, in predicting the disappearance of the nation state. Saint-Simon had drawn up plans for a European Parliament; his followers had dreamed of uniting West and East. But the most expressly cosmopolitan socialist was Fourier, who looked forward to a time when phalansteries spread over the entire globe, when national differences (symptoms of backwardness and deviation from the universal human norm) would be eradicated, and the whole human race speak the same language.[41]

The Petrashevtsy were also strongly influenced by the ideas of the French socialists, and especially the Saint-Simonians, on art. In opposition to romantic writers such as Théophile Gautier, who supported the idea of art for art's sake, the Saint-Simonians developed the idea of the social function of art. Saint-Simon had believed that men possessed three cardinal capacities − reason, industry and sentiment. His disciples elevated the role of sentiment, of art, above the others. In their eyes, art, more than anything else, reflected the nature of an age. Great art was only born in organic ages when men were united and believed in something. It was also through art, more than anything else, that men were inspired to action. 'The artist alone is worthy of guiding humanity.' The artists of their day had a great mission: to take up the great new unifying ideas − association, progress, brotherhood, love − preached by the Saint-Simonians, thus reviving art, and to usher in the new organic epoch of socialism. A whole generation of writers, including Alfred de Vigny, Heinrich Heine, Thomas Carlyle, Victor Hugo, were inspired by this theory. Its influence appeared most strongly of all in the socialist novels of George Sand. The Fourierists adopted a more philistine, didactic and utilitarian version of it.[42] Writers close to them included the novelist Eugène Sue and popular poets such as Béranger and Louis Festau.

One of the aspects of French socialism to be enthusiastically adopted by the Russians was the emancipation of women. With two notable exceptions, Proudhon and Cabet, all the French socialists were in favour of it. The Saint-Simonians had campaigned for the reintroduction of divorce and demanded equality and the right of inconstancy for women – the extreme nature of Prosper Enfantin's views on women was the major cause of the collapse of the movement.[43] George Sand was probably the most influential advocate of womens' liberation in the forties. She herself had escaped to Paris and freedom from a brutal and boorish husband. In novels such as *Indiana* and *Valentina* she portrayed the vile position of women trapped in loveless marriages. She argued that the marriage of women against their will was worse than prostitution and defended her heroines right to leave their husbands in search of love, developing the classic concept of the *free union*. This was a free and equal contract, entered into by a man and a woman without a priest but before the face of God and made sacred by the genuine nature of their love. George Sand's heroines were chaste and virtuous, her concept of love holy, an elevated ideal rather than a sexual passion.[44] Fourier's feminism was much more extreme and centred on the abolition of the family. He reserves some of his most devastating criticism for the position of women in Civilisation – sold in marriage to the highest bidder, confined to the home, forced to devote themselves to housework and child-rearing, activities for which, in his view, three-quarters of them have not the slightest inclination. In Harmony, women would be emancipated by collective living and the social upbringing of children, have complete equality of rights with men and complete freedom of choice in love. Fourier was the originator of the famous phrase, 'The extension of the privileges of woman is the essential principle of all progress.'[45]

The Petrashevtsy considered with interest the various ways suggested by the French utopians for implementing their ideas: persuasion, experiment, and political reform. Saint-Simon and Fourier shared a profound distrust of politics and said that their systems were apolitical. They were both quite happy to appeal to powerful people of quite posite political complexions for help in implementing their theories. They also (and particularly the Saint-Simonians) had a touching faith in the sheer moral power of their ideas to convert the world. The Saint-Simonians turned themselve into missionaries and set out, often on foot, preaching the Saint-Simonian religion all over Europe. For Fourier, Cabet and, in England, Owen, however, preaching was only a preliminary. When enough people had been converted and enough capital collected, the truth and practicality of their ideas was to be irrefutably demonstrated to the world by means of an experiment in association on a miniature scale. A multitude of socialist experiments were attempted in the forties. A few of these − a phalansterian bakery, Fourierist penal colonies at Mettray and Ostwald, Owen's factory at New Lanark − were highly successful; the more ambitious experiments, and especially those in America (Owen at New Harmony, Cabet at Nauvoo) were spectacular failures.[46] Other socialists and in particular Louis Blanc, Lamennais and Leroux, were encouraged by the advent of Louis Philippe to hope that socialism might be introduced through parliament, and agitated for universal suffrage.[47] The largest group of Fourierists, led by Considerant, also shed some of their apoliticism in the course of the forties.

The other way through which socialism might be implemented was through revolution. Though this was to become the classic (Marxist) solution, in the 1840s it was rejected by virtually every socialist thinker. Socialism in France arose as a reaction against the French Revolution, whose rivers of blood had failed to solve the problem of social misery. Saint-Simon and Fourier had both lived through the horrors of the revolution and both had conceived a total aversion to violence.[48] According to the socialists of the thirties and forties, the revolution had caused as much harm as it had promised good. It had left men hostile and divided; its only positive achievement was a collection of punitive laws; the problem of working-class pauperism remained and was growing worse. There was, as a result, the imminent threat of a new revolution, which would cause yet more destruction and misery. The socialists looked on their theories as an alternative, as a means of reconciling classes and averting revolution. Almost all of them agreed with Cabet, 'If I held a revolution in my hand, I would keep my hand closed, even if this should mean my death in exile.'[49]

It was on this question that the Petrashevtsy differed most strikingly from the French utopians. The Petrashevtsy looked to the republican tradition of radical conspiracy. The ideas of Babeuf's *Société des Égaux*, the achievement of equality through conspiracy, insurrection and revolutionary dictatorship, had been kept alive by his disciple Philippe Buonarotti after Babeuf's execution in 1797. After the restoration, neo-Babouvists were active in various conspiracies against the monarchy – first the *Société des Carbonaris*, which played an important part in the overthrow of Charles X; then the radical republican societies, *La Société des Amis du Peuple* and *La Société des Droits de l'Homme*, whose leaders, the Babouvists Voyer d'Argenson, Blanqui and Francois Raspail, spent all their time plotting and were frequently arrested; and finally the more clearly socialist *La Société des Familles*, (1834) and *La Société des Saisons* (1837), created by Barbès and Blanqui, authors of a disastrous attempt at insurrection on 12–13 May 1839. Though the neo-Babouvists had socialist and especially communist tendencies, they were republicans and professional revolutionaries first of all, much less interested in what would happen after the revolution than in how to bring it about. As Blanqui said, 'Communism (i.e. Cabetism) and Proudhonism stand by a river bank arguing whether the field on the other side is maize or wheat; let's cross and see.'[50]

The collective libraries

Almost all the Petrashevtsy were well acquainted with all the theories outlined above. Many of them knew the different doctrines in a great degree of detail, were experts on the nuances of their meaning and the exact issues dividing the socialist tendencies. With few exceptions, they read French easily. They read not only the works of the best-known socialists, but also the most obscure pamphlets written by their minor disciples. There was hardly any work by any French social-ist published during the 1840s which failed, somehow or other, to come to their hands. The main means by which the Petrashevtsy were able to achieve this degree of familiarity with French socialist ideas was the establishment of collective libraries. These made a wide selec-tion of French socialist literature available to even the poorest of them.

By far the largest of these libraries was that housed in Petrashevskii's flat. It was, his acquaintances agreed, the 'main enticement' to visit him. The 'first and most important' means through which Petrashevskii carried out socialist propaganda was 'by ordering the greatest possible number of books and giving them to people to read'.[51] He lent out books both from the collective store in his flat and from his extensive personal library.

The collective library was organised in Spring 1846. Petrashevskii, leading members of his original circle (Kaidanov, Pleshcheev and Danilevskii) and Maikov and his friends (Saltykov, Shtrandman and Esakov) met at Shtrandman's house to discuss 'how it would be useful to club together to purchase a large quantity of foreign books'. The nine of them agreed on the need for a library but not on its purpose. For Petrashevskii a library was primarily an instrument of propaganda. He therefore wanted to order short simple works, brochures and leaflets, designed for introducing people to socialist ideas. Maikov and his friends were less interested in the direct propaganda of socialism. They wanted to pool their resources to obtain long, difficult academic works, major texts, which they needed for their own studies but which, as Shtrandman explained were 'too expensive for impecunious people'. These included historical texts, the works of the political economists, books on the natural sciences (Danilevskii's speciality), and the collected works of various other authors. Saltykov, in addition, demanded books on his pet subject, the penal system. When they came to make a choice of titles from a huge list of books, brought by Petrashevskii, a furious argument broke out. Almost all the books proposed by Petrashevskii were 'rejected unanimously' by Maikov and his friends. Petrashevskii, however, was in a strong position since it was he who had the list and the contacts with booksellers. He managed to insist on being in sole charge of the library, collected twenty silver roubles from each of the others and went ahead and ordered the books he wanted. These were almost exclusively books on socialism, most of them brochures and periodicals, as Saltykov remarked in disgust: 'worthless both in their content and in their price'.[52] After this, Maikov and Shtrandman refused to have anything more to do with the library and they soon left Petrashevskii's circle altogether.

In spite of this row, the library was soon enlarged greatly and it became immensely popular with Petrashevskii's visitors. It was very efficiently organised. Speshnev explained how:

> One had to put in a certain sum of money (I think no less than fifteen and not more than thirty silver roubles) and with this money he (Petrashevskii) bought books. These books did not belong to anyone, but, however, each of the shareholders had the right to read them all … in the three years in which this was done, a great quantity of books was collected … when the steamships began running, the shareholders met one Friday, Petrashevskii

brought all the new catalogues and from them they chose books for the whole amount.[53]

When Kashkin and his friends organised their own circle in 1848, they set up a similar library, which Konstantin Debu took charge of — 'Each of us suggested a book which he wanted and everyone was asked, "To buy", or, "Not to buy"; each of us said "Yes" or "No" and we wrote down the number of votes. Everyone agreed on socialist books and most of them were of this type'.[54] According to Speshnev, Petrashevskii was expert at getting hold of books and procured every book that was wanted. His chief bookseller was a Frenchman called Joseph Lurie, who had connections with the Garnier brothers in Paris. When, on 28 March 1849, Petrashevskii unwittingly gave the spy Petr Antonelli a list of books he was ordering from Lurie, it turned out to include over two hundred titles, almost all of them foreign and almost all of them banned. The Commission of Inquiry was astonished by 'the large quantity of forbidden works which Petrashevskii's library contains. One can say without exaggeration that he possesses all the most impious and revolutionary books which have been published abroad'. In his study, according to Kropotov, 'Expensive editions were piled on the floor, the tables and the window sills, books about anything and everything.'

Petrashevskii tried to persuade all his guests to subscribe to the collective library. Since few of them could afford to set up comparable libraries of their own, they usually agreed. On leaving his house, they always carried with them new books to read, which they later returned and exchanged for others. Petrashevskii also willingly shared his own personal library 'not only with his friends but also with people he didn't know well but who seemed decent to him, and he did this through a conviction of its social use'. In the previous eight years, he admitted in 1849, several hundred people had visited him and left for different towns throughout Russia, taking his books with them. Akhsharumov testified 'People read the books with pleasure and this more than anything else had an influence on them.'[55]

The Petrashevtsy's attitude to the French socialists

Approximately ninety per-cent of the books mentioned as being in Petrashevskii's library were in French.[56] By far the largest number of these (123 titles) were about socialism. The high esteem in which the

Petrashevtsy held Fourier can be seen from the fact that among them, works on Fourierism predominate (forty-nine titles), including, as well as the voluminous writings of Fourier himself (in several editions) and the Fourierist journal *La Phalange*, the writings of twenty-five of his disciples. These range from the classic expositions of Fourierism: Victor Considerant's *Destinée sociale* (1837–8), Gatti de Gamond's *Fourier et son système* (1838), Gabrielle Gabet's *Traité élémentaire de la science de l'homme* (1842), Charles Pellarin's *Charles Fourier, sa vie et sa theorie* (1843), Cantagrel's *Le Fou du Palais Royal* (1845), Hypollite Renaud's *Solidarité* (1841) and Alphonse Toussenel's *L'Esprit des bêtes* (1847), to pamphlets composed by little known figures such as J.B. Krantz, F.L.A. Tamisier and Maurize. Many of the Petrashevtsy possessed their own copies of Fourier's collected works, or at least individual volumes of them (including Speshnev, Nikolai and Vladimir Kaidanov, Akhsharumov, Konstantin Debu and Khanykov). The works of Fourier, Considerant and *La Phalange* were those most often borrowed from the collective library; Ipollit Debu later read *Destinée sociale* during the seige of Sebastopol.[58]

Public references to Fourier were comparatively frequent in Russia. The first mention of Fourier's name in print was a eulogistic obituary in *Literaturnoe pribavlenie k Russkomu invalidu* in 1837. This was based very closely on the speech Considerant made at Fourier's tomb, published in *La Phalange*. Fourier's 'immortal theory' it declares, 'far surpasses the works of the very greatest geniuses and will never have its equal on earth'. Fourier himself was 'the Columbus of the social world'. Discussion of Fourierism could be found in the French newspapers (available in coffee houses) and in reviews in Russian journals of 'the innumerable multitude of works appearing every day from the school of Fourier'.[59] Some of the Petrashevtsy seem to have been introduced to Fourier at university. The ascetic and radical-minded Poroshin, Professor of Economics and Statistics at St. Petersburg University, devoted a large part of his lectures to an exposition of the ideas of the French socialists and especially Fourier, whose theories, he taught, contained, 'something grandiose and not far from the truth'.[60]

Fourier was considered the greatest socialist thinker by a majority of the Petrashevtsy (the major exceptions were Maikov and Miliutin, who preferred Saint-Simon, and Speshnev, who favoured the communists and Proudhon). The Petrashevtsy were idealistic and enthusiastic and had a tendency to get carried away by the poetry of Fourier. At times they made extravagantly Fourierist statements. Petrashevskii, on reading Fourier for the first time, in January 1844, declared:

> It has surpassed all my expectations. It has surpassed what I consider possible, and you know that there's not much I don't consider possible! I hadn't till now imagined that the mind of a genius could achieve the depth of understanding of the whole world which is revealed in the works of the great Fourier ... in his person I would be ready to believe in the incarnation of the divinity ... there is no longer any reason for humanity to waste time racking its brains over inventions and discoveries. He has covered everything ... there remains only the realisation of everything in practice and the humble analysis of his revelation.

Other Petrashevtsy spoke of Fourier in no less exalted fashion. Vladimir Kaidanov, in Rostov, for instance, was brought by Considerant's works to 'such ecstasy that I couldn't read them straight through. Several times I had to throw the book down and walk up and down the room for half an hour in order to calm myself and go on reading'.[61] Fourier's works were studied attentively by the members of different circles: at Petrashevskii's, Petrashevskii and Danilevskii gave a series of lectures on them; at Debu's a group met 'to resolve obscure questions in Fourier's theory; at Speshnev's, Timkovskii read out his translation of Cantagrel's *Le Fou du Palais Royal*.[62]

The culmination of the interest in Fourier was the dinner held to commemorate the anniversary of Fourier's birthday on 7 April 1849 at Esakov's flat. As Esakov said, it was 'the first celebration in honour of Fourier in our country'. Fourier's birthday was an occasion celebrated by Fourierists all over the world, from Paris to New York, from Rio to Rome. In Paris, the Fourierists sat at a table a hundred feet long, with guests harmoniously arranged in groups of twenty. Speeches were made, toasts drunk and songs sung, in anticipation of the day:

> Quand notre humanité, puissante et glorieuse
> Accomplira sa loi rayonnante at joyeuse.

The Russians tried to imitate this on a smaller scale. Eleven people participated: Petrashevskii, Speshnev, Khanykov, Akhsharumov, Kashkin, the Debu brothers, the Evropeus brothers, Esakov and Vashchenko (Danilevskii was invited but took fright at the last moment and stayed away). Speeches were made by Khanykov, Akhsharumov and Petrashevskii. Khanykov's was a 'panegyric' to Fourier, looking forward to 'the transformation of the whole planet and the humanity which lives upon it'; Akhsharumov called on his friends to 'cover the whole poverty-stricken earth with palaces, fruits and decorate it with flowers'; Petrashevskii was booed when he tried to bring un-Fourierist political subjects into his contribution. They drank toasts after the speeches — to Fourier, to the knowledge of reality, to the spreading of Fourier's teaching and to the friendship and solidarity of those present. Kashkin then read a Russian translation of Béranger's famous poem, *Les Fous*, about Fourier, Saint-Simon and Enfantin. The message of the poem was, as Akhsharumov said, that all eccentrics are laughed at, but that it is the eccentrics who make the discoveries which change the life of man. Finally, Ippolit Debu proposed that they should undertake a joint translation of *Théorie de l'unité universelle*, Fourier's largest and most obscure work. This would, he suggested, both make it available to others and enable them to understand it better themselves. All eleven met at Vashchenko's the following Monday, divided it up into eleven parts of 150 pages each and drew lots for who got which. Some of them started work at once — Akhsharumov and Kashkin's translations were found among their papers. The Commission of Inquiry regarded this dinner as one of the chief political crimes of the Petrashevtsy. After reviewing the evidence, the Commission concluded, 'Fourier's system, more than all the other socialist systems, is capable of attracting inexperienced minds and impressionable young men.'[63]

The Petrashevtsy were far more strongly influenced by the theories of Fourier than by those of the other great utopian socialist, Saint-Simon. The hey-day of Saint-Simonism in Russia, as in France had been the thirties. The spectacular trial of the Saint-Simonians for alleged immoralities in their retreat at Ménilmontant was widely reported in all the French newspapers and had a great impact in Russia. And so, when Herzen and his circle (Ogarev, Nikolai Satin, Nikolai Sazonov) developed an interest in socialism, it was inevitably the pamphlets of Saint-Simon and his followers, their tracts and their trial, which came into their hands. A surprising number of different sorts of people were attracted to Saint-Simonism in the thirties: V. S. Pecherin, later a Redemptorist monk; the 'mad-man' and Catholic sympathiser Chaadaev; Turgenev, who though always a cautious liberal rather than a socialist, took part in the fiery Saint-Simonian debates in the Rue Taitbout in Paris in October 1830; and even Field-Marshal Bariatinskii, a most unlikely socialist.[64] This was linked to the fact that the elements of Saint-Simonism which appealed to and were adopted by the Russians of the thirties were the religious and ethical rather than the socialist and economic ones. The

Russian Saint-Simonism of the 1830s could not really be called socialism. However, Herzen, an early acquaintance with Saint-Simonism was to have lasting effects on the ideas of those who later became committed socialists. He wrote, 'Saint-Simonism lay at the foundations of our convictions and remained in its essentials unalterably so'. And it was to Saint-Simon that Belinskii looked when he became interested in socialism.[65] The romantic and ethical character of Saint-Simonism fitted in with the introspective, philosophical mood of Russia in the thirties. In the forties, as the political climate brightened, the Russian radicals looked to Fourierism, which envisaged immediate action. Herzen (writing much later) put the Petrashevtsy's Fourierism down to the difference of temperament between the inhabitants of Moscow and St. Petersburg, 'Saint-Simonism, vague, religious and at the same time analytic, suited the Muscovites remarkably well'. On the other hand, 'in St. Petersburg, they like regimentation, discipline, application' and therefore the Phalanstery. But it was really more a question of time than place. Even Herzen (though he later conveniently forgot this), felt the pull of Fourierism in the forties. 'Fourierism of course has most deeply of all plumbed the question of socialism', he wrote in 1843.[66]

However, in spite of the stronger appeal of Fourierism, the influence of Saint-Simonism continued to be felt in the Russia of the 1840s. Enfantin's *Correspondance politique et religieuse* was, for example, enthusiastically reviewed in *Otechestvennye zapiski* in 1848.[67] Even such an ardent Fourierist as Petrashevskii sported long hair and a beard, a Saint-Simonian fashion. Petrashevskii's library contained both the works of Saint-Simon (though these seem to have been taken out only by Maikov and Golovinskii) and the most important summary of his followers' ideas, *Doctrine de Saint-Simon. Exposition. Première année 1828–29* (which was more widely read). The Petrashevtsy refused to adopt Saint-Simonism as a system. There was almost unanimous dislike of the elitist aspects of its theory, although they were in general more indebted to it than they cared to admit. They were greatly influenced by Saint-Simonism (in particular the ideas of Bazard) in their interpretation of history. They also drew considerably on it for their ideas on art and on the position of women in the future society. A few of the Petrashevtsy felt, like Herzen, that Fourierism was excessively detailed, and made Saint-Simonism their preferred socialist doctrine. The 'Saint-Simonian' current among the Petrashevtsy was especially strong among the members of Maikov's circle. The influence of Saint-Simon is extremely obvious in the writings of both Maikov and Saltykov.

Saltykov's short stories, *Contradictions* and *A Tangled Affair*, not only echo, but in places directly paraphrase Saint-Simon.

As much as on Saint-Simon and the Saint-Simonians, the Petrashevtsy drew on the newer, more democratic versions of the doctrine, developed by Pierre Leroux and popularised through the novels of George Sand. The extraordinary popularity of George Sand's novels in Russia has often been documented.[68] Thirteen of them were translated and serialised in Russian journals in the 1840s (the majority in *Otechestvennye zapiski*). These included the very markedly socialist *Horace, Mauprat, Jacques, Jeanne* and *Le Pêché de M. Antoine*, (which ends with the foundation of a socialist commune). Sand was Belinskii's heroine. He gravely overestimated her talents, referring to her as 'the leading poet and novelist of the age' and making her works the subject of numerous reviews and articles.[69] Much Russian literature of the day bore the marks of her influence, in particular, love stories such as Herzen's *Who is to Blame?* and Druzhinin's *Polin'ka Saks*. The Petrashevtsy seem to have been interested in the strictly socialist aspect of her novels as much as in her advocacy of the rights of women. Dostoevskii who was himself strongly influenced by Sand and was to retain his enthusiasm for her throughout his life, recalled on her death in 1876 how 'thousands' of Russians in the 1840s had been converted to socialism through her novels. He called her, 'One of the most brilliant, stern and just representatives of the contemporaneous western new people, who ... boldly proclaimed that the renovation of humanity must be radical and social.'

Pleshcheev, in a poem entitled *An Acquaintance of Mine*, painted a portrait of a typical 'liberal *enragé*', who 'nourished a grand passion for George Sand and for Leroux'. Saltykov later described how:

> The idea of France and Paris is for me inseparably connected with memories of my youth, of the forties. Yes, and not only for me personally, but for my contemporaries, in these two words there was something radiant, glowing, that warmed our life ... we adhered ... not to the France of Louis-Philippe and Guizot, but the France of Saint-Simon, Cabet, Fourier, Louis Blanc, and especially *George Sand*. From there, there flowed to us a faith in humanity, from there, there shone to us a certainty that the 'golden age' was not behind but ahead of us ... in a word, everything good, everything desirable and admirable − it all came from there.

Leroux's own writings, which had a tendency to be both mystical and turgid and were less popular in Russia, were reviewed occasionally in the radical journals.[70] The collective library contained his *De l'Humanité*

(1840); the *Encyclopedie nouvelle*, (1836–43), edited by Leroux jointly with Jean Renaud; and *La Revue indépendante*, a journal produced by Leroux in collaboration with Sand.

That more pragmatic seceder from Saint-Simonism, Louis Blanc, was also extremely popular among the Petrashevtsy, as among all the radical intelligentsia. He was admired both as a socialist and as a historian. Almost all the Petrashevtsy were familiar with his histories of the 1830s and of the French revolution. Both his *Histoire de dix ans 1830–40* (1831–4), and the first two volumes of his *Histoire de la Révolution francaise* (1847) were found in the collective library, together with the basic statement of his socialist ideas, *Organisation du travail* (this, one of the most popular socialist works of the day, went through ten editions 1839–48). Some of the more left-wing Petrashevtsy, such as Pleshcheev and Dostoevskii, came to believe that his theories and in particular his ideas on the equitable distribution of wealth, were the best conceived by any socialist. Their interest became focussed on him in 1848, when he became the only socialist to join the provisional government and they followed his activities at the Luxembourg Commission with rapt attention. The young Chernyshevskii, an especially fervent admirer of Louis Blanc, chronicled his excitement in his diary, summarising his views as those of 'a red republican and socialist ... more and more an adherent of Louis Blanc'.[71]

The Petrashevtsy were fascinated by both the ideas and personality of Proudhon, with whom they had what can best be described as a love/hate relationship. Speshnev, like Herzen, was attracted by Proudhon's outrageousness and individualism. Both of them admired him particularly for the way in which, in 1848, alone among the socialists he criticised the republic, preserving the intransigence of his views when faced with the prospect of power. Speshnev regarded him as one of the few 'pure' socialists in France, his proposals to the National Assembly as truly revolutionary. Chernyshevskii admired Proudhon for the same reasons and placed him second to Louis Blanc in his list of socialists. The specialists in political economy among the Petrashevtsy, Miliutin and Jastrzebski, were influenced by Proudhon's economic theories, especially the idea, expressed in *Contradictions économiques*, that every economic phenomenon has a good side, to be preserved, and a bad side, to be overcome. However, the Petrashevtsy were also aware of the other, moderate side of Proudhon's ideas and subjected aspects of his *Contradictions économiques* to severe criticism for their equivocation: Speshnev, in his *Letters to Edmund Chojecki*, attacked Proudhon's ideas on God;

Miliutin, in *Malthus and his Opponents* and Saltykov in his first story, significantly entitled *Contradictions*, made strong objections to his theory of equilibrium between contradictory forces, as nothing more than a justification of the golden mean. Their ambivalent attitude towards Proudhon was clearly revealed one evening at Petrashevskii's, when the visitors discussed the relative merits of Fourier and Proudhon. Fourier, they talked about 'with loud praise'; Proudhon, on the other hand, 'they both praised and abused'.[72] Proudhon's two best-known works, *Qu'est-ce que la propriété?* (1840) and *Système des Contradictions économiques ou Philosophie de la misère* (1846), were both in the collective library and frequently borrowed.

The Petrashevtsy were less interested in Christian socialism, but they expressed great admiration for the democratic fervour of Lamennais' *Paroles d'un croyant*, another socialist classic and best-seller. The collective library had a copy (although the Russian government regarded this work as especially seditious and had it 'unconditionally banned') and the Petrashevtsy made the first Russian translation of it. A few of the Petrashevtsy, including Pleshcheev, Dostoevskii and Durov, seem to have sympathised with the vague sort of deism espoused by Leroux and Sand.

The utopian communist systems were not generally popular among the Petrashevtsy. Many of them had read Cabet's works (his *Voyage en Icarie*, 1840, and *Le Vrai Christianisme suivant Jesus-Christ*, 1846, were both in the collective library), but his system was actively and almost unanimously disliked. Vladimir Kaidanov, for example, wrote to his brother, 'As far as Cabet is concerned, send him to me only in the case of your finding out if he wrote anything better than his *Voyage en Icarie*.' Like Herzen, who referred disdainfully to Icaria as 'a communist monastery', the Petrashevtsy objected both to Cabet's religiosity and to the monotonous, repressive equality of his system. The revolutionary communism of Cabet's ex-secretary and chief foe, Theodore Dézamy, an atheist and materialist, was, on the other hand, the preferred system of Nikolai Speshnev, the most radical of the Petrashevtsy and the only one to declare himself a communist. Dézamy's *Le Jésuitisme vaincu et anéanti par le socialisme* (1845) was found in Speshnev's possession on his arrest. Others, including Timkovskii, had by this time come to sympathise with his ideas.[73]

Newcomers to the circles were often introduced to socialism through one of the general accounts kept in the collective library. These included: in French, Louis Reybaud's detailed but hostile *Études sur les reformateurs contemporains ou socialistes modernes* (1841) and Francois Villegardelle's more sympathetic *Histoire des idées sociales*, (1846); and, in German, Lorenz von Stein's *Der Sozialismus und Kommunismus des heutigen Frankreichs* (1842) and Karl Biederman's *Vorlesungen Über Sozialismus und soziale Fragen*, (1847), which both Tol' and Vladimir Kaidanov undertook to translate for their non-German speaking friends.

The Petrashevtsy's interests thus ranged across the whole spectrum of utopian socialist thought in France. They studied all the systems and studied them in depth. They sometimes made extravagant professions of faith in Fourier. But, the Petrashevtsy were not unqualified adherents of any one socialist doctrine. Even Petrashevskii admitted, 'I am not a completely pure Fourierist.' They criticised all of them. They culled ideas here and there from different theories, as it suited them. They were occasionally frivolous, but their eclecticism derived from a constant, strong, underlying current of serious intent. Their main aim was to make something out of French socialism which was applicable to their own lives and to the Russian situation. They were interested in using these ideas in Russia, rather than in studying them for their own sake. They believed, as Maikov said, that the tasks of 'Russian science' lay not in the blind imitation but 'in the critical study, the systematic adaptation to its life' of the ideas of the French and other nations.[74]

French socialism in the hands of the Petrashevtsy was bound to change its nature, because the circumstances to which they tried to adapt it were so very different from those in which French socialism had arisen in France.

The context in which French socialism flourished in the 1840s was the 'bourgeois monarchy' of Louis-Philippe. In France, there had been a great revolution. The absolutist and aristocratic regime which had stood for centuries had been overturned almost at one blow. Serfdom had been abolished and the mass of French peasants had been confirmed as proprietors of their smallholdings. Basic political freedoms, freedom of speech, press and assembly, had been permanently gained, the rule of law established. In spite of a high property qualification for the vote, France had representative government. The overthrow of Charles X in 1830 and the accession of Louis-Philippe had marked the end of the last attempt to revive the seigneurial regime. The way was opened up for the industrial development of France. The term 'industrial revolution' was coined in 1837 by Jerome Blanqui. Rapid industrial growth, mechanisation, concentration, urbanisation, the frequent cycles of boom and slump, brought with them not only the appearance of a sizeable working class, but for the first time, the phenomenon of working class pauperism. The potential political power of the workers became apparent during the July Revolution, when they played a decisive part on the barricades; the problem of their low pay and appalling living and working conditions was brought to the fore in 1831 by the insurrection of the starving silk-workers of Lyons, who rose beneath the banner 'Vivre en travaillant, ou mourir en combattant' and held the town for ten days. These events were decisive for many who became socialists in France in the 1830s and 1840s. Socialism arose in France from a realisation that the Revolution's solutions had all been political, that it had failed to answer the problems of social misery and that, though the peasants might be better off than before the Revolution, the plight of the lower classes in the cities had grown much worse. The failure of the Revolution of 1789–93 to enact any social legislation made its political achievements meaningless for the lower classes. As Louis Blanc wrote:

> Political freedom, freedom of conscience, freedom of industry, conquests so profitable for the bourgeoisie, were for them but imaginary conquests, since, though they had the *right* to profit from them, they did not have the *ability* to do so.[75]

In contrast, socialism arose among an educated minority in Russia as a reaction against an essentially feudal regime. In Russia there had been no revolution. The country was governed by an autocratic monarch. There was no freedom of speech, no freedom of the press, no freedom of assembly, almost no legal freedom. The essential class division was between just over half a million gentry and forty million peasants, twenty-two million of whom were serfs. The 'bourgeoisie' was insignificant in numbers and influence; the towns and industry undeveloped and backward. The radical intelligentsia turned to socialism as a protest against the lack of political and personal freedom in Russia. It was, first of all, a personal protest. They were rebelling against their own situation as isolated and alienated intellectuals, against the atmosphere and restrictions of the autocracy and bureaucracy, which stifled them as individuals, hindered their personal development. Secondly, it was a much broader ethical and humanitarian revolt against the barbaric injustices, wretched conditions and inhumanities suffered by the majority of the population, who were state peasants or serfs. The Russians took up socialist rather than purely democratic demands because they were aware of the terrible human consequences of capitalism in Europe. They had read numerous descriptions of the misery of the working classes in

England and France by liberal and socialist economists such as Vidal, Buret and Villermé. They were anxious to avoid such consequences in their own country, in which they could dimly perceive the beginnings of a similar development.

The problems the Petrashevtsy were trying to solve were thus very different from those facing the French socialists. This led them to pick out ideas here and there from French socialism and adapt them to fit Russian conditions. They put them together and developed them, often in the most unlikely combinations. They combined them with ideas from other sources − in particular the philosophy of the German left-Hegelians and the theories of the political economists − and with original and peculiarly Russian ideas which they thought up themselves. They were still in the process of working out their theory: as Speshnev said, speaking of himself, 'he was a man who had not yet settled, was still working, studying, and his system was only gradually coming together, changing in its details and becoming clearer to him'.[76] But, as I hope to show, by 1849, the Petrashevtsy, basing themselves on French socialism, had come a long way towards forming a Russian socialism adapted to Russian needs.

IV — THE PHILOSOPHICAL IDEAS OF THE PETRASHEVTSY

In the 1830s and 1840s, if socialism meant France, philosophy meant Germany. The dominant influence of the time was Hegelianism. Hegelianism arose as a reaction against the rigid rationalism, the empiricism and materialism of the seventeenth and eigthteenth centuries, putting in their place a profoundly metaphysical view of the unitary nature of world history, the integration of the particular and the universal, the individual and society. The heyday of the ideas of Hegel, in their purer form, was the mid and late 1830s. It was at this time that advanced Russians, such as Bakunin and Turgenev, made the pilgrimage to the lecture halls of Berlin University; at this time that Hegel's ideas aroused a ferment in the Stankevich circle. The 1840s were still truly the age of Hegel, but by then a differentiation had begun to take place among his followers due to the continued political immobility of Prussia under the new king, Frederick William IV, and the ambiguities contained in Hegel's ideas. His followers separated into conservatives, who took his dictum, 'What is rational is real', as a justification of the existing order, the Prussian state, and the radical left- or 'young' Hegelians, who interpreted it as an argument for subverting the existing order, as irrational. The writings of the left-Hegelians were more materialist and individualist than those of Hegel, their ideas harking back more closely to the eighteenth-century enlightenment.

The French socialists (with the partial exceptions of Proudhon and Leroux) were ignorant of German philosophy and expressed their contempt of it. Fourier was especially hostile. In this case, the Petrashevtsy did not share his views. When, one Friday at Petrashevskii's, Timkovskii naively read a Fourierist speech attacking philosophy, Petrashevskii put him down sharply for his ignorance of 'the influence of philosophical systems on socialist development'.[1]

The Petrashevtsy loved and respected philosophy. Their aim was to give the ideas of the French socialists added depth, rationality and insight, by combining them with philosophical concepts, fitting them into a philosophical framework, at the same time bringing out the practical and political implications of the ideas of German philosophy.

In philosophy, the Petrashevtsy took their cue from Herzen and Belinskii. Both had, by the early 1840s, denounced Hegel's system as monolithic, as exalting absolutes – Reason, History, Progress, the State – above the individual. Though still very much influenced by Hegel, they had adopted left-Hegelian positions. They drew, in particular, upon Feuerbach, accepting his claim that the Hegelian Idea was just a disguised form of the Christian God; and (to a lesser degree) his materialistic conception of human nature. The Petrashevtsy were greatly influenced by Herzen's popularisation of left-Hegelian ideas in *Dilettantism in Science* and *Letters on the Study of Nature*, published in *Otechestvennye zapiski* in 1843 and 1845–6.

The Petrashevtsy differed from Herzen and Belinskii in that, being younger, they had not 'lived through' a period of immersion in Hegelian philosophy. Only a few of them (Petrashevskii and Speshnev for example), had read Hegel. Their ideas were more directly inspired by Feuerbach and, as a result, were both less sophisticated and more clearly materialist. They read the works of the left-Hegelians: Feuerbach, Strauss, Bruno and Edgar Bauer, Arnold Ruge, Max Stirner. Some, for example, Petrashevskii, Speshnev, Tol', read them in the German original; some, including Maikov and Ippolit Debu, in Littré's French translations; others just read summaries of their ideas in Victor Cousin's books and articles in the *Revue indépendante*. Feuerbach's 'unconditionally banned' *Das Wesen des Christenthums* (1841) and Strauss's *Das Leben Jesu* (1835) were among the most popular books in Petrashevskii's library. Katenev made a translation of *Die Religion der Zukunft*, by Feuerbach's brother Friedrich, and circulated it among his friends.[2]

In the philosophical arena, the democratic socialism of the Petrashevtsy manifested itself as a passionate defence of the autonomy of the human individual and the wish to incorporate this idea into some sort of historical framework, which would show history as the rational progress of mankind towards individual and collective freedom. The central tenets of their philosophy were derived from a fusion of Feuerbach's and Fourier's ideas and included: an insistence on the importance of man and human nature, an attack on concepts, religious or metaphysical, placed above the individual. But, unlike these two thinkers, who viewed human nature as essentially unchanging and static, the Petrashevtsy attempted (even if this sometimes led them to contradict themselves) to place human development within a historical context, which they derived mostly from Saint-Simon, but partly from Hegel. In addition, the most intellectual of the Petrashevtsy, especially Maikov and Miliutin, tried to evolve a new philosophy of science, basing themselves on Comte; the most revolutionary, especially Speshnev and Engel'son (like Herzen after 1848), inclined towards the extreme individualism of Stirner.

Attacks on religion and idealism

Among the Petrashevtsy, as among the French socialists, some were religious, some not. They all shared a respect for Christ and the early Christians and recognised the usefulness of appropriating them to the socialist tradition. But the Russians were on the whole more overtly and militantly atheist than the French. In France, beginning from the eighteenth century, there had been attempts to modernise Roman Catholicism, by refining and humanising it – attempts which had led finally to the Christian socialism of Lamennais and Abbé Constant. Both the Roman Catholic and the Protestant churches were intellectually alive, capable of appealing to educated people. The socialists found them impossible to scorn and saw that it was essential to take account of them. The Russian Orthodox religion, in contrast, was leaden and ritualised, intellectually sterile and obsolescent. The Church had been part of the state apparatus since the reign of Peter I. Religion had never had a strong hold over the educated members of Russian society and the Russian socialists found it easy to shake off.

Those of the Petrashevtsy who retained a belief in God, for example Maikov and Dostoevskii, tended to believe in the purified social Christianity of Lamennais, rather than the dogmas of the Orthodox Church. There were a few, but only a few, truly mystical socialists among Petrashevskii's visitors including Ol'dekop, Timkovskii and the poet Apollon Grigor'ev.[3] The majority of the Petrashevtsy had no patience with mysticism. When Grigor'ev became reviews' editor of *Finskii vestnik* in 1846 and began a consistent propaganda of Christian socialist ideas, linking Fourierism with mysticism, they retaliated by inserting a caustic review of Grigor'ev's poetry (probably written by Durov). While approving Grigor'ev's socialism, it condemned the mysticism of his *Hymns*, and ends with the hope that, 'the cobwebs of mysticism won't strangle the author's eagle's dissatisfaction'.[4] Furious at receiving such insults in his own paper, Grigor'ev stormed out of *Finskii vestnik* leaving the field clear for the anti-religious tendency. Many of the Petrashevtsy, however, like the French socialists and like Herzen and Belinskii, retained a reverence for Christ and the early Christians, whom they regarded as the first socialists, and, like the Saint-Simonians, tended to speak of socialism as a new and more rational form of the Christian religion. The *Pocket Dictionary*, for example, contains an ecstatic account of how:

> There was a time when humanity was awoken by a divine idea, when, in a Roman province, in oppressed Judea, the word of love and freedom rang out and quickly spread over the world and shook the thrones of Caesars and vice-regents. Man ... was reconciled by the words, 'Love your neighbour', 'Look on your neighbour as your brother ...' a simple parable showed him the indivisibility of the goods of nature and the equality of rights of every living creature to its treasury.

Even Speshnev, an avowed atheist, praised the first Christians for aspiring to achieve, 'the fraternity *ordained* among men'.[5] However, the Petrashevtsy leant away from the idea of a 'God–Man' to that of a 'Man–God' i.e. a human doctrine based on the idea of restoring to man the attributes (goodness, justice, etc.), which had been taken away from him and transposed into the divinity. This idea was a logical extension of New Christianity, implicit in many of the writings of the French socialists, but was developed to its fullest degree by the German left-Hegelians, especially Feuerbach and Strauss. It was essentially atheist and reduced Christ to the status of an ordinary man. Katenev, for example, claimed 'Instead of the Son of God, there was simply an intelligent man ... in this sense I, Katenev, am a God.'[6] However, the theory preserved the moral–religious ideas of Christianity, and Christ was regarded at least by some of its exponents (e.g. J.S. Mill) as a particularly perfect example of man.

But some of the Petrashevtsy went further. They not only denied there was anything special about Christ, they openly attacked him. Petrashevskii referred contemptuously to 'the famous demagogue Christ, who ended his career rather unsuccessfully', and to 'the name of Christ and that in which we don't believe'. Petrashevskii headed a militant anti-religious tendency among the radical intelligentsia. His attitude to religion can be seen from the famous occasion when he donned woman's clothes and went to a service in the women's half of the Kazan cathedral. Thanks to his long black beard, his presence was soon spotted. According to the story, a police officer came up to him and said, 'Madam, it seems to me that you are a man'. Petrashevskii replied, 'Sir, it seems to me that you are an old woman.' Leaving the police officer dumbfounded, Petrashevskii made his escape and reached home safely. Petrashevskii also held parties on Good Friday and regaled his guests with rum punch, cheese, Easter cake and ham as if it were Easter Sunday. He waged a personal propaganda war against religion. Few people who came within its range emerged unscathed. Mordvinov related how Petrashevskii did not believe in anything and laughed at his Church-going and Epiphany water. On one occasion, Petrashevskii even compared Moses to an ass.[7] Among the other openly anti-religious Petrashevtsy were Speshnev and Tol'. Tol' was so desparately anxious to refute the existence of God that he 'snatched hours from sleep' to do so. Speshnev was the most coldly atheist of all, in his own words, 'such an inveterate atheist and materialist of the school of Dézamy that the very word 'spirit' brings an evil sneer to your lips, a man who not only believes in no symbol of faith, no mystery ... but believes in nothing at all and recognises only what he sees, hears or reaches by the path of logical deduction'. Encouraged by Petrashevskii, the two of them made speeches at his Fridays attacking religion: Tol' a series of lectures on the origins of religion deducing it from fear; and Speshnev one speech in which, using the arguments of the German left-Hegelians, he denied the existence of God.[8]

The fervent atheism of a section of the Petrashevtsy is explained by the fact that they associated religion with oppression and tyranny. There were three main reasons for this. First, they saw religion as an instrument of intellectual terror, the means by which the Tsar cowed the people and legitimised his reign of violence and arbitrariness. According to them, religion 'crushed the development of the mind' and 'destroyed morality', and was used 'to maintain the people in still greater ignorance and oppression'. Kaidanov said, 'the fear of the knout is religion'. In this they were strongly influenced by Belinskii, who, in his *Letter to Gogol*, called religion 'the prop of the knout and the servant of despotism'.[9] Secondly, God was not just used by tyrants, he was a tyrant himself. The incompatibility of human suffering with the idea of the goodness of God was perhaps the most powerful argument used by the radicals of the 1840s to deny the existence of God. In *Dmitry Kalinin*, Belinskii had denounced 'the tyrant God' who had 'surrendered the unhappy earth as a tribute to the Devil'. He asked, 'Can it really be true that eternal bliss must be bought at the price of the most frightful sufferings? It's rather expensive.' Dostoevskii repeats this argument almost word for word in *The Brothers Karamazov*. It was also used by Petrashevskii by Kashkin, by Engel'son.[10] Man's emancipation from religion begins, Engel'son wrote, when he realises that God is the source of all the misery and evil on earth and concludes that it is admissible to try to escape from him 'as from the plague and the locusts', which leads him naturally to atheism. As Petrashevskii argued, their atheism was 'practical ... inspired by life itself'. In the eyes of the most radical of the Petrashevtsy, God was a tyrant not just because he made men suffer, he was a tyrant and man's enemy *per se*, as an authority set up over man. This was the third and decisive reason for the rejection of religion. Speshnev, for example, praises Proudhon for separating and opposing God and man, for showing that what was good for God was bad for man. However, he criticises Proudhon for just presenting the contradiction between God and man. In his view, Proudhon should have solved it, annihilating God and accepting that, 'There is no God and there are no gods, but only finite beings.'[11]

The Petrashevtsy wanted *ni Dieu ni maître*. Their rejection of God was bound up with their rejection of all authorities whether religious or moral, set up over the individual. The Petrashevtsy's critique of God was part of their critique of all idealist systems, and in particular, of German philosophy. Their critique of idealism was drawn from the writings of the German left-Hegelians, especially Feuerbach, and also owed a great deal to the re-interpretation of these ideas by Herzen in his *Dilettantism in Science*. It formed an essential link in their philosophical theory, but is one of the least original parts of it. The Petrashevtsy attacked idealism and religion for scorning matter and exalting the spirit; for arbitrarily generalising the attributes of man's spirit into an Absolute Idea, placed over man; and for using this Absolute to justify a system in which some men prospered at the expense of others.

According to the Petrashevtsy, religion and idealism had both wrongly separated man's soul from his body, spirit from matter, and placed the former above the latter. Spirit was then labelled the principle of good, matter the principle of evil. Both religious fanatics such as the Jansenists and philosophers, such as Kant, had depicted man's existence as a perpetual struggle between them. The Petrashevtsy denounced this 'battle of the good and evil principles in man' as unreal — the 'fruit of the false principle which wants to place human reason above the laws of nature', of 'the arbitrary, illusory separation of spirit and matter.[12]

Just like the religious theorists, Kant, Fichte, Schelling and Hegel first exalted man's spiritual qualities and then went on to deprive man of them and transfer them to some sort of absolute spirit, to which the whole world and the whole of world history was subordinated. As Feuerbach had said, 'The essence of theology is the essence of man, *transcendent*, outside man; the essence of Hegel's logic is transcendent thought, the thought of man placed *outside him*.' The Petrashevtsy, following Herzen, ridiculed the philosophers who tried to cut themselves off from their own material nature and from the real world, by raising themselves up and submerging themselves in the spiritual world. Maikov wrote ironically in *Otechestvennye zapiski*:

> Thought is cut off from life, absorbed in the contemplation of itself and bears no relation to reality .. on the wings of synthesis one can fly to such a height that the blood turns to ice and the human body freezes, to a height which no flyer has ever reached, but whither, with a cigar between their teeth thousands of scholars have soared.[13]

Since the theories of the idealists were based, not on the observation of real facts, but on ideas inborn in the human mind, they were obviously unscientific and untrue. The philosophers merely spun hypotheses in the air and then used 'these phantoms' to explain all the phenomena they encountered, regardless of whether or not the facts fitted in with them. In a critique partly derived from Stirner, Speshnev explained how, with their hypotheses, the idealists just created a fantasy world, a false spirit world alongside the real world, 'All metaphysics fears reality. It considers the actually real something other than the thing itself (essence, idea etc.), the real world is for it a great masquerade and its fantastical world — true reality.' The idealists' theories bore no relation to the real world, however much they attempted to twist the facts to fit in with them. In a speech, *The Tasks of Social Science*, which he read out to his circle, Kashkin compared the philosophers to the Chinese emperor, who happily believed himself the ruler of the whole globe, while all the time the whole globe, with the exception of China, was completely independent of him.[14]

The imaginary picture of the world created by the idealists, however, was more than just false and unscientific, its implications were dangerous and reactionary. Philosophy, like religion, had become the tool of the ruling classes and was used to justify the existing order. Hegel's formula 'What is rational is real and what is real (i.e. actual) is rational', was used to show the legitimacy of everything in existence. The Absolute Idea, as Saltykov said, was used to rework and purify everything so that even the dirty, poverty-stricken Russian peasant, 'Ugly Proshka', emerged from its unquenchable fire, 'ironed, cleansed, unrecognisable'. Kashkin quoted Herzen's disgust with the 'glassy calm' of the philosophers who saw in Hegel's formula irrefutable proof that 'humanity has achieved the *absolute* form of being': 'They are not embarrassed by the facts — they despise them. Ask them why, given this absolute form of

being, workers in Manchester and Birmingham are dying of hunger: they
will say this is an accident.'[15] The ideas of the philosophers had been
taken out of the sphere of abstract reason, into social life, by the political
economists, who had developed a systematic justification of the existing
economic order and of working class pauperism. This form of metaphysics was the target of the especial venom of Miliutin in his economic
articles and of Saltykov in his story *Contradictions*. The Petrashevtsy
refused to accept that a world in which individuals suffered could be
absolute, the best of all possible worlds and impossible to change. Here
their ideas were again similar to those of Belinskii, who rejected Hegel
because he placed the welfare of the Absolute over that of the individual
man, just as religion had that of God: 'You may laugh if you like, but
I still maintain that the fate of the subject, the fate of the individual is
more important than the fate of the whole world and the health of the
Chinese Emperor (i.e. Hegel's *Allgemeinheit*).'[16]

A materialistic monism

The Petrashevtsy believed that man should no longer be forced to
recognise the rationality of an irrational world in which people suffered.
It was time for science to 'descend from its throne to life'. They called
for the rehabilitation of matter, for a science based on the study of
reality, for the absolute to be toppled from its pedestal and no longer
oppress man. He should be given back his own authority, be left free
to act and change things. The reunion of science with life, of spirit with
matter, was, the Petrashevtsy thought, already underway. It had been
begun, paradoxically, by Hegel, who had reunited spirit and matter by
his theory of the identity of thought and being, though at the same time,
by making his idea the foundation of both, raising idealism to its greatest
height. Feuerbach had taken the next and decisive step and left idealism
behind. He called his philosophy, 'the realisation of Hegelian philosophy
and at the same time its negation'.[17] Feuerbach denied that the nature
and acts of man and society in any given age were determined by the
working in them of an identical absolute spirit. The Absolute Spirit and
God were formed from the attributes of the human species as personified
in finite beings, alienated from man and placed above him. Man had
unconsciously surrendered these attributes of justice, goodness,
harmony, unity, permanence etc. to God (who promised paradise in a
future life) or to the Absolute (which offered the comfort of a dream

world) as compensation for the fact that owing to the inadequacy of the material conditions in which they lived, men had not been able to realise these attributes and were miserable on earth.

Feuerbach replaced the philosophy of the Absolute with a philosophy of nature. Man was a sensual being, part of nature and subject to its laws. It was the sum of the material conditions surrounding him at any given time which had the decisive influence on his thoughts and actions, the nature of his society. He had to achieve self-consciousness by claiming his attributes back, bringing them out of the sky, out of God, out of the Absolute, into himself, and then, by studying and mastering the laws of nature to transform his life. The *Pocket Dictionary* tells us that Feuerbach's naturalism or anthropotheism:

> Regards the universal acceptance of God in the positive religions as the result of man's deification of his personality and the general laws of his thought; all religions which the historical development of mankind presents to us are considered as only the gradual preparation of mankind for *anthropotheism* or full *self-consciousness* and the *consciousness of the living laws of nature.*

The Petrashevtsy defined naturalism as 'a teaching which only accepts man in nature as the supreme being'[18] and made this statement the central principle of their philosophy. Their philosophy of man was more original than their critique of idealism. They attempted to combine the philosophical ideas of the left-Hegelians with those of the French socialists, (something that Marx was also working on at this time, though in a rather different way). By mixing and fusing the theories of Feuerbach and Fourier, they formed a philosophy of man and nature which was at once both rational and romantic. Feuerbach's philosophy was a critique of Hegelianism, Fourier's was an empirical reaction to the chaos of capitalism, but the two had much in common – they both sprang, on the one hand from the scientific materialism of the eighteenth century, and on the other from a passionate libertarianism, a desire for human emancipation. The Petrashevtsy drew from them an insistence on the importance of matter, the idea of the unity of the world, of nature, the idea that man was part of nature and primarily a sensual being. This had a double implication – man as part of nature was subject to its laws, the study of man was a branch of the natural sciences (as August Comte had said) and required rational, positive methods; however, man also possessed, in his reason, an instrument which allowed him to emancipate himself from nature, by mastering her laws and using them to secure the full development of his capacities, the full satisfaction of his needs.

The Petrashevtsy had a great respect for matter. Like the Saint-Simonians, they wanted to rehabilitate it, they believed that philosophy should embrace, 'not a single aspect of being, *spirit*, but also the *flesh*'. Petrashevskii had, 'thought about matter and spirit and become convinced that there is nothing in the world but matter'. However, he was not a 'vulgar' materialist. He attacked the 'childish' view of materialism, according to which man was nothing more than a higher animal and had no aim but the satisfaction of his bodily needs, and recognised that there were spiritual phenomena which could neither be measured nor touched, which yielded neither to sight, or hearing or taste — such as the imagination, memory, mind, will etc. Petrashevskii merely considered that these too were part of nature and could be explained in the same way as visible phenomena.[19]

Everything that existed, whether matter or spirit, was linked as part of an indissoluble whole-nature. All the Petrashevtsy shared this belief in 'the unity of everything'. They derived it in part from Feuerbach's materialistic re-interpretation of Hegel's and especially Schelling's Absolute; in part from Fourier, who had developed the idea that, 'Everything is linked in the system of the universe, and there is unity of action between all its parts', into a huge and complex theory of analogies. Petrashevskii said many times that there would be no place for any separation of spirit and matter in the consciousness of the healthy man who had developed in harmony with the whole of nature. He would see all natural phenomena as closely connected with each other and imbued with one universal and all powerful life force. Balasoglo, too, spoke of the 'unity of the totality' of nature — 'that life alone which is solid and real'.[20]

The Petrashevtsy looked at the phenomena of nature objectively, saw them as existing in space and time. Petrashevskii believed that every natural phenomenon had its legitimate duration, its beginning and end. However, nature itself was eternal. Matter was indissoluble, 'In nature nothing is lost'. The contradiction nature formed as an eternal whole with finite parts was solved dialectically by Herzen by the principle of eternal movement, the eternal transition of one part, one moment, into another. The Petrashevtsy expressed the same idea. Maikov, for example, described the constant substitution of one form for another, through the transfer of particles of matter, through attraction and repulsion, the changes in forms and flowers. Everything in nature was found in close connection and dependence on everything else. The principle of connections between all the existing phenomena of nature was seen not just as a mechanistic interaction of mutually dependent and similar atoms, but as the interdependence and interaction of living, diverse, ever-changing forces. Ippolit Debu, using Fourierist terminology, wrote, 'There is nothing *simple* in nature, everything is *complex* (*composé*), one thing turns into another, connects with a third, depends on a fourth, and the fourth is connected with the second, in dependence on the third etc.' Every phenomenon was at once a part and a result of the entire movement.[21]

The phenomena were thus constantly changing and they were never repeated. The article *Neology* in the *Pocket Dictionary* is entirely devoted to the idea that the ceaselessness of innovations is the external expression of the life principle in nature. In nature there is 'no complete reappearance for anything, there is no resurrection, no complete reproduction of a force which one day outlives its time'. However, in spite of this, 'the mass of forces acting in nature is from eternity perpetually one'. The variety of ever-changing phenomena was formed from the multiple combinations of the same perpetually-acting laws of nature. Man and nature were powerless to produce anything new, but could only re-organise what already exists. Individual parts of nature might change, but the sum of forces in the universe remains the same.[22]

Man stood at the centre of this materialistic monism. This idea was present in Feuerbach, but it was developed to its extreme by Fourier, who based his theory of analogies on the Renaissance idea of man as the microcosm, the mirror, of the universe.[23] Though rejecting Fourier's cosmogony, the Petrashevtsy had a tremendous weakness for the poetical analogies, which they saw as an allegorical illustration of the idea of the unity of man and nature as found in German philosophy. They took their cue from *Esprit des bêtes* (1847) by Alphonse Toussenel, (a Fourierist and famous anti-semite), a treatise on 'passionate zoology' in which all the animals reflect human characteristics. In 1848 *Otechestvennye zapiski* reproduced a rapturous review of this book, translated from the French of Emile Pellétan. The author used the review as an excuse to outline Fourier's theory of analogies and, among other things, makes the point about the similarity between Fourier's analogies and the German Absolute. Akhsharumov wrote in the same spirit:

Many phenomena cause one to suspect that the whole of humanity with its feelings, sufferings, pleasures, with its dreams and ideas is expressed in the vegetable, mineral and animal kingdoms. Can it be true that the magnificently spread tail of the peacock strewn all over with brightly jewelled flowers, blazes before our eyes without sense, without a meaning, that it expresses nothing? ... Does the nightingale with its light velvety note sing in the woods in spring a meaningless song?

He was sure that it must be possible to penetrate the mysteries of nature's symbolism, to unravel, for example, the caballistic writing on the spider's back and thus 'enter into a close relationship with everything in the universe'. Tolbin and Ippolit Debu expressed similar ideas.[24]

There were several logical consequences of man's unity with nature. First, as part of nature, man was primarily sensual. As Feuerbach said, 'Being is the subject, thought the predicate.' In the individual man cognition of the nature surrounding him preceded the moment of self-consciousness. As Tol' explained, in his lecture on religion, man was motivated by his feelings, his instincts, reason was secondary, 'Feeling exists first and then mind appears to verify it and prove that it has a firm basis ... nothing enters reason without first passing through the feelings.'[25] The more enthusiastic Petrashevtsy delved deep into the intricacies of man's instincts and made special studies of Fourier's 'scale of passions'. The most detailed is found in Beklemishev's *Correspondence of Two Landowners*, handwritten copies of which were passed round the members of Petrashevskii's circle and which, in its comprehensiveness and clarity, compared well with any exposition of Fourier's theory produced by his followers in France. Danilevskii also wrote a long account of the theory of the passions while in prison, at his interrogator's request. Others, including Khanykov, Chernyshevskii and Timkovskii, ventured into the esoteric analysis of the possible combinations of the passions contained in Fourier's manuscripts, published posthumously in *La Phalange*. Chernyshevskii, for example, laboriously translated 145 pages of the extraordinarily obscure *Du clavier puissanciel des caractères*, and read his translation out at one of his university classes.[26]

A second consequence of man's unity with nature was to make him dependent on nature, subject to its laws. Petrashevskii recounts how, 'I was forced by cold reasoning to recognise the complete dependence of all living phenomena in men on the universal laws of nature'. Ippolit Debu gave a materialist explanation of how there is no break anywhere in man's connection with everything existing:

> Man lives, but in order to live he needs food, he eats, assimilates to his body animals and plants, therefore his life depends on the life of others.

The plant world is dependent on the climate, i.e. the temperature, the humidity, density or rarity of the air, on the winds, electricity, the clarity of the sky etc; in other words, is dependent on the general phenomena of the earth's surface, which in turn depend on the position of the Earth in our solar system and the latter links in with the whole of the universe.[27]

If man was part of nature and strictly governed by nature's laws, the destiny of man and of human society could only be deduced from the study of human nature. The study of human nature had to be part (and the most important part) of the natural sciences. As Miliutin wrote, 'The consciousness of the basic principles and actual laws of social life, can only be achieved by means of an assiduous and successful study of the nature and activities of man'; or as Dostoevskii more succinctly put it, 'Man is a mystery. This mystery must be solved and if you spend your whole life working at it I won't say you will have wasted your time.'[28] The concept of the study of man as a science is present in the writings of the French socialists and Feuerbach, but was developed by Auguste Comte, the founder of positivism. The Petrashevtsy, especially Maikov and Miliutin were generally sympathetic to positivism and intensely interested in the latest discoveries of the natural sciences which they believed had to be made the basis of the study of man.

The reconciliation of science and freedom

Their interest was related to the great development of the natural sciences in the first half of the nineteenth century. In the West, there were George Buffon, George Cuvier, Wilhelm Humbolt, Pierre Laplace, William and John Herschel, Louis de Lagrange; in Russia, Karl Rul'e, Pavel I'lenkov, Karl Ber, Christian Pander, G.E. Sharovskii, P.F. Goriakov, lesser known but still influential representatives of a whole row of natural sciences. Their works were read in popularised versions in *Otechestvennye zapiski* and *Sovremennik* by the whole of the educated Russian public. Among the Petrashevtsy, L'vov, Mombelli, Filippov, Danilevskii, Golovinskii and Ippolit Debu were particularly interested in the natural sciences. They threw themselves into the study of physiology, anthropology, anatomy, all the sciences connected with man. Ippolit Debu even wrote a poem to Cuvier, who:

Unravelled the ancient world from its wreckage,
And wonderful, perished creatures,
Took from his fingers and brought back to life.

Some of them (including Chernyshevskii, Mombelli and Ippolit Debu) showed a particular interest in the writings of the French mechanical materialist George Cabanis. Cabanis, a doctor, had developed a totally physiological explanation for all man's actions, and made the famous pronouncement, 'The brain secretes thought as the liver secretes bile.' His ideas crept into Russian universities through Russian professors sent abroad. However, the Petrashevtsy were not quite 'so much materialists' as to be completely happy with this explanation.[29]

The two Petrashevtsy most concerned with the question of raising the study of man to the level of a science and working out the principles of a new, scientific social philosophy were Maikov and Miliutin, less political and more academically-minded than the others. In this they often did little more than paraphrase Comte's ideas on the introduction of the positive method into the social sciences. The account of the descriptive and dynamic methods, in Miliutin's review *A Study of National Wealth* by Ia. Butkovskii (the first Russian textbook on political economy) is, as Miliutin himself admits, taken directly from Book Four of the *Cours de philosophie positive*. According to Miliutin, Comte, 'explains in great detail and very satisfactorily, the method of positive working out of the social sciences', how they could be woken out of their 'theological' and 'metaphysical' slumbers, by the patient analysis of individual facts. Maikov was particularly interested in developing Comte's idea that a new encyclopedia might be achieved, when the social sciences were raised to the positive level and devotes an enormous article, *The Social Sciences in Russia*, to this question. He dissects the three main social sciences which he sees as political economy, law (which includes philosophy) and pedagogy (morals) to show them (i) in their independent aspect; (ii) their relationship to each other, and (iii) their relationship to other wholes, i.e. to the other sciences. He was particularly anxious to demonstrate that the contemporary conflicts between the different sciences were unnatural and would cease once they were reorganised as a united whole. Only then would social science take its proper place as the crown of the other sciences. It took longer for the social science to reach the positive stage, 'in virtue of its greater complexity, its more complete speciality and its more direct personality' i.e. it was the most sophisticated and the closest to man. Not all the Petrashevtsy however, shared Maikov and Miliutin's admiration for Comte's version of the form the new encyclopaedia was to take. The eccentric and enterprising Balasoglo, for example, drew up a system of classification all of his own. This was based on the idea of 'predominant aspects', in some ways similar to Fourier's theory of different passions predominating in different individuals and different parts of the universe.[30]

However, even Maikov and Miliutin could be critical of Comte. They believed he had taken empiricism too far. By aspiring to an endless splintering of knowledge on the basis of experience, he was turning away from science, which always had had as its object the completely opposite task – the generalisation of knowledge by means of speculation. Saltykov painted a horrible picture of analysis without synthesis:

> Imagine a man to whom at birth was given the ability that whatever he turned to, whatever he glanced at, would in an instant be decomposed for him into its component parts ... his situation would be terrible ... there would be no beauty, everywhere he would see a coarse heap of the most ugly elementary particles – in a picture by Briullov he would see only paints, canvas and oil.[31]

Maikov believed in the necessity of an integral method, a new logic. This would combine analysis and synthesis, empiricism and speculation, the methods of philosophy and the natural sciences. Man acquired knowledge of the external world through a two-fold process: (i) analysis, the capacity of thought to divide the cognised object into its component parts, and (ii) synthesis, the capacity of thought to join the parts into a single whole. Without analysis there was no knowledge of the parts, without synthesis no knowledge of the whole. Therefore, 'In science as the most perfect form of human knowledge, these two methods, these two forms of mental activity must be placed in the very closest connection.' However, of the two, the analytic method, or empirical knowledge, came first, synthesis and speculation second, but not separate, as a higher development of the same process. The features of this new logic – its combination of opposite methods, its acknowledgement of the primacy of analysis and empiricism over synthesis and speculation, were carefully conceived to correspond to the real world, the relationship of thought and being in nature, as the Petrashevtsy saw it. In their view, as Maikov said, science had to serve, 'as a mirror of existence'.[32]

Thought, reason, was part of nature, but it was at the same time the instrument of man's liberation from nature. The Petrashevtsy combined their rationalist ideas on science with a romantic vision of mankind struggling through history to develop its reason, overcome and escape from nature. Man achieved his final liberation from nature, paradoxically, by reuniting himself with it, by achieving an understanding of nature's laws and organising his life and society in accordance with them. Chernosvitov wrote, 'the starting point of free will is to follow the laws of nature' (and in particular, human nature).[33] The idea that freedom consisted in accepting nature's laws derives from Spinoza and is one of the central concepts of both Feuerbach's and Fourier's system.

Man was the most perfect product of the creative, omnipotent, forces of nature because he possessed reason. Man's reason was not something divorced from nature, but on the contrary, part of it, the highest development of nature. It was in fact, 'the consciousness of nature about itself'. This idea, shared by the Petrashevtsy and Herzen was inspired by Feuerbach, and through him, by Schelling, from whom Feuerbach took most of his philosophy of nature (though giving it a materialistic twist). In his soul man carried the idea, the thought of everything existing. The laws of thought were the consciousness of the laws of being, which lay hidden in nature, waiting for man's reason to come along and wake them up. Without man nature was therefore incomplete. Ippolit Debu wrote:

> If there was no man, nature would remain just as beautiful as it is at present, just as rational, just as variegated in its unity; in spite of this, without the presence of man, it would be dead, aimless and in its rationality, irrational. What point would there be in God's gift of nature, what point in beauty, what point in the harmony of the worlds and the laws directing them, what point in the meridian of stars with their wonderful, shimmering light, what point in the rays of the sun, playing on the surface of the water ... what point in all this if there is no creature which understands the laws of nature and its poetry?

Reason was 'the light of nature', it explained, enlightened, rectified and completed nature. All nature's aspirations and efforts were achieved through man. As Akhsharumov said, 'Nature in the human world uses man as her instrument: he as her active principle carried out in his person, expresses, the laws inspired by her — the general laws of the whole universe with which the whole of his life is found in close connection.'[34]

However, the reason of the individual was powerless on its own. Without other men, the individual was lost in the ocean of nature, unable to comprehend either himself as a man, or nature as nature. This was Feuerbach's idea. He explains it by saying that the first object against which the individual's pride stumbles is another I, another man. This object is the beginning of his knowledge of the outside world, 'I reconcile myself, I become friendly with the world only through my fellow man.' Petrashevskii summed this up, 'Man as an individual, placed face to face with nature, is nothing, man is powerful as a species.'

The knowledge of a single man was limited, but the reason of men taken collectively, of humanity, the species, was unlimited. The origin of man's life as a species being, was, according to Herzen, contained in his capacity of memory, 'Nature remembers nothing, for her there is no past, but man carries his whole past in himself; therefore man represents himself not only as an individual, but also as a species.' Petrashevskii stresses the importance of language, man's capacity for expressing and generalising human thought, in enabling the species to preserve the results of its previous development and thus making infinite progress possible.[35]

According to this theory, the species life of man embraced humanity past, present and future. Humanity was an indissoluble whole. As man was connected with the whole of nature, so all men were connected with each other, each generation with the next. The individual was but, 'a link in the single chain of his fellow creatures, one note in the great chord of humanity'. Nature's reason developed towards self-consciousness and man progressed towards an understanding of nature, through the history of humanity. Change in history was explained by the irrepressible striving of the reason of humanity for full development. If one looked at the past, Debu said, one would see that, 'The whole life of humanity, for thousands of years, has striven and strives to understand, evaluate and make use of what surrounds it.'[36]

History and progress

Feuerbach had replaced the Absolute spirit with the Human spirit, but he had not been interested in the historical possibilities of his theory. Along with Hegel's idealism, he had abandoned the dialectic, and his view of the world was essentially static, ahistorical. Other left-Hegelians, however, for example Bruno Bauer, had adopted the idea of the human spirit while retaining Hegel's idea of dialectical development in history.[37] This was in general what the Petrashevtsy did. They fitted Feuerbach's concept of humanity in with the idea of historical laws and progress in history as found in Hegel, and more particularly, in Saint-Simon. Once the Absolute spirit had been replaced by humanity, there were striking similarities between the two theories. From Hegel and Saint-Simon the Petrashevtsy drew a most un-Feuerbachian and un-Fourierist interest in history. They developed in detail a historical theory, based on the concept of reason as part of nature, which they attempted to reconcile (in a sometimes contradictory way) with the Fourierist idea of an unchangeable human nature.

The Petrashevtsy's acceptance of historical laws derived from their desire to believe in the future of man. They refused to accept that man had been abandoned to, 'the meaningless arbitrariness of blind chance'. There had to be laws for history to become a science, for mankind to be able to predict its future and to guarantee that it would one day arrive on the threshold of an ideal society. Like Saint-Simon the Petrashevtsy regarded the past, present and future as terms of a single and identical series of events. A detailed knowledge of the past, Petrashevskii believed, 'can make everyone the master of the future'. Their ideas about the future were scientific, not utopian, Saltykov argued, because they deduced their utopia from the historical development of reality.[38]

In the Petrashevtsy's view, the laws of history led man inexorably towards ever better things. Like Saint-Simon, and especially his mentor Condorcet, the majority of the Petrashevtsy were believers in progress. They thought not only that humanity had a golden future but that 'the perfectibility of mankind is truly indefinite'.[39] They combined this with the idea of the constant dialectical movement of the human spirit to ever higher levels, which was expressed in the writings of some of the left-Hegelians, who based themselves on their master's *Phenomenology* rather than his *Logic*. Their sense of rationality and their love of freedom caused the Petrashevtsy to take ideas of progress (and other ideas) to their extreme, to their logical conclusion.

They poured scorn on the failure of Rousseau and Fourier to overthrow such backward, religious conceptions as the original ideal condition of man and the Fall,[40] and argued that humanity's history was a progress from savagery towards a golden age, which as Saint-Simon had said, lay in the future. Saltykov put Saint-Simon's words into his hero's mouth, 'We don't live in the golden age, Tat'iana Ignat'eva, the golden age is ahead of us, as one of your favourite writers says.' The Petrashevtsy were particularly concerned to vindicate the idea of progress because it was by no means generally accepted in Russia. They directed their writings specifically against the Slavophiles' yearning for the restoration of an idealised Russian past. It was completely impossible for humanity to go backwards, Balasoglo declared, as impossible as for a river to flow uphill or for a tree to grow from the top down. Petra-shevskii pointed out the degradation and brutality of the so-called 'heroic' aspects of Russia's past: 'The past cannot be brought back, today no-one, not even the Kirghiz who camps on the wide Baraban steppe, is impressed by the valour of Sviatoslav, who slept on a sweaty felt blanket in the mud and drank wine mixed half-and-half with blood from the still warm skull of his enemy.'[41]

The law of progress had two sides to it — it was impossible for humanity to go backwards, it was also impossible for it to reach a final point. As Belinskii, looking back in horror on his period of reconciliation with reality, put it in 1844, 'There is no limit to human progress, never will humanity say to itself: stop there is nowhere further to go!' The Petrashevtsy shared this view. Change and progress were absolutely essential attributes of the life of humanity. Saltykov, an especially fervent supporter of this idea, said that, if man and nature merged in a final synthesis, if history ended, 'the period of death will begin'. The progress of mankind had to take place and took place constantly, every day, in all human societies.[42] This distinguished the Petrashevtsy from the French socialists, who (with the exception of Leroux) tended to wrap things up, to cut history off at the point of socialism and invent final versions of the new society.

In their treatment of history, the Petrashevtsy quite consciously combined the dialectic of Hegel with the dialectic of Saint-Simon — Petrashevskii, for example, uses the Hegelian term *synthesis* as a synonym for the Saint-Simonian term *organic epoch*.[43] Hegel was concerned with the Absolute Spirit, Saint-Simon with human society, but both saw the dialectic as the moving principle of history. According to this dialectic, as interpreted by the Petrashevtsy, history was the successive development of one set of phenomena out of others. Each incomplete form of social life prepared the way for another more perfect one, for example, barbarism for feudalism, feudalism for civilisation. Each form (i.e. synthesis or organic epoch) provided a solution to the problems of humanity which though incomplete, satisfied the requirements of the day. Each was developed 'to the last extreme, as if salvation lies in that form'. Then, when it had become obsolete, had produced its fruits, it gave rise to a new principle, its negation. A battle ensued between old and new, in which, 'after a long and bitter struggle', man passed through antagonism, contradiction, opposition, to a complete rejection of his previous beliefs. The ground was cleared for a new organic epoch, a new synthesis, in which the best elements of the old were preserved, but in a new form, allowing new progress.[44] The Petrashevtsy adopted with especial enthusiasm Saint-Simon's idea of a great critical epoch, a great period of destruction, beginning with Luther and culminating in the French revolution, which had finally cleared away the last remnants of the medieval order. The idea that they were living among the ruins of the old society, in a sort of echoing emptiness and vacuum, held a great appeal for them because it seemed to provide a general social explanation of the personal feeling of despair, which they experienced as isolated individuals in backward Russian society. They referred to their era as 'black days in the history of mankind', a period in which the old idols had been toppled from their pedestals, and new ones not yet formed. This theory also, in its insistence that the old order had collapsed, that the time had come to create a new one, to act, seemed to offer them the hope of emerging from the limbo in which they lived. Saltykov parodied the feelings of the Petrashevtsy in a satirical sketch of his friend Pleshcheev (Aleksis in *A Tangled Affair*), who was: 'ready to place his head on the block in order to prove that the period of destruction had passed and that now it was necessary to *create, create, create*'.[45]

The motor of history, which developed dialectically through the historical process, was, as has been said, the reason of humanity, i.e. ideas. Petrashevskii explained that, 'In humanity ideas play the same role as forces in nature and epochs of new tendencies in the development of humanity are determined by the appearance of ideas which had a guiding influence on the development of mankind.'[46] In spite of this, it was in some ways a materialist theory. The development of new ideas in history was prompted by the variety of the demands of human nature. These prevent man from ever being content with the established means of satisfying his needs and force him ceaselessly to search for new ones, which correspond more exactly to his nature. Though the original definition of reason comes from Feuerbach, in the development of this idea in a historical context, the Petrashevtsy were influenced chiefly by Saint-Simon. It led them, like Saint-Simon, to stress the importance of technology in human progress, 'Not the strategy and tactics of Napoleon, but the force of compressed steam, was fated to transform the earth and elevate mankind.' Again like Saint-Simon, the Petrashevtsy sometimes spoke of the dialectical development of history as a battle between the oppressed and oppressing classes. In his speech on Fourier's birthday in 1849, Khanykov spoke of:

A law which runs through the whole of history in different forms, the law of the conquerors and the conquered, which manifested itself: in the East, through the battle of castes; in Greece, through the battle between the demos and the eupadrids; in Rome, the plebians and the patricians; in the Middle Ages, all sorts of struggles for the emancipation of the individual from authority, battles between sects, parties, new classes which were forming at that time, and most typically, a battle of peasants and town communes and vassals; and today, a battle of the proletarians against the capitalists.

The idea of class struggle was brought out more clearly here than in most of the writings of the French socialists and bears a striking resemblance to the opening passage of Marx's *Communist Manifesto*, which it is just possible Khanykov might have read.[47]

The Petrashevtsy (and in particular Maikov) outlined in sometimes excessive detail their view of the intellectual stages through which humanity rose to a greater degree of self-consciousness and a greater understanding of nature. They were partly influenced by Feuerbach, but primarily by Comte's law of three states – theological (fetishism, polytheism and monotheism), metaphysical and positive. They preferred it to the original Saint-Simonian version (which ended with monotheism) because of its scientific and atheist elements.

The Petrashevtsy explained religion as just the lowest phase of human thought, the product of a period in which man was still totally dependent on, totally dominated by, nature and had not yet achieved any understanding of her workings. In his speech on religion, Tol' explained how the first manifestation of religion, fetishism, arose from man's feeling of subordination to the rude but gigantic forces of nature, his total ignoranc of it, which caused him to feel fear towards it, mingled with respect, and instantly to deify every object that attracted his attention. Maikov described how, 'A will o'the wisp in the graveyard becomes the lost soul of a dead man, an echo in the forest the cry of a woodgoblin … the imagination loses itself in the splendours of creation and peoples the world with spirits.' The second two phases of religion, polytheism and monotheism, were marked by a tentative development of human thought. As Tol' said, at first man worshipped what struck him immediately, then he began to worship its causes in a collection of higher phenomena, and finally he arrived at the idea of one cause for all things. However, they were essentially only modifications of fetishism. Man's continuing ignorance of and subordination to natural phenomena could be seen, for example, from his faith in miracles.[48]

The next stage, metaphysics, was, as Speshnev said, 'an ambiguous thing'. On the one hand, it was just a modification of theology in which through ignorance of the real causes of things, men invented false ones – this time, instead of God, an Absolute. Looked at from another point of view, metaphysics was the complete opposite of theology. Theology was the extreme of feeling, materialism; metaphysics, the extreme of thought, idealism. As Maikov said, 'the awakening of the independence of thought' was manifested in a desperate rebellion against nature, in which man tried to 'tear himself out of the real world and create an opposite world'.[49]

In the third state, positivism, which man had now entered, he rejected all the false essences placed above him and brings his thought back into himself, down to earth and takes on the study of what was accessible, what was under his nose, accepting reality as 'the only sphere of activity to which man is drawn by the needs and activities of his nature'. Through the proper study of reality, of nature, everything would become known, the more enthusiastic and optimistic socialists among the Petrashevtsy believed. Man would, Petrashevskii declared, 'with time and through the consciousness of world laws, fully become the sovereign and the organiser of the whole of visible nature, in which there is nothing that cannot be subordinated to him as to the conscious and self-aware principle of creative activity.' The more scholarly Maikov and Miliutin, however, like Comte, blanched at the prospect of total knowledge.[50]

Man would use his understanding of the laws of nature as the basis for the transformation of his life. There were two aspects to this. First, he would harness the laws of nature, through new inventions, new developments of technology, improving the material conditions of his life beyond all recognition. Debu outlined the immensity of science's progress so far:

> Man was created bare, without means of protection or clothing – he did not possess the fur coat which covers the wild beasts, nor horns, nor the strength and ferocity of the tiger; but he possessed reason. Through reason he subordinated the wild beasts and transferred part of his labours to them; through reason he comprehended the forces of nature and already he travels as fast as a bird from one place to another on steamships and with the speed of lightning conveys his thoughts along thin wires for a thousand, ten thousand versts. What will the future hold?

Petrashevskii and Herzen agreed that 'steam' was transforming man's life, that the invention of machines, by providing the means to free man

from the burden of ceaseless labour, formed an essential preliminary to
'the resolution of the most important social question'.[51] Secondly, man
would also, by reorganising society in accordance with the laws of human
nature, transform the social conditions of his life. The Petrashevtsy
believed that only in a society which allowed man to develop the full
potential of his nature and to satisfy all his needs, inclinations and tastes,
material and spiritual, would man be truly free and happy. The idea that
freedom lay in the ability to satisfy all one's natural desires struck a great
chord among the Petrashevtsy. Chernosvitov, for example, made a
Russian abridgement of the treatise on free will published as a prologue
to Fourier's *Théorie de l'unité universelle*. Here Fourier jeered at the
so-called freedom of Civilisation, in which man possesses the negative
freedom to opt for greater or lesser privations and torments, but not
the positive freedom of being able to choose the life he really wanted.
The Petrashevtsy also encountered the idea that man's freedom and
happiness were directly linked with the acceptance of human nature as
the supreme law in the writings of the left-Hegelians, in particular *Die
Religion der Zukunft*. The definition of freedom accepted by the
Petrashevtsy was that composed by Akhsharumov, 'The free man is he
who can fulfil all his desires, all his whims, which not only do not appear
without reason, but are directly linked with the basic forces directing
our whole life.'[52]

The individualists: Maikov and Speshnev

The theory that has been presented so far thus provided a definition of
individual freedom which accorded with the requirements of science.
This was accepted by the majority of the Petrashevtsy. But some of them,
notably Maikov and Speshnev, felt that as it stood, it laid too little
emphasis on individual freedom. They refused to accept all its determinist
elements – the concept of man as wholly subordinate to nature and part
of an indissoluble, monolithic humanity. Maikov and Speshnev attacked
these notions in quite different ways, but both regarded them as intoler-
able because of the restrictions they placed on the freedom of action of
the individual, for them the primary object of philosophy.

Maikov, unlike the majority of the Petrashevtsy, accepted Comte's
idea that science, the positive method, only allowed one to co-ordinate

a certain number of natural phenomena, but did not explain the essence of things. To explain the essence of things, Maikov argued (following Kant) one had to postulate the existence of another sphere, separate from and superior to the realm of natural laws − the sphere of God and free will. Maikov's emphasis on the freedom of the individual was thus connected with his retention of religious beliefs. His essential idea was that the exceptional individual could, by the exercise of his free will, overcome the limits set by natural laws and through this process, move history forward. In this Maikov was, as he admitted, strongly influenced by the writings of the French historian Jules Michelet, another passionate champion of individual liberty.[53]

Maikov developed this theory in the course of a public polemic with Belinskii in the Russian press of 1846−7.[54] This took the form of a dispute over the nature of the poetry of the peasant writer, Aleksei Kol'tsov. This dispute was ostensibly over the question of nationality (*narodnost*), but the central issue was free will and the explanation of the appearance of 'great men' in history. Both accepted the concept of 'great men' and explained this by the idea of a division of society into a conservative majority and a minority of exceptional individuals, an élite, through whom progress was accomplished. Maikov, however, attacked Belinskii for what he felt was the latter's excessive espousal of moral determinism.

Belinskii saw the great individuals who changed history as the product of their social, economic and national environment, as men who were great by virtue of their ability to formulate precisely the progressive ideas and aspirations existing unconsciously in the majority at any one epoch. Even after he, in theory, discarded his Hegelianism, he clung to the determinist idea that 'every great man achieves the task of his time, resolves the contemporary questions, expresses through his actions the spirit of the time in which he was born and grew up'. Similar ideas were expressed by Petrashevskii in the *Pocket Dictionary*, and by Miliutin in his economic articles.[55] It was historical circumstances that determined the appearance of great leaders − wars produced great generals, revolutions great orators. The individual who tried to disregard the circumstances would fail, however hard he tried.

Maikov refused to accept this. In his view, 'A man in whom the external circumstances of his life, a whole panorama of the facts of his origin and development are reflected as in a mirror, is a vegetable, not a free and reasonable being, created in the *image and likeness* of God.' His version of the majority/minority theory was a division of mankind into a majority, who were not free, but lived a passive mechanical existence in submission to the laws of nature (summed up as climate, environment, race and fate); and a minority, of whom great men were merely the most outstanding representatives, who gained freedom and produced great ideas by opposing themselves to the majority, by tearing themselves out of their environment and disregarding historical circumstances. The ideas of great individuals were gradually channelled into humanity through the minority. The more a man freed himself from his environment, the greater he became, the larger his contribution to the development of humanity. The outstanding example of a truly great individual, was, Maikov believed, Christ. His doctrine, 'achieved such a remarkable independence from phenomena fateful for millions of beings called free and reasonable', and he was elevated to such a degree above the laws of historical phenomena, that mankind had not yet caught up with it, not yet fully understood and realised it.[56]

Speshnev's philosophical ideas are set out in two letters to his friend Edmund Chojecki, a Polish journalist, criticising the left-Hegelian philosophy of another Pole, Heinrich Kamienski. Speshnev took his theory of individualism and free will several steps further than Maikov. He wanted to emancipate all men, not just great individuals, from the concept of humanity and from law and authority altogether. His philosophy was inspired by the amoralism and egoism of Max Stirner, author of *Der Einzige und sein Eigentum*.[57]

Like Stirner, Speshnev attacked Feuerbach for stopping half-way, for knocking down the religious and the Hegelian Absolutes only to replace them with another — the Human Absolute. Humanity was just another Absolute, just another authority over the individual, an 'essence over us'. Feuerbach had again separated body and spirit and labelled the latter superior. Speshnev expostulates, 'Isn't it ridiculous, to posit man as a being with a double content, like two cases, one locked up inside the other, or like a jewel locked up in a casket, in one word, as one being, *Geist* (spirit), shut up inside another, *Körper* (body)?' According to him, this made anthropotheism nothing more than another religion, the last metamorphosis of the Christian religion. It had replaced the 'God–Man' by the 'Man–God', but there was no essential difference between the two. Humanity, just like Christianity, was 'an abstract and glorified image of man'.[58]

Speshnev added to his critique of Feuerbach a violent attack on the concept of the oneness of humanity in history, as it appeared in the writings of the French socialists and especially Pierre Leroux. Through his acceptance of metemphsychosis, Leroux had carried the denial of the individual and the exaltation of humanity to its furthest possible point. Speshnev turned his considerable powers of irony to the task of demolishing such theories and advocating in their place the simple idea of the autonomy of the individual. Although we do not know the positive beginnings of the human world, he wrote:

> We do know the names of dozens of men who have moved science and industry forward, who have brought it to the condition in which we find it today: the names of Copernicus, Galileo, Kepler, Newton, Herschel, Columbus, Cook, Jenner, Davy, Watt, Fulton, Euclid, Archimedes, Lavoisier, Shakespeare, Goethe, Schiller, Byron, my God! the names of hundreds of other men who had gradually advanced science, created works of art, invented productive processes; the names of historical figures, who, one after the other, changed social institutions, who dedicated themselves to the abolition of slavery, who destroyed feudalism and founded the state etc. You may positively know many names, but you are nonetheless mistaken, this is the result of an optical illusion. Scientific inventions, works of art, social institutions – all these are products of the Absolute, of the absolute human essence.

Speshnev made himself, like Stirner, the champion of the individual against all authorities, all generalities, 'the enemy of every higher power', of religion, Humanity and morality. For the whole man, the ego, there were no higher essences. No God, no Humanity, no principles, no right and wrong existed. Nothing was sacred. Might was right. The individual himself, his will, his ego, his self-interest – this was the criterion. 'I do everything on my account'. This was the bare violence that lay at the heart of Stirner's philosophy: 'When the world comes in my way – and it comes in my way everywhere – I consume it to quiet the hunger of my egoism. For me no-one is a person to be respected ... but solely ... an object, in which I take an interest or else I do not, an interesting or uninteresting object, a usable or unusable person.' Speshnev accepted without qualm all the sinister implications of Stirner's theory. He proclaimed his total indifference to moral questions. In his view such categories as beauty and ugliness, good and bad, noble and base were merely a matter of taste. It was Speshnev that Dostoevskii was thinking of when, in *The Devils*, he described Stavrogin as a man for whom 'good and evil do not exist and are but a prejudice'. In his personal life, Speshnev acted deliberately, as far as possible, according to Stirner's egoism. It seems to have been easy for him to do this because he was by temperament and inclination an egoist. He wrote to his mother in

1846, 'In the world I am capable of loving myself, much, much and others, little, little.' His whole history, from his schooldays, shows him to have been a man with a cold rational brain and a complete absence of scruples.[60]

Speshnev converted his closest friend at this period, the charming but neurotic Vladimir Engel'son, to his philosophy of egoism. In 1854, Engel'son explained to Herzen how he had preserved what he called his 'Speshnevskoi point of view', how he therefore held his fellow men in contempt and was not prepared to contemplate any closer association with them than the loose and temporary alliances of egoists acting for coincidentally similar aims, advocated by Stirner. Herzen himself in 1849, disillusioned by the failure of the revolution in France, had for a short period succumbed to the fascination of Stirner's theory. In his collection of essays, *From the Other Shore*, he, like Speshnev, extended his critique of religion and idealism to cover Feuerbach and the concept of Progress too, announcing, 'we shall find no haven but in ourselves'.[61]

The ideas of the Petrashevtsy were thus not entirely homogenous. There was, however, a definite core of ideas, accepted more or less wholeheartedly by the majority of the philosophically-minded Petrashevtsy – Petrashevskii, Ippolit Debu, Balasoglo, Tol', Khanykov, Mombelli, Kashkin, Miliutin, Saltykov, and, with reservations, by Maikov and Speshnev. This can be summed up very roughly as follows. Although some of the Petrashevtsy believed in God, they were on the whole less religious, more atheist than the contemporary French socialists. The reason for this lay in the association of religion with tyranny, both the tyranny of the Tsar over his subjects and of a heartless God over a suffering humanity. They merged their critique of religion with an attack on the Absolute of Hegel and Schelling. Both God and the Absolute were illusory essences formed of man's attributes placed over man. And, just as religion served as the prop of Tsarism in Russia, so idealist philosophy, through the notion 'the rational is real' served as the justification of the despotism of the bourgeoisie in the West. The Petrashevtsy called for the reunion of spirit and matter, science and life and developed a materialist theory of nature as a unity, of man as part of this unity, a sensual being and subject to its laws. This idea had both rational and romantic implications. On the one hand, if man was part of nature and subject to its laws, the study of human nature was part of the natural sciences and like them had, as Comte had said, to be raised to the positive, scientific stage. On the other hand, man possessed reason,

which, though part of nature, was also the instrument of man's liberation
from it, his means of escaping from brute, passive submission to nature's
laws. Human reason developed through the history of humanity, pro-
ceeding through dialectical stages to an ever-greater understanding of
nature, until finally it reached self-consciousness. In the stage of full self-
consciousness, humanity achieved a full understanding of, full mastery
of, the laws of nature. But paradoxically, what this self-consciousness
enabled man to realise, was that his freedom, his liberation from nature,
lay precisely in returning to nature, in transforming and reorganising
his life in accordance with the dictates of her laws and in particular, with
the laws of his own nature.

This theory was formed under the influence of German philosophy
and French socialism. It combined a sensual, romantic view of human
nature, derived from Feuerbach and Fourier; and a more rational,
scientific theory of history, drawn in part from Hegel and Bruno Bauer,
but chiefly from Saint-Simon, the Saint-Simonians and Comte.
Petrashevskii and his closest associates — Debu, Balasoglo, Tol',
Mombelli, Khanykov and Kashkin — were more attracted to the anthropological Feuerbachian aspect of the theory; Maikov, Miliutin and
Saltykov to the stress on history and science. There was an obvious
tension between the idea of a static, unchanging human nature and the
theory of historical change, which the Petrashevtsy attempted to resolve
here through the concept of the development of human reason to a
comprehension to the laws of its own nature, and which will become
more apparent when the economic and political applications of these
ideas are discussed.

The idea of individual freedom lay at the centre of the Petrashevtsy's
philosophy — the idea of man throwing off the authority of God, the
Absolute and finally achieving freedom from subordination to nature
through the consciousness of her laws. The final aim was romantic and
sensual — freedom for men to give themselves up wholly to their natural
instincts, and harmlessly to satisfy their every desire. However, because
of their respect for science, most of the Petrashevtsy were unable to
contemplate an idea of freedom which could not be combined with an
acceptance of the laws of nature and history. Maikov and Speshnev were
the only ones to demand a greater degree of freedom for the individual
— the freedom to raise himself above and discard these laws.

The Petrashevtsy's philosophical ideas were not the most original
part of their theory. They were not only indebted to the German left-
Hegelians, but also drew heavily on Belinskii's and above all Herzen's

interpretation of them. However, the Petrashevtsy were not very interested in Hegel and were more directly inspired by Feuerbach. They were less concerned with history and more inclined to materialism than Herzen or Belinskii. Anthropological materialism was for them the central tenet and, when it conflicted with their historical ideas, took precedence.

The other thinker whose development bears close parallels to that of the Petrashevtsy, who also, though in a different manner, fused the ideas of the German philosophers and French socialism, was, of course, Karl Marx. The theories of the Petrashevtsy cannot, however, really be compared with those of Marx. Their philosophy was a compilation of ideas from different sources, rather than a completely new theory. Marx had immersed himself in philosophy, worked his way through it to historical materialism. The Petrashevtsy had, right from the beginning, a pragmatic attitude to philosophy. They were not so much interested in it for its own sake as for the political conclusions which could be drawn from it. They went into philosophy to look for a theory which would justify and provide a solid and rational foundation for their urge to action, their wish to change existing society. Herzen described how

> The Petrashevtsy rushed ardently and boldly into action ... the heirs of the strongly aroused intellectual activity of the forties, they went straight from German philosophy to the phalange of Fourier.[62]

V — THE CRITIQUE OF CIVILISATION

The Petrashevtsy's attitude to Western European society was crucial in turning them from democrats into socialists. Their socialism was, to a large extent, a reaction against Western capitalism (which they usually called by the Fourierist term 'Civilisation').

   The evaluation of capitalist society was one of the main issues dividing the different currents of thought among the Russian intelligentsia of the 1840s. The Slavophiles consistently exposed and attacked capitalism from a romantic–conservative standpoint, vaunting the superiority of the values of an idealised, pre-capitalist old Russia. The position of the Westerners was more complicated. Their main enemy was the pre-capitalist society of serf and autocratic Russia. Their goal was to transform Russia through the adoption of Western values and practices. Implicit in this was a conviction of the superiority of Western social forms and the Western path of development. The more liberal Westerners (especially the merchant's son Botkin), following this line of reasoning, regarded capitalism as progressive and pointed to the growing wealth and democratic freedoms of England and France as proof of this. The radicals, however, found it very hard to reconcile themselves to the social reality of Europe. Their response to it took different forms. Herzen's was the most extreme. He left Russia for Europe in 1847, spending part of his time in Italy, but most in Paris. The rapid disillusionment caused by first-hand experience of the West was chronicles in his *Letters from France and Italy* and *Letters from the Avenue Marigny*. Herzen's revulsion was of a cultural nature. It took the form of an aristocratic disdain of middle class modes and values. It was virtually devoid of political or economic content. Herzen saw 'bourgeois society' as the culmination of the decadence of the 'old world' (i.e. Europe). He included the whole of that society in his condemnation, workers as well as the bourgeoisie, socialists as well as capitalists. It was all vulgar, mediocre, corrupt. This led him eventually to break with Westernism and to turn towards Russian values, adopting a position which had some points in common with that of the Slavophiles. Belinskii was more hesitant in his verdict on Europe. His views remained very much within the framework of Westernism. He felt that European society was imperfect. But this was because it had failed adequately to impose its own principles, as developed in the Enlightenment and French revolution. Belinskii believed in bourgeois democratic principles. And, though he disliked the bourgeoisie and preferred the socialists, he felt that the bourgeoisie was a historical necessity. Progress depended on them and a bourgeoisie was therefore (unfortunately) desirable in Russia.[1]

The Petrashevtsy's position was slightly different from either Herzen's or Belinskii's. Like Herzen, they adopted a stance of uncompromising hostility to capitalism. Petrashevskii said 'We have condemned the present social order to death.'[2] But, like Belinskii, they remained within the Western tradition, in that they continued to believe that Western society was progressive and that Western ideas were of value and relevance to Russia. The inspiration for their attacks on the evils of capitalism and their ideas for solutions to them, came from Western sources – from the French socialists and liberal political economists, especially Fourier and Sismondi. The Petrashevtsy's critique was strongly anthropological in nature and, above all, focussed on the increasing pauperisation of the masses. They emphasised social misery as capitalism's salient feature, were alarmed at the small beginnings of similar developments, which they could detect in their country and turned to socialism as a way of avoiding capitalism in Russia (see Chapter VI). All this foreshadowed later Populist theory. The Petrashevtsy's continuing belief in the progressive nature of Western society, however, places them firmly in the Enlightenment tradition in Russia. In this combination of Enlightenment and Populist elements, their theories bear a resemblance to those developed by Chernyshevskii in the early sixties.

The Petrashevtsy's critique of bourgeois society embraced both the main aspects of the capitalist society of France and England and Russia, as far as similar phenomena could be observed there. Their attitude seems to have been that, in terms of educational and moral structures, there was very little difference between them; in tems of industrialisation, Russia was developing rapidly in the same direction. Their exposés were based on two, sometimes contradictory methods: the anthropological and the historical. Of the two, more important was their anthropological theory of society and socialism, inspired by Fourier and Feuerbach but outlined in a manner peculiar to themselves. Everything was judged according to certain eternal, absolute principles of morality and justice, morality and justice being defined as that which corresponded to the

laws of nature, and more particularly, to human nature.[3] The Petrashevtsy denounced 'Civilisation' as *abnormal*, unjust and unnatural, a
society which contradicted and repressed human nature. Its economic
system was condemned because it made the satisfaction of the demand's
of man's nature, both material and spiritual, impossible; its systems of
morality and education because they told men that this non-satisfaction
was right and taught them to resist and repress their own nature. Civilised
society was thus absolutely wrong, the complete opposite of what it
should be. As a result, it warped and twisted men, made them mere
caricatures of their true selves. The socialists' aim was to discover
Civilisation's opposite — the *normal* or just and natural state of society,
a society which corresponded to and gave full freedom to human nature.
The *Pocket Dictionary*, under *Normal State*, defines a '*normally-
developed* or well-organised society', as that which:

> provides each of its members with means for the satisfaction of their needs
> in proportion to their demands and places every man in such a ... relation-
> ship to the whole of society, that he, in giving himself up wholly to his
> natural impulses, in no way disrupts the harmony of the social relations,
> but through his actions benefits not only himself, but the whole of society,
> without sacrificing his self-interest.

The mention of self-interest, with its echoes of Mill, foreshadows
Chernyshevskii's more utilitarian theory of socialism, based on the idea
of man as a selfish being. But for the Petrashevtsy, the idea of self-
interest was only incidental. What interested them above all was the idea
of individual freedom. Their aim was to reconcile individualism and
association, to create a society in which all individuals could be absolutely
free, freedom being defined as the ability to follow every inclination,
indulge every whim of one's nature. A socialist society was defined by
Kashkin as one which guaranteed, as well as political freedom and
equality 'general human freedom'.[4]

The second method used by the Petrashevtsy to criticise Civilisation
was historical. They attempted to combine the anthropological ideas of
Feuerbach and Fourier with a Saint-Simonian appreciation of relativity
and historical change. This led them to state that as well as absolutely
true and permanent laws (the laws of human nature), there were relatively
true impermanent ones (the laws of history). An example of relatively
true laws were those of capitalism. Capitalism like every other historical
system arose from a certain level of the productive forces and was
progressive and legitimate for a certain period. During this period the

economic laws according to which it operated were valid and true; all its economic phenomena – competition, machines, the division of labour etc. – brought benefit to man in the form of an incredible increase in wealth; all its social institutions were progressive. But capitalism soon became obsolete and retrogressive. Its laws were by now invalid, (or had assumed perverted forms, like Malthus's law of population), its economic phenomena had developed bad as well as good sides and had created the terrible scourge of pauperism. The political economists who continued to uphold and justify them were trying to hold back the course of history by passing off laws that were historically, relatively true, as eternally and absolutely true. Mankind was now straining towards a new development, a socialist system, which would retain and develop the good aspects of capitalism, (the increase in wealth) while shedding the bad, and create a new prosperity for all men.

The anthropological and historical methods co-exist uneasily in the social criticism of the Petrashevtsy. There was a constant tension and sometimes a flagrant contradiction between the two. It was difficult to maintain simultaneously that capitalism went against human nature, was loathsome, totally wrong and had to be destroyed and that capitalism was initially progressive and had good sides which would be preserved under socialism. The Petrashevtsy, however, did not see, or did not care to see, this problem.

The Petrashevtsy put these two methods together to make vituperative attacks on every aspect of existing society: on its repression and perversion of human nature, on its false education and morality; on the unjust economic system of capitalism, which while creating immense wealth, had reduced the mass of the population through pauperism to the status of animals; on the political economists who justified this system; and on all other theories which stopped short of a complete transformation of society. They called for its total reorganisation on the general socialist principles of the redistribution of wealth and the organisation of labour. However, they subjected the different solutions offered by the different French socialists to stringent criticism from the point of view of their own particular version of the anthropological principle. Fourier's phalanstery seemed to them the most satisfactory, because it not only offered to share out prosperity more equally among all men, but was deliberately devised to allow the maximum freedom to each individual to follow the demands of his nature. All the Petrashevtsy accepted its main principles – even the dissidents, Speshnev and the radicals, who wanted to combine Fourierism with communism and Maikov and his circle, who wanted to work out a less utopian system.

Critique of morality and education

The Petrashevtsy criticised the conventional system of morality and education from the anthropological point of view. Their ideas on these subjects were a development of the ideas of Fourier and of Rousseau.

Like Fourier, the Petrashevtsy rejected the existing system of morality and existing concepts of vice and crime. According to them, man was naturally, inherently, good.[5] In his stories, Dostoevskii showed the 'little men', the Charlie Chaplins of this world, Devushkin, Prokharchin, Polzhunkov, preserving their natural virtue against all odds. Evil in man arose not from human nature but from the repression of human nature, of the passions, from the material and spiritual deprivation of the individual in society. This deprivation was reinforced by the priests and philosophers who legitimised it and labelled resistance to, repression of, one's nature as 'virtue'. However, man's passions could never be totally repressed. When they were denied their natural outlets, their legitimate satisfaction, they sought unnatural, illegitimate paths and took on warped and twisted forms. Akhsharumov described how, 'In our society, where there is no outlet for the passions, where they are all either repressed or take on a distorted development ... (man) becomes repulsive, unbearable, evil, quarrelsome; love is replaced by debauchery; luxury by theft, drunkenness; intrigue by gambling; ambition by touchiness, egoism.' Laziness, drunkenness, fear, meanness, revenge and envy were all false, temporary manifestations of the passions (what Fourier had called 'subversive recurrences') produced by the bad organisation of society. It was society which perverted the passions, not nature; society which produced the 'moral monster'; society, not the criminal, which should be held responsible for crime.[6]

The Petrashevtsy's explanation of vice, crime and social antagonism was a development of ideas found in Fourier. They invented a whole theory of the psychological impoverishment and warping of men in society and tried to show that all men's bad qualities, all their evil actions had purely social causes. Their fascination with this idea was partly due to the fact they were aware that the drabness of their own lives, as petty civil servants etc. had had a deleterious effect on their own psychological make-up. The most detailed explanation of it is to be found in Dostoevskii's early stories. In these he protested indirectly against social conditions by showing how society causes the psychological deformation of the individuals. He traced the origin of vice to the desperate struggle of the little man, the man who is poor and occupies an inferior position in society, to preserve his self-respect, to keep up appearances before himself and before the rest of the world and explicitly stated that, 'Vice is a human thing, something you pick up, it's not born with you – here today it can be gone tomorrow.'[7] His characters – Devushkin and Old Pokrovskii in *Poor Folk*, Efimov in *Netochka Nezvanova*, Emelian in *An Honest Thief* – take to drink when they fail in the struggle for social recognition. In *Mr Prokharchin*, Dostoevskii showed how poverty and a sense of social insecurity can give rise to avarice. *The Double* presented the insecurity of a man who has risen just far enough in society to become a prey to ambition, but not quite far enough to be able to realise his ambitions, and showed how this can lead to madness. Dostoevskii gave a talk on the vice of ambition and its social causes at Petrashevskii's. He also observed other evil effects, not so much vices as unnatural characteristics, arising from the social and material insecurity of the poor man – quietness, suspiciousness, an aversion to the company of their fellow men, exaggerated feelings of humility and worthlessness.[8] Though Dostoevskii's main concern was always the poor man, he also showed that the unnatural organisation of contemporary society acted differently, but no less adversely, on the characters of the rich. In *Netochka Nezvanova*, Katia, the little rich girl, succumbs to the vice of pride. Dostoevskii talks of it in explicitly Fourierist terms, it was

> the chief vice of the princess, or rather, the chief principle of her character, which irrepressibly strove to take on its natural form, but existed in a state of deviation ... everything in her was good, not one of her vices was born with her – all were inculcated and all were found in a condition of struggle. Everywhere one could see a good beginning, adopting for a time a false form.[9]

The analysis of the effects of social circumstances on character also forms one of the chief features of the short stories of Durov, Saltykov and Tolbin (see Chapter VII).

The same factors which led to psychological deformation, to vice, in the majority, led a minority to crime. According to Petrashevskii, a crime merely indicated that, 'The person committing it had some natural need which could not be satisfied by the established path.'[10] Crime was more prevalent among the lower classes, the Petrashevtsy thought, because they had more needs, especially material ones, which remained unsatisfied. A review of the Swedish King Oscar's *Punishments and Corrective Institutions* in *Finskii vestnik*, for example, probably by Golovinskii, analysed the chief causes of crime and found them to be ignorance and poverty.[11] The Petrashevtsy argued that absolutely all crime, even murder, had social causes, the criminal could always be excused by the circumstances. Crime was just another aspect of the perversion of the passions. In prison, Petrashevskii imagined himself on the way to Siberia:

> next to a hardened criminal on whose conscience lie ten murders ... sitting at a halt and sharing a crust of dry bread ... we fall into conversation ... I tell him about the phalanstery − what its like there and why ... I explain why people become criminals and he, sighing deeply, tells me the story of his life. From his story I see that much that is great has perished in this man through circumstances, a strong soul broken by the weight of misfortune ... Perhaps in the conclusion to his story, he will say, 'Yes, if it had been as you say, if people had lived like that, I would not have been a criminal' and I, if the weight of my chains allows, will stretch out my hand to him and say, 'Let us be brothers' ... beside me I see not a criminal but an unlucky, perhaps initially misunderstood man like myself.[12]

The Petrashevtsy derived the extreme radicalism of their views on crime in part from Eugène Sue's detailed study of the criminal classes in *Mystères de Paris*, through which he attempts to show that all human instincts, even love of killing, can be turned to good. Saltykov praised Sue because 'He justifies *suicide* and *all the crimes* which people unfortunately commit.'[13]

The Petrashevtsy tended also to attribute all the enmity of mankind − of man against man, of class against class, of nation against nation − to the perversion of the passions and a social system which opposed instead of uniting them. Petrashevskii repeated Considerant's description of the prevailing social bedlam, 'It is in turmoil, all the passions are at boiling point and there is no corresponding satisfaction for them; the enmity of the poor towards the rich is manifested in full force.' The Petrashevtsy do not appear to have worried about the apparent contradiction between this explanation of the class struggle and the Saint-Simonian idea of the historical progress of mankind through the class struggle and history as a gradual lessening of antagonisms. Akhsharumov in his poem, *Europe 1845*, ascribes all the wars of Western history to the 'subversive flight' of the passions.[14]

The only way to eliminate vice and crime, the Petrashevtsy felt, was to tackle the real culprit – society. The remedy for all evils lay in changing the form of the social organisation to make possible the satisfaction of all man's needs, all his passions, both material and spiritual. In such a society, 'There will be no poor, no needy, therefore all those weaknesses, vices and crimes, which flow from envy, destitution, desperation, will no longer exist; morals will be transformed and man will be reborn in both a moral and a physical sense ... there will be no more criminals.'[15]

An essential part of the reorganisation of society and the formation of a new morality was the reform of the education system. The Petrashevtsy's expert on education was Saltykov, who developed his ideas in a series of reviews of children's books written for *Otechestvennye zapiski* and *Sovremennik*, in 1847 and 1848.[16] The Petrashevtsy argued that education, like everything else, had to be adapted to man. Its particular job was to help every individual to recognise and develop the full potential of his nature. They took the idea of 'education according to nature' from Rousseau, its originator, and from Fourier and Saint-Simon, who developed it. They also bitterly criticised the existing system of education, which instilled in children the principles of Civilisation's false morality and began at an early age the process of alienating man both from the real world and from his own nature. Their attack was directed chiefly at the education system in Russia.

The content of education in Russia – fairy tales, moral preaching and meaningless facts – was viewed with great disapproval by the Petrashevtsy. They were convinced, as Saltykov said, that 'It is particularly dangerous to joke with children and of all jokes, the telling of fairy tales is the most unsuitable for a child'. Fantasy was so harmful for children because, as Rousseau had explained in *Émile*, they mistook it for the truth.[17] The Petrashevtsy also shared Fourier's aversion to moral teaching. Saltykov described how, when men begin to grow up, a struggle takes place within them between the unnatural moral principles instilled in them in childhood and the calls of their own nature, 'a terrible feverish drama, which prevents the man from leading a positive life'.[18] The stultification of children was completed by the compulsory memorisation of masses of unnecessary figures and facts. As a result their brains became overcrowded, they were 'seasoned and stuffed like a roast grouse'.[19] Their education made them capable of receiving and repeating information, but not of understanding it, or of thinking for themselves. They emerged paralysed, unfit for real life, like Saltykov's heroes — Nagibin, Michulin, Brusin — knowing nothing of any practical use. Saltykov hinted at the government's political interest in keeping education as distant from the real world and thus as harmless as possible, in turning its pupils into robots who submissively accepted the existing order of things.[20]

The key to understanding what was wrong with the existing system of education and how it should be changed was the child's relationship to nature. As things were, there was always a terrible tension between the two. The Petrashevtsy's feelings about the separation of nature and education were summed up by Balasoglo. He told the story of his own instinctive attraction to nature, his banishment to school:

> Opening his eyes on God's world, the young soul ready for expression and nourishment, or if you like, *education*, begins there on its own to look at the world ... examines the rays of the rising sun; the breeze of the wind rustling the leaves of the quivering trees and the twittering birds jumping from branch to branch; the flash of glass glinting in the window of a far house; and the gentle babble of the stream's waters to the sandy shore ... the whole sweet-smelling world of the early morning ... and all this together, and part, and again as one sort of whole, beckons, calls, attracts the innocent watcher — seems to wink and bow to him — seems to great him with a smile of some unfathomable bliss and say to him with its eye, 'Hello child! know me — this is I'
> — Who is this? So beautiful! The young souls asks itself ...
> — This is nature ...
> — What are you doing there, you lazy thing? It's time to go to school! a voice rings out, alas! a voice very familiar to the soul and the soul, shaking and hanging its head, wanders like an unshorn sheep to *school* ...
>
> Here is nature for you! the first view of her divine face, the first glance, the first kiss of her powerful being — it's already a crime, a sin, *idleness* ...
>
> The soul goes to school, sits on a bench, turns over the pages, marks and cleans the board and covers a quire of papers with writing, ... The tutor praises its quick understanding, is proud of its parrotings, proclaims its intelligence to the whole school! ... But what if they knew, it thinks to itself, that I have just for the fourth time forgotten all the grammar which I have only just spouted off my brain for the fourth time ... and that I never understood any of it and I don't understand it now, I'm not capable of it, and I won't ever get to understanding it in the future!!!? What if they knew that I certainly won't know anything when I leave, out! ... that I *learn* only in order to leave as soon as possible. Yes, to get out to freedom!

Elsewhere he speaks of the 'excess of feelings of hatred, repulsion, loathing which the system of its *education* succeeded in developing in it!'[21]

The education of the child had to begin by introducing him to nature, as Rousseau had said, not by divorcing him from it. Its purpose was, as the Saint-Simonians, and more strongly Fourier, had said, to discover and develop the child's natural capacities. Saltykov put these two ideas together, though on the whole preferring the more utilitarian tone of Rousseau to the fanciful theories of Fourier. His suggestions are similar to those advanced by Belinskii, another admirer of Rousseau. The central idea was a sensual one — man was part of nature, was at first wholly subordinated to it and only gradually separated himself out of it and developed his reason.[22] Like Rousseau, Saltykov and Belinskii stressed that the education of the body should begin before that of the mind, 'Let children play, be noisy, romp.' Their formal education should start with the study of that which was closest and most comprehensible to the child, nature and the natural sciences. The study of the human world should come later and be approached through the study of man's simplest needs and the means of satisfying them. Both Belinskii and Saltykov praised a Russian translation of *Robinson Crusoe*, regarded by Rousseau as 'the best treatise on education according to nature'. Saltykov calls it the most useful of all children's books because:

> Its basic idea is the analysis of the most simple needs of man, those most easily understood by children. On reading it, the child automatically thinks about the objects which are nearest and most familiar to him and in this way learns to think about everything vital, learns to think and live at the same time.[23]

Though he discarded as fantastic the complex mechanism of education in Harmony — miniature tools, little hordes, opera etc., Saltykov (unlike Belinskii) had a great admiration for Fourier's theory of education, and in particular the idea that its task was, 'to promote the discovery of the INSTINCTUAL VOCATIONS of the very young and to apply the individual to the diverse functions to which nature has destined him'. This admiration was shared by other Petrashevtsy — Akhsharumov translated the chapters on education from Fourier's *Théorie de l'unité universelle*; Petrashevskii recommended every father to read *Education attrayante dedié aux mères de familles* (Considerant's slightly simpler exposition of this theory) and to follow this method of education. Saltykov borrowed this book both from Petrashevskii and from Zotov (editor of *Illiustratsiia* and another visitor to Petrashevskii's circle) and used it in writing his reviews. He told his public, 'Every tutor should have in mind the discovery of the child's capacities with the aim of their full and harmonious development by means of education.' His account of the harmful influence of the family in misdirecting their children's inclinations directly echoes passages in Fourier and Considerant.[24]

Critique of the economic system of 'Civilisation'

No more than the reigning systems of morality and education was the existing economic system seen to correspond to the demands of human nature. Indeed it was, according to the Petrashevtsy, the fundamental cause of human unhappiness, because it made it impossible for the majority of men to satisfy their basic material needs.

The Petrashevtsy, unlike Herzen and Belinskii, were as much, if not more, interested in political economy as philosophy. This interest had, in many cases been inspired by Viktor Poroshin's lectures on economics and statistics, which they attended at St. Petersburg University. There were two experts on political economy among the Petrashevtsy – Vladimir Miliutin and Jan-Ferdinand Jastrzebski. Miliutin, who was only twenty-one and writing his doctorate, published a brilliant series of economic articles in *Otechestvennye zapiski* in 1847. (*Malthus and his Opponents, Proletariat and Pauperism in England and France*, and two reviews of *A Study of National Wealth* by Aleksandr Butovskii, were the most important of these). Jastrzebski taught political economy at three different educational establishments in St. Petersburg.[25] He also, during the winter of 1848–9, gave a series of lectures on the subject at Petrashevskii's. These were 'bursting with liberal phrases', full of outrageous jokes and extremely popular with his audience. He was also probably the author of a series of articles (even more radical than Miliutin's), published in *Finskii vestnik* in 1846 and 1847 (including *A Biography of Sir Robert Peel*, reviews of *The Repeal of the Corn Laws in England*, by Iakov Linovskii, *A Political Economy of Agriculture*, by Poroshin, and Butovskii's book).[26] Other Petrashevtsy with a particular interest in political economy were Ippolit Debu, who took a further degree in it, Osokin, who taught it at Kazan University, Maikov and Speshnev.[27]

This was a time when the discipline of political economy in its traditional form was disintegrating. The classical school of economists, the outstanding representatives of which had been Smith and Ricardo, had been founded in the late eighteenth century and flourished in the first two decades of the nineteenth. Its writings had taken the form of a straightforward description and explanation of the workings of the early capitalist economy. The benefits of such an economy to the whole human race were regarded by them as, and appeared on the basis of the available data to be, unquestionable. By the 1830s the development of capitalism had reached a point where the pauperism of a section of the lower classes and the conflict of interest between worker and capitalist could no longer be ignored. This led to a division of political economists into 'vulgar' economists, such as Say and Bastiat, who devoted themselves to justifying the capitalist system; and liberal, humanitarian and socialist economists, whose leading figure was Sismondi and who devoted themselves to attacking it. The Petrashevtsy sided with the latter and developed a critique of the capitalist system (especially the pauperism it caused) and of the orthodox economists, which drew both from Sismondi and liberal economists such as Eugène Buret and from socialists such as Fourier and Proudhon.

The Petrashevtsy saw political economy as the most important of the social sciences. Its importance derived from its aim, which, they believed, was to assure the material welfare of man, the essential condition for social welfare. According to Dostoevskii, 'Socialism is just the same as political economy, but in another form.'[28] Both Miliutin and *Finskii vestnik* begin their reviews of *A Study of National Wealth* by laying down as an axiom that, 'the material welfare of man' was 'the one and only subject of political economy'. From this it followed that the task of political economists was not just to explain the workings of the present system, but to judge it according to the criterion of man's material welfare, and, if it was found lacking, to work out a better system. The Petrashevtsy had no doubt that the capitalist economic system did not guarantee the material welfare of man, because under this system a majority of the population, the working classes, were reduced to the position of paupers. Like the French socialists of the 1840s, though not like Saint-Simon and Fourier, who had written before the problem had really become visible, the Petrashevtsy regarded the pauperism of the working classes as 'the vital question of our time', the rationale for socialism, which was, as Golovinsky put it, 'a protest of hunger'.[29]

The Petrashevtsy's critique of capitalism was thus directed at the phenomenon of pauperism as it had developed in England and France, and as, from their observations of the life of the lower classes in St. Petersburg, they believed it was beginning to develop in Russia. In their critique they combined the anthropological and historical methods.

On the one hand, pauperism was obviously and utterly unjust and unnatural. The Petrashevtsy cried out against the gulf between rich and poor in terms worthy of Lamennais. Saltykov and Dostoevskii, for example, tried to make plain in their short stories that social contrasts could be found in Russia as extreme and unjust as any in Western Europe. In *A Tangled Affair*, Saltykov described the cold, wet St. Petersburg night as seen by the rich man, speeding along Nevskii Prospekt in a carriage drawn by four roan horses – not only bearable, but even attractive. In contrast, his hero, the poverty-stricken Michulin, who tramps home on foot to an unheated room, with the wind whispering maliciously in his ears, is struck by the contrast and begins to think 'black and subversive thoughts'. In *Poor Folk*, Makar Devushkin is provoked to rebellious thoughts by a walk along a fashionable shopping street. He marvels at the sumptuous shops and houses, the carriages with windows like crystal, linings made of silk and velvet and lackeys dressed in epaulettes and wearing swords, full of princesses and countesses hurrying to balls and cries out, 'How is it that you are so unfortunate Barbara, how is it that *you* are so much worse off than other people?'[30]

The most serious work on pauperism published in Russia in the 1840s was a monumental study in four parts by Miliutin, *Proletariat and Pauperism in England and France*. These put together and analysed material from the first liberal accounts of the phenomenon (mostly French). Miliutin's sources included Buret's *De la misère des classes laborieuses en Angleterre et en France*, Leon Faucher's *Etude sur l'Angleterre*, Villermé's *Tableau de l'état physique et moral des ouvriers employés dans les manufactures de coton, de laine et de soie*, Villeneuve-Bargemont's *Economie politique chrétienne* and other works found in Petrashevskii's library.[31] Miliutin examined in detail the appalling working and living conditions of the English and French workers and described how these led to both the physical and moral deterioration of the working class. He explained how their health was ruined by labour of fifteen to sixteen hours a day; how the constant repetition of a single action caused some parts of their bodies to develop monstrously, others to wither away; how they worked in stifling atmospheres, often full of harmful fumes, which causes them to catch strange illnesses, such as the fatal lung disease invariably contracted by the Sheffield grinders. Miliutin devoted a great deal of space to describing the child workers, 'ill, feeble, ignorant, crushed physically and morally' and showers Robert Owen with praise for his attempts to help them.[32] For their exhausting, debilitating labour, the workers received a pitifully low pay, wages on which they could only afford to live on the verge of starvation, in the most appalling conditions, and this of course, caused their physical state to deteriorate still further. After a survey of workers' habitations in London, Manchester, Liverpool, Mulhouse and Roubaix, Miliutin concludes, 'The places in which the poor live are a thousand times more disgusting and dirty than the sheds in which pigs and cows are kept.' According to *Finskii vestnik*, 'Damp cellars in which all possible sorts of gasses except oxygen abound form the dwelling of the English worker.' Infectious fevers raged there, and the mortality rate was higher.[33] The conditions in which the worker lived and worked degraded him both physically and morally, reduced him to a mockery of his true nature, a squalid drunken figure no better than an animal. Like Buret, Miliutin spoke of the dissolution of the 'industrial family', the abyss between worker and capitalist, and worker and worker, the weakening of family ties, depravity in the factory, children growing up on the streets, reared 'on opium instead of milk'. Poverty caused many men to turn to crime, women to prostitution. Drink was the universal means of forgetfulness. *Finskii vestnik* describes how, after a sixteen hour labour in the factory, the worker crosses the threshold of his own home with a sinking heart, he finds there his wife and children in rags, begging him for bread, 'and in order to achieve sweet forgetfulness of his situation, he goes to a gin-shop and there drowns himself in drink'. In a special section on 'dirt and drunkenness', Miliutin describes the 'silent reverence' with which the British workers down their gin.[34]

Chilled by the pauperism of England and France, the Petrashevtsy and their contemporaries looked around themselves and saw that similar phenomena were emerging in St. Petersburg. This was brought out by a series of statistical surveys of the capital undertaken by Konstantin Arsen'ev (1833), Ivan Pushkar'ev (1835) and Konstantin Veselovskii (1847).[35] The lower classes numbered (according to Veselovskii) about 230,000 i.e. 50 per cent of the population.[36] This, however, was not a real working class — they were mostly peasants, who, though they might work in a factory or shop or for a contractor still had to pay a quit-rent to their master. And, though by the early 1840s St. Petersburg had about ten large mechanised cotton and metal-working factories, the typical feature of early urbanisation, here as elsewhere, was the artisan workshops, where the workers were cramped together in appalling conditions. It was these that the Petrashevtsy observed and wrote about in their sketches and short stories. In *Khalatnik*, for example, Durov asks his readers:

> If you have ever, by any unforeseen chance, or simply out of curiosity, glanced into the workshop of a Russian tailor, cobbler, or locksmith? If so, I'm sure that you will a second time avoid such a misfortune at all costs and never in your life forget the unpleasant impression produced on you by the black greasy walls of the workshop and the compressed, stifling air and the dirty faces of the boys sitting on the floor with their bare legs folded under them in all corners of this dark, stinking dwelling.

He calls it 'a god-forsaken hole ... a picture from Dante's *Inferno*, a black, terrible picture, capable of filling your soul with fright'. As Poroshin explained, working in such conditions had the same dreadful physical effects as in the West. He called the life of child apprentices in the St. Petersburg sewing industry 'a mutilation', describing how tuberculosis and scrofula raged among them, catching their chests, filling their eyes with blood, causing a swelling of the glands, a discharge from the ears. [37] The Third Admiralty District, the centre of trade and the most populated part of St. Petersburg consisted of large stone houses of three or four storeys, which were already what would now be called slum tenements. Most of this was cheap accommodation, rented out to poor artisans, poor *meshchane* and *chinovniki* for not more than 150 roubles a year, without the use of a kitchen – the inhabitants had to take their meals in taverns. The poorest rented corners of rooms, like Dostoevskii's heroes – Devushkin, Ordynov, Prokharchin – or lived in 'burrows, in damp and cold cellars' or 'a nest under the roof in the attic, literally only a shelter from the rain and the cold'. Arsen'ev's description of a St. Petersburg cellar rivals contemporary accounts of Paris or London:

> No-one ordinarily cares about the cleanliness of the air; the windows are almost never opened; in the winter, to maintain the warmth, the charcoal fumes from the stove are shut in. There too, not infrequently, food is prepared, bread is baked, water is poured on the floor, wet washing is dried, chickens are kept etc. If to these pathogenic causes one adds inactivity, idleness and too long sleep, then one can easily understand why dangerous illnesses frequently appear amongst them, and in particular, scurvy and basement fevers.

A government commission for the study of the life of St. Petersburg labourers in 1847 discovered 'up to fifty people of different ages and both sexes living in one room'.[38]

The Petrashevtsy hearily shared the Fourierist detestation of the city, 'the city' for them meaning St. Petersburg — the only real city in Russia in the sense that only here were people unnaturally crammed together in a huge human Noah's ark, requiring intensive servicing by cafes, cookshops, porters, laundresses, cobblers and everything else imaginable. St. Petersburg was bigger and wealthier than any other town in Russia, its population growing faster than that of London or Paris (from 220,200–483,000 in the period 1800–46).[39] The Petrashevtsy hated St. Petersburg with particular violence because for them it was more than just a centre of pauperism, it was a symbol of the dead hand of Tsarist tyranny and of their own personal and political impotence and misery. It was the headquarters of absolutism. Katenev called it

> '... great city of Peter,
> New capital of depravity,
> Home of fetters and the axe,
> Of suffering, hatred, malice.'

Saltykov and Akhsharumov wrote of it as a parasite, which lived off the rest of the country 'drinking its blood'.[40] The elegant architecture of St. Petersburg, the famous straight lines of the streets and canals, the regularity of the buildings, was perceived by the Petrashevtsy as an expression of the deathly and lowering spirit of despotism. An almost physical revulsion of St. Petersburg is revealed in the writings of the natural school in the forties — in those of Gogol, Nekrasov, Apollon Grigor'ev, as well as Dostoevskii, Pleshcheev, Saltykov.[41] The Petrashevtsy looked at the capital through the eyes of the poor *raznochinets*, who came to St. Petersburg from the provinces to seek an outlet for his talents, but who, without money or protection, inevitably failed to find it. In Saltykov's words, it was, 'a city of sorrows and never-satisfied desires, of ... how much bitter disappointment'.[42] Like the Fourierists, the Petrashevtsy looked forward to a time when all big cities would be destroyed, their populations transferred to smaller units in the countryside. Akhsharumov prophecied the advent of new rural palaces:

> Capitals will be razed
> From the face of the earth, they will be no more;
> And with them all their groans, all their suffering
> Will be buried in the ground.

In their place the columns of new buildings
Will proudly rise like palms.[43]

As well as describing the terrible, unnatural state of affairs caused by
the present economic system, the Petrashevtsy approached it more
scientifically, as a system which had developed historically, and attempted a detailed analysis of its workings. This aspect of their criticism
is fairly standard, relies heavily on the writings of the French socialists
and is therefore of less interest than the anthropological part.

Drawing on Sismondi and Proudhon, Miliutin argued that capitalism
had a good and a bad side, and was, as Sismondi had said, 'a two-edged
sword'. It was, in its beginning, its principle, like every other historical
system, progressive and legitimate. The phenomena of capitalism,
competition, the introduction of machines, the division of labour, were
essentially good and designed to benefit the human race. It was these
phenomena that were responsible for the flourishing of the Western
states, whose wealth had increased beyond all recognition in the previous
fifty years.[44] However, as capitalism developed, it also began to produce evil effects, i.e. pauperism. The Petrashevtsy drew a clear distinction between poverty, which had always existed where man had not
sufficient means for the satisfaction of his needs, and pauperism,
conscious poverty, which was born of the *contrast* between rich and
poor, existed only in wealthy, 'civilised' countries and arose as a consequence of the development of capitalism.[45]

In their analysis of the bad sides of the phenomena of capitalism,
the Petrashevtsy borrowed from Louis Blanc and Fourier as well as
Proudhon and Sismondi. The placed particular emphasis on the ruinous
effects of competition on the workers, explaining how the 'whip hand
of hunger' placed the workers in complete subservience to the capitalists,
who were able to exploit them mercilessly. An anonymous article on
vampires in *Finskii vestnik* included the factory owners among the chief
representatives of this species; Herzen called them cannibals. The worst
sort of capitalist, the Petrashevtsy believed (though they did not attack
them quite as obsessively as Fourier) was the merchant-speculator, who
unlike the other capitalists did not even create any material values.
Petrashevskii called them 'pimps who take a huge percentage for their
pimping'.[46] They were also very much conscious of the evil effect of
machines, which for the workers merely brought the threat of unemployment. They noted that this threat had even made its appearance in Russia,
where the construction of the St. Petersburg–Moscow railway (the

first in the country) was causing a 'panic fear' among the long-distance coachmen.[47]

The Petrashevtsy traced these bad sides of capitalism to the disorganised, chaotic state of industry, and, above all, to the division between worker and capitalist, the concentration of capital in the hands of a 'few chosen ones'. Like the Saint-Simonians they looked at this division as the last metamorphosis of a relationship of exploitation which had existed throughout history, between master and slave, lord and serf etc. and believed that it was 'doomed to disappear' as mankind progressed.[48] The solution lay in the organisation of production, and the redistribution of wealth through a more equitable division of the product of industry, which were to be the chief features of socialism, the historical stage which would replace capitalism.

The capitalists as well as the workers, the Petrashevtsy believed, had an interest in organising industry, because they too suffered from its present chaotic state and in particular from competition. Like Fourier and Louis Blanc, the Petrashevtsy emphasised that *all* the members of society were at war with one another. Capitalism was a system from which no-one benefited. In his first review of *A Study of National Wealth*, Miliutin quotes in full the famous description of the contemporary state of England from the preface to the second edition of Sismondi's *Nouveaux principes*. Sismondi writes of the incredible wealth of England and the happiness that this wealth was supposed to bring, 'I seek this happiness in all classes and I cannot find it anywhere' and concludes, 'What are the facts of this immense accumulated wealth? Have they had any other effect than to share out the worries, the privations, the danger of complete ruin among all classes?'[49]

Critique of political economy

The Petrashevtsy's critique of the classical political economists and above all *Malthus and his Opponents*, the article which made Miliutin's name, forms one of the most lucid and radical parts of their theory. They attacked the orthodox political economists, who had made themselves into apologists for capitalism, just as they had attacked capitalism, i.e. from both the anthropological and the historical points of view. However, in this case, the historical method was of supreme importance. The main thrust of their argument was that, through the adoption of a false and incomplete *aim* (wealth rather than welfare), the economists had come to concentrate on the good and ignore the bad sides of capitalism, i.e. they ignored pauperism. This idea, first put forward by Sismondi in 1819, formed the crux of all socialist theories of political economy. Miliutin explained that there was an essential difference between the two concepts, 'When we talk about welfare we have always in mind a certain condition of man, in which he possesses a sufficient quantity of means for the satisfaction of human needs and desires; when we talk about wealth, we ... understand the actual means of satisfaction of human needs, i.e. things, products and goods subject to exchange.' The first was the end, the second the means. The economists, and most of all Ricardo, had forgotten this and turned political economy into an abstract science of wealth and the increase of wealth. Man appeared in their theories not as 'man proper' but only as the representative of a productive force – capital or labour.[50]

In addition, the political economists had adopted a false *method*, (descriptive rather than historical). Incorrectly assuming that the method of the natural sciences was fully applicable to political economy, they, 'took the *actual* state of the contemporary social system as normal'. They failed to compare it with other historical systems and thus did not recognise the temporary historical nature of capitalism, the only relative validity and truth many of its laws, but took them as absolute and eternally true. As Debu wrote, 'The economists confuse the necessary, *general laws*, which are unchangeable and the *particular* laws which we can change at our will.' This led them to a position similar to a right-Hegelian interpretation of the formula, 'what is real is rational', to the idea that the existing system was the only one possible, that everything took place for the best, even the pauperism of the lower classes.[51] Saltykov's story *Contradictions* is an attack on this view both as put forward by the political economists and, in particular by Proudhon (as the title shows). Nagibin's career is a pathetic example of Proudhon's theory that contradictions cannot be resolved and man should therefore accept them. Throughout the story he wavers between the world view of the 'ridiculous utopians', who refuse to accept poverty, accuse reality of unnaturalness and wish to change it, and that of the 'niggardly economists', who believe that poverty, 'flows inevitably from the very nature of things ... it is and this should be enough to justify it'. Finally he adopts the position of his dreadful friend Valinskii, who accepts life as it is, and settles down contentedly to a passionless, petty existence. Saltykov scathingly calls it, 'such a harmony as the minds of neither Fourier nor Saint-Simon ever rose to, or any of those who would venture in this field'.[52]

The Petrashevtsy, in particular Miliutin, *Finskii vestnik* and Osokin, tried to show that the laws worked out by political economists were relative, only valid for a certain historical epoch, after which they became obsolete. They did this by tracing the development of political economy through history and showing how each theory of political economy – mercantilism, the physiocratic school, *laissez faire* – had corresponded to a particular stage of development of the productive forces. The formula, *laissez faire, laissez passer*, on which the present theory of political economy was based was, when it was first proclaimed by Adam Smith, progressive, it had met the needs of the time, i.e. the emancipation of industry from controls and its adoption had led to the great development of industry from the end of the eighteenth century. The Petrashevtsy defended Smith against French socialists such as Leroux and his brother, arguing that it had been perfectly legitimate, in the initial stages of industrial development, to believe that the immense increase in wealth resulting from *laissez faire* would benefit all mankind. Smith could not be blamed for not foreseeing the evil consequences, the pauperism, which only developed after his death.[53]

By now, however, the system of *laissez faire* was obsolete, the growth of pauperism had made it obvious that it no longer benefited or brought happiness to mankind. There were two ways, both of them unjustifiable and reactionary, in which Smith's followers tried to legitimise the continuation of *laissez faire*. The first was simple hypocrisy – the method adopted by Say, Ricardo and the majority of economists. They justified *laissez faire* by ignoring pauperism, by trying to pretend that it didn't exist, or was an accident, and that the existing system still really benefited everyone.[54] The second method, adopted by Malthus, was to deny that the economis system could or should benefit everyone. Malthus brought *laissez faire* up to date by recognising that pauperism existed, but continued to justify it by inventing a law of population which proved that the majority were doomed to and should therefore accept as natural, eternal poverty and suffering.[55] The Petrashevtsy brought the anthropological method into their criticism of Malthus and argued that his law of population contradicted the only absolute eternal laws, the laws of human nature, according to which wealth and happiness were the destiny of man. If poverty and suffering really were the 'inevitable' law of existence, the human race might just as well commit suicide there and then, 'Death! Here is the last word of science, here is the most essential law of nature!'[56] The Petrashevtsy tried to show that Malthus's law was an example of a temporary and relative law, 'correct for our time' but not for all time. According to them, human nature only operated according to Malthus's law, i.e. people only reproduced in geometrical proportion, under the existing circumstances of pauperism. If pauperism was eliminated and living standards were higher, people would naturally have fewer children. Miliutin had particular praise for the idea that there were natural limits to reproduction which resulted from the relationship between food and fertility, as suggested in passing by Fourier and developed in detail by the English radical Thomas Doubleday, according to whom, population always multiplied in inverse proportion to the quality and quantity of the food.[57]

The Petrashevtsy also denounced all remedies for pauperism suggested by the political economists and other supporters of *laissez faire* as half-measures, false measures. None of them, in their view, solved the problem, they merely, by alleviating pauperism, served to perpetuate both it and the existing system.

Their anthropological principles led the Petrashevtsy to reject out of hand all suggestions for reducing the rate of reproduction of the workers which relied on them refraining from sex, and which thus involved them in denying their own nature. The theory of moral restraint was first formulated by Malthus to placate the public after the horrified reaction to the publication of his law of population. Malthus said that, though the rate of man's reproduction still doomed them to eternal poverty, they could improve their position slightly by voluntarily giving up sex. The idea was taken up in different ways by Malthus's opponents, including both Sismondi and Proudhon.[58] The Petrashevtsy found these arguments totally unacceptable because they contradicted human nature and placed man's reason in opposition to his instincts. In *Contradictions*, for example, Saltykov jeers at the idea of moral restraint, depicting poor Nagibin placed between Scylla and Charybdis, 'Either love and die from hunger, or eat a stale crust of bread and don't dare think about anything else!' Miliutin brusquely refutes it as incompatible with the 'normal state' of man, which, 'consists in the harmonious development of all his forces, in the equal satisfaction of his needs'.[59]

Another measure commonly supposed to benefit the working class was the introduction of free trade. This meant, above all, free trade in grain. The period between the foundation of the Anti-Corn Law League in 1838 and Peel's conversion to Corn Law repeal in 1845–6 was a time of furious debates on the subject in England. The landowning interest stood for protection; the manufacturing interest, represented by the Anti-Corn Law League and led by Cobden, for free trade. English liberal opinion generally supported Cobden; the radical working-class Chartists opposed the League and were suspicious of its motives. Russia, as a large exporter of grain, had a particular interest in the matter. The commonly-held liberal view, shared in Russia by most of the Westerners, was that, as the members of the Anti-Corn Law League said, repeal would benefit both capitalists, for whom cheap imports of grain would mean lower wages, enabling them to sell their products more cheaply and competitively abroad; and workers, who would be able to buy cheaper bread. When Cobden visited St. Petersburg in September 1848, even the socialist-inclined Poroshin attended a public dinner held in his honour and wrote enthusiastic accounts of it for the Russian press. Though recognising that the members of the League were manufacturers and wanted repeal chiefly to enable them to lower wages, he was sure that 'fortunately their interest in this case coincides with the general'.[60]

The Petrashevtsy were more suspicious. A radical and perceptive account of the free trade movement was given by *Finskii vestnik* in *A Biography of Sir Robert Peel* and a review of Linovskii's *The Repeal of the Corn Laws in England*, both published in September 1846. The author of these two articles was in principle in favour of free trade. Under socialism, when the human race was united, it would bring untold benefits. However, 'Although the abolition of the Corn Laws in other circumstances would be beneficial, now its merit is purely negative'. Repeal, in his eyes, was a class measure. The League had 'emerged from the entrails of the bourgeoisie' and shared its interests. Its aim was simply to increase the profits of the manufacturers and to achieve, 'the fall of the great English aristocracy and the transfer of power to the middle classes'. In this, it was using Peel as its instrument. Its speeches about its concern for the workers were the purest hypocrisy. As Poroshin had seen, but refused to recognise, repeal would make bread cheaper but it would not lead to a better standard of living for the working class because wages would also fall. The English workers had realised this and had not joined the League. Instead they had turned to the Chartists. The author makes plain his sympathy with the Chartists, who, led by Feargus O'Connor, had 'beautifully exposed the sophisms of the League'. He expresses his support for the Chartists's demands and particularly for the socialist aspect of their ideas, explaining how they had said, 'that Peel's measure does not help the poor classes, that pauperism will still rage in England ... that before the freedom of industry there should be its organisation. And many other *truths*'.[61]

Another means of alleviating pauperism, then very much in vogue, was philanthropy. In St. Petersburg itself, the word philanthropy was 'on everybody's lips', especially after the foundation of the *Society for Visiting the Poor*, a charitable society on the Western model, by Prince Odoevskii in 1847.[62] The idea that charity was a noble act, which benefited both giver and recipient, was generally accepted in Russian intellectual circles. Only the extreme radicals and in particular the Petrashevtsy, spoke out against it. A controversy about the value of charity was sparked off by Nikolai Mel'gunov, (a utopian friend of Herzen's) who wrote a series of articles stating the socialist view that the aim ought to be not to alleviate pauperism by charity, but to reorganise society so that there would be no pauperism, no rich and no poor and thus no need for charity. The reactionary Shevyrev replied with a satirical drama, *The Last Poor Man on Earth or a Humane Utopia*, which depicted a world without charity, in which, 'the rich didn't give, the poor don't ask and die from hunger'. In the Petrashevtsy's view, the motives behind charity were suspect. Charity was a means by which the rich appeased their own consciences at the expense of the poor. Charity did not benefit, but rather harmed the recipient, by creating in him, 'new needs which he didn't have till then', making it impossible for him ever again to be content with his previous joyless life. Charity also, by depriving the poor man of the need and wish to work removed the sole incentive which could retain and save his human dignity in the struggle with fate. It thus became, 'an active instrument for the development of pauperism and for the demoralisation of the working classes'.[63]

The Petrashevtsy were equally sceptical about the results of new partial measures to alleviate pauperism – education, political rights, savings banks and colonisation – suggested by a new 'philanthropic' school of political economists (Michel Chevalier, Jerome Blanqui, Buret, Villeneuve-Bargemont and others), and agreed on the 'complete impossibility of defeating pauperism' by these means.[64]

Socialist solutions

No parial solution, no remedy which preserved the existing order, could hope to have success or do anything other than bring greater harm to the workers. The Petrashevtsy believed, 'Palliative medicine does not cure the most radical ills ... to do something by halves is worse than not to do it at all.' The transformation had to be total. They had a great admiration for Sismondi, the first economist to realise this and the great 'destroyer' of the system of Smith. However, like most destroyers, the Petrashevtsy felt (echoing Saint-Simon) he was unable to build. Though he saw the need for a 'New Deal', he had failed to provide anything substantial.[65] For solutions they looked to the socialists.

The aim of political economy was redefined by the Petrashevtsy, according to the anthropological principle, as the discovery of a system which corresponded to human nature. It had to be a system which not only eliminated pauperism and guaranteed material welfare to all men, but which also satisfied man's spiritual nature, in which they would be free to follow their every inclination, to develop their full potential, satisfy their every desire and to do this without harming others. The Petrashevtsy agreed that this could only be achieved on the basis of the general socialist principles of a more equitable distribution of wealth and the organisation of labour.

The source of Europe's terrible pauperism was seen as the injustice of the laws according to which wealth was distributed among the various classes of producers and the chaotic, irrational nature of the economic system. Wealth had to be redistributed according to more just principles, i.e. according to principles which corresponded to man's nature. The Petrashevtsy (and especially Dostoevskii in his short stories) divided society up in a Saint-Simonian way into workers and idlers and poured contempt upon the latter. Man, they argued, was by nature created with arms and legs, a worker. His destiny was to create happiness and freedom for himself through labour.[66] Labour was the sole source of wealth. Adam Smith had been the first to see this, but he had not realised the implications of his words, i.e. that labour should be given the prime consideration in the distribution of wealth. The idea had been taken up by the socialists, in particular by Proudhon, who attacked the unjust preference shown to capital (consolidated labour) over labour. The *Pocket Dictionary*, referring boldly to his *Qu'est ce que la propriété?*, set out Proudhon's argument that men had been turned into slaves by their own consolidated labour, 'illegally and unjustly' appropriated by a few capitalists. The source of the tyranny of capital, the Petrashevtsy (and especially Maikov) argued, again echoing Proudhon, lay in the system of wage labour.[67] All the socialists agreed that the new system of distribution of wealth would be based on the abolition of wages and the restoration to the workers of the right to the products of their labour, which had been usurped by capital.

A new system of distribution, however, could only be introduced within the context of the organisation of industry. Petrashevskii called 'the question of the organisation of production the vital question of modern society'.[68] Production was to be organised by the *association* of capitalist and worker. The Petrashevtsy, like the French socialists, believed firmly in the possibility of ending the antagonism between worker and capitalist, making their interests identical and, finally, eliminating the differences between the two. Again influenced particularly by Proudhon, they (especially Maikov and Miliutin) regarded with alarm and suspicion the attempts of workers to unite in opposition to the capitalists.[69] At this time it was understandable to see workers' coalitions as divisive — trade unions were still in their infancy and even the best supported strikes, such as those at Lyons in 1831 and 1834, ended in failure.

The Petrashevtsy studied and criticised the various ways of redistributing wealth and associating capitalist and worker suggested by the different French socialists. They judged them according to the degree of freedom which they accorded to the individual and the degree to which they corresponded to human nature.

All the socialist schemes for the redistribution of wealth agreed that the lion's share of the social product should go to labour. They differed, however, over how much should be given to labour and how much (if any) to other factors in production — capital and talent. The Saint-Simonian solution, 'from each according to his capacities, to each according to his works', met with least sympathy among the Petrashevtsy. They regarded the idea of rewarding people according to their capacities as undemocratic, elitist and unjust. It would merely replace the aristocracy of blood and the aristocracy of wealth, with a new 'aristocracy of talent'.[70] In contrast, the Fourierist principle, which gave the greatest share of the social product, (five twelfths), to labour, but which also rewarded capital, (four twelfths), and talent (three twelfths), appealed more to the Petrashevtsy and was wholly accepted by the more moderate of them. In the entry for *Organisation of Production* in the *Pocket Dictionary*, the most explicit propaganda of Fourierism to pass the censor in Russia, Petrashevskii recommends the teaching of Fourier because, 'It does not exclude and does not sacrifice any one of the agents of production to another and through this makes the establishment of the solidarity of interests *unconditionally possible*, while in no way injuring the already established social relations.'[71] However, to a large number of the more radical Petrashevtsy — including Speshnev, Pleshcheev, Dostoevskii, *Finskii vestnik*, Balasoglo and (on occasions) Petrashevskii himself — Fourier's retention of a share for capital (even though he intended all men to become capitalists) and, especially, for talent, (they were swayed by Proudhon's vigorous denial of talent, an echo of the Babouvist tradition) smacked of élitism and anti-democratism. They argued that the personality of each individual was of equal value, whatever the amount of his capital, whatever the measure of his talent.[72] Everyone should receive an equal reward for work done to the best of his ability. These Petrashevtsy accepted the general communist formula, devised by Louis Blanc, 'from each according to his capacities, to each according to his needs,' as, in Pleshcheev's words, 'more just than the formula of Fourier'.[73]

The Petrashevtsy also studied and criticised all the different ways of organising labour, all the different forms of association suggested by the different French socialists and communists.

Least popular among them were the statist ideas of the Saint-Simonians, Cabet and Louis Blanc, which in their eyes were tinged with despotism. They were particularly anxious to criticise the excessive anti-individualism of the proposals of Louis Blanc, for whom they had otherwise so much respect as a practical socialist. Maikov felt that Blanc's too-complete communalism, his total elimination of competition, would 'exclude all individual initiative from the sphere of human activity and would thus plunge it into death-like stagnation'.[74]

The idea of basing socialism on credit, on a series of free contracts between individuals, as put forward by Proudhon, Owen and, earlier by John Law, appealed more strongly to the Petrashevtsy as permitting an extension of individual freedom. Proudhon's project for a mutual bank was welcomed by *Sovremennik*, by Jastrzębski, and above all, by Speshnev. In August 1848 he wrote to his mother in breathless excitement about the famous occasion (31 July 1848) when Proudhon got up on the tribune and, amidst furious clamour, read out his plan to the French Assembly:

> Proudhon made a proposal that the rich should be made to contribute a third of their incomes for the general use. Theirs was the speaker and spoke at length against Proudhon and socialism. On the next day, Proudhon replied with a speech lasting three hours, in some way so provocative that the Assembly forbade its publication, announcing that anyone who revealed its contents would be brought to trial.

Speshnev commented gleefully, 'This shakes the foundations of the social order and forms the first step towards the implementation of his theory.'[75]

Law's disastrous attempt to introduce a system of free credit and paper money into France in the eighteenth century had been retold from the utopian socialist point of view by Blanc in his *Histoire de la Révolution francaise*. Blanc made Law out to be a democrat and socialist, 'the enfranchisement of the people was his aim and credit his means'. The Russians were very interested in this chapter on Law. According to *Sovremennik*, it expressed, 'a completely original and correct opinion about the intentions and actions of this man, one of the most interesting and misunderstood politicians of the great eighteenth century'. A shortened version of it, including some of its most radical passages, was translated and reprinted by the editors of *Finskii vestnik* in a fit of exceptional daring (the book was banned), in March 1847. They added a preface emphasising the importance of mistakes such as Law's for providing guidance on the 'organisation of welfare', (i.e. the introduction of socialism), in the future.[76]

The Petrashevtsy also had a great respect for Owen, derived from his foundation of a (short-lived) system of free credit, the Equitable Labour Exchange, and his establishment of associations. The *Pocket Dictionary* has a special entry for *Owenism*, which praises Owen's principles of free and mutual co-operation and tells us that New Lanark, founded according to these principles, was soon named by the English 'a picture of comfort, happiness, order and prosperity'.[77]

The Petrashevtsy were, however, mainly interested in Owenism because of its similarities to Fourierism. A majority of the Petrashevtsy 'very hotly defended the absolute prosperity of the human race in the phalanstery according to Fourier's system'.[78] Though they had reservations about some aspects of Fourier's system, they agreed that Fourier had come closest to devising the perfect form of association, the one which corresponded most exactly to the needs of human nature. They were attracted to the phalanstery because it proposed to organise labour and vastly increase the wealth of mankind, not only without harming, but on the contrary, vastly increasing, the liberty of the individual. It both associated and emancipated individuals.

The Petrashevtsy were greatly interested in the enormous economies and the immense wealth that Fourierism would bring. Petrashevskii, for example, carefully calculated what Fourierism would mean for the Russian village, estimating the economy of labour when thirty or forty village cooks replaced 300 or 400 peasant wives each with their own little stove, at 4,927 roubles p.a. the saving on fuel at another 7,000 roubles. Beklemishev marvelled at the wealth that would be produced when social parasites – women, children, merchants, policemen, judges – were put to useful work, 'Just think how many hands, completely idle now, will then return to productive labour, how greatly the income of the producers will increase and the expenses of the consumer diminish!'[79]

But the wonderful thing about the phalanstery in the Petrashevtsy's eyes was, that as well as being rich, the individual was made free. He was free to choose what jobs he worked in, when and how he worked and how long for, and since work had become a pleasure, 'a joy instead of a burden', he would freely choose to work.[80] Both work and living in the phalanstery were organised so as to combine the advantages of association with the retention of individual freedom. In the phalanstery each individual had complete freedom to follow his inclinations not only in choice of job, but also of type of dwelling and mode of life, in dress, in food and in love, in a society organised so that he could do this without harming others. Fourier's system was an attempt, as Petrashevskii said, 'to unite the advantages of the private household (*ménage morcelé*), with the advantages of a communal household (*ménage associé*) ... the comforts of individual life ... with the comforts of life in a community or commune'. The retention of an element of individualism and free choice within association appealed even to the communist Speshnev. He praised the Moravian communes of the followers of John Hus because, 'The mixed couples don't live in communal houses. In general no-one is *forced* to live in a communal house – the most privileged of all are the hermits.'[81] An essential element of the individual freedom of the phalanstery was the partial retention of private property. Like Fourier and also like Proudhon, most of the Petrashevtsy regarded private property as the basic guarantee of individual liberty and security. Poroshin, for example, argued, like Proudhon, that 'the form of property which exists today should be left and only the abuses abolished'; and praised Fourier because, 'He does not destroy property completely, but gives it a new aspect, lays down the rule that it should be proportional to everyone'.[82] The Petrashevtsy's emphasis on property derived from the Russian situation, in which the peasants and poor gentry dreamed of owning a piece of land, their nightmare was the communal forms of life as realised in the Tsar's barracks (hence the aversion to Cabet.)

The Petrashevtsy thus liked Fourier's phalanstery because it was an attempt to create a society which offered total freedom to the individual, by offering total freedom to human nature. Life and work in the phalanstery were designed to make it possible for all men to follow their every inclination in order to develop each of their capacities to its full potential, to satisfy their every need, both material and spiritual.

A large number, probably a majority of the Petrashevtsy, who formed the solid core of the movement, felt that the phalanstery provided a genuinely satisfactory model of 'the normal state of society' i.e. a society which corresponded to human nature.[83] A minority however, while accepting Fourier's basic principles, and in particular the theory of attractive labour, believed that his version could be improved upon. This included both the more radical Petrashevtsy, headed by Speshnev and the more cautious and theoretically-minded members of Maikov's circle.

The radical Petrashevtsy wanted to add to Fourierism elements drawn from communist systems. A good number of them, as we have seen, were in favour of the communist principle of distribution of wealth. A mixture of the two systems, based on combining the Fourierist organisation of labour with the communist principle of equal distribution had been suggested in France both by the radical group of Fourierists led by Gatti de Gamond and Cyzinski and by the communist Dézamy.[84] The idea was to infuse the spirit of freedom into the otherwise rather despotic organisation of Cabet and Buonarroti's communism, and the spirit of democracy into the slightly elitist system of Fourier. According to Speshnev:

> The most just social form that thought could conceive (was) a social system which will transform self-interest into solidarity, social interest, where all men will work because they want to, not just to get paid. In one word, this will be a society where production will be regulated by the great principles of Fourier and consumption by the general communist principle of equal distribution.

Under Speshnev's influence, Timkovskii made a similar suggestion at Petrashevskii's.[85]

The members of Maikov's circle — especially Maikov, Miliutin and Saltykov, more interested in theory, less anxious to act, had reservations about accepting any socialist system put forward so far. In this they stood closer to Herzen and Belinskii than to the other Petrashevtsy. They felt that there were two serious faults in Fourier's system.

First, while Fourierism theoretically allowed complete liberty to man, it also seemed regimented and excessively detailed. Fourier had over-enthusiastically tried to fix so much of the future that man was left with no freedom for improvisation. Saltykov reproached Fourier for 'ruling out the future, garnishing it with the smallest details ... so that his great and fundamental ideas ... were pushed into the background ... and forgotten, or at least fragmented into tiny pieces'.[86] (This had always been Herzen's complaint about Fourierism.) The second and major reproach levelled at Fourier and at the French socialists in general, was that their systems were utopian. Because of this Maikov produced his own solution, for a profit-sharing scheme, the *dolshchina*. Maikov was aware that this idea might seem half-hearted, but he argued that at least it was scientific. Miliutin also felt that the socialist systems of the day belonged, 'indisputably in the category of utopias'. He accused the socialists of despising everything that involved the positive study of facts and trying to discover rational principles not by means of observation and reason, but by some sort of mysterious inspiration.[87]

However, though the present socialist systems were utopian, Miliutin still felt they were useful. Using an argument adapted from Leroux's *Encyclopédie nouvelle*, he called utopias the moving principle of history, 'It is obvious that if man did not have the ability to counterpose to the real facts his ideal utopia, there would be no development ... no progress.' And, gradually, socialism was becoming more scientific, beginning to employ the positive methods of political economy as well as the imagination. Though they had not yet come completely down to earth, the socialists were preparing 'a great and successful future' which would, 'efface for ever the traces of the distress and suffering in which contemporary society is so rich'. *Finskii vestnik*'s study of socialism and political economy brought him to a similar conclusion.[88]

The Petrashevtsy thus judged existing society, and, in particular, the capitalism of the West, as *abnormal*, unnatural, on the grounds that it allowed men no possibilities of satisfying either their material or spiritual needs and as a result warped and perverted human nature. They shared a prevailing optimism that a satisfactory socialist solution, a 'normal society', that corresponded to human nature, could be worked out and implemented in the near future. Their socialism was a response both to Western capitalism and to Western socialist theories. They were the first people in Russia to look at Western economic systems and ideas with the aim of working out a coherent body of socialist theory. Their emphasis on the anthropological principle, their concept of socialism as a 'normal state of society' and their interest in political economy, sets them apart from any other group of thinkers in Russia at this time. Their attempt to base their analysis of capitalism and theory of socialism on a combination of anthropological and historical methods, though not entirely satisfactory, was also new. The Petrashevtsy were eclectic in their theories, untidy in their methods, but for a reason. They wanted to develop a theory of socialism which, as Speshnev said, could be 'adapted to Russia'.[89] Their interest in capitalism and Western socialism was connected with the fact that they thought capitalism was beginning to develop in and western socialism was applicable to, Russia i.e. these were things which concerned *them*.

VI—RUSSIAN SOLUTIONS

There has been a tendency to dismiss the Petrashevtsy as dreamers, who imported their ideas wholesale from Europe and knew and cared little about their native land. The Petrashevtsy's declarations of internationalism have encouraged them to be seen as standing apart from the other intellectual trends of the time.

In fact, the whole of the Russian intelligentsia of the 1840s, including both Slavophiles and Westerners, was preoccupied with Russian issues. The least 'Russian' were the liberal Westerners. But, even Turgenev, often thought of as particularly 'European' was at this time writing his *Sketches from a Hunter's Album*, a portrayal of Russian peasant life. The intelligentsia divided not over their concern for Russia, but over the extent to which they believed Western ideas could be of use in solving its problems. The interest in Russia in educated society by the 1840s was more general than in preceding generations. This was partly connected with the growing plebeian contingent in its midst. The young intellectuals of the 1840s were no longer brought up to speak French as their first language; they mostly came from impoverished gentry families, their comparative poverty bringing them closer to the people; they no longer automatically travelled abroad (Speshnev was the only one of the Petrashevtsy to have done so). Belinskii first brought this new provincial atmosphere into the intelligentsia; the Petrashevtsy were his closest successors.

This feature of the Petrashevtsy has been neglected because their interest in Western ideas and systems, and in particular in Fourierism, did lead them to strike sometimes extreme cosmopolitan attitudes. They received from Fourier a theoretical disdain for nationality, the idea that nations and national characteristics were obstacles to be overcome on the path towards universal human unity, the merging of all nations into one people. This distinguished them from Belinskii, who, starting from a more Hegelian viewpoint, believed that nationalities formed the essential components of the future synthesis of mankind. The pros and cons of nationalities were debated by Maikov and Belinskii in the pages of

Otechestvennye zapiski and *Sovremennik* in 1846–7. Maikov accused Belinskii of reactionary Russian chauvinism; Belinskii reproached Maikov for his 'fantastic cosmopolitanism'. This polemic helped to obscure the basic similarities of the views of the Petrashevtsy and Belinskii on Russia.

Though they believed that national differences would eventually disappear, the Petrashevtsy saw no contradiction in regarding themselves first and foremost as Russians. Far from ignoring the problems of Russia, they were, like Belinskii, interested in Western ideas only as far as they could be applied to Russia. Petrashevskii wrote, 'On us lies no small task, the task of adapting the general principles which science has worked out in the West to our own reality.'[1] The Petrashevtsy shared the general sense of insult and outrage, felt by Russian intellectuals at the European habit of dismissing everything Russian as backward and barbarous. For them this was epitomised by *Lettres de Russie. La Russie en 1839*, by the Marquis de Custine, the first detailed account of the nature of autocracy in Russia, which referred to the Russians as 'not yet civilised … regimented Tatars, nothing more'[2] and which became a best-seller in the West. Their sense of national pride led them, like Herzen and Belinskii, to seize on the fact of Russia's comparative historical youth. The advantages of this were stressed with particular insistence by Russian intellectuals, in general, as a form of compensation for the inferiority complex which they have always had *vis-à-vis* the West. The idea that the West was old and decrepit, that Russia had only just begun to live, had first been put forward to Chaadaev, in his *Apologie d'un fou* (1837): 'The future is ours!' In the same way, the Petrashevtsy called Russia, 'a young society, boiling with a surplus of energy', 'a wonderful, new unknown country' and prophesied, 'a great and mighty future awaits Russia and the Russians'.[3]

At their meetings, the Petrashevtsy divided their time fairly equally between abstract discussions of philosophy and Fourierism and practical questions of Russian life. Petrashevskii, in particular, urged his friends, 'Let us not push reality aside with a smile of disdain … first we must study reality.'[4] The comparatively plebeian nature of their origins made the Petrashevtsy perhaps more acutely aware than their elders of the difficulties inherent in this. They were very conscious of the gulf which separated even the *raznochintsy*, as members of the educated tip of the huge social pyramid of the Russian empire, living in the capital, from the people – a problem which was later to obsess the populist movement. An anonymous letter to Petrashevskii explains, 'We love what is native, Russian, and every innovation is dear to our hearts, but the trouble is that we are insufficiently acquainted with our country and therefore cannot fully sympathise with it.'[5] In addition to their lack of personal contact, there was a dearth of published information about the life of the people. The main written sources were descriptions by foreigners and emigrés, imported from abroad. Of these the most important and widely circulated were, besides Custine's book, Frédéric Lacroix's *Mystères de Russie* (1844); *La Russie sous Nicholas I* (1845) by Ivan Golovin, one of the first political emigres; and Baron August von Haxthausen's famous work, one of the first to draw attention to the peasant commune: *Studien über die inneren Zustände, das Volksleben und insbesondere die ländlichen Einrichtungen Russlands* (1847). Putting these accounts together with their own observations, the Petrashevtsy produced as thorough a critique of the regime as was possible in the 1840s. They painted a grim picture of the all-pervading despotism of the Russian state, of the stifling of individual freedom and initiative in all areas of life and of the suffering and degradation of the mass of the population, who lived in a condition of virtual slavery. Their critique was twofold. On the one hand, they depicted the arbitrariness, injustice and corruption of the institutions of the Russian state and called for the introduction of democratic principles (though they wavered over whether democratic reforms might be introduced by the autocratic state, or only by their ideal government, a republic). This was what could be called the Petrashevtsy's minimum programme – the demand for the guarantees of individual liberty and security which the French revolution had already secured in the West. However, the Petrashevtsy did not just want political change. Democratisation was merely the essential precondition for further changes – the implementation of their 'maximum programme', which was socialist. This is obvious from their views on the most important reform of all – the abolition of serfdom. They wanted to abolish serfdom, but not in order to create a landless proletariat, and to free Russia to follow in the path of capitalist development. Their studies of pauperism in the West made them anxious to avoid it at all costs. They were struck by the similarities between the communal owner-ship of land as practised in the Russian village and Fourier's phalansteries and this led them to advocate a Russian socialism based on the *mir*. A growing interest in Russia's past had led the commune to become a sub-ject of discussion in the forties (though to nothing like the extent of the next decade). Westernising historians such as Kavelin and Sergei Solov'ev pointed to it as a survival of primitive kinship relations; the Slavophiles,

especially Konstantin Aksakov, saw it as the prime example of a society
held together by moral bonds, 'an association of people who have renounced their personal egoism, their individuality and express common
accord'.[6] The commune had more than once been linked with socialism,
especially by the Slavophiles, who said that it made socialism unnecessary
in Russia, as it offered all the advantages which socialism (falsely)
claimed for itself. However, the Petrashevtsy seem to have been the only
people in the forties to suggest that it was possible to avoid capitalism
and the creation of a proletariat in Russia (they used the term 'pauperisation'); that Russia could pass directly from feudalism to socialism;
and that this could be done by establishing socialism on the basis of the
Russian peasant *obshchina* or *mir*. The Petrashevtsy thus anticipated
Herzen, to whom this idea is usually attributed. The first reference to
it occurs in the *Pocket Dictionary* in 1845; Herzen formulated his theory
in 1851. The Petrashevtsy were not interested merely in suggesting this
idea, but were determined to act on it and initiated a number of attempts
at founding socialist associations, which made them the first to try to
implement socialism in Russia. The Petrashevtsy's attitude to Russia was
summed up by *Finskii vestnik* in 1846 and 1847:

> If we learn a salutory lesson from the path which economic development
> has taken in the West, then we can combine greater material prosperity
> with a just and as far as possible equal distribution of goods ... despite
> all the abnormality of this situation (serfdom), which contradicts the
> requirements of science, we can see the indications of a glorious future
> in our communal conception of the right of ownership – the land belongs
> to us, the right of ownership belongs not to any individual person, but
> to the *obshchina*, the *mir* ... We think that Russia presents a vast field
> not only for theory, but for the application of political economic truths
> and that these questions are therefore much more important here than
> in the West.[7]

Nationality

The Petrashevtsy's position on nationality came straight from Fourier.
As Petrashevskii said, 'Socialism is a cosmopolitan doctrine, which
stands higher than nationalities ... for socialists differing nations do not
exist, there are only people'.[8] The Petrashevtsy's cosmopolitanism was
utopian in nature, derived from working backwards from an abstract
idea. They regarded national characteristics as deviations from the one

'universally human character', which all men would attain if and when it became possible for them to achieve the full, all-round development of their attributes and the full satisfaction of their needs. They arose from the subordination of men to diferent external circumstances, which caused their natures to develop in a one-sided manner. An article in *Otechestvennye zapiski* in 1848, for example, defines nationality as 'the preferential development of one or another of the general human capacities at the expense of the others'. The more backward a people, the more it was subjected to external circumstances, the more its members would deviate from 'the ideal type of the true man' and the more pronounced its nationality would be. Only by shedding its national attributes could a people progress to the 'height of human cosmopolitan development.'[9]

These cosmopolitan ideas were developed by Maikov in a review of *The Poems of Kol'tsov*, his first major article as chief critic of *Otechestvennye zapiski*, written under the direct influence of the Petra-shevtsy and as an attack on Belinskii. A year earlier, in *Finskii vestnik*, before he joined the Petrashevskii circle circle he had put forward Belinskii's argument that 'Nationality is one of the conditions of human development.' Maikov, as we have seen, was more concerned than the majority of the Petrashevtsy with the question of individual freedom and in his hands their cosmopolitanism acquired a distinctive individualist twist. The more pronounced the national characteristics of an individual, the further he was from the ideal of the truly free man, who would not be distinguished by any one national characteristic but would combine in his person 'the harmonious development of them all'. At present, Maikov argued, only a few exceptional individuals, 'great men', achieved this ideal. He called his division of mankind into a majority, who were subordinated to external circumstances and not free, and a minority, who obtained freedom through opposing themselves to external cir-cumstances; the *law of nationality*. The majority displayed national characteristics; the minority shed these and raised themselves to the level of autonomous individuals imbued with universally human values. Maikov argued that the genius of writers such as Gogol and Kol'tsov lay in their ability to raise themselves above their nationality and depict universally human types. This gave their writings a universal, eternally valid human appeal, in contrast to the purely temporary, historical appeal of more limited 'national' authors.[10]

Belinskii, in his first article as critic of *Sovremennik, A Review of Russian Literature in 1846*, replied to Maikov with a strong defence of nationality. He approached the subject from a more historical and Hegelian point of view. According to him, 'What *individuality* is in relation to the idea of *man, nationality* is in relation to the idea of *humanity* ... Without nationalities, humanity would be a dead logical abstraction, a word without content, a meaningless sound.' Humanity progressed through history through the intermediary of nations. These were its essential constituent parts. The more they developed, i.e. the more pronounced their national characteristics, the greater the variety among the parts and the richer and fuller would be the life of the whole. Humanity, in its proper development, was a great synthesis, in which were integrated a vast variety of national elements. To some of Belinskii's friends, this seemed like a surrender to the Slavophiles, but Belinskii stopped far short of their idealisation of the national virtues of the Russian peasant mass and, like Maikov, considered that progress was accomplished through individuals. The difference was that, in Belinskii's view, the exceptional individuals did not renounce the national characteristics of the majority, but, on the contrary, embodied them in a fuller, more conscious form. Belinskii ascribed the genius of Gogol and Kol'tsov to their ability to depict not 'truly human' but 'truly national' types, to bring out and embody the character of the Russian people.[11]

The apparent divergence between their views led some historians to portray Belinskii as a realistic apostle of Russian national freedom, Maikov and the Petrashevtsy as feckless cosmopolitans, interested only in the study of Western ideas and oblivious to the possibility of adapting socialism to Russia.[12] But, in reality, in spite of their differences, they agreed in their final aims — the unity of nations and the universal satisfaction of man's needs. And, whether they considered that this future unity should take a national or a cosmopolitan form, they believed that, here and how, Russia had a part, and an important part, to play in humanity's progress. Belinskii said, 'Yes, we have a national life, we are called upon to speak our word, our message to the world'; Petrashevskii echoed him, 'the time will come for the Russian mind ... to say a sensible word in the conversation of humanity'.[13]

The need for the democratisation of Russia — the minimum programme

The Petrashevtsy were very much concerned with the concrete problems of Russian life. Their general feelings about Russia were expressed by Khanykov, 'My fatherland is in chains, my fatherland is enslaved.' Petrashevskii spoke of the 'thousand injustices' sapping the strength of the Russian people and called Russia, 'a stinking society where it is impossible not only to think but even to breathe freely like a human being'.[14] They analysed and criticised, as far as was possible for them, every aspect of the Russian state and institutions, and drew the bleakest picture of its despotism, arbitrariness, injustice and corruption. They called for the democratisation of Russia — the extension to Russian life of those political rights and freedoms for the individual which had already been won in the West.

The government of Nicholas I was, in the Petrashevtsy's eyes, despotism. It both oppressed and impoverished the country. In theory, the Petrashevtsy argued that the ideal form of government, the one which allowed the greatest freedom to the individual, was a republic. They envisaged the socialist future as a stateless society — an anarchist federation of free communes. In practice, though they were aware of the class nature of all states, they were prone to a delusion which crops up regularly among radicals at all stages of Russian history — that the autocratic state might act in a progressive way and help the cause of reform.

The Petrashevtsy unanimously denounced the government of Nicholas I as despotism.[15] Their opposition to absolutism was concentrated into a personal animosity towards Nicholas I. This was connected with the fact that they lived in St. Petersburg and so Nicholas was very close — they could see him in the streets, the parks, the theatres. They were anxious to banish the illusion (held by the peasants) that Nicholas I was a kind 'little father' to his people, that the abuses and injustices were the work of his evil advisers, the landowners. The violence of the language they used in speaking of the Tsar was one of the chief reasons for the severity of their sentences in 1849. Mombelli, for example, had written, 'No, Emperor Nikolai is not a man but a monster, a wild beast, he is that Antichrist of whom it is spoken in the Apocalypse'; Shaposhnikov conceded that 'Nikolai Pavlovich' had strength of mind, but how was this expressed, 'in hanging, killing, destroying everything beautiful'.[16] Though they were aware that serfdom was the real brake on economic progress, the Petrashevtsy also tended to speak as if Nicholas was personally responsible for the poverty of the vast mass of the population. The Tsar's extravagance was an obvious and visible cause of the wastage of precious capital. When asked by friends what he meant by the initials, 'N.P.', Shaposhnikov said abruptly, 'a robber'. The Petrashevtsy inveighed against Nicholas for depriving industry and agriculture of desperately-needed credit by squandering money on palaces and barracks.[17] Their tendency to blame Nicholas rather than the system was carried to its extreme by Tolstov, who compiled an enormous list of Nicholas's various crimes and concluded, 'He is the source of the general distress ... he does not love his subjects, he is an egotist. He himself knows that he has wronged his subjects and is squeezing them in an iron fist.' To test whether Nicholas I really was suffering from a guilty conscience, Tolstov and Khanykov even went to a royal command performance at the Marinskii Theatre, to try and stare him out of countenance.[18]

In principle, the Petrashevtsy, as one would expect, were in favour of a republic. It was the ideal form of government, the only one which was 'truly human', i.e. which guaranteed the liberty and security of 'each individual separately'. Younger and rasher Petrashevtsy, such as Katenev and Tolstov, openly carried on agitation for a republic among their friends. Katenev even went about in republican dress, consisting of white trousers with large checks, a round white hat, a long white waistcoat, a black frockcoat, and a thick cane with a head depicting one of the French revolutionaries.[19] It was, however, very dangerous to talk openly about a republic in Russia, much more dangerous than to talk about Fourierism. The Petrashevtsy therefore tended to cloak their arguments for a republic in the guise of a discussion of Greek and Roman history, of which they had detailed knowledge. They used the example of ancient Greece to emphasise the 'great moral power' of republic. Only in a republic, only when individual liberties were guaranteed, could the arts, science and industry flourish. Poroshin, for example, introduces three pages of quotations from Thuycydides's account of Pericles's speeches on the Athenian constitution into his book on economics to emphasise this. In addition, comparisons between the institutions of the Roman republic and those of the Empire were a convenient way of showing the advantages of republican over autocratic government. Balasoglo rebukes Gibbon for trying to maintain that the 'free institutions' of the Republic could survive under the Empire; Durov praises Demetrius Laberius, who turned mime into a political weapon, for 'attacking the abuses and despotism of Caesar' and describes how, in one of his plays, Demetrius himself ran out onto the stage dressed as a slave, 'and said in a penetrating voice "it's all over, Romans! Freedom is lost!"' Praise of the American and French revolutionary constitutions, though more risky, was also occasionally smuggled in.[20] The *Pocket Dictionary* outlined the main provisions of the French Constitution of 1789 which set up a constitutional monarchy and Akhsharumov drew up a plan for a constitutional monarchy in Russia. The Petrashevtsy recognised that a constitutional monarchy had its advantages, but only as a stepping stone to a republic.[21] In the long term, many of them wanted to do away with the state and all its institutions and envisaged some sort of anarchist federation of free communes, as advocated by Fourier and Proudhon. According to Akhsharumov, 'The state should perish, along with its bureaucracy and tsars, its armies, its capital cities, its laws and temples. In its place, small communities should be set up ... which would constitute wholes and be ... independent from each other and represent, so to speak, microcosms of humanity.'[22]

In practice, the Petrashevtsy wavered on the question of the state. Like many other Russian radicals, including both Herzen and Belinskii, since the absolutist state controlled all aspects of Russian life, they thought, it was the best, if not the only possible, instrument of reform. Though they exaggerated the extent of its power, it was true, as the Petrashevtsy said, that the state had played an important if not the major role in Russian history. Russia was a vast, backward country with few natural defences and, as Balasoglo said, it was only through the concentration of resources in a strong state, that she had beaten off invaders from East and West. The state had also played a progressive role in Russian history, in that (though mainly for reasons of defence) it had been largely responsible for the importation of Western institutions and ideas. There were thus considerable grounds in Russia for the belief that the state, 'stood above all classes' and furthered progress.[23] The Petrashevtsy felt that this was true, above all, of the reforms of Peter the Great. Like all the Westerners, they tended to idealise Peter, who had dragged the boyars out of barbarism by their beards. Struck by the revolutionary nature of his reforms, the Petrashevtsy went as far as to speak of Peter as their predecessor.

Balasoglo claimed, 'Peter prepared the way for our time. He foresaw the contemporary thought of Europe.' Although the government of Nicholas I, being closer at hand, did not quite live up to the Petrashevtsy's

rose-coloured image of Peter, right up to February 1848, the state did
seem to be the major progressive force in Russian life. As Balasoglo
wrote, 'The government of Russia organises and maintains the army,
navy, harbours, administration, relations with foreign powers, factories,
workshops, even agriculture. It is founding *gymnaziia* and *uchilishcha*,
cadet corps, universities, opening more and more faculties of more and
more sciences.'[24] Nicholas had also given some rights to the towns,
passed some measures to help the serfs and was even, it was widely
rumoured, considering emancipation. Russia had no 'civil society' which
could generate reforms from within itself, merely a few thousand
obstinate, boorish landowners, forty million utterly ignorant peasants
and tiny circles of intelligentsia who were isolated from the rest of the
population. Before 1848, it was understandable that the radical intelligentsia felt they had no choice but to look in the government's
direction, however much this contradicted their fundamental dislike of
despotism. Dostoevskii was thus not wholly insincere, just telling half
the truth, when he told his interrogators, 'Everything that has been good
in Russia ... has always come from above, from the throne', and even
Petrashevskii saw no inconsistency in appealing from his prison to
Nicholas to found the first phalanstery.[25] Most of the Petrashevtsy
looked to the state reluctantly, for opportunist reasons, as a concession
to necessity. There were a few exceptions, however, who accepted the
state on principle. Among these were some of the more moderate
Petrashevtsy whose socialism, like Fourier's, was apolitical and who had
no intention of challenging the existing form of government. The best
example of this is Danilevskii who was later to go over to the side of
absolutism.[26] Then there were those, in particular, Maikov and Miliutin
who could not be called political moderates, but who accepted Louis
Blanc's argument that the state could act impartially and that its great
power meant that it *had* to be used in the introduction of socialism.
Maikov asked, 'Who besides an enlightened and impartial government
can lead society out of the false track along which it is rushing to ruin?
... what force can establish harmony between the hostile classes of
society, if not the government?'[27]

But though the Petrashevtsy hoped that the state might act in an
impartial spirit, they were aware that this was not how it acted at present.
The examples of France and England, which in spite of their constitutions
were still ruled by privileged classes, helped them to see this. (Miliutin,
in particular, stressed the power of the English upper classes). Soviet
authorities on Saltykov have put forward an interpretation of the dream

of a pyramid in *A Tangled Affair* as an allegory of the class nature of the Russian state. Saltykov seems to have derived the idea of a social pyramid from Saint-Simon. Saint-Simon's pyramid had a granite base – the working class; middle layers of 'precious metals' – scholars, artists etc.; an upper part – nobles, landowners and other 'rich parasites' holding up the 'magnificent diamond' – the power of the King, carved from golden gypsum. Saltykov's pyramid is a psychological device (one of the first examples in Russian literature of a dream being used in this way). The columns forming it were not made of granite, but of 'an infinite multitude of people standing one on top of the other', so that those at the bottom could scarcely breathe from the weight oppressing them.[28] Other Petrashevtsy emphasised the 'caste' nature of the Russian state, run in the interests of the landowners by a monarchy, which was 'just the summit of the aristocratic part of the hierarchy, body and soul belonging to it'. The secret of the state's real character was jealously kept from the people by the statesmen and the secret councillors, who had formed themselves into a new class of obscurantists. It was, as Engel'son said, 'a conspiracy of those who have property against those who have not'.[29]

The chief instruments of this state power were the army, the bureaucracy and the legal system. Here the Petrashevtsy found brutality, ignorance and corruption. The reform of the state apparatus naturally seemed more feasible than the abolition of the institution of autocracy. They viewed it as an immediate, practical question and placed a great deal of emphasis on it. They called for democratisation in all areas, according to a programme which they derived from their study of representative government in France and England, and in particular, of the reforms introduced in France in the revolutionary and Napoleonic periods.

The Petrashevtsy described in detail the dreadful conditions of soldiers' lives, the harsh punishments used in the army and suggested ways of ameliorating their conditions derived from an idealised picture of the French revolutionary armies. A significant number of them were or had been in the army as junior officers, including Mombelli, Grigor'ev, the Dostoevskii brothers, Kuz'min, Pal'm, L'vov, Chernosvitov, and thus had first-hand knowledge of the lives of the common soldiers. Mombelli and Grigor'ev both wrote painful accounts of army conditions. Mombelli's took the form of a diary and includes a bloodcurdling description of the *fel'd-sherbel*, a punishment in which the soldier had to run a gauntlet of knotted whips – in his case the victim died after 3,000 blows. Grigor'ev's was a short story, *A Soldier's Tale*, in which an old soldier,

Ivan Kremnev, looks back on the succession of miseries which have made up his life. A serf, sent into the army as a punishment by his owner, he was disciplined, beaten, broken like a mangy cur, 'the food was rubbish, the pay paltry, a dog's life!' When he 'got his ticket' and went home, his father, mother and sister were dead, his home had been given to someone else, and, as he was too old and decrepit to work, he was soon forced to beg on the streets.[30] The Petrashevtsy's accounts of army life were in no way exaggerated or atypical. The term of service was twenty-five years, the harsh conditions and cruel treatment meant that even in peace-time a large number of soldiers died before completing it. The Petrashevtsy's solution was, first, to found a National Guard on the French model, which would enable the size of the standing army to be cut by half, and, secondly, to reform the standing army according to a very idealised picture of the Napoleonic army:

> There's little conscription there … the pay and food are good: the soldiers know nothing of the birch … there is only one punishment, which is arrest, as for officers here; and the soldiers choose their officers from among themselves. There everyone serves to a man, both the landowner and the merchant and our brother muzhik. There's freedom for you.[31]

Since a majority of Petrashevtsy occupied minor posts in the civil service, they all knew well about conditions there. If cruelty was the ruling principle in the army, in the overgrown state bureaucracy the Petrashevtsy felt, it was chaos. The *Pocket Dictionary*, in a sly reference to Russia, says, 'Anarchy sometimes also reigns in states where *apparently* law and order exist in the administration, but in fact there are no solid enactments and no strict fulfilment of them.'[32] According to the Petrashevtsy, civil servants were ignorant, corrupt and behaved like despots towards their subordinates. Routine and prejudice, not knowledge and virtue, guided their actions and the main principle on which they operated was muddling through. The higher officials were allowed an arbitrary freedom which was a result of and a direct corollary to the arbitrary freedom allowed to the landowners. As the landowners ruled over their serfs, so the *chinovniki* ruled over the rest of the population. The higher officials took it out on the lower, the lower on their petitioners. Outlining the defencelessness of the population as a whole, Filippov moaned:

> We have no protection from their arbitrariness … to complain is to undergo fresh insults and humiliations … in Russia every chief is a despot and there is no guarantee of personal security for the weak, whom everyone who is of higher rank can crush like a worm.

The low wages paid to civil servants intensified the problem. Corruption was universal, bribe-taking so common that Meier got one of his students to write a dissertation on it. Mombelli tells a typical story of two police officers, especially picked for their 'disinterestedness, efficiency, zeal, honesty, nobility etc.' who were sent to arrest the participants in an illegal gambling game. After accepting a bribe of 2,000 silver roubles each, the zealous officers returned to announce that they had found the company playing whist![33]

Some of the Petrashevtsy (Pleshcheev in particular) felt that reform had to be begun from the bottom. They had naïve and idealistic ideas of setting out like white knights into the wilds of the provincial administration, taking humble posts there and spreading, by their own example, the principles of justice and virtue. In Kazan, Meier had similar hopes for his students.[34] The majority of the Petrashevtsy, however, conceded that there was a need for more radical reforms. Inspired by the declaration of the French constitution of 1789 that, 'All citizens have equal rights to the occupation of all posts within exception', they called for the opening up of the civil service to all classes (the entry to all but the lowest ranks of the civil service was restricted to the gentry) and the filling of all posts with 'elected representatives of the people'.[35] In addition, Petrashevskii attempted, through his own personal initiative, to force the elected bodies which already existed (the Nobles' Assemblies and the newly-reformed Town Dumas) in the direction of greater democracy and widen the scope of their powers. He tried to introduce a discussion of his plan for emancipating the serfs into the St. Petersburg Assembly of the Nobility and to stand for election to the newly established post of secretary to the St. Petersburg Duma, which he hoped to make 'an influential position'. The limitations of the government's enthusiasm for democracy were shown by the outcome of Petrashevskii's efforts − he was declared ineligible for election to the Duma; forbidden to speak at the Nobles' Assembly and an intensive police watch was put on him. Other Petrashevtsy argued, with some justification, that nothing could be expected from these bodies as long as Tsarism existed. Kuz'min, for example, explained how the government party in Tambov, where he lived, controlled elections to the Nobles Assembly, by acting in the most unscrupulous way − even resorting to arresting and imprisoning its opponents to keep them out of the way for the duration of the elections.[36]

The reform of the legal system was, Petrashevskii believed, most vital of all. Many of the Petrashevtsy had studied law (since law was the basic

requirement for entry into the civil service). Both Petrashevskii and
Golovinskii were lawyers by profession and had a special interest in the
question. Golovinskii seems to have been the author of radical articles
on law in *Finskii vestnik*; both he and Petrashevskii spoke regularly at
the Fridays on this question.[37] The Russian legal system was, in spite
of attempts at reform, as Petrashevsky said, a jungle — the laws were
confused, complicated, contradictory and all legal proceedings were
shrouded in secrecy. Court cases dragged on for years. Appeals were
so expensive that very few could afford them. Lawyers were poorly
trained, poorly paid and sold justice summarily to the highest bidder.
The public were often ignorant of the existence of laws that might help
them. The *Pocket Dictionary* called Russia a country, 'where justice has
never, for one moment, been impartial, where the legal system acts as
the guardian of every kind of injustice!' Chernosvitov was a typical
victim of this system. To fight a decision in which the Yaroslavl civil court
had awarded an inheritance he thought was due to him to a richer and
more influential claimant, he had had to borrow half the value of the
inheritance, 'a case of crying injustice!'[38]

The Petrashevtsy saw the solution in the introduction into Russia of
features of the more democratic judicial systems of England and France.
The first, and most important, principle was publicity. Legal proceedings
had to be opened 'to the whole world'. Only then could impartiality be
guaranteed. Publicity would also make proceedings much quicker —
cases which took eight years could be settled in one.[39] The second principle was the involvement of the public in the actual decision — making
of the courts, through the introduction of trial by jury. The Petrashevtsy,
and especially Petrashevskii, tended to idealise the English jury system
as the 'best and most perfect' legal institution in the world. Only with
the jury could justice be achieved, for only then were circumstances, as
well as the crime, taken into consideration in determining a man's
sentence. Only with a jury did human sympathy enter the courts.[40] The
Petrashevtsy also called for changes in the criminal law. Petrashevskii
began a laborious analysis of the criminal code in 1845, which he promised would excel Montesquieu's *Esprit des Lois*, and continued it in
prison. Among the reforms advocated by the Petrashevtsy were the abolition of the death penalty and corporal punishment and the reorganisation,
or still better, the abolition of the prison system. Saltykov, for example,
made a special study of the prison system,[41] and Shtrandman wrote in
Sovremennik that, '*Corporal punishment in every case debases human
dignity ... forces the man to despise himself*, and finally, *enrages him*'.

In addition, Petrashevskii was one of the first and more dogged champions of the idea of beginning reform by campaigning for the implementation of at least those laws that already existed, or as he called it, *legality*. In 1846 he set up a law office, employing Baranovskii as his assistant, and Petr Egorov, a sympathetic teacher from the Larin gymnasium, as his clerk, and placed an advertisement in the *Sanktpeterburgskie vedomosti* to the effect that, 'Butashevich-Petrashevskii announces that he will intercede without payment in the court cases of all poor people who do not have the money to hire lawyers and from rich people he will take only the very smallest fee.' However, since the cases brought to him were mainly private suits about money matters, not the complaints about government abuses he had been hoping for, Petrashevskii decided to concentrate on bringing cases on his own behalf. Following the letter of the law strictly, he took his complaints against the Chief of the St. Petersburg Police and the Governor General of St. Petersburg (for disqualifying him from the elections to the Town Duma) from court to court, until he reached the Senate. There, in spite of the 'ironic laughter' with which his pleas were received, he demanded, as an old law permitted, that he be allowed to present his case orally to the assembled senators. Their refusal reached him in prison.[42] In Siberia he was to continue an unceasing struggle for 'legality' until his death in 1866.

The Petrashevtsy, and especially the writers among them, were also convinced that there was no possibility of reforming Russia, no hope of exposing and destroying abuses, until there was freedom of speech and of the press, until the government tolerated criticism and the formation of an opposition. The *Pocket Dictionary* tells us that, 'to live without criticism without discussing one's own and other people's affairs, is to vegetate like a plant'. In his *Petersburg Feuilletons*, Dostoevskii describes the 'piercing feeling of desolation, caused by the question, "What's the news?"'[43] They condemned the censorship both because it stifled public opinion and initiative and because it was ruining literature. At his trial, Dostoevskii spoke out boldly against its 'exorbitant severity'. Most of the Petrashevtsy-writers had suffered personally from the harshness of the censor. The *Pocket Dictionary* was banned and burnt; Dostoevskii's *Prokharchin* was mutilated; Durov's preface of the works of Khmel'nitskii had its most witty passages cut out. The Petrashevtsy saw free speech as one of the most fundamental natural rights of the individual. Dostoevskii asked, 'Why was reason stimulated in me? What is knowledge if I do not have the right to voice my personal opinion or to disagree with opinions which are regarded as authoritative?' Freedom of speech was also one of the essential guarantees of the individual's political freedom. Only in a state where people could speak out freely against the government, i.e. where opposition was tolerated, was the individual secure against its arbitrary actions. The Petrashevtsy were very firm believers in political opposition (which for them meant parliamentary government). The *Pocket Dictionary*, for example, has a special entry for *Opposition*, which outlines Guizot's ideas on the nature and principles of different forms of political opposition.[44]

A socialist solution to the peasant question – the maximum programme

The Petrashevtsy's immediate programme of reform for Russia was thus based on the democratisation of the state and the guarantee of basic freedoms for the individual. In Russia, however, democracy would have no meaning for more than half the population without the implementation of another reform – the abolition of serfdom. On this, the most important question in Russia, the Petrashevtsy's ideas passed from democracy to socialism.

In the Petrashevtsy's eyes, the Russian serfs lived in a condition of slavery. They protested against the injustices of serfdom and tried to expose the humanitarian hypocrisy of so-called liberal serfowners. They were also among the first to identify serfdom as the cause of Russia's economic stagnation.

The Petrashevtsy, like most of the French writers on the subject referred to the serfs as slaves, to bring out the abjectness of the Russian serfs' position.[45] The Russian serf suffered from a far greater degree of oppression than his medieval European counterpart: whereas the medieval serf had been tied to the land, the Russian serf could be separated from it and sold without it at his master's whim. The use of the word slave was also a convenient device for slipping their assault on serfdom past the censor – the Petrashevtsy could pretend they were talking about slavery in ancient Greece or Rome or the United States. The abstract argument against slavery could not have been simpler and was openly taught by radical professors at the university, 'Men are by nature equal in rights and therefore slavery shouldn't exist.' In their published articles, the Petrashevtsy turned to Ancient Greece and Rome to argue that all constitutions were illusions, no reforms had any meaning, as long as a state remained based on slavery, and spoke with scorn of the 'Athenian or the Roman citizen who drowned in comfort and luxury, trampling on the individuality of millions of men.' They used the example of the United States to lament that, 'In spite of the fact that mother nature created both hands (i.e. all men) with equal rights, in spite of the democracy of North America and of the French Revolution which proclaimed equality, no-one has restored the lost rights of the left hand.'[46] Most important of all, references to the campaign for its abolition in the West Indies, enabled the Petrashevtsy to show that, though slavery persisted, its injustice was universally recognised – it was on the way out. The *Pocket Dictionary* devotes two long articles, *Negro* and *Negrophile*, to this subject, and showers praise on the 'heroic efforts' of the 'noble champions of the truth' who succeeded in abolishing slavery in the English colonies in 1833.[47]

It was much more difficult to speak about 'the Russian slaves' in print. Outspoken attacks on serfdom could only be circulated in manuscript form. The most outstanding of these were Belinskii's *Letter to Gogol* and Grigor'ev's *A Soldier's Tale*. In his letter, greeted with rapture by the Petrashevtsy, Belinskii declares that Russia, 'still presents the dire spectacle of a country where men traffic in men without even having the excuse so insidiously exploited by the American plantation owners who claim that a negro is not a man'. In *A Soldier's Tale*, the serf Kremnev describes in detail how he came to be sent into the army for beating up his master, after the latter raped his beloved younger sister.[48] The government's sensitivity to attacks on serfdom can be seen from the fact that for writing *A Soldier's Tale*, Grigor'ev, aged twenty, was sentenced to fifteen years hard labour; for merely reading Belinskii's letter, Dostoevskii got ten. However, milder, yet realistic portrayals of peasant life could slip past the censor if they were presented in fictional form – the best examples of this were Turgen'ev's *Sketches from a Hunter's Album* and Grigorovich's *The Village*[3] both published in *Sovremennik* (1847–8). The landowners' cruelty to their serfs was also attacked in non-fictional articles in the radical journals by Shtrandman, who managed to get away with this through a skilful use of irony; and by Tolbin and others under the disguise of a debate on 'kindness to animals'. Poroshin was one of those who, in *Sanktpeterburgskie vedomosti* and *Otechestvennye zapiski* began 'an energetic protest' against the ill treatment of animals, and in particular, the beating of horses. *Sovremennik* and *Finskii vestnik* called this 'hypocritical liberalism' and tried to draw attention away from horses to the treatment of serfs. An 'A Physiological Sketch about Animal Lovers' published in *Finskii vestnik* (December 1847), Tolbin launched a sarcastic attack on the landowners and especially their wives, who treated their animals better than they did their serfs. One woman, for example, orders her servant to go to buy beef for her 'doggie'; 'Good beef, not the sort you buy for serfs', another sends for a vet for her dog Azor, rather than a doctor for her coachmen, 'Of course the coachman can wait ... and even, between ourselves, if he went and died, you'll agree you can find a thousand coachmen, but you won't find another Azor!'[49]

Serfdom was thus an unjust, cruel and barbarous institution which reduced the serf below the status of an animal. In addition, the Petrashevtsy argued, it brought no benefit to the landowner, but was the cause of the backwardness of Russia's agriculture. There were practical and economic as well as abstract and humanitarian reasons for its abolition. The theory of the economic disadvantages of serfdom had just begun to be put forward by liberals such as Andrei Zablotskii-Desiatovskii and reforming landowners, such as Herzen's friend Ogarev. In a famous article, *The Cause of the Instability of Corn Prices in Russia* (1847), Zablotskii argued that since serfs worked for nothing, the cost of labour did not enter into the price of the grain. But since serf labour was also obligatory, the landowner had to sell his grain at all costs, even at low market prices. The cause of 'the unsettled, chaotic state of agriculture' was therefore 'the unnatural, anti-economic distribution of productive forces'. The Petrashevtsy were among the first to take this idea up. *Finskii vestnik put* put it more bluntly, 'The system of serfdom which exists here means that the landowner, even if he considers it unprofitable, must cultivate the land.' Shtrandman, reviewing articles by G. Kozlov and Ogarev, argued that *barshchina*, forced labour, was expensive and wasteful and concluded that it was this 'abnormal organisation of the productive forces' which was responsible for the 'primitive' state of Russian agriculture. The Petrashevtsy were aware of the tendency of landowners in grain-producing areas to intensify the *barshchina* system in a last-ditch attempt to make serfdom profitable. Shtrandman cites with horror the methods used by landowners to force peasants back from *obrok*, the quit-rent system, to *barshchina* − locking them up, beating them and threatening to send them into the army.[50]

Discussion of emancipation was encouraged by the belief that Nicholas I was in favour of freeing the serfs. At least before 1848, there were grounds for thinking this. In 1842 Nicholas told the State Council.

'There is no doubt that serfdom in the form in which we have it now is clearly and obviously bad for everyone ... it is at least necessary to prepare the way for a very gradual transition to another order of things.' He established a large number of secret committees to discuss the peasant question and took some steps to help the serfs: a decree of 1842 about 'obligated peasants'; a decree of 1847 allowing serfs on estates sold at public auction to buy their freedom; and the introduction of inventories regulating relations between master and serf in the Western provinces. Though these were very tentative and largely ineffective, they at least showed good will. As a result, everyone talked about the abolition of serfdom, it became, as Beklemishev said, the question which 'occupies the whole of Russia'.[51] All the Petrashevtsy, and indeed, all the liberal intelligentsia, were wholeheartedly in favour of emancipation and were not afraid to admit it. Miliukov boldly told his interrogators, 'If you call a liberal tendency my ideas about serfdom and wish for emancipation as the source of enlightenment and happiness for the whole people, then this tendency appeared in me long ago.' In April 1849, in his farewell lecture, Meier spoke out openly in front of the whole of Kazan University, 'I believe in the proximity of a revolution in the internal life of our society. Everyone who has a human heart involuntarily recognises all the absurdity of serfdom.'[52] The question was merely whether the serfs should be liberated with or without land, with or without the payment of compensation to the gentry. In the press, since any mention of emancipation was strictly forbidden, the discussion of the forms it might take was usually hidden as a discussion of the relative merits of the English and French landholding systems. In private, it was possible to speak more freely. The Petrashevtsy discussed a multitude of projects – their own and other people's. Some of these were moderate, others revolutionary, but all of them agreed that the creation of a proletariat had to be avoided at all costs – emancipation should take place with land.

England represented the type of emancipation the Petrashevtsy definitely did not want. Serfdom had given way to capitalism in agriculture. A tiny group of aristocrats retained the ownership of huge estates, comprising almost all the land in the country. The majority of the peasants had been expropriated and had become landless labourers or workers in the towns. The Petrashevtsy embarked on a public debate with Poroshin whose *A Political Economy of Agriculture* (1846) was seen as a betrayal in radical circles. In his university lectures, Poroshin had denounced the rule of the English landowning aristocracy. But, after a visit to England (where he received lavish hospitality from English lords), he changed his mind. His book begins with a panegyric to the 'rural happiness' created by English improving landowners who had 'raised agriculture to the status of an art' and concludes that the aristocracy has been 'of undeniable service to the people'.[53] Maikov, Miliutin and *Finskii vestnik* pointed out that the 'agricultural art' of the English aristocracy was based on the labour of a penniless, landless, agricultural proletariat, unemployed for half the year, 'Agriculture flourishes as an art in England, but at the sacrifice of what? Of the most sacred right of the working class − the right to a comfortable existence. Yes, let the best of all arts perish if such are its consequences!' The Petrashevtsy believed that the only way to protect the lower classes from destitution was to give them land. The example of this sort of emancipation was France, where the great estates had been split up into tiny plots and several million peasants participated in the rights of landownership. However, they recognised that division of the land had its disadvantages − it made it impossible to cultivate the land on a large scale or use improved methods of farming and was 'thus death to production'. They wanted to combine the advantages of both small-scale and large-scale landholdings − the French universalisation of property with the English efficiency. This could be done, Miliutin said, through 'the *association* of small landowners, uniting to cultivate their plots with common forces and common means ... the right to landed property can be splintered to extremes, but the actual subject of the property, land ... should stay whole and undivided.' In their discussion of the English system, the Petrashevtsy also, by their rejection of all theories of rent as 'based on false premises' rejected the idea that mere ownership of land conferred any rights on the holder whether the right of demanding rent, or (by implication) the right of demanding compensation on surrender of the land.[54]

When the Petrashevtsy discussed emancipation openly, in private conversation, the need to free the serfs with land was paramount. The creation of twenty million proletarians was a prospect which not only appalled the Petrashevtsy, but which also terrified the Russian government. For the Petrashevtsy the granting of land to the peasants was a way of avoiding capitalism and passing directly to socialism.[55] The government and liberal bureaucrats supported it for more practical reasons, as the only way to avoid 'an uprising of the peasants against their supposed oppressors' and mass emigration which would 'completely ruin the landowners' by depriving them of labourers.[56] The problem was that the majority of the landowners were not in favour of emancipation, still less of giving up their right to the land. As Kuz'min said, they were boorish, backward and reactionary, they 'behave like dogs and have antique, prejudiced ideas about things'.[57] There were two main approaches to dealing with the landowners. One, adopted by the liberal bureaucrats and the more moderate of the Petrashevtsy, was to take account of their interests and attempt to win them over to emancipation by awarding them compensation for their land. The other, more radical and utopian, adopted by the majority of the Petrashevtsy, was to reject the idea that the gentry had any right to the land and favour their expropriation without the payment of any compensation, whatever problems this might cause.

Projects designed to mollify the landowners were composed by Nikolai Ushakov (a zoologist and liberal landowner, who visited Petrashevskii's) and Beklemishev. Beklemishev attempted to devise a formula for emancipation which demanded from the landowners, 'sacrifices so insignificant they are not worth mentioning'. His proposals leave the owners with a great deal of land (about half the average estate); oblige the peasants to pay the whole value of the land given to them (plus interest); and to continue working for their masters as wage labourers for a period of three years. In February 1848, Petrashevskii too composed a moderate and practical plan for emancipation, *On Ways of Increasing the Value of Settled Estates*, intended for immediate adoption by the government. He lithographed it, distributed it to his friends, to prominent members of the Petersburg gentry, and attempted to read it out at the Nobles' Assembly (but was prevented). This was based on an extension of the decrees of 1842 and 1847 and allowed merchants the right of buying settled estates on condition they turned the serfs living on them into obligated peasants, i.e. free peasants paying an annual rent for the use of the land; Petrashevskii estimated that this would vastly increase the value of estates by leading to the injection of large amounts (up to 500 million paper roubles worth) of merchant capital into agriculture.[58]

The majority of the Petrashevtsy opposed Petrashevskii's project. Khanykov's reaction was, 'But this is betrayal!' Vladimir Kaidanov objected strongly to the favour shown by Petrashevskii to the merchants and refused to distribute the letter among the Rostov gentry:

> I cannot preach what I don't strongly sympathise with and I have no sympathy for this project or for any plant which leads to the creation of an arch-mercantile feudalism and a financial aristocracy ... I will not do

anything to benefit this class which I have never liked and for which, after reading Fourier, I feel total revulsion. And so, that's an end to it. He cannot count on me.[59]

The main reason for the Petrashevtsy's hostility to the plan was that Petrashevskii's advocacy of turning the serfs into obligated peasants looked to them like acceptance of the principle that they should pay compensation. Their argument was that the landowner's enjoyment of the land was not a *right* but a *privilege* which was granted as a favour by the government and could be withdrawn at any time. There were therefore no grounds for compensation. The Petrashevtsy, as Speshnev said, wanted 'the immediate and total abolition of serfdom'.[60] *A Project for the Emancipation of the Serfs*, which Petrashevskii wrote slightly later (1848-9) and which contained his principled position, was more to their taste. Here he rejects the government's reform plans and all liberal projects and proposes a 'total solution', the 'immediate and unconditional emancipation of the serfs with the land which they have been working, without any compensation for the landowners'. He justifies this by claiming that the gentry have usurped the land and by denying that they have any right to the exclusive possession of it:

> (1) the human race is the joint owner of the globe, and (2) every individual member of humanity has a right to the possession of that part of the globe which falls to his share on the equal division of the globe among its inhabitants'

i.e. this was a *socialist* formula for emancipation.[61] For the Petrashevtsy, emancipation was the prelude to the socialist reorganisation of Russia. Socialism, the Petrashevtsy thought, could be established earlier and more successfully in Russia than the West, because Russia had not yet undergone an industrial transformation. The peasants were not yet paupers but still lived on the land, and most important of all, still preserved the medieval tradition of the communal ownership of the land in the form of the Russian *obshchina* or *mir*. Inspired partly by the Slavophiles, partly by Haxthausen, partly by Fourierism, the Petrashevtsy anticipated Herzen by almost six years in putting forward the idea that the *obshchina* might be the basis on which to construct the future socialist society.

The idea that the commune shielded the peasant from pauperism had first been put forward by the Slavophiles. Khomiakov wrote in 1842, 'The peasant is never completely isolated, thanks to the commune. He never has been and never will be, similar to the proletariat of Europe.' The Petrashevtsy elaborated on this. They observed that 'pauperism, that scourge of the West, has still, thank God, not yet penetrated into Russia'. The Russian peasant still lived on the land, still cultivated his own plot. This guaranteed him against misery and meant that, unlike the French or English proletarian, he was 'nourished, housed and warmed'. This was partly due to serfdom, which tied the peasant to the land, and also acted as a crude form of association — the landowner, at least in theory, helped his serfs in time of trouble; partly due to the survival of the traditional communal institutions, the *artel* and *mir*, which protected the welfare of and provided land for each of their members.[62]

As early as 1845, the Petrashevtsy drew attention to the survival of communal institutions in Russia and pointed to the potential of the *obshchina*. The *Pocket Dictionary*, under 'commune', explained that the medieval commune of Europe was 'exactly the same thing as the Russian *obshchina*', emphasising that once they had emancipated themselves from the power of their feudal lords the European communes had become rich, powerful, independent societies, the instruments of the overthrow of the feudal system.[63] The Petrashevtsy's interest in the *obshchina* was intensified by the publication in 1847 of *Studien über die inneren Zustände, das Volksleben und insbesondere the ländlichen Einrichtungen Russlands*, by the Prussian ethnologist Haxthausen, who had been led by his search for the survivals of medieval communes to Russia. Haxthausen pointed out, 'the perfect equality of rights' which reigned in the *mir*, as a result of the communal ownership and occasional redistribution of the land, and the fact that, as every Russian belonged to a commune, there were 'no born proletarians in Russia'.[64] This book was available in French and German (though its translation into Russian was forbidden) and widely read and reviewed. *Finskii vestnik* declared that Haxthausen had discovered 'Eldorado in Russia'. In 1846 and in particular, in 1847 (under the stimulation of Haxthausen), the journal put forward the idea that, once the peasants were freed and confirmed in their ownership of the land, the communal ownership of land in the *mir* could become a bulwark against the expropriation of the peasants and be made the basis of a socialist communal ownership. concluding, 'We can see the indication of a glorious future in our communal conception of the right of ownership.'[65] This was the whole core of later *narodnik* theory.

The *obshchina* became a general subject of discussion among the Petrashevtsy in 1847 and was talked about even in 'apolitical' circles of Kashkin and Durov. Golovinskii, for example, insisted on the socialist

nature of *obshchina* property, 'Village, i.e. peasant, land belongs not
to any individual but to the whole *mir* − the *obshchina*, which divides
it equally between the members of the *mir*'. Grigor'ev drew attention
to other socialist aspects of the *mir* − the *artel* or collective of workers
who hired themselves out to do jobs; and the social strip of land cultivated by all the able members of the *mir* collectively on behalf of thoe
who were unable to work. 'What is the *artel*, if not an instinctive invention of the Russian mind, which long ago gave socialism its due merit?
What is our charitable social tillage ... again socialism.' Speshnev
emphasised the democratic nature of the *mir* assembly, in which all heads
of households had a vote and wrote a speech beginning, 'Gentlemen!
Our parliament! Our *mir* assembly!' Petrashevskii explained how the
mir protected the peasant from pauperism:

> The greater and more perfect the social development, the more the objects
> of common use, common possession (communist institutions), the cheaper
> the enjoyment of them through clubbing together (*par association*) ...
> Look at your village, at your peasant, in spite of his carelessness not
> reduced to the destitution which should arise from his laziness, seek the
> reason − you will find that it is the repartition of the fields, the common
> use of the lands.[66]

The purpose of the Slavophiles and of Haxthausen (a conservative landowner) had been to demonstrate that socialism and revolution were unnecessary in Russia, since 'the utopia of the European revolutionists
already exists here'. The Petrashevtsy, however, did not idealise the
obshchina. As Petrashevskii's remarks above show, they were aware of
the backwardness, stagnation, ignorance, dirt and degradation of
Russian peasant life. The *obshchina* was for them (as it was to be for
Herzen later) not the end, but just the beginning of the question of
socialism, the point from which the future socialist society would be
launched. As Debu said, the *obshchina* was discussed 'among the
Fourierists' as the basis on which to establish the Fourierist phalanstery.[67] The Petrashevtsy were naturally drawn to the *obshchina*
because of its obvious similarities to the particular form of socialist
society advocated by Fourier, based on small agricultural communes.
They were encouraged in the idea of establishing Fourierism in the
Russian village by Gatti de Gamond's *Fourier et son système*, which
though it does not mention the *obshchina*, argues that 'Poland and
Russia are perhaps the countries in the world the most capable of realising
the *système sociétaire*, immediately and on a large scale ... the abolition

of slavery can be immediately carried out to the profit of the masters and the profit of the slaves by the application of the principles of association.'[68] Their views on the introduction of socialism in Russia were summed up by Petrashevskii, 'I wanted a full and complete reform of social life. I believed in the phalanstery as the key, the touchstone of such a reform.'[69]

The Petrashevtsy did not merely suggest this idea but were determined to act on it. They studied the attempt by contemporary French socialists — especially the Fourierists — to set up socialist communes. Quite a lot of information about this was available in Russia. In 1842, for example, *Otechestvennye zapiski* informed its readers of the Fourierist Arthur Young's purchase of the former Benedictine abbey of Cisteaux, 'in order to found in it a Fourierist phalange'; of the acquisition by another group of Fourierists of a rich estate in Brazil; and of Charles Pellarin's offer to the Fourierists of a large piece of land in Texas.[70] The Petrashevtsy viewed with special enthusiasm the attempts of the Fourierist leader, Considerant, to raise money, either by public subscription or by government loan, to found a phalanstery near Paris. While in prison, Petrashevskii made a will, leaving Considerant a third of his property, 'for the purposes of founding a phalanstery'.[71]

The Petrashevtsy regarded it as their 'mission' to be the first to introduce socialism in Russia,[72] and initiated a number of attempts at founding trial associations. They optimistically hoped that the Tsar would be willing, if not to finance, at least to tolerate, experiments in communal living. Petrashevskii dreamt up a plan for financing a Russian phalanstery by legalising and taxing tobacco smoking in public (at that time forbidden). If a tenth of the 400,000 inhabitants of St. Petersburg smoked three cigars a day as they walked through the streets, he calculated, this would bring in 146,000 silver roubles a year! More seriously, he argued that legally, landowners could carry out socialist experiments on their private estates, without even having to ask the governments permission for this, backing up his point with quotations from the Code of Laws.[73] The few Petrashevtsy who were rich enough to possess land and serfs contemplated setting up phalansteries for their peasants. The majority had to be content with more modest forms of social experiment. Some of the poorer of them, including Dostoevskii, grouped together and founded the first of the city communes which were to become so popular in the sixties. Though the peasant phalansteries either never got off the ground or were disastrous failures, the city communes flourished.

Since they mostly lived in cold, bleak, rented rooms and took their meals alone in taverns and coffee houses, the poorer Petrashevtsy were naturally attracted by the advantages, social as well as material, of communal living and eating. We know of two examples of the communal flat set up by the Petrashevtsy in the 1840s.

For the first, our source is Dostoevskii. It began with a series of co-operative dinners in which the Maikovs, Butkov, Pleshcheev and others took part. Dostoevskii loved these dinners, 'the soul rejoices to see the poor proletarian sit down in good company to eat a good dinner and even drink champagne.' Once he was sent off in search of Butkov, who had stayed at home for lack of the two roubles with which to pay his share and they all chipped in to pay for him. The communal organisation was soon extended to ordinary eating, Dostoevskii explained, 'I take my dinner with a group. Six people who know each other, including Grigorovich and myself have got together at the Beketovs. Each pays fifteen silver kopecks a day and we have two good simple dishes and are quite satisfied.' The next step was communal living: 'We have found a spacious apartment and all the expenses of the rent and upkeep do not exceed 1,200 paper roubles a year for each person. Such are the great benefits of association.' Dostoevskii enjoyed this so much he felt reborn both physically and morally.

There are references to another, earlier experiment in an intriguing letter of Petrashevskii's written in 1844. The letter's recipient, whose identity is unfortunately unknown, appears to have started a similar collective in the provinces, somewhere near Moscow. Petrashevskii writes, 'As it is obvious from your remarks that the advice I gave you on parting about communal living or the establishment of a *menage associé* did not fall on barren soil, I have devoted myself to the matter as if I were a real member of your *association gastronomique* or *de votre menage associé*', and offers to enlist the services of his friend Pavlov to help him buy in bulk from Moscow. Petrashevskii estimates the savings resulting from communal living at a third. To these, he empha-sises, must be added the spiritual benefits, 'the *plaisirs animiques*, such as the mutual exchange of opinions, services and debts, which will give rise amongst you to *harmonie parfaite et unité fraternelle*'.[75] The col-lective principle was also in operation at Pal'm and Durov's evenings – each visitor paid three silver roubles a month towards the dinner and the hire of the piano.[76]

The three Petrashevtsy rich enough to think about setting up phalan-steries for their peasants were Kashkin, Speshnev and Petrashevskii himself. Kashkin planned to ask the government's permission to establish a 'model farm' on his parents' estate in Kaluga province.[77] Speshnev spent a considerable amount of time in Kursk province devoting himself to the improvement of his estate. It was to Speshnev that Pleshcheev gave Beklemishev's essay, *The Advantages of Association in Comparison with 'Morcellisme' in Different Branches of Labour*, an account of the benefits which would result from the transformation of the peasant obshchina into a Fourierist phalanstery.[78] Beklemishev wrote:

> Imagine that *community* exists, that the pitiful, dirty huts of our peasants have disappeared but in one village … that they all, let us say 200 families, live in one building, each having a separate appartment … imagine that an association has been set up, that all the village's land, until now split into hundreds of strips, has been joined together and has become the common possession of the *obshchina* as if of one man.

The peasants would have fresh bread every day, eat meat, make cheese, things that were impossibly expensive for the isolated peasant family. Communal laundries with piped water, drying and ironing rooms would mean that the peasant woman no longer had to go to wash clothes in the cold river, she would no longer bring illness back with her into the household. There would be communal cooking, communal marketing, communal child-care, even central heating. Unfortunately, we do not know whether Speshnev successfully implemented any of these ideas on his estate.

However, there is a story, though its authenticity is questionable, that Petrashevskii did try to set up a phalanstery for his peasants. Semevskii, the early authority on the Petrashevtsy, accepted it; some later Soviet historians, headed by Leikina-Svirskaia, have rejected it.[79] It is true that the only source is Vladimir Zotov, who was not a particularly close friend of Petrashevskii's but I feel that it should not be dismissed entirely; it is difficult to believe that Petrashevskii, the indefatigable agitator, did not try any experiments with his peasants; the outcome is predictable and is symptomatic of the gulf that existed between the early Russian radicals and the people. According to the story, the elder of a village of seven households which was situated in a particularly unpleasant marshy spot, came to Petrashevskii and begged for help in repairing their dilapidated huts. Then Petrashevskii asked:

> Wouldn't it be better for the peasants, if instead of reconstructing their huts in a spot which was known to be unhealthy, they built in the pine forest, on dry ground, one large hut into which all seven families would

move, each with a separate room, but a common kitchen for cooking, a hall for common winter work and gatherings, and outbuildings and barns for domestic utensils, food stores and tools which should be held in common like everything else in the household. The master expounded all the advantages of such community at length, promising of course to build it all at his own expense ... The elder listened, bowed low ... and to all questions, 'Really, won't this be better and more to your advantage?' replied, 'As you wish, you know best, we are ignorant people; what you order, we will do'. The master tried in vain to get from him his own opinion on the convenience of such a community.

Petrashevskii and the peasants built a phalanstery in the forest, and towards winter, everything was ready. But, the night before they were due to move in, the peasants burned the building to the ground and, with it, everything he had bought for them. Zotov says this happened in 1847.[80]

Episodes such as Petrashevskii's attempt to transport the Russian serf into a socialist paradise, or Beklemishev's ideas of introducing central heating into the Russian village, reveal the utopian and naive elements always present in the Petrashevtsy's thinking. However, the Petrashevtsy did make their own country their chief occupation. They made an analysis of the ills besetting Russia which, considering the difficulties of collecting information under Tsarism, was thorough. It was the work of a collective — of a comparatively large group of young men who pooled the fruits of their personal observations and private study. Though the Petrashevtsy, like all Westerners and liberals oppositionists of the time, saw one of the most important needs for Russia to be the guarantee of basic political freedoms — the democratisation of the government, army, administration and legal system, freedom of speech and of the press and the emancipation of the serfs — they went further, in seeing these reforms, and emancipation in particular, as the prelude to the introduction of socialism in Russia. Their interest in and discussion of the peasant commune is especially striking. Their suggestion that the survival of the commune made Russia more suitable ground for establishing socialism than Western Europe, that the evils of pauperism might be avoided in Russia by founding socialist communes on the basis of the peasant *obshchina*, anticipated Herzen and foreshadows the ideas of the later populist movement. They were the first to try to establish socialist associations in Russia. However, in 1848, revolution in Europe ended all hopes of the Russian government tolerating, let alone encouraging socialist experiments under its nose.

VII — PROPAGANDA AND LITERATURE

The Petrashevtsy were determined to spread their ideas as widely as possible. When Timkovskii asked the point of Petrashevskii's meetings, he was told, 'The aim is *the realisation of social reforms* and for this the first and most important means is *propaganda*, which they want to organise on a large scale.' Serebriakov, an unintelligent and uneducated minor civil servant, who blundered into the Fridays, recalled the frequency with which the word 'propaganda' cropped up in conversation, 'I thought to myself, this is some academic term, but it turned out not to be that at all.'[1] The first step was to make socialism known to those most capable of understanding it — the educated section of the Russian public. The main means through which they attempted to do this were entirely legal and consisted of: personal agitation among their friends and acquaintances and the formation of circles; attempts to indoctrinate the younger generation made by those of the Petrashevtsy who taught in secondary schools; and efforts to reach a larger number of people through literature and the journals. These were the easier and more obvious means available to Russian radicals for the propagation of their ideas. In their adoption of them the Petrashevtsy were influenced by other leading radicals, and, especially, by Belinskii.

Personal agitation was the simplest sort of propaganda. Akhsharumov wrote, 'We must begin by spreading our ideas in our circle. We must recruit people of different characters, different walks of life, both men and women.'[2] Petrashevskii devoted himself full-time, obsessively to propaganda, roaming St. Petersburg in quest of recruits to his circle. After him, the most persistent agitators were Ippolit Debu, who converted his brother Konstantin, Akhsharumov, Evropeus and Kashkin to socialism; Khanykov, who was active among the university students and through whose efforts Chernyshevskii, among others, became a socialist; and Shaposhnikov, who made extravagant speeches about socialism to the army officers, cadets, teachers and civil servants who came to buy tobacco and cigarettes from his shop in the Petrogradskaia district. Many of Shaposhnikov's friends were also members of the

Lamartine Club, a left-wing literary society which met on Friday just off Nevskii Prospekt. In Tambov, Kuz'min made lists of his acquaintances and tried to assess their susceptibility to socialist ideas.[3]

The importance of teaching as a way of getting radical ideas across to larger groups of people had been recognised by both Herzen and Belinskii. According to Belinskii, teaching was one of the 'only two means of action' feasible in the Russia of Nicholas I.[4] Petrashevskii placed a particular emphasis on teaching as propaganda and the teachers among the Petrashevtsy were active and influential in converting their pupils to their ideas.

However, it was above all in literature that the Petrashevtsy concentrated their activity. In their attempts to use literature as propaganda, the Petrashevtsy were consciously following the example and precepts of Belinskii. Inspired partly by the Saint-Simonians' ideas on art, Belinskii wrote, that Russian society was 'crushed under a heavy yoke'. Gloom, melancholy and apathy reigned. Only literature, despite the barbarous censorship, showed 'signs of life and forward movement' and offered an outlet for the 'fresh forces' of Russian society, seething and struggling for expression. Because only they had an opportunity to speak out, Russian writers had a responsibility to act as the leaders of society, the champions of the opposition to autocracy.[5] The Petrashevtsy took up Belinskii's ideas on the social role of art, in some cases giving them a more utilitarian form. This led to furious debates on the subject — between Belinskii and Maikov in the pages of *Sovremennik* and *Otechestvennye zapiski*; and between the 'scientists' and 'writers' in Petrashevskii's circle. The Petrashevtsy, and Maikov in particular, also attempted to formulate an anthropological theory of art, as a complement to their anthropological ideas on philosophy and a corrective to what they regarded as Belinskii's unscientific artistic categories.

A large number of Petrashevtsy (as many as forty according to Semevskii) were engaged in literary activity. Some of these, such as Durov and Tolbin, were professional writers; others, such as Saltykov and Pal'm, combined literature and the civil service. They were involved in producing all sorts of different types of radical literature. Their best-known publishing venture was the extraordinarily revolutionary *Pocket Dictionary of Foreign Words*, most of which was written either by Maikov or by Petrashevskii; others of them, and in particular the indomitable Balasoglo, participated in a series of attempts at founding artistic and scientific journals, literary societies etc; and from the years 1845–8 the Petrashevtsy were also the dominant, if not the controlling influence in the radical journal *Finskii vestnik*. In addition to *Finskii vestnik*, they also published articles and stories in a large number of other newspapers and journals of the day. The most prominent writers of fiction among the Petrashevtsy were Dostoevskii, Saltykov, Pleshcheev, Durov, Pal'm and Tolbin. They wrote radical poetry, *ocherki* or sketches of lower class life, and, above all, short stories. The fiction of the Petrashevtsy shows the combined influence of French socialist and native Russian sources − in prose George Sand and Eugène Sue, combined with Gogol; and in poetry Béranger and Auguste Barbier, combined with Lermontov and, to a lesser extent, Pushkin. The Petrashevtsy-writers sought to integrate the socialist tone of the French writers into the Russian literary tradition.

Propaganda in schools

The teachers among the Petrashevtsy − Jastrzębski, Tol', Petr Beletskii, L'vov, Miliukov, Maderski, Mikhailov, Vvedenskii, Vladimir Kuznetsov, M. Ia. Morozov and others − were among the first to attempt consciously to influence their pupils in a radical direction. In addition, Petrashevskii attached a great deal of importance to instilling socialist ideas into the heads of the younger generation.

Petrashevskii tried to secure influence at his old school, the Lycée. Though the most select educational institution of the Empire, the Lycée had a history of radicalism − it had produced Pushkin and many of the Decembrists, as well as a large number of the Petrashevtsy. In 1844 Petrashevskii began to visit the Lycée regularly. His application for a job as law teacher there was turned down on the grounds that, 'He wanted to be a teacher purely with the aim of spreading liberal ideas among young people.' In spite of this Petrashevskii managed to make his influence felt. In September 1844 the Lycée authorities discovered that three pupils, Aleksei Unkovskii, Vladimir Konstantinov and Aleksander Burtysk, aged between fourteen and sixteen, had been secretly visiting him. On examination, they were found to have been, 'enticed into this acquaintance by the vain fascination of the new ideas with which Petrashevskii attracted their minds ... The influence of this acquaintance on them was displayed in a sceptical attitude towards matters of religion and the present social system.'[6] Unkovskii was expelled but retained his connection with Petrashevskii and his socialist convictions. In a letter written in 1845 (tongue-in-cheek for the censor's benefit) Ivan Pavlov,

a friend of Petrashevskii's, expelled from the Lycée in 1842, describes
a visit Unkovskii, full of (in this case misplaced) revolutionary fervour,
paid to him in Moscow:

> He — (in a pathetic tone) — Ivan Vasilevich!
> I — What?
> He — (still more pathetically) — Take me into your brotherhood.
> I — (goggling) — What brotherhood?
> He — Don't try to hide it. I know everything. Your activity,
> your influence, your mode of thought. I have already heard of
> you in Petersburg from Petrashevskii.[7]

After the failure of his application to the Lycée, Petrashevskii began
to encourage other members of the circle, including Tolstov and the spy
Antonelli, to get teaching jobs in schools, in order to disseminate 'human
ideas' there.[8]

The most politically active teachers among the Petrashevtsy were
Jastrzębski, Beletskii, Tol', L'vov, Miliukov and Vvedenskii, who
though not actually a member of Petrashevskii's circle was very close
to it. Their efforts at enlightened teaching were bedevilled by the official
programmes, which laid down exactly what had to be taught in each
lesson and which textbooks should be used (the programme composed
by General Rostovtsev for military educational institutions, at which
most of the Petrashevtsy taught, was particularly rigid). There was also
the problem of the examinations, which were oral, and at which pupils
were liable to blurt out any radical ideas they had been taught and give
their teachers away. In spite of this Jastrzębski, Beletskii, Tol' and
Vvedenskii in particular, managed consistently to introduce radical concepts into their lessons. The nature and success of their teaching is
described in memoirs left by their former pupils.

The Petrashevets who had the most profound influence on his pupils
was Jastrzębski, who taught political economy and statistics in the
Nobles' Regiment, the Technical Institute and the Institute of the Corps
of Communications Engineers. While carrying out the official programme conscientiously, he managed to make his teaching subtly
subversive. One of his pupils, Mikhail Veniukov, recalls:

> He knew how to use this course magnificently, to arouse in us ... a deep
> dissatisfaction with a social order in which the poor and weak were com-
> pletely sacrificed to the strong and rich. He did this so skilfully that at
> the examinations, in the presence of the authorities, not one of us would
> speak out against the principles of the orthodox Smith—Say school, but
> in the depths of our souls, we suffered from the consciousness of the
> injustice of these principles.

In his lessons, he outlined the theories of the classical economists, not forgetting to praise them, and the theories of 'Babeuf ... Rousseau, Saint-Simon, Fourier and Louis Blanc', not forgetting to denounce them as 'harmful', but merely by the lavish use of irony and the hint here and there, steering his pupils towards his own preference for the latter. Veniukov compares the radical influence of Jastrzębski in the Noble's Regiment with that which Herzen's story *The Notes of Dr. Krupov* was producing on Russian society at the time.[9]

Beletskii tried to apply similar methods in teaching history to the pupils of the First and Second Army Cadet Corps. He boasted that he had a class who, at their exams would advocate the 'nonsensical principles' of Rostovtsev's programme, but who in reality subscribed to socialist convictions and that, 'from this class will come people who will move Russia forward'. Beletskii's example, however, shows the pitfalls inherent in radical teaching. Beletskii was arrogant and quarrelsome by nature and did not possess Jastrzębski's dexterity in teaching, while apparently not teaching, socialist ideas. He was encouraged by the indulgent attitude of his headmaster Orest Likhonin, who attended his classes and condoned his methods and he went a little too far. Matters came to a head over his remarks about religion, which sparked off a feud with the Scripture teacher, Deacon Nadein. In one of Nadein's classes, an eleven year old named Elagin had suddenly asked him, 'Is it true sir that Abraham did not exist?' The astonished Nadein interrogated the boys and discovered that Beletskii had told them that Abraham was merely 'a myth representing the pastoral way of life of the ancient Jews'. Beletskii was only saved from serious trouble and the loss of his job by the protection of Likhonin and the loyalty of his pupils, who, like Jastrzębski's did not betray their teacher when it came to the examinations.[10]

Tol' taught history at the school of the Military Cantonists (for conscripted Jewish boys) and Russian literature at the Chief Engineering School. He was bitterly critical of Rostovtsev's programme and lamented the fact that, 'This book is probably also translated into foreign languages and Rostovtsev will not only be put to shame all over the world, but it will probably be recorded in history that there was once such a pig in Russia.' He campaigned to get his history syllabus narrowed, which he told his friends would enable him to, 'teach history of course from the most orthodox books ... but relate it in accordance with the plans of our society.'[11]

Vvedenskii, though he stuck to his own circle, was considered by many to be 'a soul-mate of Petrashevskii's'. As well as translating Dickens, he was one of the most enlightened teachers of literature of the forties (like Jastrzębski, he taught in the Noble's Regiment). He managed to expand a paragraph in the programme into a series of lectures on the *encyclopédistes*:

> He officially called Voltaire, Diderot, D'Alembert, Rousseau, Helvétius, Holbach etc. 'destroyers' as Smaragdov (the official textbook) did, but *privatim*, their destructive theories were expounded so that it was clear that they were restorers of human rights, people who were ... only put in the Bastille by worthless men like Louis XV.

Veniukov recalls how the pupils went away from Vvedenskii's lessons to read Rousseau and Voltaire; A.M. Miklashevskii how Vvedenskii inspired them to compose a radical literary journal.[12]

Other teachers among the Petrashevtsy did not have a consistent plan and restricted their radicalism to the odd remark. L'vov explained how he introduced politics into his chemistry lessons. For example, one day in 1848, when he had been burning phosphorous and his pupils noticed that after the blinding light which it gave out, the light from the lamp in the room seemed dark, he noted that, 'We only understood the whole brightness of light when we are deprived of it' and added, 'For example, there's a rumour that they're going to close the universities; if you don't learn now, you'll be sorry later.' In a similar way, Miliukov, a teacher of literature and author of *A Sketch of the History of Russian Poetry*, a satirical book in the style of Belinskii, had cured his pupils of the habit of running out of the classroom to kiss the hands of passing priests by telling them that this was one of the favourite tricks of Chichikov, the anti-hero of Gogol's *Dead Souls*.[13]

The theory of Art – Art as propaganda

In the twenties and thirties, the dominant currents in Russian literature had ben classicism and romanticism. In the forties, under the aegis of Belinskii, realism replaced it. Classicism and romanticism were attacked as exaggerated and unnatural, depicting only one side of life – the great, elevated and exciting. The writer's task was seen, by the new 'natural school', to show life as it was, its bad and disgusting as well as its good and beautiful sides, and to adopt a critical attitude to what he depicted. Art thus acquired a social purpose. Almost all the leading writers and critics of the decade were adherents to this theory — Herzen, Nekrasov, Turgenev, Aleksandr Druzhinin, Vladimir Dal', Dostoevskii, Maikov, Saltykov, even, to some extent, Vladimir Sollugub, Vladimir Odoevskii and Apollon Maikov. The ideas of the natural school were attacked by the government camp, which denounced them as subversive, and the Slavophiles, who clung to romanticism, but neither of these groups produced any notable artistic works. The break-up of the natural school into supporters of the more utilitarian theories subsequently associated with Chernyshevskii and advocates of a purer art took place later, in the context of Belinskii's death and the political reaction after 1848 and accompanied a growing rift between radicals and liberals at this time.

In the 1840s, all the Petrashevtsy subscribed to the natural school theories. Within the natural school, they stood very close to Belinskii. Not too much importance should therefore be attributed to the often furious debates on literary questions between Maikov and Belinskii and between different members of the Petrashevskii circle. They all belonged to the same literary camp. The arguments were about different interpretations and developments of generally accepted ideas.

Differences between Maikov and Belinskii over the nature of art stemmed from Maikov's greater degree of interest in utopian socialism (in particular the anthropological ideas of Fourier and Feuerbach) and from his insistence on explaining everything scientifically. In 1847, Maikov, aged twenty-three, began his career as chief critic of *Otechestvennye zapiski* with an attack on the criteria for literary criticism established by Belinskii, arguing (with some justification) that Belinskii's categories, talent, extraordinary talent, talent of genius, genius etc., were subjective and arbitary and therefore inadequate. Maikov took upon himself the task of developing Belinskii's theory and giving the ideas of the natural school 'a scientific foundation'. Maikov's criticisms of Belinskii were shared by other Petrashevtsy, including Dostoevskii, and his theory of art found general acceptance among them.[14] It also seems to have a considerable influence on the development of Chernyshevskii's artistic theories.[15]

Maikov's theory was an original attempt to apply the ideas of anthropological materialism and utopian socialism to art, to work out an explanation of art that both justified the natural school and fitted in with the philosophy of the Petrashevtsy. In his writings, Maikov was influenced to some extent by the Saint—Simonians and more so by Feuerbach (like theirs his was a sensualist theory) but the theory as he developed it was new. He took as his starting point one of Feuerbach's central philosophical principles, 'Each of us understands and explains to himself everything solely in comparison with himself.'[16] From this Maikov deduced the *Law of Human Sympathy*. According to this, art was the process of humanising the object depicted, of making it accessible (or sympathetic) to the feelings of all men. He wrote, 'The secret of creativity consists in the ability to portray reality faithfully from its sympathetic side', or in other words, 'Artistic creativity is a reworking of reality carried out without changing its forms but by bringing them into the world of human interests'. This process took place through the application not of the artist's reason but of his feelings to the object depicted, through his feeling of either 'living love' or 'repulsion' for it. Only if the artist managed to achieve a feeling of identity with the object and depict in his portrayal of it what it had in common with man, would art become human, something that other people could identify with and feel with. Art, as Chernyshevskii later wrote, had 'purely human aims ... *similis simili gaudet*'.[17]

Transformed by the artist's eye, not only objects of the human world, but also of nature, could appeal to man's feelings. This was because of the fundamental identity of man and nature, one of the Petrashevtsy's basic philosophical ideas. As a result of this identity, man sympathised with nature and recognised his own moods and emotions in it. He instinctively understands a storm, for example, Maikov wrote in the *Pocket Dictionary*:

> For in the human soul there is a completely corresponding phenomenon. We call storms in nature a desperate struggle of the elements amongst themselves; here is resistance and triumph and defeat, phenomena with which we are completely familiar with from our own experience.

A similar explanation of man's interest in seascape was put forward by Tolbin in *Finskii vestnik*:

> The noise, movement and even the calm of the sea are enchanting, but only in relation to man; the sea charms us only because it can inspire the rational being with a multitude of ideas of every sort, solemn and gloomy and great, and can open up his soul to every sort of impression, both sad and joyful.[18]

Maikov made this theory into a justification of the natural school in literature (and genre-painting in art) by insisting that whatever the subject of art, nature or man, it would mean nothing to other men, unless the original appeal of the object to the feelings had been faithfully translated by the artist, i.e. unless it had been depicted realistically. The task of the artist and writer was to remain close to the real world, to depict life as it was and accord equal value to all aspects of reality. As Chernyshevskii was to say, 'The sphere of art ... embraces everything that in reality (in nature and life) interests man'. The artist thus had a right, indeed a duty, to include the ugly as well as the beautiful sides of life.[19]

This theory of naturalism was developed logically by Maikov into an explanation of the social role of art. By depicting his feelings about the objects he portrayed — his instinctive revulsion from the evil and attraction to the good in them — the artist automatically became a social critic.

Maikov and other Petrashevtsy laid great emphasis on depicting the bad sides of life. The artist's task was a Fourierist one — by depicting ugliness and evil in their surroundings, to show that in all cases society, not men, was to blame, and induce the reader or viewer to pity its victims. If, for example, Miliukov argued, one were to rewrite Aleksandr Griboedov's comedy *Woe from Wit*, today, one would not pour scorn on the scoundrel Molchalin as Griboedov did, but 'try to indicate why this man has reached such debasement. Perhaps he was reduced to it by need, by circumstances from which he had no escape' and to make the audience 'pity him from their soul'.[20] By depicting both his revulsion from evil and the social causes of it, the writer was effectively calling for social change.

However, it was also necessary for the author to depict his attraction to the good aspects of life. Here, their utopian socialism led the Petrashevtsy to differ from Belinskii, who had limited the task of the natural school to criticising reality, while admitting that this 'purely negative tendency' was a one-sided extreme.[21] The Petrashevtsy's insistence on the need to depict the good side as well as the bad, to make literature optimistic, was a natural result of a belief in the eventual triumph of socialism. Maikov argued, 'the creation of an ideal alone can give sense and firmness to analysis and negation'; *Finskii vestnik* called for a poet who, 'has a firm faith in the coming future ... for whom the dream of a bright future full of life is real and brightens up the semi-darkness of the present'. The ideal to which they pointed in literature was the socialist ideal of the natural, healthy man, the man who has fully developed his potential, who finds happiness and satisfaction in love and work. They ridiculed the ideal heroes of the romantics — pale and puny with sunken chests. The best example of the socialist ideal of 'passion and labour in their natural equilibrium', Maikov believed, was found in the verses of the peasant poet Aleksei Kol'tsov. His poetry was, 'a direct summons to the full enjoyment of that life, the simple laws of which contemporary wisdom strives to define by the paths of criticism and utopia'.[22]

The basic idea of the social purpose of art was accepted by Maikov and by all the Petrashevtsy. Their favourite French authors were those who deliberately modelled their writings according to the Saint-Simonian theory of art, and in particular, George Sand. The Petrashevtsy, like Belinskii, agreed that the reproduction of reality was not art, unless it was guided by an idea. In attacks on the Russian adherents of pure art, especially the reactionary Bulgarin, the Petrashevtsy frequently reiterated this principle. Tolbin, for example, asked 'What is art, if it doesn't express an idea? It isn't art at all.' By idea, the Petrashevtsy made it clear they meant social purpose. To distinguish themselves clearly from the champions of pure art, they adopted the term *tendency* or *contemporary tendency* to designate art with a political or socialist aim. Maikov demanded from literature, 'before all else, a contemporary tendency'. Works which had no relation to society or humanity, the *Pocket Dictionary* dogmatically asserted, 'are not today accepted as literary'.[23]

But, although there was a basic consensus that art should have a social aim, there was disagreement over the relative importance of social and aesthetic considerations. Belinskii and the Petrashevtsy-writers, especially Dostoevskii, Durov and Pal'm, considered literary merit on the whole more important than social content. Maikov, Petrashevskii, Balasoglo and other 'men of science' in Petrashevskii's circle, who did not write fiction themselves, were, on the other hand, inclined to judge literature purely according to its use as propaganda.

These divisions were not completely clear-cut. Belinskii at times stated that a books' propagandistic value was more important than its artistic merit.[24] However, contemporaries regarded Maikov's attitude to art as more didactic than Belinskii's. According to Annenkov, 'Maikov put aside the whole aesthetic, moral and polemical baggage of Belinskii and for a criterion of judging works of art took the number and importance of the human and social questions raised by them and the methods by which the author points them out and solves them.'[25]

This was an exaggeration — Maikov did draw a line between the artistic idea, inspired by feeling, and the didactic idea, which arose from reason[26] — but it was true as a whole. The difference between Maikov and Belinskii was clearly brought out by their discussion of *belles lettres*, a term used for light literature (poetry, essays, criticism, short stories) which often had a didactic as well as an artistic element. Belinskii argued that the artistic content of *belles lettres* was more important than their didactic content; Maikov believed, 'The idea should attract the attention-of the critic more than all the other elements'. Belinskii drew a sharp distinction between artistic and scientific forms and regarded the *belle lettrist* as obliged to use the former; Maikov, however, thought that the *belle lettrist* should employ a mixture of the two. By uniting art and science they would do a two-fold service — to art, by giving it the logical foundation it so badly needed; and to science, by bringing it into closer connection with life. He was sure that artistic literature would be improved by 'its invasion by works of a chiefly didactic nature'. The difference was brought out in their attitude to Herzen's didactic stories. Maikov praised him for uniting science and life; Belinskii accused him of being too philosophical and said that this detracted from the general value of his works.[27]

The same questions were debated much less politely at Petrashevskii's. Petrashevskii like Maikov, favoured a union of art and science, even suggesting the formation of a club where scientists and writers could wine, dine and exchange ideas. If anything more so than Maikov, his idea was that literature should serve political ends. He called for writers to express, 'the ideas dear to them', explaining that by this he meant, 'the system of Fourier'. His position was accepted by many of the more scientific members of his circle, especially Balasoglo, but writers such as Durov, Dostoevskii and Pal'm, while accepting the social function of literature, felt that he went too far. The argument broke out over a discussion of the works of the fabulist Ivan Krylov. Petrashevskii claimed that Krylov, whose simple fables lacked a socialist tone, was not a great artist and that he could in no way be compared to Gogol. Durov retorted that Krylov was a genius and a truly popular writer. Durov said that Petrashevskii was incapable of understanding art; Pal'm called him 'a dry man without a heart'. Pal'm later admitted that he and Durov carried their remarks to 'unjustified extremes'. At the next Friday (23 April 1849), the 'scientists' got their own back. Petrashevskii made a speech about, 'How writers should act in order to be sure of having an effect on the public', in which he launched into a diatribe against the writers in his circle, and especially Fedor and Mikhail Dostoevskii, for failing to make a proper study of science (i.e. socialism) and for not stating socialist principles clearly enough in their stories. After supper, Balasoglo, 'touched to the quick' by Petrashevskii's speech, rushed into the fray 'and really laid into the poor, unfortunate writers! He said that they were trivial men without any education who idled their time away but were as puffed up with pride as any cock!' He accused Dostoevskii and Durov (quite unfairly) of not having read, 'one decent book' – neither Fourier, nor Proudhon nor even Helvétius'.[28] Dostoevskii retorted that art had no need of a tendency, 'The author only has to worry about the artistic aspect and the idea will come out by itself.' Some commentators have seen this as a relapse into the theory of art for art's sake. However, Dostoevskii's stories themselves show that this is not true. He was merely defending his own, indirect, psychological method of protest in literature and reacting, quite understandably, against being told what to do by Petrashevskii.[29]

The two sides also disagreed in their opinions of the relative merits of the leading socialist novelists of the day, George Sand and Eugène Sue. Both of these writers used their novels to preach socialist ideas, the difference was a question of nuance. Sand's socialism took the form of lofty ideals, Sue preached his much more openly and brashly. All the Petrashevtsy, like almost all Russian radicals of the day, were great admirers of George Sand. However, while Maikov, Petrashevskii and the 'men of science' placed Sue on the same exalted level as Sand, Belinskii and the Petrashevtsy-writers found the level of didacticism in Sue unacceptable and argued that his novels were inferior to Sand's. For example, when Petrashevskii bracketed Sand and Sue together as great socialist writers and pointed to their novels as an illustration of how writers should use literature to 'instil one's ideas into the public', Durov retorted that he did not see how he could possibly place Sue on the same level as Sand, since 'the former is not worth a finger of the latter'.[30]

In spite of all this, there was no disagreement between Belinskii and Maikov, Petrashevskii, Balasoglo, Durov, Pal'm, Dostoevskii and other Petrashevtsy on the fundamental question – that art should be the expression of a social idea. It was only over the method by which this social idea should be expressed that they argued. Dostoevskii himself admitted this at his trial, 'In the end it turned out that Petrashevskii and I had the same ideas about literature but that we misunderstood one another', partly, 'as a result of pride.'[31]

Publishing ventures

The main outlet for the literary and propagandistic activities of the Petrashevtsy was the journal. They wrote for a large number of publications – as well as the three main radical journals of the day, *Finskii vestnik, Otechestvennye zapiski* and *Sovremennik*, for *Illiustratsiia*, (edited by Petrashevskii's friend Zotov), *Repertuar i panteon, Moskovskoi gorodskoi Listok, Literaturnaia gazeta, Biblioteka dlia chteniia, Sanktpeterburgskie vedomosti* and Katenev and Grigorii Danilevskii even, rather surprisingly, published their stories in *Vedomosti Sanktpeterburgskoi politsii*, the police gazette. They also embarked on a number of publishing ventures of their own. These included the two parts of the *Pocket Dictionary of Foreign Words* (1845–6) which (especially the second), openly preached socialism and formed the most radical piece of literature published in Russia in the 1840s; a remarkable number of scientific and literary projects of Balasoglo's; and an attempt to take over the journal *Finskii vestnik*, which though it never rivalled *Otechestvennye zapiski* or *Sovremennik* in circulation, became under their influence often more radical than either.

The Pocket Dictionary of Foreign Words Introduced into the Russian Language, (its full title) was edited by Nikolai Kirillov, a Staff Captain in the Guards' Artillery, who also taught in the Pavlovsk Cadet Corps and acted as Secretary of the charitable *Society for Visiting the Poor*. He was a timid figure, easily dominated by his two chief contributors, Maikov and Petrashevskii. The *Pocket Dictionary* was first advertised in December 1844 as, 'nothing less than a short encyclopedia of the arts and sciences or, more exactly, a short encyclopedia of concepts introduced to us by European scholarship'. It was to include an explanation of four thousand different terms. The chief inspiration for it appears to have been Pierre Leroux and Jean Reynaud's radical *Encyclopédie nouvelle*.[32]

The first instalment, *A–Mar*, appeared in 1845. Its content was largely determined by Maikov, a great admirer of Leroux's encyclopedia. He had already been sacked from a job on the *Encyclopedic Dictionary* of Karl Krai, because, the editors said, his notes, 'were composed in the spirit of Leroux, whose dictionary we could not be and did not want to be guided by'. Maikov believed that dictionaries should be used 'as a means for the spreading of new views and the destruction of the old'.[33] In the *Pocket Dictionary* he made his general theme the critical appraisal of canonised authorities, the need to attack idealism, the

demand for the analytic as opposed to the synthetic method. Though
what he wrote was radical in tone, he confined himself mainly to
questions of philosophy and aesthetics (entries for, *Analysis and Synthesis, Idealism, Materialism, Critic, Landscape Painting, Literature
etc.*) The other chief contributors to the first part were Shtrandman, and
Petrashevskii (who wrote some of the more political articles, *Aristocracy,
Anarchy, Constitution etc.*) Minor contributors included Ivan Maslov,
a friend of Belinskii and Nekrasov's, and Dmitrii Kropotov, whom
Petrashevskii recruited to his Fridays (author of *Labyrinth, Lexicon,
Oasis, Obelisk* and others). Kirillov insisted on 'simplicity and clear
language, without inappropriate erudition'. The dictionary was a great
success and was greeted with enthusiasm by Belinskii.[34] However, after
the publication of the first part, there appears to have been some sort
of crisis. According to Kropotov, Kirillov was let down by one contribu-
tor, who wrote 500 or 600 entries, in three days, all far too short and
completely incomprehensible.[35] Maikov dropped out – his excuse was
that he had just started work on *Finskii vestnik*, but he had also just
quarreled with Petrashevskii. The second instalment, Mar–Ord, (published in April 1846), was almost entirely written by Petrashevskii. It
was much more radical than the first part and bore a closer resemblance
to the socialist tract than a dictionary. The short factual articles which
had taken up a lot of space in the first part were omitted and replaced
by a series of long articles (the first part had 176 pages and 1,424 entries;
the second 148 pages and 364 entries). Engel'son later explained how
Petrashevskii won Kirillov's favour by offering to work for a very small
salary:

> The literary entrepreneur, delighted by this advantageous proposition, left
> the choice of words to be interpreted to Petrashevskii. The latter eagerly
> seized the opportunity to propagate his ideas through a book which looked
> completely innocent: he enlarged its scope, mixed proper names with the
> common nouns, introduced into the Russian language on his own initiative
> foreign words not used in it before; all this in order to expound under
> various headings the principles of socialist theories.[36]

The result is the best extant summary of the ideas of Petrashevskii and
his circle. It contains four main types of material. First, philosophical
articles advocating atheism and anthropological materialism, some of
which (for example *Naturalism*) are direct expositions of Feuerbach.
Secondly, explanations of socialist theories, including Fourierist ideas
on human nature (*Natural Condition*); the Saint-Simonian theory of

history (*Organic Epoch*); the principle of association (*Owenism*), and Fourier's and Proudhon's ideas on economics (*Organisation of Production*). Thirdly, articles advocating revolution, the most important of which, *National Assembly*, enumerates the fundamental articles of the French revolutionary constitution of 1789.[37] And, fourthly, a 'virulent critique' of the state of Russia — serfdom was attacked in *Negro* and *Negrophile* and criticism of other aspects of the Tsarist system smuggled past the censor by the lavish use of irony, (for example, the discussion of Captain Kopeikin in *Knightly Order*). To make sure his readers understood, Petrashevskii had explained *Irony* in the first part of the dictionary, citing Machievelli's *Prince*. As Liprandi said, Petrashevskii used 'the most perfidious praise of Russia' to 'hide his meaning'.[38] Petrashevskii also used the dictionary to recommend certain key socialist works to the interested reader, including Proudhon's *Qu'est-ce que la propriété?*, Fourier's *Le Nouveau monde*, and *La Fausse industrie* and Villegardelle's *Histoire des ideés sociales*, and quoted openly from Béranger.[39]

Petrashevskii managed to get this anthology of socialist propaganda past the rather dimwitted censor, Aleksandr Krylov, by systematically confusing him.[40] He had gone too far however, and a month after the dictionary's publication (14 March 1846), Mikhail Musin-Pushkin's Chief Censorship Committee caught up with it, dismissed Krylov and ordered all copies to be confiscated from the bookshops and printers and burnt. Only 400 out of 2,000 survived. The first part, however, was sold freely until April 1849 when the Buturlin Committee examined it and ordered it to be withdrawn from sale as 'extremely dangerous'. By December 1852 1,236 copies had been burnt.[41] In spite of all the authorities' efforts, however, the dictionary was widely read and known to radicals of the day — the first part was easy to get hold of, the second was passed from hand to hand. Both parts were found in Nekrasov's library; Herzen took it with him to Paris where he introduced it to Bakunin; Bervi-Flerovskii and all his friends knew it well. A Czech *Dictionary of Foreign Words* was published by F. M. Klaçel in 1849 in imitation of it. Its popularity and scarcity forced the price of the first part up from one rouble in 1845 to ten in the 1850s.[42] It remained the most radical piece of literature to be published for many years, and its appearance in the Russia of Nicholas I was, as Engel'son said, 'a surprising fact' and on the Petrashevtsy's part, a notable achievement.

Balasoglo, who, through the painful process of his own self-education, had learned the inadequacy of existing textbooks, devoted himself to popularising the arts and sciences[43] and dreamed up an extraordinary number of projects – for artistic journals, literary societies, a reclassification of the sciences, textbooks – some of which were partly successful, others which never saw the light of day.

In his unfinished composition, *An Exposition of the Sciences*, begun in 1848, a half-autobiographical, half-scientific treatise, Balasoglo tells the story of his own struggle, as 'a simple soul' who 'must and wants and thirsts to know the world just as it is', to educate himself, his constant hopes and disappointments. He recounts his progressive disillusionment with existing artistic and scientific works, from Gibbon to Leroux's *Encyclopédie nouvelle*, which, he discovers, are written not for an ordinary man like him, but for specialists who know everything already. He feels excluded and rejected in the world of knowledge, just as he did when all the belles refused to dance with him, the one time he ever went to a ball:

> And all the soul could do was to go from room to room and watch others enjoying themselves, not understanding anything … the soul … cursing to itself every member of this strange inaccessible and incomprehensible crowd, rushed from the ball to his quiet garret, never again to look upon a similar gathering.[44]

On leaving the navy in 1838, Balasoglo embarked on an attempt to remedy this situation. He began by publishing, together with his friend Petr Nor'ev, a young architect, an anthology of rather bad poetry, *The Poems of Veronov* (many of them about his search for knowledge).[45] Then, in 1839, the two of them started work on the *Pamiatnik iskusstv*, which they intended to be, 'a contemporary encyclopedia of the arts' published in serial form. However, their efforts were frustrated by their commercially-minded publisher, Mr. Fisher, who paid them miserable wages and censored their material, and in 1841 they walked out, having wasted, Balasoglo said, some of 'the best years of our lives in vain'.[46]

Balasoglo's next project (1844 or 1845) was for a literary society which would try to make it easier for writers to get their books published and for the public to read them. Its members would be capitalists, scholars and writers, who would collect money and use it to set up a bookshop, which would sell the books of any author who brought them, at the price the author wanted; attached to it, a library, started by levying ten copies from each author who sold in the shop; and a printshop, which would print the works of any author for a certain fee and others, selected by the society's committee, free of charge. Balasoglo read this project out at Petrashevskii's and hunted fruitlessly, for capitalists to finance it.[47]

Undaunted by his failure, he embarked on a new venture, the *Listok Isskustv*. This was to be a cheap, but high quality serial publication covering all aspects of art: painting, sculpture, architecture and interior decorating, music, literature and theatre, the application of art to the sciences; and designed to make them easily accessible to the public. Balasoglo declared, 'This will be a real service to art!' He cajoled Vladimir Akhsharumov into giving him a thousand roubles to finance it and planned to set up a printing press in a house another Petrashevets, Kuz'min, was intending to buy, to make the publication completely independent. It began to come out in 1846 and included contributions from Pal'm, Durov, Apollon Maikov and other Petrashevtsy, but later got into trouble with the censor and was never completed.[48]

After this, Balasoglo began work on *An Exposition of the Sciences*. He intended to conclude his survey of the inadequacy of existing works with a call for the reclassification of the sciences (according to a system all of his own) and the publication of a collection of simple textbooks on all subjects, 'linked organically by a single universal human logic'. He had already decided which of his friends among the Petrashevtsy were to write which of these books, when he was thwarted again, this time by his arrest.[49] The only popular textbook he managed to get published was his *The Letter E, a Guide to its Use in Writing*, which was based on the theory that, 'One can only speak and write correctly, when one has become familiar with the whole natural science of the language, which develops endlessly, like a forest of pines, oaks and cedars, from a few original roots, or rather, seeds!'[50]

The Petrashevtsy recognised that the most important means available in the 1840s for the communication of ideas was the journal. As well as writing extensively for established journals, it was their constant preoccupation to get their hands on one of their own.[51] As early as 1841 Petrashevskii planned a journal, which was to be 'Russian, for Russians and then for Europe' and invited a number of students from the Lycée to take part in it, including Vladimir Stepanov, who was expelled, and the seventeen-year-old Saltykov, who got low marks in the final examination as a result of this.[52]

The journal a number of Petrashevtsy were deeply involved in and attempted to take over, was *Finskii vestnik*. Fedor Dershau, a minor writer sympathetic to the Petrashevtsy, persuaded the government to allow him to publish a journal by saying that its purpose would be to acquaint the Russian public with the culture of Scandinavia and (more interesting from the government's point of view) 'to spread the Russian language in Finland.'[53] The journal's real aims were quite different. They were outlined by Maikov in the first issue, which appeared in 1845. Here he announced that the journal was going to take a political stance and had no intention of 'preaching neutrality in the battle of opinions'. Its priority was not the study of Scandinavian but of Russian life, 'We have reached the age of self-consciousness; we are beginning to turn to the critical study of ourselves'; its secondary aim, 'the critical study of all elements of (Western) civilisation'. Maikov's article on the social sciences, published in the first issue, was intended as the first step in this.[54]

Maikov left after the first issue, but in spite of this, *Finskii vestnik* stuck very closely to his programme for the three years 1845–8. Most of the contributors were political radicals and many Petrashevtsy were involved in it, including Pal'm, Durov and Tolbin, who wrote sketches, stories and poems for it; Miliukov, its chief literary critic at the end of 1846 and beginning of 1847; one of the Petrashevtsy, probably Jastrzębski, was the author of its economic articles, the most left-wing to get past the censor in the 1840s; Golovinskii probably wrote its reviews of legal literature; and Mombelli was listed in the index as the author of an article, *Asian Cholera*, though this never appeared. Even Belinskii was involved – he and Nekrasov stepped in and edited the second issue in 1845 after Maikov's departure.[55] Between them, they made the journal the most radical of any in the 1840s. The more right-wing Vasilii Grigor'ev, who eventually took over *Finskii vestnik* remarked in disgust that 'The majority of the writers are impossibly infected with the Western (and in 1848 this meant socialist) spirit.'[56] The journal's importance and radicalism has been overlooked because of its brief and stormy history. After Maikov and Belinskii, there was a succession of chief editors, whose views often clashed with those of the radical contributors. For most of the journal's life, the radicals managed to keep the upper hand, and edged out editors they regarded as too right-wing – including Al'bert Starchevskii (editor of Nos. 3–6, second half of 1845) and Apollon Grigor'ev, (Nos. 7–9, first half of 1846). A full-scale battle for control of *Finskii vestnik* broke out after the appointment as editors of Grigor'ev and Pavel Savel'er who though they had some sympathies with socialism, wanted to introduce a 'religious-patriotic spirit' into the journal. Dershau fell ill and Grigor'ev and Petrashevskii competed to buy the journal from him. Dershau seems to have favoured Petrashevskii – he invited him and all his friends to a party for contributors on New Year's Eve 1848, but the deal fell through, 'for financial reasons' and ownership of *Finskii vestnik* passed to Grigor'ev. He had little joy of it. The transaction was only completed at the end of 1848, by which time the February revolution in France, which 'made it impossible to print anything',[57] had virtually killed off the journal. After changing hands several times more and changing its name to *Severnoe obozrenie*, it finally folded up at the beginning of 1850.

The literature of the Petrashevtsy

Given the exaggerated importance of literature in Russian conditions, it was natural that many of the Petrashevtsy should have literary ambitions. Less to be expected was that two great writers, one outstanding poet and a number of good minor writers should emerge from the midst of these impoverished gentry, petty civil servants etc. The quality of the young men attracted to the Petrashevtsy is evidence of the importance that the socialist movement was already assuming in Russia. The literary merit of Dostoevskii's and Saltykov's first stories, published in the 1840s, was immediately acclaimed by the critics, who placed them among the leading writers of the day — Turgenev, Herzen, Goncharov, if not Gogol. Pleshcheev's poetic talent also gained instant recognition.

The writers among the Petrashevtsy were concerned above all with producing good literature. Though their stories have a socialist tone they are first literature and, a long way second, propaganda. Pleshcheev's revolutionary poems, Durov and Tolbin's sketches of lower class life, and to a certain extent Saltykov's stories — have an obvious propaganda content. But most of their writings, and in particular their short stories, are far less didactic than those of George Sand or Eugène Sue. The need for socialism is only hinted at indirectly. Both the exigencies of literature and of the censorship, the Petrashevtsy writers felt, justified this (Saltykov was, after all, banished to Viatka for his too openly socialist story, *A Tangled Affair*). It was this indirect nature of their socialist propaganda that infuriated the cruder and more philistine Petrashevskii.

Poetry and sketches of Russian life were the literary forms in which the Petrashevtsy expressed their socialist convictions most openly. In contrast to the 1830s when the poetry of Pushkin and Lermontov had dominated the artistic scene, in the 1840s poetry was generally frowned upon in radical circles because it was not as easy to give it a 'tendency' as it was prose. Belinskii, Petrashevskii and even Saltykov agreed that the disappearance of the poem was a 'sign of the maturity of Russian literature'.[58] As a result, to be acceptable, poetry had to have a more markedly socialist tone than the short story. As Maikov wrote, 'Verses to country girls and the moon have gone for ever. Another epoch has dawned.'[59] The Petrashevtsy's chief poetical model was Béranger, with his gay, popular, political songs (*goguettes*) in which he praised Saint-Simon and Fourier, attacked tyrants and kings. The Petrashevtsy-poets were also heavily influenced by Russian poetry, by Pushkin and, above all, by Lermontov. They reiterated Lermontov's feelings of torment and bitter dissatisfaction with the world, attempting to give them a socialist interpretation.[60]

Pleshcheev, one of the most revolutionary of the Petrashevtsy, published his first book of poems in 1846, when he was twenty-one. He was at once recognised by Maikov as, 'undoubtedly the best poet of the present time', 'a poet with a mission,' who, 'strongly sympathises with the questions of his age'.[61] As well as Béranger and Lermontov, he was influenced by Lamennais, whose *Paroles d'un croyant* he helped to translate illegally into Russian.[62] His verses have the same apocalyptic fervour, the same vision of blood and battles, the same faith in the eventual triumph of the people against their tyrants. His most famous poem has been called 'the Russian Marseillaise', and is a direct call to revolutionary action, beginning, 'Forward without fear and doubt, To glorious deeds my friends.'[63] Directly echoing the ideas of the Petrashevtsy, in this and other poems, he defines the poet's task as 'to proclaim the love of learning to the poor and the rich'. He calls on his friends to 'fight under the banner of science' for 'the holy law of truth'. He believes that truth will only be achieved as a result of a bloody popular struggle. When 'the longed-for hour strikes', 'the sleeping peoples' will arise and form 'the holy host of freedom'. He is sure that truth will triumph and 'the hatred of the peoples will die down' ... 'Man has not long to await that time, he will not suffer and be tormented long', 'I have already seen the dawn of holy redemption in the skies!'[64] Some of these poems were slipped past the censor by pretending they were translations, others − *New Year 1848, In Spirit Brothers I am with you,* − were banned and circulated in manuscript form among his friends. Some of his uncensored poems, *The Righteous* and *To N. A. Mordvinov*, which places his friend among those, 'ready to stand in the ranks of the defenders of freedom', have only been rediscovered in the last few years.[65]

Durov and Pal'm also wrote a fair amount of poetry. This was also obviously socialist, but it was less full of revolutionary fervour and optimism than Pleshcheev's. Durov's poetical model was Auguste Barbier, whom he was the first to translate into Russian. Barbier, a poet generally popular among the Petrashevtsy, specialised in vigorous, often crude, exposés of the evils of French society: as Miliukov said, he 'presented to society's view the pus of its spiritual wounds'.[66] Durov's view of the poet's role was, unlike Pleshcheev's, largely negative, to express 'dissatisfaction with life and fate'. The depressing nature of most of his poetry is shown by a typical passage:

> Wherever you go, wherever you cast your eye –
> Everywhere you meet either a pale rank of paupers,
> Or the yellow faces of those returning from exile,
> Or a coffin and a funeral procession ...

Pal'm's poems were also gloomy and despondent. In *When I Look at the Town Buildings*, for example, he attacks the city – a 'lumber room' of human passions, bitter reproaches, fatal tragedies, in which the individual can never hope to make his voice felt. However, their poetry had some bright spots, some hopes for the socialist future. Durov's version of Barbier's *Chiani*, for example, deals with the possibility of liberating Italy from the Austrians, and tells us, 'you can always rely on the people', calling them 'earth in which a powerful sap ferments eternally, giving life to everything'.[67]

Two other Petrashevtsy, Akhsharumov and Balasoglo, also wrote poems, and two famous poets, Apollon Maikov, Valerian's elder brother and Apollon Grigor'ev, also visited Petrashevsky's circle. Akhsharumov wrote extremely feeble poetry, full of extravagant visions of a harmonious Fourierist future. Balasoglo's collection of verse, *The Poems of Veronov*, (1838), reflects his intellectual frustration in the period before he met the Petrashevtsy. During the period of their visits to Petrashevskii's, the poetry of Apollon Maikov and Apollon Grigor'ev briefly reflected the influence of the circle, though they soon went different ways. This is most obvious in Maikov's *Two Fates* and *Mashen'ka* and Grigor'ev's *The Town* and *When the Bell Triumphantly Tolls*, which laments the lost freedom of Novgorod and expresses the certainty that, 'the bloody hour of retribution' will come.[68]

The other literary form used by the Petrashevtsy for the direct expression of socialist ideas was the *ocherk* or short sketch, a new literary form, specifically designed to meet the demands of the natural school – the reproduction of scenes from life, and in particular as Belinskii (a great protagonist of the *ocherk*) emphasised, the depiction of types.[69] It was essentially a democratic form of literature, used for describing the seamy sides of life and in particular, the life of the lower classes in the capital, though there was the occasional *ocherk* about upper class types.

The *ocherki* of Durov and Tolbin, mainly published in *Finskii vestnik*, were particularly outstanding for their democratic flavour. In 1847 Durov threw up his job as a translator to concentrate entirely on writing and produced a series of sketches devoted to the lower classes. In *Khalatnik*, he describes the cramped, unhealthy working conditions of the young tailors' apprentices and their thieving, fighting and malicious pranks. He points out the social causes of this behaviour − they were torn too young from their parents, put to work and had no time to enjoy themselves as children. He concludes, 'The souls of these apprentices are no worse than those of any other Russian souls.' In *Petersburg Van'ka*, he depicts the long hours, low pay and drunken despair of the capital's coachmen. This incensed Bulgarin who wrote an *ocherk* of his own, *The Night Coachman*, to show that, 'the honest man can be happy in any station of life'. *Luka Lukich* is devoted to the knave, who in the provinces is quickly recognised and exposed, but in Petersburg does well and earns popular respect; *Tetin'ka* shows how harsh circumstances force a peasant woman to steal.[70]

Tolbin excelled at the description of the dregs of Petersburg life, partly because of his own experience of it. Like Durov he earned his living by writing, but he could not afford a roof over his head and kicked about the city, sleeping on other people's floors. He also had a predilection for wine and gambling. He said, 'Only a tenth of my work is done in the study; my chief work is on the streets ... I learn from life, I look with both eyes on subjects scattered all over the town.'[71] The low life of the capital parades through his *ocherki* − the ragpickers, the salesman from Yaroslavl, the professional billiard players, who ply their 'art' in taverns, 'in the most picturesque places along the Obvodii canal, where there are usually barges, full of all sorts of rubbish'. Some of his *ocherki* are just humorous sketches, others, especially those written in 1847−8 when he became a regular visitor to Petrashevskii's, are bitter protests against the system. Among these are *Pen-Pushers*, about the miserable copyists who live, 'in corners, behind a ripped curtain of coarse cloth, serving instead of a screen', who set up their stools in the street and, driven by need, are 'ready to witness, for a double price, *for* and *against*, in the same case'. *Street Musicians* is the heart-rending story of the Savoyard children with their monkeys and barrel-organs who die of hunger in the streets. Tolbin openly expresses his sympathy for these types – even the billiard player and the man who steals a beaver collar – and makes it clear that he prefers them to the hypocritical rich.[72] The latter are savagely attacked in another series of *ocherki* – in *Animal Lovers*, the story of the landowners who treat dogs better than children; *Mon chers*, about the petty, useless life of the young dandy; and in *Hungarians*, a description of the Hungarian soldier billeted in the Russian provincial town, who never does a useful day's work, or has a sensible thought, or experiences real feeling, in his life.[73]

The stories of the Petrashevtsy fit into the general literary current of the 1840s and are in many ways similar to those of other writers, who were affiliated to the natural school, but who were not involved with the Petrashevtsy or attracted to socialist politics. Like all the writers of the period they tended to write. long short stories rather than novels, designed for the main public forum of the day, the journal. The themes they chose for their stories were those favoured by a majority of their contemporaries. These included a reinterpretation and a reappraisal of a theme which had come to be traditional in Russian literature, the theme of the *lishnyi chelovek*, the romantic superfluous man, the most famous examples of which are Pushkin's Eugène Onegin and Lermontov's Pechorin, but which goes back to Griboedov; the theme of the life of the 'little man', the poor *chinovnik* or teacher, the general theme of the natural school, which owed its origin to Gogol; and, thirdly, the theme of the position of women, a subject which, as a result of the great influence of George Sand in Russia, received attention from all the more progressive writers of the day, in particular Herzen and Druzhinin.

However, though they operated within the general framework of the natural school and took for their stories the themes common at the time, the Petrashevtsy looked at these subjects from their own particular, socialist point of view. Like other writers, for example Turgenev, they mocked the romantic, superflous man. But, in a way that otherwise only Herzen did at this time, they went on openly to identify society as the cause of his predicament. Their treatment of the theme of the little man forms perhaps the most interesting part of their writings. Basing themselves on the Fourierist philosophy of human nature, they attempted to show how social circumstances affect character, how man's quirks, vices and crimes arise from external circumstances brought to bear on them in the course of their life. This was something new in Russian literature. The Petrashevtsy's depiction of the position of women, though sometimes extreme, was more derivative.

The hey-day of Russian romanticism had been the thirties. By the mid 1840s, the more progressive writers had reached the conclusion that the *lishnyi chelovek* was not a hero tragically alienated from his surroundings but a pathetic case, a pointless, useless man. The more moderate writers, for example Turgenev in his series of weak and feeble romantic heroes, confined themselves to depicting and lamenting the pitifulness of the *lishnyi chelovek*'s situation. The more radical — Herzen, through Bel'tov in *Who is to Blame?*, and the Petrashevtsy — tried to explain how this alienation had occurred and called for something to be done about it. They explained it by the rift between education and social reality. The enlightened education which so many gentry youth received in the thirties and forties gave them an idea of the world which in no way corresponded to barbarous Russia and aroused in them aspirations which could not be satisfied within the narrow range of opportunities open to them in the army or bureaucracy. As a result, when they left school or university, either despising reality, or terrified by it, the young intelligents took refuge in self-indulgent posturing or dreams and eventually became completely paralysed, incapable of any sort of action. In their fiction the Petrashevtsy make clear that though they understand it, they have lost patience with this sort of behaviour. The moral of their stories is that the correct response to the unpleasantness of reality in Nicholas' Russia is not to run away from it but to come down to earth and struggle with it. Their Fourierism led the Petrashevtsy to analyse the social causes of the phenomenon of the *lishnyi chelovek* with great care, illustrating how the romantic malady affected both rich and poor.

Pal'm's stories are mostly devoted to an attack on the familiar Pechorin type of romantic — the rich spoilt sons of the upper classes. The two best examples of this are his *Jacques Bichovkin* (deliberately called after Sand's romantic hero Jacques) and Prince Rassvetov, hero of *The Joke*, who, in spite of their noble characters and the noble aspirations they conceived at university, in real life achieved nothing and brought harm and unpleasantness to others, turning into posturing fools with 'empty heads and hearts'. Pal'm asks, Why did this happen? and points to social reality as the culprit, 'The present is boring and sterile, the future dark, where can one find satisfaction?' Pleshcheev wrote a story on the same theme, also called *The Joke*, as a complement to Pal'm's. Though Pal'm and Pleshcheev's attitude is more hostile, their characters bear many similarities to Beltov, the restless nobleman of

Herzen's *Who is to Blame?*, who, largely, out of frustration and boredom, disrupts the conjugal idyll of a young couple in a provincial town.[74]

More original were the Petrashevtsy's attempts to show how poor men were spoilt for life by an education that filled them with too many high ideals. Their attitude is here more sympathetic, because the subject was closer to their own experience. They felt that they had only been saved from a similar fate by their discovery of socialism.

Saltykov was particularly interested in the educational aspect. The activity of his heroes Nagibin and Brusin was 'paralysed' because they were 'not given a practical understanding of reality'. Saltykov points out that the paralysis induced in his heroes by their elevated education was intensified by their poverty which made it even more difficult for them to act.[75]

The idea of a link between poverty and romanticism was developed by Pleshcheev and Dostoevskii in their studies of the dreamer. The dreamer was a particular psychological type. He was intelligent and educated but poor. Terrified by the harshness of real life, instead of getting himself a job and a wife and the modest comfortable existence he really wanted, the dreamer ran away into a corner and hid himself, compensating for his inability to cope with reality by indulging in extravagant dreams. Lomt'ev, hero of Pleshcheev's *Friendly Advice*, for example, on finishing at university; lived a solitary, lazy dreamy life. '"I shall rest a little", he said, though there was nothing to rest from.' As a result, when he falls in love, he has no money or prospects to offer the girl and she, though she loves him, marries his friend Okolesin. The hero of Dostoevskii's story *White Nights*, which he dedicated to Pleshcheev, lives in the same way:

> What is real life to him? in his corrupted eyes ... we live so torpidly, slowly, insipidly ... poor things, thinks our dreamer and it is no wonder that he thinks it! ... Look at those magic phantoms, which so endlessly, so whimsically, so carelessly and freely group before him.

His romance ends in the same way as Lomt'ev's. Dostoevskii also studied the phenomenon of the dreamer in *The Landlady* and *Netochka Nezvanova*.[76]

The second main theme of the Petrashevtsy's stories, the life of the little man, had been introduced into Russian literature by Gogol. Gogol had attempted to make the subject of fiction the depiction of real life and had set the example for the whole of the natural school in the 1840s.

He had exposed the injustices of Russian society simply by describing them, by collecting (in Maikov's words) 'the artistic statistics of Russia'.[77] For the Petrashevtsy this was just the background. Inspired by Fourier, they were interested in exposing the injustices of society not just by describing them but by showing their effect on the personalities of the individuals who made up this society. This psychological method was quite new in Russian literature. It was first used by Dostoevskii in his second story, *The Double* (his first story, *Poor Folk*, had been written in the straight descriptive manner of Gogol). Most of the other Petrashevtsy writers also used it in their stories. It is this that marks them as a *group* of writers and distinguishes them from other writers of the time. The Petrashevtsy regarded it as a more sophisticated development of Gogol's analysis, built on his achievement. Maikov, for example, asked, 'If the author of *The Double* had been born eight years earlier (i.e. before the publication of *Dead Souls*) could he have been such a psychologist?' He pointed out that Dostoevskii's psychological stories contained just as much social protest as Gogol's — it was merely that it was formulated more subtly, indirectly and, he thought, in a more penetrating manner. According to him, Dostoevskii 'penetrates so deeply into the human soul ... that the impression created by *The Double* may be compared only with that of an inquisitive person penetrating into the chemical composition of matter'. Maikov went on, expressing himself ironically for the censor's benefit, to explain the point of the story — all Goliadkin's defects were caused in him by *'the surprising harmony reigning in human society'*, i.e. by the injustices of the social system.[78] Maikov, as an admirer of Fourier, understood and sympathised with the aims of the psychological method. For other radicals, including both Belinskii and Petrashevskii (whose love of directness proved stronger than his Fourierism), it was too subtle, the points too obscure. Belinskii had praised *Poor Folk* to the skies, but disliked the psychological method of *The Double* and the fantastic, Hoffmanesque elements Dostoevskii used to emphasise his ideas. He completely revised his opinion of Dostoevskii and referred to his subsequent stories as 'rubbish'.[79]

Regardless of their critics, the writers among the Petrashevtsy produced a detailed expose of how social conditions affect character. The social/psychological content of Dostoevskii's other early stories has already been discussed in Chapter V. The same theme recurs in the stories of the other Petrashevtsy. They portray the quietness, timidity and insecurity of the little man; the social causes of madness, of avarice and, in general, how people's characters change according to circumstances.

Their little men reveal many of the characteristics of Dostoevskii's heroes. They are shy and quiet, hide themselves away from other people and live in conditions of poverty. Saltykov's Michulin, for example, lives in 'a very small room with one half-obscured window overlooking a rubbish tip'. As his money runs out and hopes of a job fade, he becomes increasingly unconfident and misanthropic and avoids other people.[80]

Tolbin's story, *The Black Day*, like Dostoveskii's *The Double* is devoted to the poor man's insecurity, his desperate struggle to preserve his dignity. Like Dostoveskii's Goliadkin, who complains that he is not a 'doormat', Tolbin's hero protests. 'You lie, brother, I will show you that I am a man and not a worm, a citizen under the protection of the laws'. A whole chronicle of misfortunes befalls him on his 'black day': a mosquito bites him on the nose; he is late for work, his boss makes cruel fun of him in the office; he wants to answer back but cannot, for fear of losing his job; his new suit is spoilt by the rain; he forgets his purse and cannot pay the coachman; his servant is out; the shopkeeper does not recognise him and refuses to lend him the money. The point of all this is that is constitutes a perfectly normal day for the little man, who belongs among the number of people living, 'not how the ordinary mortal ought to live'. The day only seems black to him because it is the day on which the one hope that keeps his self-respect alive − his pretension to the hand of his boss's daughter − is shattered. She is already engaged and her father treats his proposal as a joke.[81]

Elsewhere Tolbin, again like Dostoevskii, shows how the struggle against poverty can lead to madness. In *Lubin'ka*, he gives a poignant account of how Makhaba, a poor orphaned Tatar girl, goes mad through her desire for a better life, symbolised by her longing for a beautiful dress. Again, in *Moths*, Tolbin emphasises that the madman who thinks he can speak the language of insects is a poor man, driven to madness by the circumstances of his life. The world of insects he creates for himself is not a fantastic world but his reproduction of the real world, hostile to the poor man.[82]

Other stories by the Petrashevtsy examine how social circumstances cause the development of vice in people. Saltykov, in *Contradictions*, explains the origins of Maria Ivanovna's miserliness in a poor and deprived childhood, which made money her 'dominating passion'. He added, 'And, in conscience, one cannot say that she was a jot to blame for this: throw her in one set of circumstances and they'll have one result, place her in other surroundings and her physiognomy will suddenly change: the same strings will give different sounds.'[83]

The theme of Durov's story, *Nobody's Child*, is how circumstances change people. The Countess K. was a 'prejudiced old enemy of present-day society', until she adopted her fourteen year-old god-daughter, Ol'enka. In the next four years the Countess grew younger, filled the house with guests and began to enjoy taking Ol'enka to balls. But, when Ol'enka left, the old woman felt suddenly alone and frightened, and a new passion, 'the inhuman, devilish attachment to money' developed in her and ousted 'the memory of the tender, gentle Ol'enka'. The character of Ol'enka's kind father was also perverted, not by an abundance but by a lack of money, until he reconciled himself to the idea of selling Ol'enka in a loveless marriage to Efrem Grigor'evich, a rich but hideous and rapacious landowner. Efrem also changes, this time for the better, as a result of his infatuation with Ol'enka. Durov explains this as an example of how, 'External circumstances, like a conscious will, force a man a level above his own mean nature, when a noble feeling ... flies into a dark soul, fills it with light and ennobles him.'[84]

The third main theme of the Petrashevtsy's stories – the emancipation of women, was again one of the most popular subjects of Russian literature in the 1840s. Interest in the question of women's emancipation was inspired by the novels of George Sand. In Russia, as V. Drashusov explained, 'no one remains indifferent to the powerful and stirring novels of this gifted woman'. Many imitated George Sand and preached the free union of the sexes – Herzen in *Who is to Blame?*; Druzhinin in *Polinaka Saks*, Petr Kudriavtsev in *Without a Dawn*; Avdot'ia Panaeva in *The Ugly Husband*. When the Petrashevtsy – Dostoevskii in *Netochka Nezvanova*, Saltykov in *Contradictions* (Tania), Durov in *Nobody's Child* (Ol'enka) – tried to give their heroines the 'elevated moral purity' of Sand's women, they were merely following literary fashion.[85] The idea of the emancipation of women had been brought into the radical movement in the late thirties and early forties by Herzen and Belinskii under the influence of Saint-Simonism.

The calls for the emancipation of women which abound both in the fiction and non-fiction of the Petrashevtsy, while they helped to root the idea in the traditions of Russian socialism, were thus not by themselves original. However, their special interest in Fourier led the Petrashevtsy to take the demand for free love further and attack the family with greater asperity than progressive writers. A few of them even accepted Fourier's sexual theory. Ipollit Debu, for example, had a habit of giving his lady friends Victor Hennequin's *Les amours au phalanstère*, a justification of it, to read, although they inevitably gave him the book back, 'shrieking with horror'.[86] In his speech on Fourier's birthday, Khanykov took the attack on the family to the extreme:

> The family is oppression, the family is despotism,
> the family is immorality, the family is depravity,
> the family is God the Oppressor ... the family is
> private property and the egotistical division of wealth,
> the family is poverty ... the family is a miasma and an
> epidemic, the family is the personnification of evil and a
> state based upon it is a poisoned organism whose ruin is
> near.[87]

Though the Petrashevtsy received their ideas on women from the French socialists, they did develop them in some interesting ways, expressing a particular contempt for society women, a particular sympathy for prostitutes and a particular concern for the problem of love and the poor man.

Durov reserved especial venom for the silliness, frivolity and bitchiness of well brought-up young ladies, and devoted a whole series of stories to the subject: *A Novel in Letters, The Mistresses, The Phantom, A Sad Tale*, and others. However, he was always careful to point out that it was society and their upbringing, not the women themselves, who were to blame for the defects of their characters. In a penetrating poem, he summed up the young girl's lot:

> With secret anguish in my heart I look at you!
> What awaits you? Dolls, which will
> At first comfort, then bore you ...
> Then, when you grow up, you yourself will be a doll for adults,
> They will dress you in velvet, call you out to show you off,
> Strictly forbid you to reveal your thoughts and feelings,
> Fetter your will (the will is most dangerous for them),
> Later, as time passes, for money (of course not for love),
> They will marry you off. To whom? This isn't your business ...
> You will live a married life, bear children, but your children
> Perhaps will resemble their father, and you scarcely loved their
> > father.[89]

The Petrashevtsy had great sympathy for the 'fallen woman', whether the unfaithful wife or the girl forced through poverty to become a prostitute. This was expressed in striking fashion by Tolbin, who, in his story *Moths*, got a justification of prostitution past the censor, by transferring it from the human to the insect world. Tolbin traces the story of his heroine, an orphaned moth, from the moment her aunt sells her off as mistress to an old drone, to her end in the gutter, a common prostitute, forced to copulate with cockroaches and worms.[90]

The problem of love for the poor man was something the French socialists had not touched on, but which naturally occurred to the Petrashevtsy as a problem they faced themselves. Durov maintained that, 'It is completely irrational for the poor man to marry for whatever reason'. Marriage without love was dishonourable and could only lead to unhappiness. But if you were poor, marriage for love also led to unhappiness. The penniless Balasoglo tried to dissuade Petrashevskii's visitors from marriage by telling the dismal story of how the passionate love of himself and his wife Maria had faded away under the pressure of material cares.[91] Saltykov describes the same problem in his stories. In *Contradictions*, Nagibin is tormented by his love for Tania, 'A woman is an object *de luxe*, which only a rich man can afford to contemplate, but for a poor man ... such a plaything is inadmissible!' An *A Tangled Affair*, Michulin has nightmares about being married to his beloved Nadya: they and their son have nothing to eat, she ceases to love him, showers him with reproaches and finally, to feed them, becomes a prostitute. This problem so worried Akhsharumov that he gave up the idea of women altogether.[92]

The Petrashevtsy were also among the first to attempt to draw women into the radical movement. Though the Fridays were very much bachelor occasions – they got drunk, smoked, told rude jokes – they were anxious to invite women and involve them in their propaganda. Tol', for example, wanted to get a job in the Pavlovsk Institute (a girls' school) because he believed, 'ideas both spread and develop more quickly through women'.[93] However, though they made a start, their efforts were not very successful. The only woman of whom they could claim, 'She does a great deal to help our society' was Iulia Zhadovskaia, author of some extremely simple and extremely sad poetry, about the misery of life on earth, especially for women. In 1849 the Third Department considered arresting her along with the rest of the Petrashevtsy but gave up for lack of evidence.[94]

Thus, though the fiction of the Petrashevtsy was less socialist than Petrashevskii hoped, it was still strongly socialist in tone. Added to the non-fiction articles and publications of the Petrashevtsy – the *Pocket Dictionary*, Balasoglo's literary and scientific ventures; and academic and critical articles of Maikov, Miliutin, Shtrandman and others, it amounts to an impressive body of material. Articles and stories by the

Petrashevtsy, both by the more prominent and more minor writers among them (such as Katenev, Grigorii Danilevskii, Mikhail Dostoevskii) and by writers who were for a short period close to the Petrashevtsy (such as Apollon Maikov and Apollon Grigor'ev) appeared in almost all but the most notoriously reactionary newspapers and journals of the day (i.e. all but *Synotechestva, Severnaia pchela* and *Moskvitianin*). And through their writings, there is no doubt, they did succeed in getting socialist ideas across to a large number of the educated young men of their own and the next generation.

VIII — 1848: REVOLUTIONARY CONSPIRACIES

The Petrashevtsy's efforts to spread socialism often took peaceful and legal forms — attempts to found socialist associations, to convert the intelligentsia to their ideas by smuggling them into print. But their socialism went further than this. With a few exceptions, they were supporters of revolution. This distinguished them sharply from the Fourierists with their peaceful, apolitical doctrines. Expressions of the Petrashevtsy's enthusiasm for revolution can be found in their writings from the early 1840s. And, from the Decembrists, to whom some of the Petrashevtsy were closely related, they inherited the idea of a revolutionary tradition in Russia.

The theoretical sympathy of the Petrashevtsy for the notion of revolution assumed a quite different complexion after the outbreak of revolution in France in February 1848. They followed the French events with breathless excitement, declaring their sympathies for the most radical socialists. As revolution swept from France across Europe, the Petrashevtsy became optimistic that Russia, too, might be engulfed by the tide. Their observation of the situation in Russia encouraged them in this view. On the one hand, Nicholas's violently reactionary response made it clear that there was no longer any use in hoping for reforms from the Tsar. On the other hand, the Petrashevtsy, looking at their country with eager, inexperienced and over-optimistic eyes, thought that they detected the elements of a revolutionary situation in Russia. They conceived the idea, which was to be so widely adopted in the seventies, of 'going to the people'. Very tentatively, they began to carry their agitation to the lower classes, in hopes of arousing them to rebellion. They were also aware of the revolutionary possibilities inherent in Russia's national question and had ties with the nationalist leader Taras Shevchenko in the Ukraine. They combined a Fourierist stress on internationalism with championship of oppressed nationalities. They argued for national independence as the prelude to the union of all nations under socialism.

The Petrashevtsy were by no means consistent in the seriousness of their revolutionary intentions. In some cases, especially the Tolstov–Katenev circle, their revolutionary ardour sprang from childishness and immaturity. Some of them seem to have thrown themselves into revolutionary plotting just for the thrill of it. Their discussions and conspiracies were based on an exaggerated assessment of the revolutionary potential of Russia, and this gives them an unreal tinge. But, the fact remains that they were the first in Russia to preach a revolutionary socialism. They did found a conspiracy to promote revolution in Russia. Some of them, above all Petrashevskii, were dedicated revolutionaries.

Though they all appear to have been in favour of secret societies, the revolutionaries among the Petrashevtsy can be divided into an extremist and a more cautious radical wing. This foreshadowed a split among Russian socialists on the question of revolution which was to reappear in the later history of the Russian radical movement. The extremists, led by Nikolai Speshnev were for revolution at once (no matter how impractical), favoured putschist and jacobin tactics and some, notably Tolstov and Katenev drew up wild plans for assassinating the Tsar. The more moderate and realistic revolutionaries, headed by Petrashevskii, were anxious to avoid the mistakes of the Decembrists. They felt that revolution should only be attempted when they were sure the people would rise to support it and that it had to be prepared by a long period of propaganda. Finally, the extremists, using the literary Pal'm–Durov circle as a cover, succeeded in forming, without Petrashevskii's knowledge, a conspiracy to promote the overthrow of the Tsar by means of a peasant revolt. They prepared a collection of propaganda for distribution among the peasantry and even bought a press on which to print it. The revolutionary nature of the Petrashevskii circle was long ignored, partly because the secret of the conspiracy's existence was very well kept – only coming to light in 1922, over seventy years later.

The Petrashevtsy's revolutionary sympathies

Even before 1848, many of the Petrashevtsy were sympathetic to the idea of revolution. Their inspiration came from two main sources – from their study of the history of revolutionary movements against feudalism, in particular the first French revolution, and, to a lesser extent, the sixteenth century Peasants' War in Germany; and from the example of the Decembrists, the first advocates of revolution in Russia.

The events of the first French revolution had long been clandestinely studied by radicals in Russia. Histories of it by Thiers, Michelet, Louis Blanc, Cabet and many others, were found in Petrashevskii's library.[1] The *Pocket Dictionary* serves as a handbook of French revolutionary terminology, with entries for *Barricades, Bastille, Guillotine, Gironde, Montagnards, National Assembly, National Guard, Notables,* among others. The entry for *National Assembly* praises the French Revolution and emphasises that its achievement was the destruction of feudal society, 'so that its resuscitation ... became a total anachronism for France'. The aim of this article was, Petrashevskii admitted, to point to revolution as the way to destroy feudalism in Russia.[2] The Petrashevtsy also used the example of the French Revolution to make plain their support for revolutionary violence and terror, criticising the Girondins, praising the Montagne and excusing the Terror by saying that, 'every revolution is more or less bloody'.[3]

The Petrashevtsy were interested in the Peasants' War in Germany as another movement for the overthrow of feudalism; the only difference between it and the French revolution was, in their view, that, 'In 1525 it was the people who were vanquished, in 1790 it was the aristocracy'. Their main source was *La guerre des paysans*, by Alexandre Weill, published in *La Phalange* in 1845, (similar in tone to Engels's *Der deutsche Bauernkrieg*, which appeared in 1850). Weill minimises the religious factor and treats the war as a matter, 'of the natural and imprescriptible rights of the cultivator in opposition to the so-called seigneurial and feudal rights' and deplores, but justifies the peasants' violence. Ippolit Debu took copious notes on Weill; the *Pocket Dictionary* uses it to outline Münzer's demands, emphasising that chief among them was the abolition of serfdom. It tells us that the success of this teaching in Germany was due to, 'the terrible oppression which the lower class of the people in Germany at that time suffered from the upper classes'. In a particularly daring passage, which the censor somehow missed, it generalises the lesson, to allow readers to draw the Russian implications, 'Some of these demands were satisfied in Germany in the course of time, but not without bloodshed, for there is no example of the restoration of violated rights without *bloody sacrifices and victimisation*!!'[4]

As well as drawing lessons from the history of other countries, the Petrashevtsy, like Herzen and Ogarev, were strongly influenced by the example of the Decembrists, to whom they were connected not only by theoretical and sentimental, but also by personal ties. Nikolai Kashkin and another Petrashevets, Fonvizin, were sons of Decembrists exiled to Siberia for their part in the rising of 14 December. Among Speshnev's female admirers was the daughter of one of the Decembrists. She wrote to him after his trial, 'God, God, God! So everything leads to this – everything goes by the old road, this man whom my soul loves so deeply, and the end of everything is the same Siberia, terrible Western Siberia with its shackles and convicts.' Chernosvitov, who had met surviving Decembrists in Siberia, was eagerly questioned at Petrashevskii's about 'their way of thought'. However, many of the Petrashevtsy were critical of the Decembrists and anxious not to repeat their mistake, not to embark on a rising without the support of the mass of the population. As Tolstov said, 'They (the government) think that now, like last time, we'll get one regiment to mutiny and we'll act by force. No – now everything is different. We won't act like that ... but only when our actions are accepted everywhere and everyone is discontented.' Petrashevskii was particularly anxious to emphasise that the Decembrists had failed because their plans were known only to a small number of people.[5]

In the years leading up to 1848, the Petrashevtsy's writings abound with references to the value of revolution. Some of these they managed to get past the censor. For example, one of the economic articles in *Finskii vestnik* (1846) insists that, 'There are circumstances when a sudden change, indeed one involving violence, murderously destroys the traditional order, but in spite of this brings undoubted benefit. Everything depends on the historical circumstances and the people carrying out the reforms.' In *A Tangled Affair*, (written September 1847 – January 1848), Saltykov presents class war as involving the extermination, not the reconciliation of the upper classes. In Ivan Michulin's dream, the hungry little boy asks, 'Mama, when will they kill the hungry wolves?', and his mother tells him, 'Soon, my dear, soon... all to the last one, not one will be left... we will be well fed... we will be merry, very merry, my dear.' Professor Petr Pletnev voiced the general amazement at the publication of the story, 'I can't help being surprised at the stupidity of the censors in allowing such works ... it proves nothing other than the necessity of the guillotine for all the rich and famous.'[6]

The outbreak of revolution in France in February 1848 crystallised the Petrashevtsy's revolutionary convictions. Like progressive youth all over Russia, they received the news of revolution with rapture and rushed for information about it – information which soon became easily available in St. Petersburg. Their heroes were the most radical socialists – Louis Blanc, Pyat, Proudhon, Blanqui, Barbès. Although the

Petrashevtsy gradually became disillusioned with the second republic, they remained convinced that the revolution marked a great step forward towards socialism. They believed that it discredited the peaceful doctrines of Fourier and showed that socialism could only be established through revolution.

'Modern history begins in 1848, the old world has been turned upside-down and a new era has begun.' These words, written by Ivan Golovin, one of the first Russian emigrés in Paris at the beginning of 1849, clearly express the mood of 1848.[7] Revolution broke out in France with the fall of Guizot's ministry on 23 February. The news reached St. Petersburg almost two weeks later, on Sunday 22nd (old calendar). Saltykov remembered:

> I was at a matinee at the Italian opera when suddenly, like an electric spark, the news penetrated the whole audience ... the old men waved their spectacles, twisted and twirled their moustaches, threatening to take up arms, the young could scarcely restrain their ecstasy ... France seemed a land of miracles.

By 2 March it had penetrated to Kazan. Osokin wrote, 'There's revolution in France. This is the news which since yesterday has spread through our town with the speed of lightning and serves as the universal subject of discussion, bewilderment, questions, guesses and suppositions.' It was quickly followed by word of revolutions in Italy, Germany, Austria, Hungary. The reactionary powers seemed to be falling like ninepins, a new life beginning all over Europe.[8] Sympathy for the revolution was almost general among the educated youth of St. Petersburg. They abandoned the journals and rushed to the newspapers. In the cafes and confectioners around Nevskii Prospekt − Izler's, Volf's, Passazh, Dominique, − the newspapers were 'devoured like oysters as they are cut, with unheard-of greed!' No-one had the patience to wait their turn, they clustered round while someone read the news out in a loud voice. Everyone quickly forgot about plays, dances, balls, there was nothing but talk about the foreign events, whenever two people met it was the inevitable topic of conversation.[9] People flocked to Petrashevskii's, which became a forum for discussion of the latest news. In Shaposhnikov's tobacco shop, the conversation turned to 'the French Revolution, equality, individual freedom and republics'. Kuz'min, marooned in Tambov, wrote to Balasoglo, 'with the most urgent request for French journals', complaining, 'I am here in complete ignorance about the events in Europe.'[10] The shopkeepers were quick to profit from the excitement and sold portraits of Ledru Rollin, Barbès, Raspail and other revolutionaries, daring to display them openly in their windows. Speshnev and Grigorii Danilevskii were among the many who hung them on their walls.[11]

The heroes of the Russian radical youth were the radicals and socialists who played the most prominent part in the revolutionary government and displayed the most eloquence in the National Assembly. Chief among these were Ledru Rollin and, especially, Louis Blanc. Aspiring orators climbed onto the tables in the cafés and read out to everyone Louis Blanc's speeches at the Luxembourg Commission. Chernyshevskii enthusiastically followed their progress day by day in the *Journal des Débats*, 'Great men! Especially I love Louis Blanc. He is a man of spirit, a great man!'[12] Next came Pyat and Proudhon, who though they had not done anything to help the workers, had made outstanding revolutionary speeches in the Assembly. The Petrashevtsy's excited approval of Proudhon's speech of 31 July 1848, which 'shook the foundations of the established order', by demanding a tax of a third on profits, has already been mentioned. Felix Pyat's famous speech made on 2 November 1848, was a defence of the principle of the right to work, thrown into jeopardy by the revolts of May and June. He justified the June days as a legitimate 'protest of misery' and ended with a threat: 'If they (the people) cannot live and work, they will die fighting!' This, perhaps the most revolutionary speech made in the whole duration of the National Assembly, was singled out by the Petrashevtsy and read aloud by Pleshcheev from *La Presse* at his flat. Petrashevskii severely upbraided Timkovskii for daring to criticise it.[13] The Petrashevtsy also expressed their admiration for Blanqui and Barbès and watched with interest and approval of the attempts of feminists, such as Jeanne Deroin, to get themselves elected to the National Assembly.[14]

However, after the first outburst of enthusiasm, the Petrashevtsy were critical of the French republic, in many ways echoing Herzen. They were aware of the emptiness of the bombastic phrases mouthed by so many leading republicans, men for whom, 'banquets, demonstrations, protests, meetings, toasts, banners are the most important part of the revolution'. They shared Herzen's disgust for the 'laudanum of Lamartine', realising that for all his brilliant speeches, his main thought was to bar the way to socialism.[15] The Petrashevtsy watched with growing alarm the gradual return of the reactionaries in France. They were saddened by the elections of 23 April, the failure of the attempt of 15 May, horrified by the repression of the June Days. Speshnev, on 5 August, wrote how:

In France all the representatives of the old order are again appearing on
the scene — all the socialists, pure and impure, have left the stage after
the July battles … The Assembly is adopting various repressive measures
— they have banned the publication of *Presse* and several other papers,
including Proudhon's paper.[16]

But the Petrashevtsy did not share the pessimism of Herzen, who
decided as early as 15 May that the revolution had been defeated. They
did not let themselves be discouraged, but were 'roused to fanaticism'
by the trials of socialists at Versailles and Bourges, each coveting, 'the
sublime role of a Barbès'. As late as April 1849, Petrashevskii remained
convinced that the socialist parties would be powerful in the Assembly
in three or four years time. After Louis Napoleon's *coup d'état* in 1851,
Engel'son, arguing against Herzen summed up the Petrashevtsy's
attitude to 1848. For Herzen 1848 was an utter flop, a shipwreck. Europe
would never create a new socialist world. For Engel'son, 1848 was 'the
first act in a great opera, performed under the title, *The Chastisement
of the Bourgeoisie!*' Though the bourgeoisie had won, things would
never be the same again, 'The bourgeoisie is collapsing from dissension
in its own womb. What will be the contents of the next act? I don't know.
But I am sure that from now on the chief role will be played by the people
and no longer by the bourgeoisie.'[17]

The Petrashevtsy were thus encouraged, not disillusioned by 1848. The
process of radicalisation they underwent in this year can be seen from
the example of Filippov, who became a revolutionary through 'reading
French journals after the revolution in the West'; and Chernyshevskii,
at the beginning of 1848 a believer and a supporter of monarchy, by the
end an atheist and revolutionary.[18] For all but a few of the Petrashevtsy
(Danilevskii, Konstantin Debu, Evropeus) the events of 1848 seemed to
discredit the peaceful theories of Fourier and justify the more revolutionary ideas of Louis Blanc, Blanqui and the communists.[19] As Timkovskii
noted with disgust, none of the Fourierists had participated in the fighting
in February or June. As Dostoevskii said, while Louis Blanc was organising workers at the Luxembourg Palace, 'The Fourierists during the whole
of the February revolution did not come out onto the streets, but stayed
in the editorial offices of their paper where they had already spent twenty
years dreaming of the future land of phalansteries.'[20] Considerant's
demands for help in establishing a trial phalanstery seemed insignificant
in comparison with plans for a socialist republic.

Though sticking to the phalanstery as an ideal, the Petrashevtsy began to believe that it could only be realised on a large scale and by means of 'a rising against the government'.[21]

The events of 1848 in Europe gave rise to a feeling that revolution in Russia too was inevitable and imminent. Balasoglo wrote, 'as a bird scents the approach of a storm, so a man has his omens ... the time of revolution is approaching'. The mood of 1848 was summed up by Pleshcheev in an uncensored (and uncensorable) poem, *New Year 1848*, circulated among his friends:

> Cries of congratulation are heard
> The sound of glasses and toasts
> Near is the hour of liberation
> Near is the hour of truth!

> Already I hear from all sides
> Curses thundering at our enemies
> Near is the hour of the last battle!
> We march boldly forward –
> And God hears our prayers
> And shatters our chains![22]

Hopes of Revolution in Russia

Events in Russia seemed to the ever-optimistic Petrashevtsy to indicate that the time might be ripe for revolution there too. On the one hand, Nicholas's behaviour made it clear that there was no longer any hope of his granting reforms; on the other, there was a perceptible increase in popular discontent.

The actions of the government, both at home and abroad, pushed the Petrashevtsy towards revolution in 1848. In the international sphere, Nicholas quickly came out into the open as the 'Gendarme of Europe', invading first Hungary (June), then Moldavia and Wallachia (July) to put down revolutions there. From mere internationalists, the Petrashevtsy became ardent anti-patriots. Mombelli melodramatically proclaimed that Europe had been divided into two warring armed camps: one, headed by France, representing the principle of good, or socialism; one, headed by Russia, representing the principle of evil, or despotism.[23]

Inside Russia, the government promptly threw off its reforming mask. There was a clamp-down on educated society. The epoch of 'censorship terror' was inaugurated the day after the French revolution by the establishment of the Menshikov Committee. Kraevskii and Nikitenko, editors of *Otechestvennye zapiski* and *Sovremennik*, were hauled before it and accused of trying to instil communism and revolution in Russia; Saltykov was exiled to Viatka for his story *A Tangled Affair*.[24] On 2 March the new state of affairs was institutionalised in the arbitrary, extra-legal Buturlin Committee. The universities also suffered: the numbers of students were drastically reduced: the powers of university councils curtailed; philosophy removed from the syllabus. Uvarov resigned the despair.

Most important of all, the government abandoned its efforts to reduce the privileges of the gentry and give new rights to the merchants, peasants and serfs. On 21 and 24 March, Nicholas informed representatives of the gentry that he relied on them for the preservation of order and that his 'unalterable will' was 'to preserve the unshakeable power and might of the serf owners over their serfs'. Discussion of emancipation became a crime. The visitors gathered at Petrashevskii's concluded, 'The Western revolutions frustrated the intentions of our government concerning the emancipation of the serfs.'[25] They felt that there was no longer any hope of a peaceful solution to the peasant question.

At the same time, circumstances in Russia gave the Petrashevtsy hope that the peasants might rise and demand freedom of their own accord. They greatly exaggerated the evidence. Discontent in Russia did not assume serious proportions in 1848. There were no indications of any likelihood of a generalised peasant revolt. However, it is true that (partly due to the influence of the European events) Russia was more than usually beset with disease, fires, famine and attacks on landowners. By late spring, with the early onset of the hot summer cholera was raging throughout European Russia. According to the official (and incomplete) figures, almost two million people caught the disease and 700,000 died. Kuz'min wrote from Tambov, 'one sees more funerals than anything else at the moment' and described the 'loud wails and sobbings' he heard constantly from the streets. In St. Petersburg the casualty rate was especially high. The capital emptied as everyone who could afford it fled to the country.[26] In addition, the hot, dry summer led to an increase in fires, terribly dangerous since almost all Russian houses were made of wood. Few were inclined to ascribe the fires to natural causes and wild rumours spread. Many thought they were the work of revolutionaries – Chernosvitov often joked, 'Isn't there a society of Illuminists behind all this?'; others, for example Tolstov, thought that they were the result of government provocation.[27] Finally, there was the worst harvest in the whole of Nicholas's thirty-year reign. Russia's serf-based agriculture was very inefficient; peasants worked with very small margins, so famine followed. Mombelli said that a cold shiver ran through his veins at the memory of the starving peasants he had seen in Vitebsk province, eating bread made out of straw, chaff and grass.[28]

The number and extent of peasant risings increased in the late forties and especially in 1848−9. The official figures give the average yearly number of big risings as sixteen in 1826−34 and thirty-four in 1845−54. Hunger and harsh conditions provoked the revolts but involved in almost all was the persistent rumour that the Tsar was going to give the serfs freedom. Rumours of freedom multiplied in 1848 as the peasants heard the news of revolution in Europe. The more serious disturbances occurred in the non-Russian borderlands − the Baltic and especially the Ukraine, a particular trouble-spot since 1846 when peasant war broke out in neighbouring Austrian Galicia. However, in 1848−9 there were spots of trouble all over central Russia, and most notably in the provinces of Ryazan, Tver, Kursk and Smolensk.[29] The Petrashevtsy sought out information about the mood of the peasants as eagerly as they sought news from France. Petrashevskii told Kuz'min, 'In the provinces adjacent to Galicia the peasants are highly disposed to cut the landowners' throats and ... this news has had the effect of recalling public attention to the emancipation of the serfs.' Tolstov bombarded Naumov with questions when he returned from Kostroma, 'What's new in Kostroma and Galicia, what are the common people saying, what's ... their mood, are they satisfied with the government's policies?' Even the spy Naumov was forced to admit that 'many of them are grumbling'. Utin told his friends of the 'general dissatisfaction and unrest' he had noticed among peasants of all sorts on his way back from Arkangelsk; Mombelli pressed Aleksei Maksheev, stationed in Orenburg, for details of discontent there. The information the Petrashevtsy gathered came in bits and pieces, from here and there, first hand, second hand, third hand. Much of it was unreliable and, taken together, the picture of unrest was not at all conclusive. However, the Petrashevtsy, spurred on by an incurable revolutionary optimism, concluded, 'We've not long to wait!'[30]

The chief factor restraining the peasants from a general uprising, the Petrashevtsy felt, was the fact that though they hated the landowners, they revered the Tsar. The peasants had to be disillusioned in the Tsar, shown that he was 'the source of the evil'. The Petrashevtsy came to regard it as their mission to do this. Unlike their predecessors the Decembrists and unlike the utopian socialists in France, they placed great

importance on the people. Akhsharumov wrote 'Everything depends on
the people, without them we cannot move, we will not move forward.'
He was the first to coin the slogan which was to have such great effect
in the seventies, 'We need to know our people better and get closer to
them.'[31] From 1848 onwards the Petrashevtsy became increasingly concerned with the question of how to spread their ideas, and particularly
ideas of revolution, among the lower classes. In December 1848, for
example, Khanykov told Chernyshevskii of the 'possibility and proximity of a revolution in Russia', pointing out to him, 'a multitude of
revolutionary elements' among the serfs, state peasants, *meshchane,
raskol'niki*, soldiers.[32] The Petrashevtsy attempted to carry their propaganda to people in all walks of life. In Pavel Kovalevskii's novel, *A Life
Summed-up*, based on the Petrashevtsy, Pavlonetskii (Petrashevskii),
answered the question, 'What shall we do now?' with:

> Everything, wherever and whenever possible: on the square (I take this
> on myself); in the barracks (let Kameev be responsible for this) (i.e. Pal'm);
> in the departments (Bukhtorin); in the corps (we'll have Polytskii) (i.e.
> E. Grebenk'a); and Sornev and Przhedetskii (Durov and Jastrzębski) where
> they wish, in the hotels and churches ... everywhere! Let the serfs follow
> us! Then we will see![33]

The Petrashevtsy did not get very far in bridging the gulf between
themselves and the people and some of their attempts to do so seem faint-
ly ridiculous, but they did at least begin to try. They started by talking
to the coachmen, the representatives of the serf class with whom they
came most directly and frequently in contact. A verbatim account of
Tolstov's gives an idea of the rather superficial way in which they pro-
ceeded. One day in 1849, on his way to see Shaposhnikov, Tolstov asked
his coachman where he was from. Having heard that he was a serf of a
landowner called Demidov and paid an *obrok'* of 120 roubles, Tolstov
said, 'Probably you work yourself to death, day and night, to earn the
money?' 'Of course sir', replied the *muzhik*. 'Your master probably plays
cards and gets drunk too.' 'Yes sir, I have heard that he plays.' On this,
Tolstov said, 'Why do you pay, haven't you heard that you are going to
get freedom from your master? ... it's your fault, you fool, why do you
pay ... don't give it to him, say no, withold it from your master. If you
withold it, others, everyone will follow you.' You *muzhik* replied, 'Oh sir,
how good this would be.' On other, similar occasions, the Petrashevtsy,
including Katenev, Jastrzębski and Chernyshevskii, tried to disabuse
their coachmen of their faith in the Tsar.[34]

More seriously, the Petrashevtsy were interested in spreading revolutionary ideas among the *raskol'niki*, the Russian schismatics. The *raskol'niki* were persecuted for their religious beliefs, they had played a prominent part in the Pugachev revolt of 1777 and this made them, Petrashevskii felt, 'the element in Russian society always ready for a terrible *Jacquerie*'. However, the Petrashevtsy recognised, the *raskol'niki* were suspicious and could only be approached through people of their own class. Petrashevskii hoped to influence the Siberian *raskol'niki* through the gold-prospector, Chernosvitov; Katenev tried to establish ties with *raskol'niki* in Moscow through the *meshchane* Naumov and Shaposhnikov (who were, unfortunately, government spies). The idea of the revolutionary potential of the *raskol'niki* was taken up by later revolutionaries, but was based on a fundamental misconception – the leading *raskol'niki* were mostly no longer rebellious peasants but well-to-do and conservative merchants.[35]

The Petrashevtsy also contemplated acting on the army. Grigor'ev's *A Soldier's Tale* was clearly intended for distribution in the barracks. Petrashevskii looked on the soldiers as part of the peasantry but was well aware of the enormous problems of conducting revolutionary agitation in Nicholas' army. When Antonelli provocatively asked him, 'Wouldn't it be a good thing to throw a few pamphlets into the army?' Petrashevskii put him sharply down, saying that the severity of the discipline, the soldiers' ignorance and traditional prejudices made this 'very difficult to do'. When Naumov asked him whether the army would put down an uprising, Petrashevskii pointed out that they had already done this once, 'They don't understand anything yet. We have first to influence them as we are beginning to do – but we won't manage this in the first year ... then, when they are ordered to fire, they will point their rifle barrels at the ground.'[36]

Another important element of discontent was the national question. In their writings, the Petrashevtsy seized every opportunity to champion oppressed nationalities Petrashevskii felt, 'States should be based on peoples and every state should contain one people.' National oppression had to cease and states be separated into their component peoples before the Fourierist goal of the elimination of national differences could begin to be achieved. The relationship between the different nationalities should be the same as that between the states of North America. All this, of course, was covertly aimed at Russia's expanding empire. The nations conquered by Russia included Finland (since 1809 a separate duchy with special rights and privileges); the Baltic states; the Ukraine or Malorossia;

the Kingdom of Poland, since the revolt of 1830 reduced to the status of a Russian province; the Caucasus and Siberia. None of these areas was satisfactorily incorporated into Russia, their inhabitants did not think of themselves as Russians and, as Jastrzębski stressed, the peasants in particular did not feel the traditional loyalty towards the Tsar. Petrashevskii argued that the unity of Russia was only maintained by military force. Revolutionaries should therefore not just agitate among the different classes of the Great Russian people but also act on the different nationalities of the Empire.[37]

The Petrashevtsy saw Poland as the most hopeful soil for rebellion. The Poles had co-operated with the Decembrists. They had rebelled *en masse* in Russian Poland in 1830, in Austrian Poland in 1846. After a popular rising in 1848 the tiny Polish duchy of Cracow lost its independence to Austria. The Russian Kingdom of Poland remained remarkably quiet throughout the 1840s but conspiracies were still regularly uncovered. In 1850 two hundred members of the *Organisation of 1848*, a revolutionary society with many similarities to the Petrashevtsy, and like them influenced by Fourier and Saint-Simon, were arrested.[38] Some of the Petrashevtsy: Jastzebski, Maderski, Nikolai Kaszewski (Kashevskii), Evstafii Marcinowski (Martsynovskii), Ignatii Poniatowski (Poniatovskii), Karl Witkowski (Vitkovskii) and Viktor Wojciechowskii (Voitsekhovskii) were themselves of Polish origin. In spite of their Fourierist internationalism, the Petrashevtsy were interested in studying the history of 1830. At Mombelli's literary evenings, for example, Maksheev read out his essay *Polish Revolution* and Mombelli his translation of the Polish nationalist Adam Mickiewicz's revolutionary poem, *To Russian Friends*.[39] Speshnev was the only Petrashevets to have actual contacts with Polish revolutionaries. Through Anna Cechanowiecki, the woman with whom he eloped abroad, he became involved in Polish patriotic circles in Dresden. Some Polish accounts say that Speshnev was initiated into their secrets and took back to Russia 'the statutes of the Polish revolutionary organisation'. Although this seems to have been wishful thinking, Speshnev did acquire one devoted Polish friend, Edmund Chojecki, who later became a follower of Proudhon.[40] However, through Saltykov, who from summer 1846 to March 1848 worked in the Polish department of the Chancellery of the War Ministry, the Petrashevtsy acquired access to secret information about Poland, including the confiscated correspondence of various Polish revolutionaries and details of the revolution in Cracow.[41]

In their estimates of the revolutionary potential of the non-Russian areas, the Petrashevtsy placed greatest emphasis after Poland, on the Ukraine. Through the poet Shevchenko, whom several of the Petrashevtsy had met in St. Petersburg in 1845 and when Mombelli in particular knew quite well, they had a direct contact with the revolutionary movement there. When he returned to the Ukraine in 1846–7 Shevchenko became the head of the left-wing of the *Society of Kyrill and Methodius*, the Ukrainian nationalist organisation. Though strongly nationalist, this group was influenced by utopian-socialist ideas and in particular by Fourier. Some of them also combined their Fourierism with ideas of revolution. Mombelli recorded the excitement produced in St. Petersburg in 1847 by the news that the society had been discovered and Shevchenko, Nikolai Kostomarov, Pantaleimon Kulish and others arrested and brought to the capital. According to him, their plan had been, by sparking off a revolution in Russia, to secure the complete secession of the Ukraine and the proclamation of a hetmanate there. Mombelli thought it a feasible plan; Petrashevskii agreed that the Ukraine was a good place to start a Russian revolution, particularly since, in spite of Shevchenko's arrest, his movement had 'put down roots' there.[42]

Shevchenko had dedicated one of his poems to the Caucasus. The long and bitter war of the Imams and their muridist followers was the battle-ground on which tens of thousands of Russian soldiers received their military training, the inspiration for stories by Pushkin, Lermontov, Tolstoi.

Petrashevskii was of course on the side of the Caucasians. He drew up a plan for a republican government for the Caucasus, which he believed, would unite the tribes and enable them to conduct the war against Russia more efficiently. He wanted Antonelli to visit the region to 'encourage revolution there' and win Caucasian support for a change of government in Russia. In the case of revolution in Russia, he alloted the Caucasus the role of 'diverting military forces away from the main theatre of action'.[43]

Other potential trouble spots were Finland and the Baltic. Finland, Petrashevskii was sure, would aid any revolution in Russia without encouragement, by trying to secede and form a separate nation. Tol', a Baltic German by birth, believed that the government's anti-Protestant policies were causing great discontent in the Baltic and hoped for a rising there, to give Russia 'a push'.[44] Then there was Siberia. Siberia was rich. There were no landowners and no serfs, no private property, everything belonged to the exchequer. To many it looked like the land of the future. Petrashevskii wrote, 'I think that Siberia is replacing the Russia of today ... a republican government will rule it.' Chernosvitov, the Siberian gold-miner, called it 'Eldorado', 'California', and happily invited all his friends to go and start a new life there. With Speshnev and Petrashevskii he discussed plans for starting the Russian revolution with an uprising in the Urals.[45]

The Petrashevtsy pinpointed the likely elements of discontent in the Russian Empire fairly accurately, although, carried away by the excitement of 1848, they overestimated the revolutionary potential of these elements in the 1840s. In their assessment of revolutionary possibilities in Russia, the serious exists side by side with the fanciful, as can be seen, for example, from Balasoglo's apocalyptic vision of what might engulf Russia:

> The soldiers will mutiny, orators will arouse the people to carnage, the rabble will pull down taverns, rape women, torture nobles and *chinovniki* – the Germans will be exterminated in one fell swoop. The Poles will kill every last one of the occupying soldiers or themselves perish to the last man beneath their bayonets; the Malorussians will most likely secede; the Cossacks will go wild as they did of old; the Caucasus will boil up like a cauldron and perhaps flood out in fierce raids on the Crimea, Moscow, Orenburg; the Bashkirs, the Kirghiz and the Mongols, who've just been waiting for this, will burst out of the steppes of Central Asia to the Volga and beyond ... Siberia will rise and throw in her lot with China ... bands of new Razins and Pugachevs will wander all over Russia ... the English will occupy the Amur.[46]

Conspiracies

Many of the Petrashevtsy were thus convinced of the potential for revolution in Russia and the need to do everything possible to hasten it. However, there were serious disagreements among them over the nature and timing of a revolutionary attempt. Throughout 1848 and 1849 there were attempts by different Petrashevtsy (and in particular by Speshnev) to form societies or conspiracies of one sort or another: in the Tolstov–Katenev circle; with Chernosvitov; with Timkovskii; with Mombelli. In each of them, conflict appeared between the extremist views of Speshnev and Petrashevskii's more cautious point of view. The conflict was brought out into the open at Petrashevskii's in a debate between Petrashevskii and Speshnev's friends, (Filippov, Mombelli, Grigor'ev and Dostoevskii) on the relative importance of emancipation and legal reform. Finally, Speshev lost patience with Petrashevskii and, using the Pal'm–Durov circle as a cover, formed a revolutionary conspiracy without him.

The views of Petrashevskii and Speshnev had a great deal in common. Both were in favour of secret societies, believing that the existence of the secret police meant that in Russia nothing could be organised successfully unless it was secret.[47] Both wanted revolution in Russia. Both believed it was the existence of serfdom that created the conditions for revolution. The difference was over timing and method. Speshnev wanted to work through a secret society for revolution in the near future and was prepared to use putschist and dictatorial methods. Petrashevskii envisaged a secret society as having an educational function, to prepare the people for revolution at some later date and insisted that this revolution had to have a democratic nature. Speshnev was a powerful and dangerous character; Petrashevskii a more consistently serious revolutionary. In Europe in 1845, Speshnev had become fascinated by conspiracies. He began by studying the early history of Christianity, then turned to everything he could get hold of about the new secret societies. His sources included *Mémoires pour servir à l'histoire du Jacobinisme* by the Jesuit Abbé Barruel, *Conspiration pour l'égalité dite de Babeuf* by Buonarotti and as well, then or later, Eugène Sue's *Le Juif errant* and Dézamy's *Le Jésuitisime vaincu et anéanti par le socialisme,* both socialist accounts of how the Jesuits organised themselves. Speshnev supplemented these authors with his personal observations of the clubs and societies of Europe.[48] His researches resulted in a book of four chapters: the first three describe the history of secret societies from the Essenes on, the fourth, which he never finished, was about the best way of organising a secret society in Russia. He burnt all but one fragment, a draft for the oath of allegiance to the *Russian Society*. It is directly influenced by Blanqui and shows Speshnev to be a supporter of putschist tactics. It begins with a pledge to insurrection:

> When the executive committee of the society, after taking the society's support, the circumstances and the occasion offered into consideration, decides that the time has come for insurrection, then I swear that I will declare my sympathies and regardless of my personal safety to take part in the fighting and to further the success of the cause as far as is in my power.[49]

Like Blanqui, Speshnev projected an association of small groups, their members ignorant of the identity of those of other groups or of the

Secret Directory. Speshnev regarded this year, 1845, as the turning point in his life, 'Now I know what I'm living for, what I want, approximately how much time I need for it.' He returned to Russia in 1847, as he himself admitted, 'dreaming of revolution' and with the aim of establishing a secret society to prepare an insurrection.[50]

Petrashevskii was not averse to secret societies. According to Engel'son, the Abbé Barruel's work was his favourite book, which he recommended to all his acquaintances. His library contained a large collection of books on conspiracies.[51] He gave Antonelli strongly Machiavellian advice on how to set up a secret society. However, whereas Speshnev was prepared to contemplate the idea of a Blanquist insurrection, Petrashevskii had taken the example of the Decembrists to heart and was convinced of the uselessness of any rising that was not supported by a majority of the population. He explained:

> Acting gradually, we should prepare means to an uprising as carefully and as surely as possible, so that the idea of a change of government does not arise in the heads of two, three or ten people, but becomes rooted in the mass of the people and appears not to have been *instilled from without* but to have arisen naturally from the state of affairs.

The purpose of a secret society was to spread enlightenment, to educate the masses and gradually convince them of the need for a change of government. It had to proceed by what Petrashevskii called 'the system of deterioration', by exposing to the public gaze the abuses and misdeeds of the Tsar and his officials and thus gradually destroying the peoples' trust in them. He particularly approved the actions of two pupils at the Law School, arrested for exposing the evil deeds of Lev Perovskii, Minister of Internal Affairs. Aware, however, of the gap between the intelligentsia and the peasants, Petrashevskii felt the process of deterioration might take a long time.[52]

There was one group which inclined definitely towards putschist and insurrectionary ideas, which had no connections with Speshnev, though it was visited by Petrashevskii and Khanykov. This was the circle which grew up around the tobacco shop of the *meshchanin* Shaposhnikov, a colourful, ebullient character, whose dream was to be an actor. His chief habitués were Tolstov and Katenev, hot-headed students with chips on their shoulders, ready for any reckless adventure. They were childish and foolish, bohemian in their life-style and it is difficult to regard them as serious revolutionaries. They carried out propaganda wherever they went (but especially in taverns), with immense enthusiasm, preaching revolution, republicanism and atheism. Shaposhnikov tried to inspire hatred of the government in 'every man who came into his shop'. They had plans for propaganda among servants, serfs and *raskol'niki*, for publishing a journal, printing 'various leaflets to instruct the people' and distributing them without being noticed in hotels and taverns.[53] (Especially when they were drunk), they indulged in loose talk, about assassinating the Tsar. On one occasion, when they were walking down the street, Shaposhnikov cried out, 'How I would love to see the Tsar hanging from this lamp-post!' Katenev declared, 'I thirst for blood ... If you like, I will kill the Tsar.' He even bought a pair of pistols from Vostrov, though whether he intended to use them to kill the Tsar or himself, was not quite clear.[54] They also nourished hopes of revolution in St. Petersburg. They paced the streets of the capital for nights on end, looking for suitable places to build barricades. According to Engel'son, a map of St. Petersburg with the spots marked was seized on their arrest.[55] The shopkeeper Petr Grigor'evich cheerfully allowed himself to get carried away by his revolutionary student friends. They were attracted to him by his habit of declaiming Shakespeare in his shop and immediately allotted him the role of orator in the coming revolution. Tolstov said, 'We are reserving him to be what we call our *Stoic Sektator* and the time will come when he will gather the people on the square with his speeches and convey our ideas to them in a comprehensible form, which we aren't able to do; he is more familiar with the common people.' The Petrashevtsy in general had a very high opinion of the art of oratory, with its revolutionary uses in mind.[56]

Petrashevskii spent his time trying to dampen this circle's revolutionary ardour and channel its members' exuberance into more serious activities. When they asked him about the timing of a revolt, he replied, '*It cannot be now*; because for a revolution one needs a convenient occasion' i.e. some sort of crisis in the state. In his more realistic estimation, though there were a number of peasant risings occurring, these were unlikely to become general and would be easily put down by the army.

He criticised Tolstov for being 'excessively fiery' and Shaposhnikov for talking 'carelessly' to his customers. In fact, Tolstov sometimes spoke in favour of Petrashevskii's gradualist policy. He told Naumov they would only act, 'when everyone is discontented and the government has become more repressive, when we are in a position to forward petitions from everyone and the government, having received this news from this and that from another province, will not know what to do'.[57]

But it was 1848, and Tolstov was unable to resist the lure of revolution.

Their imagination fired by rumours of a revolt in Moscow, they concocted a mad plan for either stabbing the Tsar or announcing his death at a public masked ball to be held in the building of the Nobles' Assembly on the night of 21 April 1849. They decided to throw two hundred forged lottery tickets into the urn at the masquerade, on which they would write news of revolt in Moscow and a call to insurrection in St. Petersburg. They started to write these out, but then lost their nerve, feeling (correctly) that the police were onto them. On 31 March, Tolstov was hauled before Dubel't, head of the Third Department, and forced to sign an undertaking not to spread any more rumours about revolt in Moscow. Several of the Petrashevtsy went to the ball, however, and were there warned by a mysterious masked lady that their arrest was imminent.[58]

Speshnev was anxious to form a secret society from the moment he arrived back in Russia in 1847. Among the Petrashevtsy his first concern was to establish his importance. This was easy to do. The rumour of his European adventures and love affairs, combined with his habitual silence, gave him a mysterious and romantic air, while he knew full well how to exploit. By dropping a hint here and there, he established the idea that he was the emissary of some international conspiracy. Petrashevskii did not believe him, but many of the others did. He had enormous personal magnetism and the ability, while giving nothing away himself, to get others to confide their secrets to him and he enjoyed manipulating and exploiting people.[59] He soon acquired an influence in Petrashevskii's circle at least equal to Petrashevskii's own. He used it to push the circle in an increasingly radical direction and to make a series of attempts to found revolutionary secret societies with various of Petrashevskii's visitors. In each case discussions broke down because of the difference of opinion between Speshnev and Petrashevskii over the nature and timing of a revolutionary attempt.

Speshnev's first attempt to form a secret society centred on Raphael Chernosvitov. Chernosvitov made a great impression on the other Petrashevtsy, as something beyond their experience, 'a man who has passed through fire and water'. Eleven years older than Petrashevskii and Speshnev, a Siberian gold-prospector by trade, he had lost a leg in the Turkish wars, been taken prisoner by the insurgent Poles in 1831 and besieged by peasant uprisings while working as an *ispravnik* in the Perm region in 1841–2. He loved attention and was delighted to find an audience to which to hold forth about his favourite topic – his heroic behaviour during the revolts in Perm and the unjust way in which his superiors had treated him. He greatly enjoyed the rebellious tone of Petrashevskii's evenings and entered into the spirit of the thing with enthusiasm, boasting of his 'unlimited influence' over Nikolai Murav'ev, the Governor-General of Siberia, over the *raskol'niki* and over the gold-miners of the Amur, who, he claimed had asked him to be their leader.[60] He spoke eagerly in favour of secret societies and, deciding that Petrashevskii's circle must be the cover for one, asked insistently to join it.[61] The more timid of the Petrashevtsy, horrified by his revolutionary speeches, believed that he was a government spy; Petrashevskii and Speshnev, on the other hand, saw him as ideal material for a conspiracy.[62]

The three of them began discussions at Petrashevskii's one Friday after all the other guests had gone. Chernosvitov told them the story of his involvement in the Siberian potato revolts – how in 1841, single handed, he had quelled a revolt in which the peasants threw the governor from his carriage and in 1842, in Shadrinsk, he and thirty soldiers of the invalid detachment had been walled up in a church and besieged by ten thousand armed peasants. He boasted that, if it had not been for his heroic actions, the revolt would have spread like wildfire through the Urals, the workers in the mines and distilleries, the convict settlers and the *raskol'niki* would have joined the peasants and the whole area would have erupted in a rising which the army was too stretched out to be able to stifle. This picture appealed greatly to Speshnev, who drew the conclusion, 'This is where the future Russian revolution must begin.' Petrashevskii did not agree, quarrelled with Speshnev and Speshnev and Chernosvitov left.[63]

Soon afterwards, Chernosvitov visited Speshnev and pressed him for details about his supposed secret society. 'To seem more important' Speshnev pretended to be a communist leader and even said that his society had a branch in Moscow.[64] They then discussed details of their revolutionary plan of action. Chernosvitov suggested they begin by raising the Perm factories, 'where there are 400,000 men with arms in their hands, just waiting for the first shot'. With this 'terrible force', they would invade the Volga region, which would soon join them 'as the peasants remember Pugachev'. If, at the same time, there was a rising in St. Petersburg and Moscow, then, 'that would be the end and the revolutionary party would have won'. At this point they decided to bring in Petrashevskii and continue the discussions at Chernosvitov's house. There Speshnev explained the plan of uprising to Petrashevskii, declaring, 'There must be a revolution' and 'The revolution which must occur

in Russia to improve the present state of life must be violent.'
Petrashevskii had no patience with these revolutionary dreams. He denounced the plan in bitter terms and retorted that, 'it was possible to
achieve everything by acting legally'. On this, Speshev and Petrashevskii
had a 'really serious quarrel' which ended when Speshnev swore at
Petrashevskii, 'took his hat and left'. Petrashevskii 'in a rage' revealed
to Chernosvitov that Speshnev was not the leader of the Russian communist party — this was a device to 'attach and interest him'. Not surprisingly, this ended the discussions.[65] It also marked the beginning of
the split between Petrashevskii and Speshnev which was gradually to
widen until Speshnev broke with Petrashevskii altogether and founded
a society without him. Chernosvitov returned to Siberia where he forgot
his conversations in St. Petersburg and led the life of an exemplary citizen
until the gendarmes came to arrest him in June 1849.[66]

Petrashevskii and Speshnev clashed again over Konstantin Timkovskii,
a minor civil servant from Reval. Brash and over-enthusiastic, in spite
of his thirty-five years, and a newcomer to socialism, he swung erratical-
ly from one socialist tendency to another. He made two speeches at
Petrashevskii's. In the first, which was fanatically Fourierist, he spoke
of the 'evils of revolution'.[67] His views changed sharply after he was
seen by Mombelli 'arm-in-arm' with Speshnev and by Chernosvitov,
mysteriously conspiring with him.[68] His second speech was 'completely
the opposite' of the first, an 'inflammatory speech in the communist
spirit'. He put forward an opportunistic and insurrectionary programme,
which was clearly a direct reflection of Speshnev's ideas. He called for
the 'cessation of all disputes over systems', the study of different systems
by circles of men of different tendencies, linked by a central committee
which would try to resolve questions on which the different systems disagreed and even suggested that phalansteries and 'communist *obshchinas*'
could be set up side-by-side, each borrowing from the other. His speech
was littered with rhetorical phrases, 'fireworks' as L'vov called them,
borrowed from the speeches of members of the French National
Assembly. He ended by declaring that socialism could only come through
revolution:

> The efforts of all true supporters of progress should be directed towards
> hastening a revolution which would happen sooner or later but which he
> would like to see before his departure for Reval, that he was ready to be
> the first to step out onto the square and if necessary to sacrifice his life
> to redeem the sacred cause of freedom.[69]

This speech aroused strong opposition and caused many of its hearers to 'turn pale with terror'. Petrashevskii was frightened that people would stop coming to him and could only bring himself to thank Timkovskii (as politeness demanded of the host) in a whisper. Afterwards, in private conversation, but loud enough for everyone to hear, he said (clearly referring to the Decembrists), that though it was easy to attract hundreds of young men out onto the square, it was also pointless — they would be shot or hung and the attempt at insurrection would only harm their cause. Speshnev and Timkovskii's brother, alone, stood up and expressed their agreement with Timkovskii and Speshnev and Petrashevskii had another quarrel, this time in public.[70] Later Petrashevskii wrote Timkovskii an enormously long and particularly Fourierist letter, in which he denounced him for trying to 'curry favour with communism' and for advocating 'the irrational waste of social forces, the destruction of hundreds of thousands of individuals',[71] rather than gradual methods. Back in Reval, Timkovskii pinned his hopes on a circle Speshnev had promised to form with himself and Danilevskii. Speshnev, however, was bored with Timkovskii's naïvety and did not not even bother to answer his letters.[72]

The most serious attempt at a revolutionary conspiracy in which Petrashevskii was involved was initiated by Mombelli, when he told him one Friday in December 1848 of his *Brotherhood of Mutual Aid*. This was a scheme he had dreamed up the previous October with the help of his best friend in the regiment, Staff Captain L'vov. At his trial, Mombelli tried very hard to prove that there was nothing political about it, it was just, 'the result of an excess of feeling, of the wish to have true and devoted friends, with whom I could bare my soul and share both grief and joy'. It was to be a mutual aid association in which progressive young men like themselves, who had no relatives, no protectors to help them, would unite to further their mutual elevation in society; its aims closer to those of the Freemasons than anything else.[73]

However, as L'vov revealed in his testimony, there was more to it than this. Right from the start, it contained a political element. As its members gained power and influence the Brotherhood would use it to initiate reforms and change society. It would act as a sort of school for political activists who, 'could play an important role in the future, if a political revolution occurred in Russia'. Mombelli had asked, 'If some men, for example the Jesuits, could unite in societies for an evil aim, why shouldn't we unite for a good aim, for brotherhood?' This idea, as L'vov admitted, comes straight from Eugène Sue's *Le Juif errant*.

Here Marius Rennepont, a persecuted Huguenot, hid his fortune, so that his descendants could use it to found 'an association for good' which would be capable of combatting the 'deadly ... pernicious association' of the Jesuits, to which he had fallen victim. Theodore Dézamy, in his *Le Jésuitisme vaincu et anéanti par le socialisme*, tried to draw up the rules for such an association.[74]

Petrashevskii became very excited when Mombelli outlined his plan and insisted he discuss it in Speshnev's presence. The three of them then decided that they needed more people to found a society and each should invite someone else. Mombelli chose L'vov and Petrashevskii, Konstantin Debu, who he knew would support him if necessary against Speshnev. Speshnev said that he 'has no-one and relies only on himself'. The group of five met between four and six times in December 1848 and January 1849 to settle the aims and organisation of the society.[75]

Petrashevskii and Speshnev both displayed great interest in Mombelli's idea because they knew about his literary evenings, now banned by the government, and they suspected (wrongly) that he 'belonged to some existing society which they could join'.[76] Under their influence Mombelli's ideas shifted a long way to the left. Petrashevskii gave him the Abbé Barruel's book to read. The author, an emigré Jesuit endowed with a powerful imagination, sets out to show that the whole of the French Revolution had been 'foreseen, meditated, planned, resolved, laid down' in conspiracies, 'long ago hatched in the secret societies' of the *Philosophes*, the Freemasons and the atheist and anarchist Illuminists. The importance of the book was that in the section on the Illuminists, it described in detail how to organise a secret society. Mombelli called the twelve volumes of Barruel's book, 'the most harmful of all those which I have ever read, because they indicate ways of practical application which otherwise would never enter one's head'. When he told the Commission if Inquiry that Barruel's book was 'harmful', Mombelli meant that he had been very strongly influenced by it. This can be seen from the fact that when the five of them discussed organisation and affiliation, he insisted not only that they should have a Central Committee, which they as founders should form; that this Committee should collect money from the members and even invest it; but also that every member on joining should have to write his biography to give the society a hold over him; and that one of the paragraphs of the oath should include the threat of the death penalty for treachery. Mombelli admitted that it became easy for him to make concessions to the 'fixed ideas' of Petrashevskii and Speshnev, 'because he had by this time come to agree with them.'[77]

However, as was to become clear when they discussed the aims of the Brotherhood, the 'fixed ideas' of Petrashevskii and Speshnev were by no means the same. Petrashevskii wanted the secret society to have a purely educational function, to conduct propaganda (especially Fourierist propaganda). For this it should form what Speshnev derisively called 'an academic committee', which would examine the nature of the state and social system and make a critical analysis of each member's proposals for the ideal society. Speshnev said that the society should be purely political and have as its aim a peasant revolt. He had been prodding Mombelli from the start to find out if there was 'something more than met the eye' (i.e. an insurrection), behind all his vague proposals.[78] In the end he lost patience and read out his own plan. This was the one Timkovskii had already outlined at Petrashevskii's:

> There are three illegal means of action − jesuitical (secret intrigue, as Mombelli, L'vov and in part Petrashevskii proposed), simple propaganda (as Debu, as enemy of secret societies, wanted) and revolt (his suggestion). None of these is certain ... and there is a better chance if all three roads are taken and for this a committee of brotherhood to set up a school of Fourierist, communist and liberal propaganda; and finally, a committee to form behind all this a secret society for revolt.[79]

It was on the word *revolt* that 'everything hinged'. Speshnev declared, 'If I need to act ... I will choose force, and as the means to this − a peasant revolt.' Mombelli and L'vov were young and unsure of themselves. Petrashevskii was set against revolution and the peaceful Fourierist Konstantin Debu backed him up. As Petrashevskii said, 'Speshnev's final aim was to start a revolution', at this point, Petrashevskii and Speshnev quarrelled yet again, Speshnev stalked out and they agreed not to continue the meetings. Petrashevskii made one attempt to revive them (largely so that he might seem in the right and Speshnev in the wrong), but it fell flat. Speshnev answered the overtures of Debu, sent as a peacemaker, with a disdainful letter, in which he said, 'that being of a completely different opinion to Petrashevskii, he didn't want to co-operate with him in any matter' and referred crushingly to their discussions as a '*chasse aux places*', hinting that he had other, more positive ties.[80]

Speshnev probably had no such ties at the time, but he soon formed them. This can be seen from the disputes which took place at Petrashevskii's in March and April 1849. We know the details of what was said because the spy Antonelli managed to infiltrate these last Fridays. The first argument was a discussion of different methods of propaganda.

Durov and Nikolai Kaidanov argued that it was pointless to inflame the lower classes against their immediate superiors, the minor officials, because the latter were also oppressed and were not to blame. Instead they should point out 'the source of the evil', i.e. attack the Tsar and the laws directly. Filippov, supported by Balasoglo and others, objected that the lower classes were too much in awe of the Tsar and his ministers. You had to begin by arousing them against their immediate bosses and then tracing the evil upwards, from the lower to the higher chiefs. This argument is important because both its substance − practical methods of conducting propaganda − and Filippov's declaration that, 'Our system of propaganda is the best and to deviate from it is to abandon the possibilities of implementing our ideas', imply the existence of a society organised for propaganda work.[81]

The second argument, which began on Friday, 1 April and was continued two weeks later on Friday, 15 April, raised more basic principles and brought the conflict between Petrashevskii's and Speshnev's ideas out into the open. It took the form of a debate about which issues should be raised first in Russia − legal reform, emancipation or freedom of the press − and it raised the basic question: reform or revolution? Speshnev himself did not take part. He had taken umbrage and refused to go on visiting Petrashevskii's after their last quarrel. The attack on Petrashevskii's ideas was carried out, and the revolutionary point of view put forward by Filippov, Mombelli, Golovinskii and Dostoevskii. These four were, as we shall see, all by now members of a secret revolutionary conspiracy, directed by Speshnev.

On the first Friday, 1 April, the argument was provoked by the nineteen-year-old Golovinskii, who suggested, that instead of Fourier, they should discuss practical questions relating to Russia. Petrashevskii agreed and at once launched into a long, convoluted speech. According to him, there were three vital issues in Russia − reform of the legal system, the peasant question and freedom of speech.[82] Freedom of speech should come last, he said. The two most important questions were emancipation of the serfs and the reform of legal procedure. Of these, before 1848, Petrashevskii had put emancipation in first place; he had written projects about it and tried to distribute them. This was because he had hoped by this to provoke the government into taking on the reform. After 1848, he stopped pressing for it because it had become clear that it could only be achieved by revolution and the people, he felt, were not ready for this. He now said that reform of the legal system should come first. He argued that the question of emancipation affected only ten or twelve million serfs. Other classes were either indifferent, or, in the case of the gentry, who would suffer great financial losses, hostile to it. The improvement of legal procedure, on the other hand, would benefit all classes and thus had a potential sixty million supporters. If everyone could be persuaded to deluge the government with petitions asking for it, Nicholas would be forced to give in. Then, once legal proceedings were public, through the cases about serfs brought to court, people's consciousnesses would be raised, everyone would realise the whole 'injustice and ugliness' of serfdom. Faced with the universal demand for its abolition, the government would be forced either to give in, or would be overthrown in a (hopefully) bloodless revolution. Petrashevskii concluded, 'We will mutually, comradely, educate ourselves and then we will peacefully reform ourselves, others, the whole of society.'

Golovinskii could hardly wait for Petrashevskii to finish. He jumped up from his armchair and began an angry, eloquent speech which 'came straight from the heart', his words tumbling over one another in his indignation. 'No!' he shouted, 'The most crying injustice is the slavery of sixty million peasants'. It was remarked to him that there were only twenty million serfs, but he replied, 'It doesn't make any difference! It is sinful and disgraceful for mankind to look indifferently at the suffering of twelve million unhappy slaves. Everyone's idea should be to attempt to free the unhappy sufferers!' There was, he said, no chance of the government emancipating the serfs. It could not free the serfs with land because it could not afford to compensate the landowners. It would not free the serfs without land or without compensating the landowners, because this would provoke a revolution. Emancipation had to take place without the government. But there was 'no exceptional difficulty' in this since the serfs themselves, 'are conscious of all the oppressiveness and all the injustice of their situation and are striving in every way to free themselves from it'. They were already murdering the gentry at a rate of over a hundred a year. Golovinskii concluded, 'For the emancipation of the serfs a rising is necessary!'[83]

His speech caused a furore. People shouted, 'So you want to go out onto the square, is that it?'; 'Are you really enticed by the prospect of a Pugachevshchina?'[84] After supper, Petrashevskii was given the right of reply and argued that emanciaption would not necessarily make the serfs better off, reform of the legal system was much 'safer and easier' to attain. Speshnev's other associates – Filippov, Mombelli and Dostoevskii then broke in to back Golovinskii up. The Golovinskii returned to the fray to say that his ideal government was a republic, but that it could not be achieved at once — during the revolutionary period, 'the serfs need a dictator to lead them'. Speshnev and his friends inclined towards Buonarotti and the Jacobins and cared little for political democracy, but it was something Petrashevskii was not prepared at any costs to sacrifice. 'What!' he interrupted, 'A dictator! who would arbitrarily command them! I will endure arbitrariness in no-one and if my best friend declared himself a dictator, I would consider myself obliged to kill him at once!'[85]

On 15 April, Speshnev's friends renewed their attack. Dostoevskii began by reading Belinskii's *Letter to Gogol*, to support their argument that serfdom was too horrible to be tolerated a moment longer. According to Antonelli, it 'produced general rapture. Jastrzębski at all passages which struck him, cried, "Just so! Just so!" Chirikov, though he did not say a word, grinned all over and muttered something to himself. Balasoglo was in a frenzy and in one word the whole company was as if electrified.' Petrashevskii made a valiant attempt to counter its effect in a speech summarising his previous ones:

> You cannot embark on a rising if you are not certain beforehand of total success, which is not possible at the present time. On the other hand, the reform of the legal system could be achieved ... by demanding from the government things which it cannot refuse, since it recognises their justice ... When legal procedure has undergone the greatest possible improvement, this will open everyone's eyes to other questions.

In reply, Golovinskii made an attempt to be conciliatory and conceded that something might be achieved through legal channels, but repeated his argument that emancipation was the most important question in Russia and that to achieve it, 'all means are good'. In general, Antonelli concluded, 'the meaning of the 15th was ... *très orageuse*.'[86] At Petrashevskii's Golovinskii, Filippov, Mombelli and Dostoevskii were speaking on behalf of a revolutionary conspiracy. Speshnev had lost patience with Petrshevskii and formed one without him, using the Pal'm—Durov circle, as a cover. The idea for the Pal'm—Durov circle to which Petrashevskii was not invited arose at a series of informal gatherings held at Pleshcheev's flat in autumn and winter 1848. Pleshcheev could not have regular meetings because he lived with his elderly mother, but he invited friends round on his birthday (22 November) and on a couple of other occasions when he had money to spare. As well as Speshnev and his friends, his guests included Mikhail

Dostoevskii, Pal'm, Durov, Shchel'kov, Tol', Miliutin, the Lamanskii brothers, Danilevskii and others. They talked about literature and about politics. Pleshcheev read out Pyat's sppech to the National Assembly and Miliukov a manuscript of Herzen's *Moscow and Petersburg*, an uncensored satirical work which attacked all aspects of life in both capitals.[87] And it was here that Speshnev first spoke about a printing press. This was an idea that occurred naturally to the frustrated writers of the 1840s. It had haunted Speshnev for a long time. Abroad, he had agreed with his Polish friend Chojecki that the latter should go to Paris and set up a typography there. Speshnev was to send him material from Russia – a history of Russia which he intended to write himself and, 'any forbidden works which are being passed from hand to hand in Petersburg'. Thus, as Engel'son boasted, he 'was the first to think of founding a free foreign journal in the Russian language', the idea which was soon to be so successfully implemented by Herzen. In Paris Chojecki became involved with the *Revue indépendante* and wrote to Speshnev asking him for articles about Russia. Speshnev told the company at Pleshcheev that he could get their writings printed abroad, they only had to write them and send them to him. However, the idea seems only to have 'embarrassed them all' and nothing came of it.[88]

The success of Pleshcheev's evenings encouraged Durov and Pal'm to form their own circle, in January 1849. A large proportion of the people they invited were 'ill-disposed towards Petrashevskii'. (Durov himself called him 'an ox and a man without a heart'). Many of them were fellow-writers whom Petrashevskii had offended by his criticisms.[89] They felt that not only did Petrashevskii not understand art, but that he did not devote enough time to it. His evenings were too much taken up with politics and Fourierism and 'were sometimes tedious and boring because of the speeches'. Durov and Pal'm's idea was to organise evenings exclusively devoted to literature and music. At the beginning, they did have a predominantly artistic tone. Before supper, Pal'm, Durov, Dostoevskii and Plescheev read their poems and short stories; after supper Kaszewski played the piano, Shchel'kov and Evgenii Lamanskii the violoncello and Durov sang. They stayed until three in the morning. All this led early commentators to take Miliukov's word for it that this was 'a small group of more moderate young men'.[90]

But the circle also included 'the most ardent people', the members of Speshnev's conspiracy, who were prepared to go to 'lengths which were not at all to the taste of Petrashevskii'. Its members were Speshnev, Mombelli, Grigor'ev, Golovinskii, Dostoevskii, Filippov, Mordvinov, probably Pleshcheev and (rather surprisingly) Miliutin. They were interested in visiting Durov's because it formed a harmless literary cover for their activities; because there they could discuss things it was not safe to mention at Petrashevskii's more open gatherings;[91] and because they hoped to persuade the writers in the circle to put their talent to work composing revolutionary propaganda for them.

The first attempt to give the meetings a directly political tone, made independently by Mombelli, was a dramatic flop. The remarks of the guests about their wish to know one another better led him precipitately to decide that he had at last found the people with whom to found his *Brotherhood of Mutual Aid*, and he read out a simplified version of the project. L'vov described the reaction, 'Mombelli was hissed, he blushed, tore up his notes. Everyone unanimously told him that we had purposely collected with the intention of eliminating all political discussion, which if he likes he can hear at Petrashevskii's.' After this Mombelli played little part in the discussions and he later quarrelled bitterly with Durov.[92]

In spite of this, little by little, politics crept into the conversation.[93] Finally, on the fifth or sixth evening, Filippov put forward the programme of Speshnev's society. He proposed that, instead of stories, they should write factual articles about Russia and its needs, each taking responsibility for the area he knew best. He called on them to 'Speak out boldly and openly ... strip bare all the injustice of our laws, all the corruption and shortcomings of our administration.' Everyone approved of the idea. Durov took on the legislative part; Dostoevskii the exposition of socialism; Filippov serfdom; Lamanskii economics; Grigor'ev the army; Minaev Russia's class system. Then the conversation turned to manuscript literature and the difficulties involved in copying uncensored material. When many of those present expressed the wish to have a copy of the articles read at the evenings, Filippov proposed that they should set up a domestic lithography. No-one disagreed and they decided to consult L'vov about the lithographic process.[94]

However, this proposal had secretly struck terror into the hearts of the more moderate writers. Dostoevskii said, 'It seemed to me that half of those present did not speak out against Filippov's idea only because they were afraid the others might suspect them of cowardice and they wanted to reject the proposal not directly but in some sort of indirect fashion.'[95] Its chief opponents were Mikhail Dostoevskii, who said afterwards that he would stop going to Durov's if Filippov did not retract his proposal; and Durov, who wanted to end his meetings as soon as possible and suggested Speshnev should take them on instead. Speshnev refused (although he had a large house all of his own) but offered to give a dinner for all concerned to show his goodwill. This was held the following week (2 April) and was the occasion on which Grigor'ev read his *Soldier's Tale*.[96]

At the next meeting at Durov's (17 April), L'vov reported that it was perfectly possible to set up a secret press, as a lithographic stone only cost twenty silver roubles. The problem was how to distribute articles once they were printed. They could not send them through the post, because it was read by the secret police. Mikhail Dostoevskii angrily pointed out that they would have to turn themselves into 'an organised club', which he protested, negated the original apolitical aim of the evenings. Fedor Dostoevskii then 'asked for the floor and talked them all out of it', persuading them tactfully that it was a rash and risky venture. He seems to have done this not because he himself disapproved of the idea but in order to stop the Pal'm–Durov circle breaking up and the conspiracy losing its cover.[97] They resolved that 'a lithography is a dangerous business' and that those who wanted to should copy things out by hand instead. They made a start by handing round Belinskii's *Letter to Gogol*, which Dostoevskii read out.[98] However, the rejection of Filippov's proposal did not allay Durov and Pal'm's fears. They had ceased (quite rightly) to trust Speshnev and his friends. They held one more evening (13 April) and then on the 18th sent out letters cancelling the next. To make quite sure, Durov went out and Pal'm retreated to bed.[99]

Speshnev's group had in fact only pretended to give up the idea of a press. In reality they merely transferred the action behind the scenes and went ahead and ordered the parts, not for a lithography, but for a typography. At their trial, Speshnev and Filippov said that this was merely a harebrained and unimportant plot between the two of them. Their other associates preserved total silence on the question, primed by Speshnev, who spread the word around after their arrest that each of them should talk about anything rather than this. The Commission of Inquiry was distracted by the sudden appearance of Chernosvitov and did not pursue the matter further. Thus, as Dostoevskii later wrote, 'a whole conspiracy vanished'.[100] This is one of the reasons why the Petrashevtsy were underestimated throughout the nineteenth century. The existence of the conspiracy did not come to light until 1922, with the publication of a letter writen by Apollon Maikov in 1885, describing a nocturnal visit paid to him by Dostoevskii. To recruit Maikov to the revolutionary group Dostoevskii had argued:

> Of course you understand that Petrashevskii is a chatterbox, that he is
> not a serious person and that nothing can possibly come of his under-
> takings, and for that reason several serious people from his circle have
> decided (secretly and without telling anyone) to form their own society
> with a secret printing press in order to print various books and journals,
> if that works out. There are seven of us now. We have chosen you to be
> the eighth. Do you want to join our society?

Its purpose was, 'to organise a coup in Russia, naturally'. Maikov writes,
'I remember Dostoevskii, like the dying Socrates before his friends,
sitting in his nightshirt with the collar unbuttoned and lavishing all his
eloquence on the sanctity of this action.' Maikov refused, but he kept
the secret for thirty-six years. He writes about it in two different letters
and there is no reason to doubt the truth of his words. Dostoevskii's
later writings are full of hints to the same effect.[101]

Speshnev and his friends had formed a conspiracy, the aim of which
was revolt, the immediate task, revolutionary propaganda. They even
set up a printing press − designed by Mordvinov, paid for by Speshnev
and ordered in parts in different places and assembled in Mordvinov's
flat. The Third Department missed it in their search because it stood in
Mordvinov's physics laboratory, among all sorts of machines, retorts
etc.[102] Speshnev tried to recruit writers and scholars − Dostoevskii,
Miliutin, Apollon Maikov − to the conspiracy with the idea of putting
their pens to propaganda use. He bound the waverers to him partly by
the sheer magnetism of his personality and partly by more Machiavellian
means − lending them money. Dostoevskii told his friend Dr Ianovskii,
'I have taken money from Speshnev (he mentioned a sum of about 500
roubles) and now *I am with him and his* ... from now on I have my own
Mephistopheles.'[103]

The process of collecting propaganda material was begun by
Pleshcheev who, in March−April 1849 went on an exploratory trip to
Moscow. His particular aim was to get hold of Turgenev's comedy *The
Hanger-on*, banned from the pages of *Otechestvennye zapiski*. He wrote
long letters back, which Dostoevskii read out at Durov's, reporting that
he had added to his list Herzen's *Before the Storm* and Belinskii's *Letter
to Gogol*, over which everyone 'was in ecstasies' in Moscow's radical
circles. He also did a bit of agitation of his own, visiting the liberal
professors Granovskii and Petr Kudriavtsev and various student circles.
Evgenii Feoktistov relates how Pleshcheev told a group of students at
his house:

That it was essential to awaken the consciousness of the people; that the best way of doing this was to translate foreign works into Russia and make a collection of speeches adapted for the people and distribute them in hand-written copies and perhaps even find a way to print them; that a society with that aim had already appeared in Petersburg.[104]

Pleshcheev only managed to find Belinskii's *Letter to Gogol*, which he sent to Durov's, care of Dostoevskii, before the others were arrested.

The members of the secret society were intending to print a large amount of propaganda. This included manuscript material by leading progressive writers, directed at the educated Russian public – Belinskii's famous *Letter to Gogol*; two works of Herzen's, *Moscow and Petersburg*, and *Before the Storm*, the first chapter of his *From the other Shore*; and Turgenev's *The Hanger-on*, one of his most outspoken attacks on the inhumanity of the Russian gentry and the sufferings of the 'little man'; uncensored works of fiction by members of the Pal'm–Durov circle, among them Durov's satirical 'tragi-comedy', *Brother and Sister*, and Pleshcheev's revolutionary poems; and socialist non-fiction by other Petrashevtsy – economic articles by Miliutin, Beklemishev's *Correspondence of Two Landowners*, a series of essays about emancipation and the adaptation of Fourierism to Russia.[105] There were also three items of propaganda of a different and far more revolutionary nature – a translation of Lamennais' *Paroles d'un croyant*, Grigor'ev's *Soldier's Tale* and Filippov's *Ten Commandments*. These were designed not for the intelligentsia but for the peasantry and call on the peasants and serfs to rise in revolt, kill the landowners, overthrow the Tsar and set up a democratic republic.

Lamennais' *Paroles d'un croyant* was the most popular of all contemporary socialist writings, translated into almost every European language, but in Russia 'unconditionally banned'. Miliukov was the first of the Petrashevtsy to realise its suitability for propaganda among the Russian peasants: the language was high-flown but the ideas were clear and simple and presented in a religious form: it talked of overthrowing tyrants and kings, but in the language of Revelations; it talked of establishing the liberty, equality and fraternity of the French Revolution, but it spoke in the language of the Gospels. He translated Lamennais' introduction, *A Testament*, putting it into Church Slavonic rather than Russian and read it out, under a new Russian title, *The New Revelations of the Metropolitan Antonius*, at Durov's. Everyone admired it greatly, especially Dostoevskii, who said that, 'The stern biblical speech of the work came out ... more strikingly than in the original.' L'vov at once took it away to copy. Pleshcheev and Mordvinov formed a project to translate the whole forty-two chapters. Pleshcheev started work on it in Moscow and tried to persuade Feokistov's student circle to help him.[106] He translated chapters 1—21 and 33 and 34; Mordvinov, 22—32 and 34—41. Their manuscript lay unnoticed in the archives of the Third Department until 1971 and still has not been examined in detail by any Soviet scholar. They stuck very close to the original, just simplifying it slightly and russifying the terms. Lamennais' attack on the authority of kings, put into Russian, becomes a denunciation of serfdom:

> And I was carried in spirit into ancient times and the earth was beautiful and rich and fertile, people were happy. I saw an evil serpent among them. His deceitful glance attracted many to him ... the serpent began to whisper in their ears ... they stood up and said, 'We are Tsars!' ... Strange things happened at that time: chains, tears and blood appeared ... the people ... let heavy chains be put upon themselves, their wives and children ... those who had said, 'We are Tsars!' dug out a vast cavern and shut up in it the whole human race.

The document goes on to predict that the people will only be freed as a result of bloody revolution, 'a war to the death'.[107]

A Soldier's Tale, by Grigor'ev, was also designed for distribution among the peasants and in particular, the common soldiers. The story is at once a protest against the landowners' cruelty to their serfs, against bad conditions in the army and a personal attack on the Tsar — it includes an account of how Nicholas I himself ran into a tavern to arrest some sailors who, half-frozen, had slipped in for a drink. The solution it offers is revolution. The old soldier explains how in France:

> The king squandered money madly, loved the rich and insulted the poor. And then, last year, the people and the soldiers made barricades out of cobblestones in the town and oh! what fun there was. A terrible punch-up. But the king and his gentlemen put up a poor show. Now they don't want tsars and govern themselves as we do in the village. A *mir* with everyone in it and elections!

Encouraged by Speshnev, Grigor'ev read this out to the members of the Pal'm—Durov circle on 2 April. The more moderate were terrified — Mikhail Dostoevskii called it criminal and Durov advised him to burn it. Speshnev, however, asked Grigor'ev to make it even 'clearer and sharper' and wanted him to read it out 'almost on the street'.[108]

Filippov had almost finished a similar, but even more revolutionary document, intended for the peasants and perhaps in particular the *raskolniki*. This was a new, revolutionary interpretation of the *Ten Commandments*. The aim was to show that the Tsar and the landowners broke the Commandments and that revolt against them was therefore justified by God. For example, the landowners broke the Fourth Commandment (Six days shalt thou labour …), by driving their poor *muzhiks* out to *barshchina* on the Sabbath Day; the Seventh (Neither shalt thou commit adultery), by raping their serf-girls and forcing serfs to marry against their will. Filippov's interpretation of the Sixth Commandment (Thou shalt not kill), however, was the most revolutionary of all and the most revealing about the aims of Speshnev's conspiracy: the landowners sin when they ill-treat and murder their serfs. The Tsar sins when he leads his people to war. But the serfs who disobey or kill their masters do not sin. They take the punishment as martyrs for their fellows. Filippov asks, 'Isn't it all right to defend yourself if robbers attack you? and the landowner who ill-treats his peasants, isn't he worse than a robber?'[109]

Thus, though they did not have time to put their ideas into practice, and though, in the context of the 1840s, their ideas of immediate action were less realistic than those of Petrashevskii, who thought that a revolution would take a long time to prepare, Speshnev and his friends had formed a revolutionary conspiracy. That its members were serious about it is underlined both by the fact that they had got as far as buying a press and by the emphasis they placed on keeping its existence secret. Their success in this was important in leading scholars long to underestimate the revolutionary nature of the Petrashevtsy circles. The Petrashevtsy in fact established a model for revolutionary activity which later revolutionaries were to adopt. Dostoevskii was later to speak with mingled pride and horror of the Petrashevtsy as the precursors of the Nechaevtsy, 'I am an old Nechaevets myself' and to assert that there was among the Petrashevtsy:

> Everything that was in the later conspiracies, which were just copies of this one, that is, a secret typography and lithography … and in just the same way, we believed that the people were with us … and we had grounds for this, since the people were serfs.[110]

In April 1849 the press was ready. The articles were ready. And then the blow came. They were betrayed by Antonelli, a Third Department agent who had wormed his way into Petrashevskii's circle. On the night of 23 April 1849, as the visitors left Petrashevskii's, the arrests began.

IX — CONCLUSION

The Petrashevtsy were humanists and materialists; anti-capitalists; democrats; the first advocates of a Russian socialism based on the *mir*; champions of a utilitarian theory of art; of the emancipation of women; and finally, supporters of revolution.

The central idea of the Petrashevtsy's philosophy was anthropological materialism, a doctrine which asserted the primacy of eternal, unchanging laws of nature and, above all, of human nature. On the basis of this, the Petrashevtsy preached a passionate left-Hegelian individualism, attacking religion, metaphysics, and all authorities placed above man, and demanded human liberation, defined as full freedom for man to satisfy his natural impulses. At the same time, they expressed a profound respect for science and felt compelled to try to fit the individual into a historical framework. The anthropological idea always came first for the Petrashevtsy and, when conflict arose between the idea of a static, unchanging human nature and theories of historical change, it took precedence. The Petrashevtsy turned their anthropological materialism into a socialist doctrine, by concluding that society should be altered so that it corresponded to the needs of human nature.

The same tension between utopian anthropological and more scientific historical ideas can be detected in the Petrashevtsy's analysis of contemporary society (which for them meant above all the developing capitalist society of Western Europe). The existing order was judged from the standpoint of human nature and condemned for failing to meet its needs: they pointed to the growing pauperism of the lower classes and the turmoil and squalor of the big cities (in Europe, and, increasingly, in Russia); the repressive principles on which the reigning systems of morality and education were based; and attacked the political economists, liberal philanthropists and others, who acted as apologists for this order. They called for its destruction and the establishment in its place of a totally new social order, which would be based on the principles of the organisation of labour and association and would ensure full freedom for human nature and the adequate satisfaction of men's needs. Yet, at the same time, the Petrashevtsy admitted their respect for a theory of historical change, according to which human society evolved to ever higher forms. They depicted the existing social order and, above all, capitalism, as one stage in this process and, as such, progressive. However, here again, the anthropological and individualist point of view tended to predominate over their respect for science and history, their hatred of the pauperism caused by capitalism over their respect for its achievements.

In spite of their interest in abstract theories and a theoretical cosmopolitanism, the Petrashevtsy's primary concern was always their own country. Their excursions into philosophy, socialist theory and political economy were regarded by them as a preliminary to working out a practical programme for Russia. They made a thorough critique of the evils of the Tsarist regime. They demanded democratic reforms — freedom of speech, press and assembly, representative government, the democratisation of the army, bureaucracy and legal system and, above all, the emancipation of the serfs. However, these reforms, especially emancipation, were seen only as a prelude to the socialist transformation of Russia. The Petrashevtsy seem to have been the first to put forward a socialist interpretation of the advantages of the survival of communal landownership in the Russian village. They suggested that the development of pauperism and establishment of capitalism could be avoided in Russia and the country pass straight from feudalism to socialism, if the peasant *mir* was used as a springboard for the foundation of socialist associations. This was the basic formula of later Russian populism.

As time went on, the Petrashevtsy became more and more determined not just to discuss, but to act towards the establishment of socialism in Russia. Their first concern was to spread socialist ideas among people like themselves i.e. among the Russian intelligentsia. They carried out propaganda among their friends, through teaching and, especially, through publishing and literature. They embarked on publishing ventures of their own, the most famous being the exceptionally revolutionary *Pocket Dictionary* and wrote articles, poems, sketches and stories for the radical journals *Otechestvennye zapiski* and *Sovremennik* and *Finskii vestnik* (which they attempted to take over). They subscribed to the 'natural school' idea that the writer had a social mission, as a result of which not only their theoretical articles but also their fiction acquired a distinctive socialist tone, and helped to make socialist ideas more widely known to young men of their own and the succeeding generation.

Many of the Petrashevtsy had long had revolutionary sympathies.

The outbreak of revolution in France in February 1848, a perceived increase in popular unrest in Russia, combined with Nicholas's reactionary response to revolution, which stripped them of illusions in a reforming Tsar, convinced them of the desirability and (quite wrongly at this time) of the possibility of a revolution in Russia. Their attention became focussed on carrying their propaganda to the lower classes – on converting peasants, serfs and soldiers to revolutionary ideas and on utilising the potential for discontent among the non-Russian nationalities of the Empire. Finally, after various attempts to form conspiracies, just before their arrest, a secret society was organised, its immediate task, the printing and distribution of propaganda, its ultimate aim, an uprising. This makes the Petrashevtsy the first sizeable group of revolutionary socialists in Russia.

These are the ideas of the Petrashevtsy as a whole, as far as generalisations can be made. But, it must be emphasised that there was a spectrum of differing views within the general socialist framework of the Petrashevtsy circles and that the views neither of the Petrashevtsy as a group nor of individuals among them can be described as homogeneous. While the prevailing tone of the Petrashevtsy circles was materialist and revolutionary, for example, there were people among them, who, while their general ideological sympathies and social outlook their acceptance of socialist ideas, such as the need for association, entitle them to be considered as Petrashevtsy, were Christians or advocates of peaceful, gradual change. The views of individual Petrashevtsy often shifted and changed (sometimes extremely rapidly) during the 1840's. The reason for this seems to have been that this was a very early stage of development both of socialist ideas and of the radical/revolutionary movement in Russia. No concrete doctrines had been laid down, ideological divisions had not yet been rigidly drawn (not yet even between liberal and radical, radical and socialist). It was a period of intellectual fluctuation and formation, an eclectic and, in some ways, encyclopedic stage. The Petrashevtsy browsed among the social, literary, philosophical and economic productions both of the West and of their Russian predecessors and contemporaries, with a view to choosing, here and there, solutons which seemed to suit them. As this would indicate, their theories were both inconsistent and, to an extent, derivative.

The dominant influences on the Petrashevtsy were the theories of French utopian socialism and the writings of the slightly older and more established Russian radicals, Herzen and Belinskii.

In the development of their ideas, the Petrashevsy were greatly indebted to the French socialists, above all Fourier, but also Saint-Simon, Proudhon, Louis Blanc and, in some cases, the communists. It was from Fourier that they drew their central idea of socialism as an anthropological doctrine, of the ideal society as one that conformed to human nature. They also owed much to him in their rejection of capitalism, their ideas on education and morality and the notion that the society of the future should be based on a federation of rural communes. Fourier's great attraction lay in the amount of liberty he appeared to offer to the individual. Though the Petrashevtsy rejected the elitist aspects of the doctrine, they took from Saint-Simon and his follower Comte their philosophy of history, their belief in progress and their respect for science, from the Saint-Simonians ideas of the utilitarian nature of art; and from both the Saint-Simonians (especially George Sand) and the Fourierists, their emphasis on the emancipation of women. The Petrashevtsy were also, to differing degrees, influenced by Proudhon's anarchism and individualism; Louis Blanc's critique of competition and ideas on association; and egalitarian ideas on the distribution of wealth advocated by Proudhon, Louis Blanc and the communists.

Although the Petrashevtsy occasionally made extravagant and frivolous declarations of their faith in Fourier, they were, in general, less fanciful than the French socialists. They changed and developed these ideas and added a perhaps more serious tone to them by combining them with ideas from other western sources: adding the anthropological materialism of Feuerbach to Fourier's theory of the passions, elements of Hegel to Saint-Simon's philosophy of history, the political economists' detailed analysis of capitalism's workings to Fourier's impressionistic denunciation of 'civilisation'. The Petrashevskii's socialism was based on a sound understanding of most of the relevant subjects.

The Petrashevtsy's adoption of French socialist ideas was driven by the problems of their own country. They adapted some aspects of French socialism to fit in with Russian conditions — Fourier's argument that capitalism should be destroyed was turned into the argument that it should never be introduced in Russia; his insistence that rural phalanteries should replace it, into the idea of establishing socialism on the basis of the peasant commune. Other French socialist ideas were rejected completely. In general, the differing circumstances and greater repression in Russia forced the Petrashevtsy towards more extreme solutions. Most of the French socialists were semi-religious; most of the Petrashevtsy atheist. The French socialists (especially the Fourierists) avoided politics; the absence of democratic freedoms in Russia led the Petrashevtsy to regard political reforms as the precondition for social change. The French socialists generally based their socialism on the idea of a class reconciliation, in which an enlightened bourgeoisie would lead and guide the proletariat; in Russia, there was no bourgeoisie or proletariat to speak of and the Petrashevtsy naturally came to rest their hopes for socialism on the peasants. The French socialists hoped to introduce their ideas peacefully and to avoid a return to the horrors of the first French Revolution; the Petrashevtsy became convinced that there was no hope of persuading Tsarism to reform itself — it had to be overthrown by violent means. The utopian socialists' deist, paternalist, peaceful theories were reworked into a materialist, populist and revolutionary form, with the ultimate goal of a socialist society specifically adapted to the Russian village. Though the Petrashevtsy's solutions were of course immensely inferior (they never got as far as a coherent doctrine), their theory bears some resemblance to that which Marx was formulating in Germany in the same period. He also combined ideas drawn from French socialism with an analysis derived from German philosophy, and from political economy and arrived at atheism, materialism and the idea of popular revolution, though in a proletarian rather than a peasant form.

The Petrashevtsy also owed much to the older radicals Herzen and Belinskii, whose articles in *Otechestvennye zapiski* and *Sovremennik* they read with the enthusiasm of all the young intelligentsia of their generation. They developed their ideas in Herzen's, and especially Belinskii's shadow. The writers among the Petrashevtsy had a particularly close association with Belinskii. They collaborated with him on *Otechestvennye zapiski* and *Sovremennik*, even for a short time, on *Finskii vestnik*; Maikov and Belinskii carried on a vigorous public debate in the journals; Dostoevskii was admitted briefly to Belinskii's circle. There is a story that the government intended to arrest Belinskii at the same time as the Petrashevtsy — Dubel't, head of the Third Department, regretted his death, as otherwise 'We would have rotted him in a fortress.'[1] The esteem in which Belinskii and Herzen were held in the Petrashevtsy circles can be seen from the way in which their works (Belinskii's *Letter to Gogol* and Herzen's *Moscow and Petersburg*) were read out at their meetings and included among the first batch of propaganda intended for Speshnev's press.

From Herzen and Belinskii, the Petrashevtsy imbibed a general humanist, radical democratic, anti-religious, anti-metaphysical outlook, a deep concern for the dignity of the human individual, hatred of injustice and oppression and a critical attitude to all aspects of Russian life, above all, serfdom. More specifically, the Petrashevtsy's left-Hegelianism was partly mediated through Herzen. His *Dilettantism in Science* and *Letters on the Study of Nature* seem to have made a great impression on them and were used as a direct source in their philosophical writings. The Petrashevtsy took the idea of the social role of art straight from Belinskii and in spite of their (especially Maikov's) differences with him, all their ideas on the subject were developed and all their fiction was written within the framework Belinskii laid down for the 'natural school'. However, unlike both Belinskii, and Herzen at this time, the Petrashevtsy were socialists. Belinskii, in spite of his pronouncements of 'socialism or death' was not a socialist in any recognised sense, adopting no socialist doctrines; Herzen only developed his agrarian socialism later, after 1848, while in exile in Europe, and its precise nature and content always remained vague. It is their acceptance of socialist doctrines, derived from the Fourierists and Saint-Simonians in France, which clearly distinguishes the Petrashevtsy from their radical contemporaries and marks them off as a separate group.

The seriousness of the Petrashevtsy's socialism has often been doubted. There is some justification for this. Few of them were consistently serious. Their socialism was often self-indulgent. Some of their antics appear frankly juvenile and bear a strong resemblance to those of French students in 1968: Petrashevskii's strange pranks; his 'Saint-Simonian' beard and wig; Katenev's white republican suit; the drawing up of a map of St. Petersburg with spots for barricades marked on it. The Petrashevtsy's ideology was in many ways muddled and inconsistent, an amalgam of bits and pieces, not yet moulded into a cohesive doctrine. They spent a good deal of time discussing abstract ideas and only in 1848 began really to consider the practical steps to be undertaken. All this makes them seem, as in some ways they were, a bunch of generous minded, enthusiastic, Bohemian youngsters.

However, though they were vague and impractical and sometimes frivolous, their ideas, though not fully formed, were well-grounded, carefully thought out and often interesting and original in their own right; their socialist convictions were in many cases deeply held. There was a strong undertone of determination always present in their discussions, even a tinge of that desperate seriousness which was to become a feature of the later populist movement (especially its *raznochintsy* members) and, in 1848, they moved towards practical application of their ideas.

The general quality of the young men attracted towards socialism and the Petrashevtsy circles was surprisingly high. Among them were

Petrashevskii, a man of exceptional energy and integrity, philosopher, writer and indefatigable agitator; Speshnev, brilliant, cynical, a political extremist endowed with terrifying personal magnetism, the power of which was to haunt Dostoevskii all his life and which he sought to portray in Stavrogin in *The Devils*; Balasoglo, self-educated, poverty-stricken, one of life's victims and yet an irrepressibly enthusiastic publicist; Beklemishev, a politically moderate Fourierist and the future governor of Mogilev; Danilevskii, later to be famous both as a natural scientist and as the ideologist of Russian Pan-Slavism; Maikov, chief critic of *Otechestvennye zapiski* at the age of twenty-three, already establishing himself as Belinskii's rival and successor, when his career was cut tragically short; Miliutin, a brilliant economist; and, finally, two great writers, Dostoevskii and Saltykov, and an outstanding poet, Pleshcheev.

In later years, many of the Petrashevtsy remained true to their convictions. Chernyshevskii, who had been linked with their circles in the 1840s, became the outstanding leader of the radical movement of the 1860's; many of the Petrashevtsy themselves became involved in the later populist movement. While it cannot be proved that the influence of the Petrashevtsy was decisive in the formulation either of Chernyshevskii's theories or in the development of later Russian socialism, it seems certain that it played a part.

It is with Chernyshevskii that the direct impact of the Petrashevtsy can most clearly be seen. Chernyshevskii, the ideological mentor of the new plebeian radical movement of the sixties, Lenin's hero, formulator of a stern utilitarian populism and a materialism almost religious in its fervour, was first introduced to socialism, to Feuerbach and to ideas of revolution, by the Petrashevtsy. Under the influence of the Petrashevtsy and, especially Khanykov, during 1848, he became inspired with a certainty of his personal mission as a socialist and revolutionary. He escaped arrest in 1849 because he frequented Vvedenskii's, rather than Petrashevskii's circle, but his ideas, friendships and sympathies in the 1840's seem to qualify him to be considered one of them. He wrote, 'I would have joined their society without hesitation, with time, of course I would have become involved.'[2] When, in 1858, he became chief critic of *Sovremennik*, he developed many ideas first elaborated by the Petrashevtsy to form the ideology of his Russian populism. His *Anthropological Principle in Philosophy* sets out the anthropological materialism of Fourier and Feuerbach.[3] His economic writings, especially his famous commentaries on Mill, are very similar to Miliutin's and show the direct influence of Fourier and Louis Blanc.[4] Probably his major contribution to Russian socialism was his development of the idea of making Russia's peasant *obshchina* into the basis of the future socialist commune or phalanstery, an idea which the Petrashevtsy introduced him to. His diary for 11 December 1848 relates how Khanykov talked to him about the revolutionary elements in the state, including 'the organisation of the peasants in the *obshchina*'. Like the Petrashevtsy, Chernyshevskii and his followers identified the *obshchina* directly with the Fourierist phalanstery. Vera Pavlovna's fourth dream in his novel *What is to be done?* is the most famous example of Fourierism applied to the Russian countryside.[5] More practically, his book was influential in advocating a form of association already attempted by the Petrashevtsy – the urban commune. Many of the ideas expressed in Chernyshevskii's *The Aesthetic Relations of Art to Reality* echo those of the Petrashevtsy, and especially Maikov, on literature.[6] And like the Petrashevtsy, but far more than them, Chernyshevskii laid a special emphasis on the emancipation of women, outlining in his novel his blueprint for a 'rational marriage'.

Chernyshevskii thus associated himself with the Petrashevtsy during his student days, had close contacts with some of the more revolutionary among them and later picked up many ideas previously developed by them in the formulation of his populist theory. Other ideas discussed in the Petrashevtsy circles were quick to reappear within the radical movement.

Akhsharumov later wrote, 'Petrashevskii's circle contained in germ all the reforms of Alexander II'.[7] On the accession of Alexander II, after the Crimean War, many demands that had been floated by the Petrashevtsy in their discussion of practical reforms for Russia – emancipation of the serfs, reform of the legal system and the censorship, the creation of a National Assembly – were raised by Herzen from his London exile and by Chernyshevskii to become the programme of a widespread opposition. Like the Petrashevtsy before 1848, the oppositionists of the fifties and sixties mingled their suspicions of Tsarism with an over-eagerness to believe in its ability to reform itself. Both Herzen and Chernyshevskii rushed to acclaim Alexander II as the 'Galilean' (i.e. Christ) in 1857 when he announced his intention of emancipating the serfs. Both were to be disappointed – the outcome was in 1861 an emancipation manifesto they both rejected; in 1865 a reform of the legal system, which, though it introduced Petrashevskii's cherished dream, the jury system, retained separate courts for the peasants; and elected, but highly restricted, provincial *zemstvo* assemblies.

The Petrashevtsy had made a very tentative approach to the question of propaganda among the lower orders of society. The new generation went much further and in 1861, three manifestos, one probably by Chernyshevskii, addressed to the serfs, the others by his friends Mikhailov and Shelgunov, addressed to the soldiers and the 'young generation' opened what has been called 'the era of proclamations'. In 1862 Herzen and Ogarev launched *Obshchee delo*, a paper directed at the middle and lower classes of the towns, and in particular, at the Old Believers. Ogarev also called for agitation among the non-Russian nationalities of the Empire.

The instruments of revolutionary action established by the most radical of the Petrashevtsy, also became those which later revolutionaries were to adopt. Though the Petrashevtsy's secret printing press came to a sad end — dismantled before it was ever used, the idea was soon revived. The first clandestine broadsheet to be printed in Russia, *Velikoross*, produced by men close to Chernyshevskii, appeared in 1861. The fact that revolutionary propaganda in Russia had to be conducted through a secret society was realised by Ogarev as early as 1857.[8] The first *Zemlia i volia*, set up by Nikolai Serno-Solov'evich after discussions with Ogarev in 1861, was, like Speshnev's Russian Society, a series of small groups of five people. From then on almost all Russian revolutionaries operated through secret societies, every group had its own illegal organ.

Finally, the quarrel between Petrashevskii and Speshnev in the 1840s provides an interesting early example of the basic quarrel between democratic populist and jacobin nihilist which was to continue on the same lines right through the Russian revolutionary movement. The questions debated at Voronezh in 1879 which led to the split of the second *Zemlia i volia* into the populist *Chernyi peredel* and the terrorist *Narodnaia volia* bore essentially the same features as those argued out in Petrashevskii's sitting room. Petrashevskii's insistence on democracy, on the need for the intelligentsia to educate themselves in careful preparation for propaganda among the people, and Akhsharumov's declaration, 'We need to understand our people better and draw closer to them',[9] foreshadowed the ideas of Lavrov and the Chaikovskists, to be embodied in the movement to the people in the 'mad summer' of 1874. Speshnev's idea of 'atheism, terrorism, communism and everything that is good in the world' and Katenev's dreams of assassinating the Tsar were also to have a long line of disciples in Russia. Side by side with the populists appeared the nihilists, insurrectionists and terrorists — the members of *Young Russia*, Ishutin's *Organisation* and *Hell*, Nechaev's

Narodnaia rasprava and some elements of *Narodnaia volia*. The first attempt to assassinate the Tsar was made by Karakazov, a member of *Hell* in 1866, *Narodnaia volia* finally succeeded in 1881. Like Speshnev, the terrorists drew their inspiration from 'an old book', Buonarotti's *Conspiration pour l'égalité*; and like him, they were influenced by Stirner's amoralism, from which they concluded that all means are justified in the revolutionary cause.

Thus, many of the ideas, platforms and programmes which were put forward in the next thirty years were present in embryonic form among the Petrashevtsy. The leaders of the revolutionary movement did not come from among the Petrashevtsy and the development of their ideas must be ascribed to a multiplicity of factors, among which the influence of the Petrashevtsy can be accorded only a modest place. Nevertheless, the Petrashevtsy undoubtedly did, both directly, through their own later activities and indirectly, through their communication of their ideas to others, make a definite contribution to the radical movement of the fifties, sixties and seventies. As well as contributing to the formation of Chernyshevskii's outlook, many Petrashevtsy, who either escaped exile to Siberia or returned from it, continued their revolutionary activities in conjunction with subsequent generations of revolutionaries in the following decades.

Only twenty-one people: Petrashevskii, Speshnev, Mombelli, Golovinskii, the Debu brothers, Akhsharumov, Khanykov, Dostoevskii, L'vov, Durov, Pleshcheev, Filippov, Grigor'ev, Tol', Jastrzębski, Kashkin, Timkovskii, Evropeus, Pal'm, and Shaposhnikov, were exiled to Siberia or the Caucasus as a result of the Petrashevskii affair. They were sentenced on 22 December 1849 in a dramatic episode, carefully and cruelly planned in advance by Nicholas I himself. They were taken from Peter and Paul Fortress to Semenovskii Square, which was full of soldiers. There the verdict — death by firing squad — was read out to them. The eyes of the first three, Petrashevskii, Mombelli and Grigor'ev, were bandaged, they were tied to posts. The drums rolled, the firing squad raised their rifles, and then the Tsar's aide-de-camp arrived, bringing the reprieve. Petrashevskii got perpetual hard labour; Mombelli and Grigor'ev fifteen years hard labour; L'vov twelve; Speshnev ten; Durov and Dostoevskii four; Jastrzębski and Tol' the mines; the rest, exile or the army. Petrashevskii, protesting vigorously, was at once put into the covered cart which was to take him to Siberia.[10]

In Siberia, many of the Petrashevtsy remained true to their convictions. When, in 1856, in honour of Alexander II's accession, their sentences were commuted from hard labour to exile, Petrashevskii, Speshnev and L'vov, settled in Irkutsk, capital of Eastern Siberia. Here, the distance from St. Petersburg allowed a comparatively liberal atmosphere to prevail. The Siberian administration was desperately short of educated, able young men like the Petrashevtsy. The Governor-General, Murav'ev, who himself inclined to liberal ideas, showed them considerable kindness. The three of them were able to found a new provincial paper, the *Irkutskie gubernskie vedomosti*, which became one of the more influential liberal organs of the day. Murav'ev showed particular favour to Speshnev (as he had to Bakunin, in Siberia at much the same time) making him head of his travelling chancery, and taking him with him to China and Japan. Petrashevskii and L'vov, however, refused to compromise or collaborate and criticised 'the shamelessness and immorality with which everything is done in the administration of Eastern Siberia'.[11] Their relations with Murav'ev steadily worsened. They came to a head in 1859 over a duel, the first to be fought in Siberia, in which one of Murav'ev's chief councillors, treacherously shot his opponent, Nekliudov, in the back. Petrashevskii roused the town, led a demonstration of two thousand to Nekliudov's grave and made speeches at his tomb. At the same time, Petrashevskii doggedly continued his personal battle for 'legality'. He showered the central government with petitions demanding a review of his case. He continued to act as a lawyer, taking up every case of injustice that came his way, and battled for publicity in the courts. Karl Ol'dekop, another Petrashevets, who had not been punished but had accidentally ended up in the Siberian judiciary, helped him.[12]

While in exile, some of the Petrashevtsy formed links with past and future revolutionaries. These included surviving Decembrists, among them Raevskii, and their wives; Polish and Ukrainian revolutionaries, including Shevchenko, whom Khanykov and Pleshcheev got to know well; Petrashevskii, Pleshcheev and L'vov also became acquainted with Mikhail Mikhailov, one of the leaders of the new revolutionary movement.[13]

Only four of the Petrashevtsy failed to return from exile. The saddest story was that of Petrashevskii himself. His insistence on standing up both for his own rights and for those of others earned him the emnity of the Siberian authorities, who persecuted him in every way they could. He was exiled progressively further and further away from centres of civilisation. He ended up in Bel'skoe, a tiny village of wooden huts in the Siberian forest, and died there in 1866, some say poisoned on

Murav'ev's orders.[14] The others were Filippov, who died in battle; Khanykov, who perished from cholera; and Grigor'ev, who went mad.

The years the Petrashevtsy spent in Siberia were the darkest years of Nicholas' reign, years of reaction and disillusionment after 1848. In 1855 Nicholas died, the Crimean War ended. The seventeen Petrashevtsy who survived regained their rights between 1857–62 and came back to a new reign and a new atmosphere. The 'thaw' was ushered in in 1856 by Alexander II's announcement of his intention of emancipating the serfs. There was huge excitement about the proposed reforms, widespread public discussion and debate, a resurgence of liberal and radical hopes and activity. Though they tended to lie low and leave the leadership to others (partly because they were already marked men under police surveillance) many of the returning exiles joined with other former Petrashevtsy (it must be remembered that another two hundred had been arrested and released, many others never arrested at all)[15] and became active members of the opposition movement.

A considerable number of the Petrashevtsy joined Chernyshevskii on *Sovremennik*. The most prominent of these was of course Saltykov, who had escaped arrest in 1849 because he was already in exile for writing *A Tangled Affair*. Though a radical satirist rather than a revolutionary, he remained faithful to many of his youthful ideas, retaining a critical, but sympathetic attitude to Fourier right until the end of his life.[16] L'vov, Aleksandr Evropeus, Pleshcheev, Durov, Pal'm, Tol' and probably Speshnev all also wrote for it.[17] L'vov had become *Sovremennik*'s Siberian correspondent while still in Irkutsk; Evropeus wrote political articles; Tol', essays developing the Petrashevtsy's ideas on education; Durov and Pal'm short stories; and Pleshcheev, who became one of the journal's chief contributors, poems and stories. Tolbin wrote for another radical journal, the first *Iskra*, first as an art reviewer, then as a satirist.

The Petrashevtsy's continued adherence to socialist ideas can be seen from a friend's testimony about Durov, 'he would carry on monologues about Proudhon, Saint-Simon, Cabet, Fourier, Considerant, for days on end, sometimes criticising their theories, sometimes agreeing with them'.[19] Pleshcheev continued to write remarkably revolutionary poems, including one about Chernyshevskii, banned until 1905. At the same time, his poems of the forties began to be used as revolutionary propaganda. *Forward!*, christened by Dobroliubov 'the Russian Marseillaise', was sung in chorus by the members of secret societies at their marches and meetings. Their continued socialist and revolutionary activity soon brought the Petrashevtsy again into trouble with the police. Mordvinov, who had got to know Chernyshevskii in Saratov in the early fifties, was arrested as early as 1855 on suspicion of being the author of an anti-government manifesto and a large amount of incriminating literature was found in his possession.[20] Pleshcheev, in constant trouble from 1858, was arrested and searched in 1863 in connection with the Chernyshevskii affair; Evropeus was arrested in 1866 in connection with Karakazov's attempt on the life of Alexander II.

Former Petrashevtsy were also prominent in the gentry opposition to Alexander II at the time of emancipation. The most active centre of gentry opposition during this period was Tver, where the leading figure was Unkovskii, who had been expelled from the Lycée in 1844 for associating with Petrashevskii. His associates included (as well as Bakunin's brothers) Evropeus, who owned land locally and Golovinskii, who had been exiled there. They first got into serious trouble in 1859 for continuing to discuss the peasant question when Alexander II had forbidden it. Unkovskii and Evropeus were singled out as the leaders and sentenced to brief periods of exile. In 1860 Saltykov arrived in Tver as Vice-Governor and immediately joined forces with the opposition. In 1862 they composed the *Address of the Repentant Noblemen*, one of the most famous documents of the sixties. This called for the land to be immediately given to the peasants, with the government not the peasants paying compensation; the abolition of the 'disgraceful' class privileges which they, as gentry enjoyed and the 'summoning of elected representatives from all the Russian land'.[20] Other Petrashevtsy were active in other areas: Kashkin was a leading member of the liberal Kaluga emancipation committee, which co-operated closely with the Tver committee; Beklemishev, on the government's side, helped to draft Alexander's rescript to the Vilna gentry, which opened the discussion of emancipation; Speshnev acted as a Peace Arbitor in Pskov province. The Third Department reported, 'Speshnev firmly stands up for the interests of the peasants. The gentry with very few exceptions hate him, but the peasants love him and he is content.'[21] Golovinskii, as a practising lawyer, was very active both in agitating for judicial reform and later, in pressing the reforms further than their authors intended. In Kazan his habit of giving free legal help to the peasants earned him the enmity of the authorities, who finally managed to obtain his banishment to Simbirsk.[22]

Other Petrashevtsy later developed links with Herzen abroad. The most important of these was via Vladimir Engel'son, Speshnev's closest friend. Engel'son was arrested in connection with the Petrashevskii affair but released in August 1849. He at once went abroad and in Nice met Herzen. They were for some time very close, Engel'son helped Herzen through his family troubles and in 1850 they even shared a house. Herzen thus had a representative of the Petrashevtsy at his elbow when he was developing his theory of Russian socialism. When Herzen went to London and set up his press, Engel'son joined him, becoming one of the chief contibutors to *Poliarnaia zvezda*. His writings are anarchist, revolutionary, show the influence of Proudhon, Stirner, Leroux and consciously reflect the ideas of the Petrashevtsy, and in particular, Speshnev. He told Herzen, 'I presented myself to you as and I remain, a "representative" of the party of my honourable friend Petrashevskii, whom you have called "reckless"'. In his frequent arguments with Herzen, Engel'son always stuck to what he called his 'Petrashevskii–Speshnevskoi' point of view.[23] Their collaboration finally broke down in 1855 and Herzen later based on Engel'son his hostile description of the 'type' of the Petrashevtsy and of the young men of the sixties (significantly, he identified the two). All the same, Engel'son succeeded in arousing in Herzen a lasting interest in the Petrashevtsy. Engel'son wrote for Herzen his own account of the affair, and Herzen published a great deal of material about the Petrashevtsy in *Kolokol*.[24] The other Petrashevets most closely linked with Herzen was Mordvinov, who, first in Saratov, then in Novgorod, worked as 'a secret agent of Iskander', sending material to Herzen in London for *Voices from Russia*. In 1860 he visited Herzen in London and went to the Isle of Wight with him.[25] The Petrashevtsy in Tver also provided Herzen with information and their activities were reported in detail in *Kolokol*.

Almost all the Petrashevtsy continued to act in accordance with their convictions – Akhsharumov, for example became a doctor and investigated the social causes of syphilis; Evgenii Lamanskii founded the first mutual credit society in Russia. The two outstanding exceptions were Danilevskii and Dostoevskii, and even they, though they went over to the side of the reactionaries, never managed to shake themselves completely free of the socialist experiences of their youth.

Danilevskii who had always been a very politically moderate Fourierist was the only one to move completely over to the other political extreme. In 1869 he published *Russia and Europe*, in which he formulated the reactionary ideology of Pan-Slavism, basing it on an original biological typology of mutually incompatible cultures. However, in spite of his 'fanatical patriotism' and hatred of revolutionaries and liberals, he never wholly renounced socialism. His goal was the expansion and greatness of the Russian state. Once this greatness was achieved, the political regime was a matter of indifference to him and he says specifically that it could be socialism.[26]

Dostoevskii's life in Siberia made him aware of the rift between the intelligensia and the people and convinced him that his socialist convictions were anti-popular and un-Russian and that the way back to the people was through their Russian Orthodox faith. From *Notes from Underground* onwards, he attacks socialism as representing the attainment of freedom and equality through despotism.[27] However, the intensity of Dostoevskii's diatribes against socialism and atheism indicates the attraction they still held for him. He fought against them for the rest of his life, but never quite managed to tear them out of himself. For example, the famous passage in *The Brothers Karamazov*, where Ivan Karamazov, paraphrasing Belinskii, argues that heavenly harmony is unacceptable, if it has to be bought with the sufferings of innocent children, shows Dostoevsky partly succumbing to the force of the arguments for atheism and socialism. In *Crime and Punishment*, the social justification for Raskolnikov's crime is powerfully put − 'dozens of families could be saved from beggary, from disintegration, from ruin, from corruption, from venereal hospitals' with the old woman's money.[28]

All through his life, the revolutionary movement was to hold a fascination for Dostoevskii. He sought out its leaders, he liked them and got on with them. He met Chernyshevskii in St. Petersburg, Herzen in London, became close friends with Ogarev in Geneva and in 1867 at the Congress of the *League for Peace and Freedom*, listened to Bakunin's famous presentation of his theses.

Socialism appears as an important theme in almost all his novels. *The Devils* is the most obvious case. The framework of the book is provided by the Nechaev affair. Into it Dostoevskii weaves the concrete experience of a revolutionary group he had acquired among the Petrashevtsy. Stavrogin is part Bakunin, part Speshnev; Petr Verkhovenskii part Nechaev, part Petrashevskii.[29] *Crime and Punishment* is an argument against nihilism, directly inspired by Vera Zasulich's justification of her assassination attempt upon General Dmitrii Trepov (Dostoevskii attended her trial). Dostoevskii chose the name *The Brothers Karamazov* for his last novel because of its similarity to that of Karakazov, the first would-be assassin of Alexander II. He intended the novel to have a sequel in which the novice monk, Alyosha, becomes a revolutionary, tries to assassinate Alexander II and ends up on the scaffold.[30]

Though he attacks socialism, Dostoevskii in many places expresses sympathy for the revolutionaries themselves. According to him, they were 'pure and radiant' of heart, sincerely seeking for the truth. They had just gone in the wrong direction and been seduced by a 'false beauty' − socialism.[31] To it he counterposed the 'true beauty' of his Christian ideal. This too was a utopia − the Orthodox idea of the universal love and brotherhood that would result from the absorption of the state by the Church. It was to be achieved by the return of the 'wandering' intelligentsia to the people, the union of the 'European' with the 'Russian' aspects of Russian life. He tried to embody it in the Christ-like figure of the Idiot. Dostoevskii repudiated the materialistic but not the humanistic side of socialism. At the very end of his life, in his last *Diary of a Writer* (1881), he used Herzen's term, 'Russian socialism', to describe his ideal.[32]

Though their ideas are frequently inconsistent and scattered through a large number of writings, the Petrashevtsy were the first in Russia to go into the question of socialism in depth and to produce a substantial body of socialist theory (this is the distinction between them and Herzen or Belinskii). And, though their behaviour reflects a strange mixture of frivolity and seriousness, though they did not get very far in implementing their ideas, the Petrashevtsy had, by 1849, taken steps towards practical action. They were the first large group of socialists in Russia and the first revolutionary socialists. In the history of the Russian radical movement, they represent a transitional stage between the gentry revolutionaries of Herzen's generation who were primarily humanists and democrats; and the truly *raznochinnye* revolutionaries of the sixties and seventies, who were socialists, often crude materialists and in some cases, terrorists. As Herzen recognised, they stood, on the whole, closer to the former than the latter. The Petrashevtsy's theories foreshadow, in many important respects, those of the later populist movement: anthropological materialism; anti-capitalism; an emphasis on the *obshchina*; a platform of democratic reforms; a concern for the emancipation of women; the split between democratic populist and jacobin nihilist and finally, the organisational model of the small conspiratorial society with a secret press. Not only were the Petrashevtsy among the first to formulate these ideas in the 1840s, many of them also played a part, if not a leading one, in the later radical movement. In the 1850s and 1860s, both as a result of their introduction of Chernyshevskii to socialism and through their own efforts − with Chernyshevskii on *Sovremennik*, with the gentry opposition during emancipation, and through links with Herzen in London — they contributed to the further development of Russian socialist ideas by a new generation of revolutionaries.

Their influence on shaping Russian populism was thus considerably greater than has usually been recognised. Liubov Dostoevskaia went as far as to claim, 'Our socialists descended from the Petrashevtsy. The Petrashevtsy sowed many seeds.'[33]

NOTES

I—INTRODUCTION

1 A.I. Herzen, *Sobranie sochinenii v tridtsati tomakh*, ed. AN SSSR, 30 vols., Moscow 1954−66, viii, 252. This is the standard edition of Herzen's works and will be referred to in future as 'Herzen'. Reference will also occasionally be made to the older and slightly fuller edition by Lemke.

2 A.V. Nikitenko, *Zapiski i dnevnik (1804−77)*, St. Petersburg 1904, i, 362; see V.G. Belinskii, *Polnoe sobranie sochinenii* (referred to in future as 'Belinskii'), 13 vols., Moscow 1953−9, xii, 339.

3 Quoted in M.T. Florinsky, *Russia. A History and an Interpretation*, New York 1953, ii, 799.

4 A.I. Herzen, *Polnoe sobranie sochinenii i pisem*, ed. M.K. Lemke, 22 vols., Petrograd 1915−25, vii, 279−80.

5 *Gosudarstvenyi sovet. 1801−1901*, St. Petersburg 1902, p.64.

6 See M.P. Pogodin, *Istoricheskie aforizmy*, Moscow 1836; *Istoriko-kriticheskie otryvki*, Moscow 1846.

7 Herzen, ix, 133. On the Slavophile/Westerner debate in the 1840s, see A. Walicki, *The Slavophile Controversy*, Oxford 1975.

8 Belinskii, xi, 556, 577; xii, 23, 66−9.

9 I. Berlin, *Russian Thinkers*, London 1978, p.149.

10 Belinskii, x, 212−20.

11 V.V. Stasov, 'Uchilishche pravovedeniia sorok let tomu nazad', *Izbrannye sochineniia v trekh tomakh*, Moscow 1952, ii, 384; I.S. Aksakov, *Pis'ma*, Moscow 1892, ii, 281; P. Pekarskii, 'Studencheskie vospominaniia o D.I. Meiere', *Bratchina. Sbornik*, St. Petersburg 1859, i, 215−16.

12 The Petrashevtsy always took the side of the Westerners against the Slavophiles. Pleshcheev, for example, on a visit to Moscow, refused on principle the offer of an introduction to Khomiakov, but went eagerly to meet Granovskii instead. *Delo petrashevtsev*, ed. AN SSSR, 3 vols., Moscow−Leningrad 1937, 1941, 1951, iii, 288, 294. This is the basic collection of published documents on the Petrashevtsy and will in future be referred to as DP.

13 N.A. Korf, 'Zapiski', vi, *Russkaia starina*, 1900, no.5, pp.278−9.

14 Tsentral'nyi Gosudarstvennyi Arkhiv Oktiabr'skoi Revoliutsii (TsGAOR), fond 801, V.I. Semevskii, Pis'mo D.D. Akhsharumova k V.I. Semevskomu, 21 October 1892.

15 A. N. Pypin, *Kharakteristiki literaturnykh mnenii ot 20kh do 50kh godov*, St. Petersburg 1890, p. 496.

16 N. S. Rusanov, 'Iz ideinoi istorii russkogo sotsializma 40kh godov', *Russkoe bogatstvo*, 1909, no. 2, p. 56. For similar views, at a slightly later date, see P. N. Sakhulin, *Russkaia literatura i sotsializm*, 2nd ed., Moscow 1924, i, 315, 332; K. A. Pazhitnov, *Razvitie sotsialisticheskikh idei v Rossii*, Petrograd 1924, p. 66.

17 M. N. Pokrovskii, *Ocherki istorii russkoi kul'tury*, Petrograd 1923, pp. 164–5.

18 G. Beshkin, *Idei Fur'e u Petrashevskogo i petrashevtsev*, Moscow–Petrograd 1923, p. 6.

19 L. Raiskii, *Sotsial'nye vozzreniia petrashevtsev*, Leningrad 1927, pp. 56, 63–4.

20 A. S. Nifontov, 'Rossiia i revoliutsiia 1848 goda', in *Revoliutsiia 1848–9*, ed. F. V. Potemkin & A. I. Molok, Moscow 1952, p. 258.

21 V. E. Evgrafov, 'Vstupitel'naia stat'ia', *Filosofskie i obshchestvenno-politicheskie proizvedeniia petrashevtsev*, Moscow 1953, p. 51. In future this collection of documents will be referred to as FOP.

22 V. R. Leikina-Svirskaia, *Petrashevtsy i obshchestvennoe dvizhenie sorokovykh godov XIXv.*, unpublished doctoral thesis, Moscow 1956, p. 33.

23 V. R. Leikina-Svirskaia, *Petrashevtsy*, Moscow–Leningrad 1965, p. 160.

24 The two best accounts of the Petrashevtsy in the English language are in J. Frank, *Dostoevsky. The Seeds of Revolt (1829–1849)*, Princeton 1976; and A. Walicki, *A History of Russian Thought from the Enlightenment to Marxism*, Oxford 1980.

II—THE PETRASHEVTSY CIRCLES

1 A. P. Miliukov, for example, destroyed a diary which he had kept since the beginning of the forties; A. V. Nikitenko's diary has a gap from April–December 1849. Mombelli's circle only came to light accidentally with the arrest of the Petrashevtsy.

2 I. P. Liprandi, 'Zapiski', *Russkaia starina*, 1872, July, pp. 73–7; Tsentral'nyi Gosudarstvennyi Voenno-Istoricheskii Arkhiv SSSR (TsGVIA), fond 9, opis' 28, 1849, no. 55, ch. 2, 11. 4ob, 130; DP, II, 405–6. See also F. M. Dostoevskii, *Diary of a Writer*, tr. B. Brasol, 2nd ed., Santa Barbara 1979, p. 147.

3 See, for example, P. Ia. Kann, *Petrashevtsy*, Leningrad 1968; F. Venturi, *Les intellectuels, le peuple et la revolution*, revised and extended French edition of the original *Il Populismo russo* (1952), Paris, 1972, i, 227.

4 See TsGVIA, fond 9, Glavnoe voenno-sudnoe upravlenie, opis' 28, 1849, delo 55, O zloumyshlennikakh Butasheviche-Petrashevskom, Speshneve i

drugikh, ch. 1–119; TsGAOR, fond 109, 111 Otdelenie, 1 ekspeditsiia, 1849, opis' 12, no. 214, Po razyskaniiu Liprandi i doneseniiam Antonelli o Butasheviche-Petrashevskomu i drugikh, ch. 3, 11. 90–114. These are the two main archival collections on the Petrashevtsy. The first contains all the documents relating to their trial, the second, the reports of the Third Department spies sent to infiltrate the circles. References to them will be abbreviated in future to TsGVIA, delo 55 and TSGAOR, no. 214.

5 Irkutsk Oblastnoi Arkhiv, N. A. Speshnev, Pis'ma k materi 1838–82, microfilm used by kind permission of E. Azhusoeva & B. Ulanovskaia ('Neizvestnye pis'ma N. A. Speshneva. Doklad materialy konferentsii *Dostoevskii i mirovaia kul'tura*, Muzei Dostoevskogo, Leningrad, 1976).

6 On Petrashevskii's father, see Gosudarstvennaia Publichnaia Biblioteka, Arkhiv K. A. Voenskogo, opis' 2, ed.khr. 299.

7 M. Gorkii, 'O petrashevtsakh, I. Turgeneve, F. Dostoevskom, L. Tolstom', *Literaturnaia kritika*, 1938, no. 6, p. 45.

8 A. Voronov, *Istoriko-statisticheskie obozrenie uchebnykh zavedenii S. Petersburgskogo uchebnogo okruga s 1829 po 1852 godu*, St. Petersburg 1854, pp. 117, 278; A. Aleshintsev, *Istoriia gimnazicheskogo obrazovaniia v Rossii XVII i XIX v.*, St. Petersburg 1912, p. 92.

9 S. P. Shevyrev, *Istoriia imperatorskogo Moskovskogo universiteta*, Moscow 1855, p. 575; on St. Petersburg University, see A. Voronov, op. cit., p. 285; V. V. Grigor'ev, *Imperatorskii Sankt-Petersburgskii universitet v techenii pervykh 50 let*, St. Petersburg 1870.

10 I. I. Davidov, 'O naznachenii russkikh universitetov', *Sovremennik*, 1849, no. 3, i, 45.

11 A. Chulinkov, 'Peterburgskii universitet polveka nazad', *Russkii arkhiv*, 1888, no. 9(3), pp. 225–6.

12 TsGVIA, delo 55, ch. 16, 1. 127.

13 Belinskii, ix, 98–9.

14 K. K. Arsen'ev, *Statisticheskie svedeniia o Sanktpeterburge*, St. Petersburg 1836, p. 117.

15 Belinskii, viii, 408; DP, iii, 364.

16 *Pis'ma k akademiku P. S. Biliarskomu*, Odessa 1907, pp. 125–6.

17 S. F. Durov, 'Neskol'ko slov o N. I. Khmel'nitskom', *Sochineniia Khmel'nitskogo*, St. Petersburg 1849, i, 4–5.

18 Pekarskii, 'Studencheskie vospominaniia', i, 210, 214; V. N. Nazar'ev, 'Zhizn' i liudi bylogo vremeni', *Istoricheskii vestnik*, 1890, December, p. 716.

19 DP, iii, 107; P. P. Semenov T'ian-Shanskii, *Memuary*, Petrograd 1917, i, 179, 189; F. M. Dostoevskii, *Pis'ma*, ed. A. S. Dolinin, Moscow–Leningrad 1928–59, i, 11; M. S. Veselovskii, quoted in W. Bruce Lincoln, *Nicholas I, Emperor and Autocrat of all the Russias*, London 1978, p. 168.

20 TsGVIA, delo 55, ch. 3, 1. 22ob; A. N. Pleshcheev, *Povesti i rasskazy*, St. Petersburg 1896–7, i, 62; N. Ia. Butkov, *Peterburgskie vershiny*, St.

Petersburg 1845–6, ii, 87–127; N.A. Nekrasov, *Sobranie sochinenii*, Moscow 1966, v, 7–49; DP, iii, 271.
21 DP, ii, 242–3.
22 K.K. Arsen'ev, *Nachertanie statistiki rossiiskogo gosudarstva*, St. Petersburg 1848, i, 211; Herzen, iv; Belinskii, xii, 385; DP, iii, 191–2.
23 R.R. Shtrandman, 'O filantropii', *Sovremennik*, 1847, no.3, iv, 50–5.
24 DP, i, 213–14; ii, 85.
25 Shtrandman, 'O filantropii', p.52; DP, i, 2–4, 116; iii, 104, 363.
26 Otdel Rukopisei Instituta Literatury AN SSSR (IRLI), raz. 1, opis' 35, no.27, Pis'ma V.A. Engel'sona k A.I. Gertsenu, pp.5–6, 13 July 1852; DP, i, 116–17.
27 DP, iii, 363–5; Tsentral'nyi Gosudarstvennyi Istoricheskii Arkhiv, g. Leningrad (TsGIAL), fond 647 A.P. Balasoglo, opis' 1, delo 5, Ob izlozhenii nauk, 1848, 11. 1–2, 7, 16.
28 TsGIAL, fond 779, opis' 4, ed.khr. 483, vol.1, Al'favitnyi spisok knig na frantsuzskom iazyke zapreshchennykh innostrannoiu tsenzuroiu dlia publiki i bezuslovno (1815–55); Iu.G. Oksman, 'Mery nikolaevskogo tsenzury protiv fur'erizma i kommunizma, *Golos minuvshego*, 1917, no.5, p.72; *Russkii invalid*, 1848, no.174.
29 TsGAOR, 111 otdelenie, 1 eksp. 1849, opis' 12, no.245, 11. 1–3ob, 147, 155, no.426.
30 Ibid., no.365, 11. 1–28.
31 A.M. Unkovskii, 'Zapiski', *Russkaia mysl'*, 1906, no.6, p.185; DP, i, 231–8; P. Efebovskii, 'Peterburgskie raznoshchiki', *Vchera i segodnia*, ed. V.A. Sollugub, St. Petersburg 1846, ii, 105–14; A.N. Pypin, *Moi zametki*, Moscow 1910, p.68; E.I. Lamanskii, 'Iz vospominanii 1840–90', *Russkaia starina*, 1915, January–March, vol.161, p.75.
32 P.V. Annenkov, 'Zamechatel'noe desiatiletie 1838–48. Iz literaturnykh vospominanii', *Vestnik Evropy*, 1880, February, ii, 506–7.
33 A.P. Miliukov, *Literaturnye vstrechi i znakomstva*, St. Petersburg 1890, pp.171–2.
34 I.I. Panaev, 'Iz literaturnykh vospominanii', *Belinskii v vospominaniiakh sovremennikov*, ed. K.I. Tiun'kin, Moscow 1977, p.261; A.Ia. Panaeva, 'Iz vospominanii', *Dostoevskii v vospominaniiakh sovremennikov*, ed. A.S. Dolinin, Moscow 1964, i, 141; DP, ii, 91.
35 Dostoevskii, *Pis'ma*, i, 103 (November 1846).
36 DP, iii, 39; D.V. Grigorovich, *Literaturnye vospominaniia*, Leningrad 1928, p.149.
37 TsGVIA, delo 55, ch.92, 1. 3 (see A.S. Dolinin ed., *F.M. Dostoevskii. Stat'i i materialy*, Moscow 1922, i, 267); M.E. Saltykov-Shchedrin, *Sobranie sochinenii v dvadtsati tomakh*, Moscow 1956–77 (in future, Saltykov), i, 281–2; TsGAOR, no.214, ch.1., 1. 137ob.
38 N.G. Chernyshevskii, *Polnoe sobranie sochinenii*, 16 vols., Moscow 1939–50

(in future, Chernyshevskii), i, 346 (28 December 1849), 395 (15 September 1850); Miliukov, *Literaturnye vstrechi*, p.72.
39 DP, i, 202, 215, 292–5.
40 *Petrashevtsy. Sbornik materialov*, ed. P.E. Shchegolov, 3 vols., Moscow–Leningrad 1923–8, iii, 60–1 (in future *Petrashevtsy*); DP, iii, 37, 107, 118, 132, 161; ii, 118; TsGAOR, no.214, ch.142, 1. 282; *Ibid.*, fond 80, V.I. Semevskii, Pis'ma D.D. Akhsharumova k V.I. Semevskomu; TsGVIA, delo 55, ch.30, 1. 45.
41 *Petrashevtsy*, iii, 64; DP, iii, 272–3.
42 A.I. Pal'm in *Iziashchnaia literatura*, 1885, no.2, p.212; V.I. Semevskii, 'Petrashevtsy S.F. Durov, A.I. Pal'm, F.M. Dostoevskii i A.N. Pleshcheev', *Golos minuvshego*, 1915, no.11, p.6. Durov had an extraordinary hatred of women and died in Pal'm's arms in Poltava in 1869.
43 TsGVIA, delo 55, ch.93, 1.6; Miliukov, *Literaturnye vstrechi*, p.175.
44 Almost the only source for this group is the agents' reports in TsGVIA, delo 55, ch.2 and 3.
45 TsGVIA, delo 55, ch.38, 11. 41–41ob.
46 DP, i, 111, 181; V.V. Bervi-Flerovskii, 'Vospominaniia tsarstvovannia Nikolaia Pervogo', *Golos minuvshego*, 1915, no.3, p.138. Nikolai and Vladimir Blagoveshchenskii were arrested in Kazan in connection with the Petrashevskii affair in 1849 (ibid., p.139; TsGAOR, no.214, ch.64, 11. 17ob–18; TsGVIA, delo 55, ch.54, 11. 30ob–40).
47 V.V. Bervi, 'Vospominaniia', p.138.
48 E.A. Belov, in *N.G. Chernyshevskii v Saratove*, Saratov 1939, pp.62–8; V.N. Nazar'ev, 'Zhizn' i liudi', p.731.
49 For Petrashevskii's relationships with student circles at the Lycée, see Chapter VI. On explusions and disturbances at the Law School, see DP, iii, 399–400. Khanykov and Filippov were suspended from the University for their agitation there, TsGVIA, delo 55, ch.120, 11. 390–390ob. On Khanykov, see Chernyshevskii's diary for 1848–9; Tolstov in TsGVIA, delo 55, ch.2, 1. 134ob. For Pleshcheev in Moscow, see Chapter VII.
50 TsGVIA, delo 55, ch.43, 11. 7, 9–9ob, 11 (letters of 8 May, 12 June, 16 October 1848); TsGAOR, no.214, ch.136, 11. 23–4, 49ob.
51 DP, ii, 414–15, 422.
52 I.P. Liprandi, 'Zapiski', p.75. He tends to exaggerate, but there is other evidence, e.g. on Tambov, IRLI, fond 265, opis' 2, Arkhiv zhurnala Russkoi stariny, no.2010; DP, ii, 241–57; on Kostroma, DP, iii, 340, 347, 350; TsGVIA, delo 55, ch.2, 11. 138–9.
53 V.A. Engel'son, 'Petrashevtsy', in A.I. Herzen, ed. Lemke, vi, 489 (this article was long ascribed to Herzen); V.R. Zotov, 'Peterburg v sorokovykh godakh', *Istoricheskii vestnik*, 1890, vol.40, pp.536–7.
54 DP, i, 122; D.D. Akhsharumov, *Iz moikh vospominanii 1849–51gg.*, St. Petersburg 1905, pp.15, 17; TsGAOR, no.214, ch.4, 1. 115; TsGVIA,

delo 55, ch. 47, 1. 8; Semenov T'ian-Shanskii, *Memuary*, i, 195.
55 TsGVIA, delo 55, ch. 55, 1. 8ob; ch. 37, 1. 7; ch. 29, 1. 4; DP, i, 152−3. Petrashevskii says his circle began in 1846, but his visitors, including Shtrandman, Esakov, Baranovskii, agree to being there in 1845.
56 On Apollon Grigor'ev and Fourierism, see Sakulin, *Russkaia literatura, i sotsializm*.
57 See DP, ii, 56−94.
58 For the times different people appeared at Petrashevskii's, see: DP, ii, 150; TsGVIA, delo 55, ch. 38, 11. 16,40; ch. 37, 11. 7ob, 8ob; ch. 29, 1. 14; ch. 42, 1. 60ob; S. A. Makashin, *Saltykov-Shchedrin. Biografiia*, Moscow 1951, pp. 324−5.
59 TsGVIA, delo 55, ch. 37, 1. 11; DP, iii, 28; Makashin, *Saltykov-Shchedrin*, p. 200.
60 TsGVIA, delo 55, ch. 37, 1. 9; ch. 92, 1. 9; Makashin, *Saltykov-Shchedrin*, p. 208.
61 Lamanskii, 'Iz vospominanii', p. 77.
62 TsGVIA, delo 55, ch. 47, 1. 8; ch. 42, 11. 9−10ob; Semenov T'ian-Shanskii, *Memuary*, p. 195; K. S. Veselovskii, 'Vospominaniia o nekotorykh litseiskikh tovarishchakh', *Russkaia starina*, 1900, nos. 7−9, p. 455.
63 DP, i, 449; 'Zapiska Generala Bronevskogo o Litsee', *Glavnoe upravlenie arkhivnym delom. Sbornik materialov i statei*, Moscow 1921, series 1, p. 42; Semenov T'ian-Shanskii, *Memuary*, p. 198; K. Lebedev, *Russkii arkhiv*, 1910, no. 11, p. 375; N. A. Tuchkova-Ogareva, *Vospominaniia*, Moscow 1959, p. 78; Chetinskii Arkhiv, 'Stateinyi spisok petrashevtsev otpravelennykh na nerchinskomu katorgu'.
64 Speshnev, *Pis'ma k materi*, 17/5 April 1846, Dresden.
65 A. I. Pal'm (P. Al'minskii), *Aleksei Slobodin*, St. Petersburg 1873, p. 327.
66 Tuchkova-Ogareva, *Vospominaniia*, pp. 76−7, 80−1.
67 Akhsharumov, *Iz moikh vospominanii*, p. 15; *Dostoevskii v protsesse petrashevtsev*, ed. N. F. Bel'chikov, Moscow 1936/71, p. 107 (in future, Bel'chikov).
68 DP, i, 333; ii, 29, 428; iii, 300; TsGVIA, delo 55, ch. 47, 11.8, 8ob, 3ob; ch. 38, 1. 13; P. A. Kuz'min, 'Iz zapisok', *Russkaia starina*, 1889, no. 2, pp. 157−8.
69 A. G. Rubinstein, 'Avtobiografiia', *Russkaia starina*, 1889, no. 11, pp. 139−40.
70 Gosudarstvennaia Biblioteka SSSR imeni V. I. Lenina, Otdel Rukopisei (BL), fond Obshchestvo istorii i drevnostei rukopisnykh (OIDR), no. 221/1,1. 99; DP, i, 105; ii, 408.

III — PETRASHEVTSY AND FRENCH SOCIALISM

1 On simplifying Fourier, see V. Considerant, 'Introduction. Système des développements de l'école sociétaire', *La Phalange*, 1845, i, p. xxv; K. Marx & F. Engels, 'The German Ideology', *Collected Works*, London 1976, v, 462. Considerant was adamant that his name should be spelt without an accent.

2 George Sand was converted to socialism by Leroux in 1835. He wrote whole chapters of her *La Comtesse de Rudolstadt*, 1841–3.

3 Ch. Fourier, *Oeuvres complètes*, Paris, 12 vols, 1966–8, Anthropos ed., i, 9, 25, 73; ii, 36; iii, 30–1, 109–23; vi, 446; x(ii), 191–2; xii, 588–96 (in future, Fourier).

4 Fourier ii (Sommaires et annonce), 145–6; i, 79–82; vi, 47–51; 'Du clavier puissanciel des caractères', *La Phalange*, 1847, August, pp. 12–14.

5 Fourier vi, 22; *Lettre au Grand Juge*, ed. Ch. Pellarin, Paris 1874, p. 15.

6 Fourier ii, 147.

7 Ibid., iii, 14–16.

8 Ibid., v, 156–62; vi, 206–14.

9 Ibid., iii, 19–25; vi, 180–201; x(ii) 73–314 (on work and education); v, 102–15, 75–9; vi, 222–4; x(ii), 141–68 (on education of the senses).

10 Ibid., viii, 344; vi, 403–13; letter to *Gazette de France*, mss. quoted in F. e. and F. P. Manuel, *Utopian Thought in the Western World*, Oxford 1979, p. 662.

11 Fourier, i, 139, 172–80; vii, 386–94. The cuts are reinstated in *Le Nouveau monde*, ed. M. Butor, Paris 1973, e.g. the love affair between a woman of eighty and a man of twenty, pp. 376–8.

12 C. H. de Saint-Simon, 'De la réorganisation de la société européene', *Oeuvres*, Paris 1966, Anthropos ed., i, 242; 'L'Industrie', vol. 4, *Oeuvres*, ii, 170–1.

13 Saint-Simon, 'De la réorganisation', p. 242; 'Du Système industriel', vol. 2, *Oeuvres*, iii, 73–4.

14 Saint-Simon, 'L'Industrie', vol. 2, p. 30; 'Du Système industriel', vol. 2, p. 26–7.

15 Saint-Simon, 'L'Organisateur', vol. i, *Oeuvres*, ii, 69; 'Opinions littéraires, philosophiques et industriels', *Oeuvres choisies*, ed. Lemonnier, Brussels 1859, iii, 59–60 (on the characteristics of creative and destructive eras); 'De la Réorganisation', pp. 173–4; 'Catéchisme des industriels', vol. 1 , *Oeuvres*, iii, 51; 'Opinions littéraires', pp. 235 ff.; 'Lettre à un Americain', *Oeuvres de Saint-Simon et d'Enfantin*, Paris 1865–78, xiii, 180–89 (on creative and destructive eras in the history of mankind).

16 Saint-Simon, 'Mémoire sur la science de l'homme, *Oeuvres*, v, 14; 'De la Réorganisation', pp. 247–8; 'Opinions littéraires', p. 261.

17 *Doctrine de Saint-Simon. Exposition. Première Année 1828–29*, new ed., Paris 1924, C. Bouglé & E. Halévy, pp. 127, 146, 492, 203–33.

18 P. Leroux, *De l'Humanité*, Paris 1840, v, 270.

19 Saint-Simon, 'Lettre d'un habitant de Genève à ses contemporains', *Oeuvres*, i, 22; 'De la Réorganisation', p. 158; 'Travail sur la gravitation universelle', *Oeuvres choisies*, ii, 219.

20 A. Comte, *Considérations philosophiques sur les sciences et les savants*, quoted in Alexandrian, *Le Socialisme romantique*, Paris 1979, p. 434.

21 A. Comte, *Cours de philosophie positive*, Paris 1830–42, iv, 14, 292, 294–409; see Saint-Simon, 'Mémoire sur la science de l'homme', p. 17.

22 Fourier, iii, 258–71; vi, 351–80.

23 Ibid., i, 41–52; iv, 254–5; vi, 459–65; xii, 15, 35–201. On this aspect of Fourier's system see R. Barthès, *Sade, Loyola, Fourier*, Paris 1971. Fourier also had a theory of metemphsychosis (iii, 309 ff; vi, 454–8).

24 Saint-Simon, 'Le Nouveau Christianisme', *Oeuvres*, iii, 116–17, 126, 173.

25 V. Considerant, 'Introduction. Système des devéloppements de l'école sociétaire', p. v; Z. Gatti de Gamond, *Fourier et son système*, 2nd ed., Paris 1839, p. v; 'Swedenborg et Fourier', *Le Nouveau monde*, 1840, no. 36.

26 *Doctrine de Saint-Simon*, pp. 404, 465; *Oeuvres de Saint-Simon et d'Enfantin*, xiv, 116.

27 F. P. Bowman, *Le Christ romantique*, Geneva 1973, p. 101.

28 Fourier, vi, 2; i, 2–4; ii (*avant propos*), 38; vi, 312 (on conflicts of interest); iv, 174–85 (on parasites); iv, 7–12 (on waste); i, 228–55; vi, 292–402; x(i), 5–114; V. Considerant, *Destinée sociale*, Paris 1835, p. 87 (on commerce); Fourier, vi, 30–1; xii, 683–717; V. Considerant, *Description du Phalanstère et considérations sur l'architectonique (1834/48)*, ed. G. Durier, Paris 1979, pp. 40–6 (on cities).

29 L. Blanc, *Organisation du travail*, 5th ed., Paris 1848, pp. 29–30.

30 J. C.-L. Simonde de Sismondi, *Nouveaux principes d'économie politique*, 2nd ed., Paris 1827, i, 113–17, 364–71, 407, 327–47; ii, 433–9 (analysis of capitalism); i, 8–9, 80, 413; ii, 336–8, 350–1, 463 (the rational organisation of industry).

31 P. J. Proudhon, 'De la Justice dans la Révolution et dans l'Eglise', 1858, *Oeuvres*, ed. Lacroix, Brussels, 1867–70, xxi, 224–5.

32 Proudhon, 'Système des contradictions économiques ou Philosophie de la misère', 1846, *Oeuvres*, v, 398.

33 Proudhon, ibid., p. 414; 'Organisation du credit et de la circulation et Solution de problème social', *Oeuvres*, vi, 92–3.

34 Saint-Simon, 'L'Organisateur', i, 17–26.

35 See Fourier, iv, 445 (Fourier sometimes varied the ratio, e.g. vi, 311–16); L. Blanc, 'La Formule du Socialisme', *Questions d'aujourd'hui et demain*, Paris 1873–84, series 5, p. 195.

36 Fourier, iv, 427–8, 455–62, 462–7; vi, 123–9; x(i), 80–350 (layout of the

phalanstery); vi, 468−9 (on choice); iii, 4; vi, 66−74; iv, 516−19; v, 384−5 (on class).

37 Ibid., iii, 19−25; iv, 337−415; vi, 55−78; x(i), 59−75; xii, 367−414 (on the groups and series); iv, 557−65; i, 172−82 (on industrial armies).

38 Blanc, *Organisation du travail*, pp. 103−6; Proudhon, 'Organisation du credit', J. Maître ed., *Dictionnaire biographique du mouvement ouvrier francais 1789−1864*, Paris 1964, iii, 258.

39 Saint-Simon, 'L'Organisateur', pp. 86, 191−92; *Doctrine de Saint-Simon*, pp. 96, 283−317; Blanc, *Organisation du travail*, pp. 102−3; 'La Révolution du février au Luxembourg', *Questions*, series 5, pp. 101−9.

40 Fourier, i, 157−9; iv, 447; vi, 288−93; Proudhon, 'Les Confessions d'un révolutionnaire', *Oeuvres*, ix, 23; 'Contradictions économiques', iv, 266−7.

41 Saint-Simon, 'De la réorganisation', p. 197; Fourier, iii, 376; vi, 230−1.

42 For Saint-Simon's ideas, see Saint-Simon, 'Opinions littéraires', pp. 210−11, 216−18; for those of his followers, *Doctrine de Saint-Simon*, pp. 142, 144; E. Barrault, *Du Passé et de l'avenir des beaux-arts*, Paris 1830; for the Fourierists, 'But social de l'art', *La Phalange*, 1836, 10 July; Ch. Pellarin, 'Critique littéraire', ibid., 1841, 17 September; *La Démocratie pacifique*, 1847, 13 February.

43 *Oeuvres de Saint-Simon et d'Enfantin*, xiv, 147−65, 171−5.

44 For instance, G. Sand, *Jacques*, Paris 1834, lettre 95; *Lélia*, Paris 1833, part 5.

45 Fourier, i, 70−1, 130−2; iv, 51−2, 96−121, see vii (on women in Civilisation); i, 133; see x(ii), 174 (women in Harmony).

46 See, for the bakery, *Le Nouveau monde*, 1839, no. 3; F. Cantagrel, *Mettray et Ostwald. Étude sur ces deux colonies agricoles*, Paris 1842. The most successful phalansterian experiment was Andre Godin's factory, 1857−1968 (see his *Solutions sociales*, Paris 1871).

47 L. Blanc, 'L'Etat', *Questions*, series 1, p. 279; P. Leroux, 'De la Ploutocratie', *Revue indépendante*, 1842, September, pp. 589−91; F. R. de Lamennais, *Du Passé et de l'avenir du peuple*, Paris 1841, ed. Garnier, pp. 311, 314−16.

48 Saint-Simon, 'Lettre à un American', pp. 170−79; Fourier, i, 2; xii, 622.

49 E. Cabet, *Voyage en Icarie*, Paris, 1840 ed., p. 565.

50 See *Dictionnaire biographique du mouvement ouvrier francais*, ii, 85.

51 *Petrashevtsy*, iii, 58; DP, iii, 115.

52 TsGVIA, delo 55, ch. 66, 1.9; ch. 37, 1. 8; Makashin, *Saltykov-Shchedrin*, pp. 203−4.

53 *Petrashevtsy*, iii, 58.

54 DP, ii, 135−6, 118, 132, 37.

55 TsGVIA, delo 55, ch. 87, 11. 6ob, 8−10; ch. 3, 1. 143; ch. 47, 1. 3ob; TsGAOR, no. 214, ch. 4, 1. 111ob; Akhsharumov, *Iz moikh vospominanii*, p. 17.

56 Our knowledge of the books in Petrashevskii's two libraries is derived from: the evidence the Petrashevtsy gave at their trial; the lists of books seized on their arrest (DP, i–iii and *Petrashevtsy*, iii, 368–71); a list of the books lent out by Petrashevskii in 1845–6 (the original is lost but Semevskii's copy is in Moskovskoe Otdelenie Arkhiva AN SSSR, fond 489, 11. 117 ff and bits of it are published in his *M. V. Butashevich–Petrashevskii i petrashevtsy*, Moscow 1922, pp. 168–71); lists of books ordered by Petrashevskii in 1848–9 (DP, i, 559–77; FOP, pp. 729–46); and V. A. Kaidanov's letters to his brother (TsGVIA, delo 55, ch. 43, 11. 7–15, TsGAOR, no. 214, ch. 136).

57 The Petrashevtsy were especially fond of Gabet, see DP ii, 319; iii, 58, 75.

58 Otdel drevnykh rukopisei i aktov, Institut Istorii AN SSSR, Leningrad (LOII), fond 48, Pis'ma I. M. Debu, ed. khr. 44, 1. 2ob (15 March 1855). The works of Fourier were taken out in 1845–6 by Jastrzębski, Kuz'min, Pleshcheev, Engel'son, A. M. Mikhailov, Baranovskii and others; Considerant's by Khovrin, Pleshcheev, Engel'son, Khanykov, Speshnev, Nikolai Kaidanov, Akhsharumov and Vashchenko; *La Phalange* by Petrashevskii, the Debu brothers Maikov, Danilevskii, Nikolai Kaidanov, Engel'son, Beklemishev and Khanykov (who passed it on to Chernyshevskii).

59 *Literaturnoe pribablenie k Russkomu invalidu*, 1837, no. 48, p. 473; *La Phalange*, 1837, 20 October; *Otechestvennye zapiski*, 1842, no. 20, vii, 44; TsGVIA, delo 55, ch. 13, 1. 47.

60 TsGVIA, delo 55, ch. 13, 11. 24–47 (extracts have been published in Semevskii, *M. V. Butashevich-Petrashevskii i petrashevtsy*, pp. 32–7). According to the official history, Poroshin was 'one of the best-loved professors in the university and obtained in it almost as great an influence as Granovskii in Moscow' (V. V. Grigor'ev, *Imperatorskii Sankt-Peterburgskii universitet*, pp. 168–70). Poroshin's lectures are known to have been attended by Petrashevskii, Khanykov, Ipollit Debu, P. I. Lamanskii and Tol'. Notes from them (for the academic year 1845–6) were seized among Khanykov's papers on his arrest. Poroshin was investigated by the Commission of Inquiry for spreading 'socialism and communism' among his students.

61 IRLI, fond 265, opis' 2, Arkhiv zhurnala Russkoi stariny, no. 2010, pis'ma Petrashevskogo k neizvestnomu; TsGVIA, delo 55, ch. 43, 1. 11ob. See DP i, 324; ii, 47, 320. The work Petrashevskii read was Fourier's *Traité de l'association domestique-agricole*.

62 DP i, 325; ii, 319, 452; iii, 34, 71, 118, 139; TsGVIA, delo 55, ch. 103, 1. 11.

63 TsGVIA, delo 55, ch. 29, 1. 5; *La Phalange*, 1840, vol. iii, no. 8, 15 April, *Le Nouveau monde*, 1840, no. 28, 11 April (poem by M. Boissy, 'Anniversaire de la naissance de Fourier'); DP, iii, 15, 31, 58–9, 74, 83, 113, 115, 120–1, 133, 147, 166, 180; TsGAOR, no. 214, ch. 142, 1. 268.

64 Herzen, viii, 161; V. S. Pecherin, *Zamogil'nye zapiski*, Moscow 1932, pp. 112–13, 30; P. Ia. Chaadaev, *Sochineniia*, Moscow 1914, pp. 179–80;

IRLI, fond 309, Bariatinskii, delo 308, 1. 135; for I. S. Turgenev, see O. V. Orlik, *Peredovaia Rossiia i revoliutsionnaia Frantsiia*, Moscow 1973, pp. 179–82, 193.

65 Herzen, viii, 162; Belinskii, xii, 53 (letter to Botkin, 28 June 1841).
66 Herzen, viii, 122; ix, 116; ii, 266–7.
67 *Otechestvennye zapiski*, 1848, no. 3, viii, 109.
68 The fullest account remains W. Karénine, *George Sand, sa vie et ses oeuvres, 1804–76*, 4 vols., Paris 1899.
69 See Belinskii, x, 106; xii, 115, 124; v, 175–6, 536; vi, 278–9, 580.
70 Dostoevskii, *Diary of a Writer*, pp. 345–7; W. Karénine, *George Sand*, i, 21–3 (this poem is not included in Pleshcheev's published works); Saltykov, xiv, 111–12; *Otechestvennye zapiski*, 1842, vol. 26, vi, p. 38; vol. 27, vii, 1; vol. 28, vii, 25–38.
71 Chernyshevskii, i, 279 (11 July 1849).
72 Speshnev, *Pis'ma k materi*, nos. 49, 50 (5 and August 1848); Herzen, x, 187–9; Chernyshevskii, i, 107 (5 September 1848); DP, iii, 430. Proudhon's works were borrowed by Saltykov, Khovrin, Maikov, Miliutin, Speshnev, Dostoevskii, Kuz'min, Pleshcheev and others (see TsGAOR, no. 214, ch. 141, 1. 128ob).
73 TsGVIA, delo 55, ch. 43, 1. 7; DP, iii, 143; Herzen, ix, 116; FOP, p. 489.
74 DP, i, 58, 114; Maikov, ii, 47; see Belinskii, ii, 53.
75 L. Blanc, *Histoire de dix ans, 1830–40*, 7th ed., Paris, 1848, iv, 244.
76 *Petrashevtsy*, iii, 70.

IV — THE PHILOSOPHICAL IDEAS
OF THE PETRASHEVTSY

1 DP, i, 531.
2 TsGVIA, delo 55, ch. 2, 11. 167–74. *Das Wesen des Christenthums* was given to Chernyshevskii by Khanykov and seized from Petrashevskii on his arrest.
3 For Dostoevskii's hostility to the Orthodox Church, see F. M. Dostoevskii, *Polnoe sobranie sochinenii*, 30 vols., Leningrad 1972– , (in future, Dostoevskii), i, 264–320 (*The Landlady*); for his religious feelings, *Diary of a Writer*, p. 148; DP, iii, 285; Bel'chikov, p. 105; F. N. L'vov, 'Zapiska o dele petrashevtsev', *Literaturnoe nasledstvo. Gertsen i Ogarev iii*, Moscow 1956, p. 188. On Maikov, see V. N. Maikov, *Sochineviia v dvukh tomakh*, Kiev 1901 (in future, Maikov), i, 44, 195, 200. On the Petrashevtsy and mysticism, TsGVIA, delo 55, ch. 37, 1. 9ob; DP, ii, 367; i, 530.
4 See 'Mesmer, Swedenborg i Fourier', *Finskii vestnik*, 1847, no. 15, vi, 3; 'Nekrolog P. A. Ballanche', ibid., 1847, no. 20, vi, 27–37; review of 'Rukovodstvo k poznaniiu zakonov', ibid., 1846, no. 9, v, 19; also no. 8, v, 31–3; no. 7, v, 15–33; 'Po povodu stikhotvorenii A. Grigor'eva. Soobshchenie', ibid., 1846, no. 9, vi, 45–9.

5 Herzen, v, 211; vii, 343; Belinskii, x, 214; FOP, pp. 330, 221; TsGAOR, fond 1071, N. A. Speshnev, opis' 1, ed.khr. 33, 11. 1–1ob; see Chernyshevskii, i, 375 (26 May 1850).

6 TsGVIA, delo 55, ch. 2, 11. 185–185ob; see ch. 25, 11. 1–10; ch. 44, 1. 3ob; D. F. Strauss, *Das Leben Jesu*, Tübingen 1835–6, ii, 733–4; L. A. Feuerbach, 'Das Wesen des Christenthums', *Sämmtliche Werke*, Leipzig, 1844–66, vii, 360.

7 DP, i, 525, 539, 194; Semenov T'ian-Shanskii, *Memuary*, i, 196; TsGAOR, no. 214, 1. 114ob; TsGVIA, delo 55, ch. 38, 1. 45ob; ch. 44, 1. 1ob.

8 DP, ii, 165; FOP, p. 491; TsGAOR, no. 214, ch. 141, 1. 287ob; DP, i, 326; ii, 180.

9 DP, ii, 180; iii, 414–15; TsGVIA, delo 55, ch. 43, 1. 30; FOP, pp. 310, 257; Belinskii, x, 214.

10 Belinskii, i, 462, 500; Dostoevskii, xiv, 224; FOP, pp. 303–5; DP, iii, 156–7; V. A. Engel'son, 'Chto takoe gosudarstvo?', *Poliarnaia zvezda*, London 1855, no. 1, p. 26.

11 FOP, p. 495; Proudhon, 'Contradictions économiques', iv, 359–61.

12 *Karmannyi slovar' inostrannykh slov, voshedshikh v sostav russkogo iazyka*, ed. N. S. Kirillov, 2 vols., St. Petersburg 1845–6, vol. i (in future, KS), 70; DP, iii, 155–6; V. A. Miliutin, *Izbrannye proizvedeniia*, Moscow 1946, (in future, Miliutin), p. 364. Vol. ii of *Karmannyi slovar'* is included in FOP.

13 L. A. Feuerbach, 'Vorläufige Thesen zur Reform der Philosophie', *Sämmtliche Werke*, ii, 247–8; Maikov, ii, 15, 264; Herzen, iii, 80; KS, i, 72; Miliutin, p. 42.

14 FOP, p. 479; KS, 9; M. Stirner, *Der Einzige und sein Eigentum*, 1845, Berlin 1924 ed., pp. 40–1 (Yes, the world is haunted!); DP, iii, 155; Herzen, iii, 80.

15 KS, 4; Herzen, iii, 48, 80–1; Maikov, ii, 45, 221; i, 248; Saltykov, ii, 263; DP, iii, 155.

16 Belinskii, xii, 22–3.

17 Herzen, iii, 48, 114–21; FOP, pp. 494–5; Maikov, ii, 16–17; Feuerbach, 'Vorläufige Thesen zur Reform der Philosophie', p. 261; 'Grundsätze der Philosophie der Zukunft', *Sämmtliche Werke*, ii, 299.

18 FOP, p. 184.

19 P. Enfantin, *La Religion saint-simonienne*, Paris 1832, 2nd ed., p. 175; FOP, pp. 125–7.

20 DP, iii, 92; i, 531, 90; ii, 21; FOP, pp. 182–3; Fourier, iv, 241 (Fourier himself compares his analogies to Schelling's Absolute, vi, 14).

21 FOP, p. 308; Herzen, iii, 18, 59; KS, 156; DP, i, 117; *Pis'ma I. M. Debu*, ed. khr. 2 (18 January 1854).

22 FOP, pp. 189, 215, 247, 345.

23 Fourier, ii, 57.

24 According to Toussenel, the pig, for example, was the emblem of the miser – only good after his death; the bickering hamster represented civilised

marriage (A. Toussenel, *Esprit des bêtes*, Paris 1847, pp. 222, 226, 243, 143−44). For similar ideas in Russia, see *Otechestvennye zapiski*, 1848, no. 3, vii, 104−9; DP, iii, 92−4, 15, 70; *Pis'ma I. M. Debu*, ed.khr. 44; V. V. Tolbin, 'Nochnye babochki', *Illiustratsiia*, 1847, no. 35−6, pp. 165−83. Fourier's account is in 'Anologie et cosmogonie', xii.

25 Feuerbach, 'Vorläufige Thesen zur Reform der Philosophie', p. 263; DP, i, 517; ii, 158; see A. N. Annenskii, 'Teoriia i praktika', *Finskii vestnik*, 1846, no. 8, v, 31−2.

26 DP, ii, 352−7, 290−7, 434; Chernyshevskii, i, 178−90 (23 November to 7 December 1848).

27 DP, i, 116; *Pis'ma I. M. Debu*, ed.khr. 2.

28 Miliutin, pp. 156−7; Dostoevskii, *Pis'ma*, ii, 550 (16 August 1839); see DP, iii, 154.

29 *Pis'ma I. M. Debu*, ed.khr. 40, 4 March 1855; ed.khr. 16, 2 December 1854; E. G. Kislytsina, ed., 'Zapiski chteniia M. E. Saltykova v sorokovykh godakh', *Izvestiia AN SSSR*, 1937, social sciences, p. 876; DP, iii, 35, 247. See P. J. G. Cabanis, *Rapports du physique et du moral de l'homme*, Paris 1824, 2nd ed., i, 33. On the popularity of the social sciences in Russia, see Herzen, iii, 93.

30 Miliutin, pp. 358−93 (see FOP, pp. 133−4; Maikov, ii, 25; DP, iii, 152); Maikov, ii, 4−40 (see A. Comte, *Cours de philosophie positive*, iv, 535); TsGIAL, fond 647, opis' 1, ed.khr. 6, 'Chernovye zametki A. P. Balasoglo k rabote po klassifikatsii nauk', 11. 2−18.

31 Saltykov, i, 137; Maikov, ii, 87−8.

32 KS, 7−10; see Herzen, iii, 97−8; Feuerbach, 'Vorläufige Thesen zur Reform der Philosophie', p. 267.

33 DP, i, 498−9.

34 FOP, p. 431; *Pis'ma I. M. Debu*, ed.khr. 2; DP, iii, 112; Herzen, iii, 126−7, 111; see F. W. J. Schelling, 'Philosophische Untersuchungen über das Wesen der menschlichen Freiheit', 1809, *Sämmtliche Werke*, Stuttgart and Ausbert 1856−61, vii, 411; Feuerbach, 'Das Wesen des Christenthums', pp. 380−2.

35 Feuerbach, op. cit., pp. 25, 126−7; FOP, pp. 319−20; Herzen, iii, 128−9.

36 FOP, p. 327; *Pis'ma I. M. Debu*, ed.khr. 2.

37 See B. Bauer, *Hegels Lehre von der Religion und Kunst vom Standpunkt des Glaubens aus betrachtet*, Leipzig 1842.

38 Belinskii, viii, 277; *Pis'ma I. M. Debu*, ed.kr. 2; DP, i, 521; Saltykov, i, 137−8.

39 Marquis de Condorcet, *Esquisse d'un tableau historique des progrès de l'esprit humain (1793)*, Paris 1971, ed. sociales, p. 77.

40 Fourier had spoken of *Edenism* as the first age of man and of some sort of planetary sickness which led to the deformation of the earth (i, 57).

41 Saltykov, i, 155; KS, 75; FOP, pp. 189−90; DP, i, 96; ii, 45.

42 Belinskii, viii, 284; Saltykov, i, 75; Miliutin, p. 69; DP, ii, 120; iii, 98.

43 FOP, p. 339.
44 Saltykov, xiii, 389; FOP, pp. 187, 339–40; *Pis'ma I. M. Debu*, ed. khr. 30; Maikov, ii, 219, 231; see Herzen, iii, 85.
45 FOP, pp. 338–9; Maikov, i, 115; ii, 172; Saltykov, vi, 387; i, 241; Miliutin, p. 68; Herzen, iii 7, 85. (See also Belinskii, xii, 70; DP, i, 439; KS, 149; Maikov, ii, 172).
46 FOP, p. 337; see Saltykov, vii, 444–5, 512; Belisnkii, xvi, 91–2; Herzen, iii, 37.
47 FOP, pp. 149 (on man's search for variety), 214 (on technology); DP, iii, 17 (on the class struggle – compare with K. Marx, 'The Communist Manifesto', *Collected Works*, London 1976, p. 482. This came out in February 1848).
48 DP, ii, 158–9; FOP, pp. 221, 268, 307–8; Maikov, i, 193–4; see Strauss, *Das Leben Jesu*, ii, 14–15.
49 FOP, pp. 480, 487; see Comte, *Cours de philosophie positive*, i, 4, 12; Maikov, ii, 96–7; Herzen, iii, 132–34.
50 FOP, p. 269; Miliutin, p. 358; DP, i, 537; Saltykov, i, 74, Herzen, iii, 75 (on the study of reality); FOP, pp. 307, 309, 347, 269; DP, i, 90 (on the possibility of knowing everything); Miliutin, p. 360; Maikov, i, 200 (their objections to this).
51 *Pis'ma I. M. Debu*, ed. khr. 2; FOP, p. 214; Herzen, iii, 94.
52 DP, i, 492–9; iii, 103; ii, 298; TsGVIA, delo 55, ch. 2, 1. 167ob. See Fourier, ii, pp. vii, xliv; F. Feuerbach, *Die Religion der Zukunft*, Nürnberg, 1843–45, 3 vol.
53 Maikov, i, 61.
54 The major articles were Maikov, review of 'Stikhotvoreniia Kol'tsova', i, 1–99; of 'Kratkoe nachertanie istorii russkoi literatury', i, 247–76; Belinskii, 'O zhizhni i sochineniiakh Kol'tsova', ix, 497–542; 'Vzgliad na russkoiu literaturu 1846 goda', x, 7–50.
55 Belinskii, x, 31; FOP, pp. 324, 327; Miliutin, p. 383.
56 Maikov, i, 58–60.
57 Henryk Kamienski (1812–65), a progressive Polish thinker, was arrested in 1845 and exiled to Viatka at the same time as Saltykov. His *Filozofia ekonomii materyalnej ludzkiego spoleczenstwa*, (1843–5), the book Speshnev read, is a rather crude attempt to deduce from Feuerbach's metaphysics the need for a communist utopia. Stirner's *Der Einzige und sein Eigentum* (1845) was kept in the collective library.
58 FOP, pp. 485, 496; see Stirner, *Der Einzige und sein Eigentum*, pp. 38, 42, 167.
59 FOP, pp. 483–4, 488, 497; Stirner, op. cit., pp. 152, 175, 282, 297, 304.
60 FOP, p. 497; Dostoevskii, xii, 113; Speshnev, *Pis'ma k materi*, (Dresden 17/5 April 1846); B. Koz'min ed., 'N. A. Speshnev o sebe samom', *Katorga i ssylka*, 1930, no. 1, pp. 95–7; 'Zapiska generala Bronevskogo o Litsee', p. 42.

61 *Pis'ma V. A. Engel'sona*, pp. 46–7, 49, 52 (especially letter of 7 October 1854); Herzen, vi, 126, 104, 34, 36, 119.
62 Herzen, x, 344.

V — THE CRITIQUE OF CIVILISATION

1 Herzen, xiii, 19–23; x, 124–30. Belinskii, in Paris in 1847, underwent a similar reaction to Herzen's, but later modified his position (Belinskii, xii, 448–50, 499 (letter to Botkin, 2–6 December 1847; to P. V. Annenkov, 15 February 1848).
2 DP, i, 159.
3 See Miliutin, p. 73.
4 FOP, pp. 238–9, 488, 497, 187; DP, i, 90, 535–6; ii, 257, 293; TsGAOR, no. 214, ch. 136, 1. 35.
5 DP, i, 284; Maikov, i, 56. See Fourier ii (*du libre arbitre*), vii, xliv.
6 DP, i, 76, 182; ii, 210, 294, 351–5; iii, 100, 113; Maikov, i, 56; see Saltykov, ix, 7–33.
7 Dostoevskii, i, 426–7; see his 'Peterburgskaia letopis', *Sanktpeterburgskie vedomosti*, 1847, no. 133.
8 On drink, see Dostoevskii i, 79 (Makar Devushkin drinks because 'Everything is ruined, my reputation, my self-respect — all that I have in the world'). On ambition, see Dostoevskii, i, 109–29, 240–63; Bel'chikov, p. 107. On quietness and humility, see Dostoevskii, i, 24, 246; ii, 16–48.
9 Dostoevskii, ii, 234. See Maikov on laziness, i, 44; ii, 174.
10 DP, i, 76.
11 Review of 'O nakazaniiakh i ispravitel'nykh zavedeniiakh, soch. shvedskogo korolia Oskara (Om Straff och Straff-Anstalter, 1840)', *Finskii vestnik*, 1845, no. 1, v, 5; see Saltykov, i, 82; DP, i, 213, 222; Miliutin, 'Proletariat i pauperism v Anglii i vo Frantsii', iii, *Otechestvennye zapiski*, 1847, no. 3–4; ii, 22 (parts iii and iv of Miliutin's article are omitted from his *Izbrannye proizvedeniia*).
12 DP, i, 84.
13 E. Sue, Mystères de Paris, ed. Libres/Hallier, Paris 1977–80, iv, 59; Saltykov, 'Neskol'ko slov o chtenii romanov', *Otechestvennye zapiski*, 1848, no. 3, vi, 40.
14 DP, i, 44; iii, 87; V. Considerant, Speech of 4 April 1849, *la Presse*, 1849, 15 April.
15 FOP, pp. 264–5; DP, i, 213; see 'O nakazaniiakh i ispravitel'nykh zavedeniiakh', pp. 1–29; Maikov, ii, 29.
16 Some of these reviews were long thought to have been written by Belinskii and were even included in his *Collected Works*, see T. I. Usakina, 'O literaturno-kriticheskoi deiatel'nosti molodogo Saltykova', *Literaturnoe*

nasledstvo, Moscow 1959, vol. 67, pp. 409–47. Only a few are represented in the latest edition of Saltykov's works, i, 327–52.

17 Saltykov, review of 'G. A. Potemkin', *Otechestvennye zapiski*, 1848, no. 1–2, vi, 47; see i, 346; Dostoevskii, ii, 165; J. J. Rousseau, *Émile ou l'éducation*, (1762), Paris 1961, Garner ed., p. 139.

18 Saltykov, review of 'Robinson Crusoe', *Otechestvennye zapiski*, 1847, no. 1–2, vi, 59; of 'Russkie skazki dlia detei', ibid., 1848, no. 1–2, vi, 44; of 'Blagovospitannoe ditia', ibid., vi, 49–50; Belinskii, x, 377–80.

19 Saltykov, review of 'Detskaia korzinochka', *Otechestvennye zapiski*, 1847, no. 1–2, vi, 62; see, i, 331; 'Obzor detskoi literatury', *Finskii vestnik*, 1847, no. 18, v, 7; KS, 158.

20 See Saltykov, i, 182, 271, 286.

21 Balasoglo, *Ob izlozhenii nauk*, 11. 40–6, 8ob; see Saltykov, i, 338–9.

22 See Maikov, i, 235.

23 Rousseau, *Émile*, pp. 113, 176, 238; Belinskii, vi, 196–9; x, 137; Saltykov, i, 330; review of 'Robinson Crusoe', p. 60.

24 Fourier, v, 3; DP, iii, 144n; i, 182; Makashin, *Saltykov-Shchedrin*, i, 250; Saltykov, i, 340. Saltykov, i, 330 directly paraphrases Fourier vi, 186.

25 These were, the Technological Institute, the Institute of the Communications Corps and the Nobles Regiment.

26 DP, i, 340; ii, 202, 204, 216. The political and philosophical tone of the articles in *Finskii vestnik* makes it fairly clear they were written by one of the more radical Petrashevtsy. Jastrzębski is the most obvious contender by far (particularly because of the articles' wit), but since there is no conclusive proof of his authorship, I will refer to the author simply as *Finskii vestnik*. See V. M. Morozov, *Russkii progressivnyi zhurnal 'Finskii vestnik'*, Candidat thesis, LGU 1961, p. 151.

27 DP, i, 446; ii, 320; iii, 63; *Biograficheskii skovar' professorov i prepodavatelei im. Kazanskogo universiteta*, ed. N. P. Zagoskin, Kazan 1904, pp. 60–1.

28 Bel'chikov, p. 146.

29 Miliutin, pp. 376–7; (Jastrzębski), review of 'Opyt o narodnom bogatstve, soch. A. I. Butovskogo, Moscow 1846', *Finskii vestnik*, 1847, no. 11, v, 111; DP, ii, 205; iii, 224.

30 Saltykov, i, 202–5; Dostoevskii, i, 85–6; see 'Parizhskie mody', *Sovremennik*, 1847, no. 7–8, v, 5–6; TsGVIA, delo 55, ch. 13, 1. 36ob; (Jastrzębski), review of 'Ob istochnikakh i upotreblenii statisticheskikh svedenii, soch. D. P. Zhuravskogo, Kiev 1846', *Finskii vestnik*, 1847, no. 1, v, 35–7.

31 See Miliutin, p. 158n; KS, 144; (Jastrzębski), review of 'Ob otmenenii khlebnykh zakonov v Anglii, soch. Ia. Linovskogo', *Finskii vestnik*, 1846, no. 11, v, 112. The collective library even had a copy of Engels' *Die Lage der arbeitender Klasse in England* (1845). A very popular work was the Fourierist Francois Vidal's *De la Répartition des richesses ou de justice distributive en économie sociale* (1846), borrowed by Saltykov, Maikov,

Speshnev, E.I. and P.I. Lamanskii, Timkovskii, Nikolai Kaidanov and Ippolit Debu.

32 Miliutin, pp. 214–21.

33 Ibid., pp. 188–96; Miliutin, 'Proletariat i pauperizm', iii, p. 11; (Jastrzębski), review of 'Ob otmenenii khlebnykh zakonov', p. 112. See M. Villermé, *Tableau de l'état physique et moral des ouvriers, employés dans les manufactures de coton, de laine et de soie*, Paris 1840, i, 100; E. Buret, *De la misère des classes laborieuses en Angleterre et en France*, Paris 1840, i, 315–79.

34 Miliutin, 'Proletariat i pauperizm', iii, pp. 1, 25–7, 32–3; Miliutin, pp. 212–14; (Jastrzębski), review of 'Ob otmenenii khlebnykh zakonov', p. 112; Buret, op. cit., ii, 45–7, 19–20; see KS, 176.

35 K.K. Arsen'ev, *Statisticheskie svedeniia o Sanktpeterburge*, St. Petersburg, 1836; I. Pushkarev, *Opisanie Peterburga*, St. Petersburg 1839; K.S. Veselovskii, 'Statistika nedvizhimykh imushchestv v Sanktpeterburge', *Zapiski russkogo geograficheskogo obshchestva*, 1849, nos. 3–4. A condensed version was published in *Otechestvennye zapiski*, 1848, no. 3.

36 Veselovskii, op. cit., p. 131; Arsen'ev, op. cit., pp. 77–8; A.A. Ekimov, 'Iz istorii razvitiia krupnoi industrii v Peterburge', *Vestnik LGU*, 1954, series 1, no. 3, p. 81.

37 S.F. Durov, 'Khalatnik', *Nevskii almanach na 1847–8*, St. Petersburg 1847, p. 189; V.S. Poroshin, 'Peterburg', *Sovremennik*, 1848, no. 1, vi, 138–40.

38 Arsen'ev, op. cit., pp. 77–8, 109–10; Veselovskii, op. cit., pp. 99–101; K.A. Pazhitnov, *Polozhenie rabochego klassa v Rossii*, Leningrad 1925, p. 170.

39 Veselovskii, op. cit., pp. 69, 77.

40 TsGVIA, delo 55, ch. 2, 1. 201ob; DP, iii, 91–2, 111–12, 360; Saltykov, iv, 311.

41 For instance, Gogol's *Nevskii Prospekt*, Nekrasov's *Peterburgskie ugly*, Ap. Grigor'ev's poems *Gorod* and *Proshchanie s Peterburgom*.

42 Saltykov, iii, 398; see TsGVIA, delo 55, ch. 13, 1. 38; Dostoevskii, 'Peterburgskaia letopis', *Sanktpeterburgskie vedomosti*, 1847, no. 93.

43 DP, iii, 88, 92; see (Jastrzębski), review of 'Opyt o narodnom bogatstve', p. 3; L. Faucher, *Étude sur Angleterre*, Paris 1845, i, 387ff (chapter on *manufactures rurales*).

44 Miliutin, pp. 116–19, 122–3, 128–9, 158–60, 162–4, 168–70, 210–11.

45 Ibid., pp. 163–8; DP, i, 444–5; ii, 205–6.

46 Miliutin, pp. 129–30, 170–3, 200; 'Basnoslovnye i deistvitel'nye vampiry', *Finskii vestnik*, 1847, no. 15, vi, 6–11; Herzen, vi, 56; DP, i, 75; ii, 347–8; Belinskii, xii, 449.

47 (Jastrzębski), review of 'Ob otmenenii khlebnykh zakonov', p. 113; DP, ii, 346–7; Saltykov, i, 235–6.

48 Miliutin, pp. 73, 161–2, 167–8, 185.

49 DP, i, 91; iii, 90–1; FOP, p. 265; Maikov, ii, 53–4; Miliutin, pp. 129, 173–4, 333–5; Sismondi, *Nouveaux principes*, preface, pp. iv–x.

50 Miliutin, pp. 307–9; 'Proletariat i pauperizm', iii, p. 149; Maikov, ii, 296; see Herzen, v, 60–1; Sismondi, *Nouveaux principes*, i, 1–8; ii, 369–70.

51 Miliutin, pp. 313–16; 'Proletariat i pauperizm', iii, p. 150; FOP, p. 346; TsGVIA, delo 55, ch. 25, 11. 2ob, 5; see Herzen, vi, 61.

52 Saltykov, i, 135, 137, 162, 164–5.

53 Miliutin, pp. 296–304; P. and J. Leroux, 'Adam Smith', *Éncyclopedie nouvelle*, ed. P. Leroux and J. Renaud, Paris 1836–43, vol. 8, p. 167.

54 Miliutin, pp. 304–5, 327–331; (Jastrzębski), review of 'Opyt o narodnom bogatstve', p. 4.

55 T. Malthus, *An Essay on the Principle of Population*, 1st ed. London 1798.

56 Miliutin, pp. 78–82; see Saltykov, i, 99.

57 (Jastrzębski), review of 'Opyt o narodnom bogatstve', pp. 8–9; Miliutin, pp. 143–9; see Fourier, vi, 337; T. Doubleday, *The True Law of Population shown to be connected with the Food of the People*, London 1842, pp. 5, 6–7.

58 Sismondi, *Nouveaux principes*, ii, 250–80, 453; Proudhon, 'Contradictions economiques', v, 366–75.

59 Saltykov, i, 106; Miliutin, pp. 87, 141–3, 150–6.

60 R. R. Shtrandman, 'Sovremennye zametki', *Sovremennik*, 1847, no. 9–10, v, 263–4; V. S. Poroshin, *O zemledelii v politiko-ekonomicheskom otnoshenii*, St. Petersburg 1846, pp. 39–44; F. Bastiat, *Cobden et la ligue anglaise pour la liberté du commerce*, Paris 1845, p. iii (used by Poroshin).

61 (Jastrzębski), 'Biografiia Sir Robert Peel', *Finskii vestnik*, 1846, no. 11, iv, 24–9; review of, 'Ob otmenenii khlebnykh zakonov', pp. 99–100, 108–9, 114, 116; of 'O zemledelii v politiko-ekonomicheskom otnoshenii, soch. V. S. Poroshina', *Finskii vestnik*, 1846, no. 11, v, 55–9; L. Faucher, *Étude sur l'Angleterre*, ii, 364.

62 Shtrandman, 'Sovremennye zametki', *Sovremennik*, 1847, no. 3, iv, 50; 'Smes', *Finskii vestnik*, 1847, no. 16, vi, 48–50; see TsGVIA, delo 55, ch. 86, 1. 30.

63 N. A. Mel'gunov began with an article in *Moskovskie vedomosti* 1847, no. 20. Shevyrev replied in no. 22. Mel'gunov then published 'Otvet Shevyrevu', in *Sovremennik* 1847, no. 5, iv (under the pseudonym L. N-v). See also Shtrandman, 'Sovremennye zametki', *Sovremennik*, 1847, no. 3, iv, 5; Saltykov, i, 84; Miliutin, 'Proletariat i pauperizm', iv, p. 142; Delo 55, ch. 13, 11, 139–40; (Jastrzębski), review of 'Ob otmenenii khlebnykh zakonov', p. 111.

64 E. G. Osokin, 'O postepennom razvitii ekonomicheskikh idei v istorii', *Zhurnal Ministerstva narodnogo prosveshcheniia*, 1845, April, pp. 79–80; DP, ii, 207; Maikov, ii, 52, 63–5; i, 191.

65 DP, iii, 92, 97; (Jastrzębski), review of 'O zemledelii', p. 92; Maikov, i, 191; E. G. Osokin, op. cit., p. 80; see Sismondi, *Nouveaux principes*, ii, 423–5.

66 Dostoevskii, i, 47, 85; ii, 275; Miliutin, p. 131; (Jastrzębski), review of 'Opyt o narodnom bogatstve', p. 4; DP, iii, 90.

67 Miliutin, p. 301, (Jastrzębski), review of 'Ob otmenenii khlebnykh zakonov', p. 120; FOP, pp. 346−7; Maikov, ii, 72−4; Proudhon, 'Qu'est-ce que la propriété?', i, 91, 95; 'Contradictions économiques', iv, 47.

68 FOP, p. 347.

69 Miliutin, pp. 175−81; Maikov, ii, 61; Proudhon, 'Contradictions économiques', v, 409.

70 (Jastrzębski), review of 'Opyt o narodnom bogatstve', p. 5; DP, i, 94; ii, 208; Maikov, ii, 54; TsGVIA, delo 55, ch. 13, 1. 46ob.

71 DP, i, 79; ii, 202, 311−13; iii, 72; TsGVIA, delo 55, ch. 37, 1. 19; Maikov, ii, 34, 56; FOP, p. 348.

72 'Obzor detskoi literatury', p. 6; (Jastrzębski), review of 'Opyt o narodnom bogatstve', p. 6; Maikov, ii, 309; see Proudhon, 'Qu'est-ce que la propriété?', pp. 97−103.

73 DP, ii, 96, 329; FOP, pp. 266, 491−2, 488; Chernyshevskii, i, 61 (30 July 1848); A. S. Dolinin ed., *F. M. Dostoevskii v vospominaniiakh sovremennikov*, i, 173.

74 Maikov, ii, 60−1; 'Frantsuzskaia literatura', *Sovremennik*, 1847, no. 7, iii, 21; this comes from Proudhon, 'Contradictions économiques', iv, 210−18.

75 Speshnev, *Pis'ma k materi*, no. 49 and 50 (5 and 9 August 1848); 'Smes', *Sovremennik*, 1847, no. 12, vi, 220; DP, ii, 209; see Saltykov, i, 237−40; DP, iii, 62.

76 'Frantsuzskaia literatura', p. 21; 'Finansovaia sistema Law', *Finskii vestnik*, 1847, no. 15, iv, 1−28; L. Blanc, 'Regénce − système de Law', *Histoire de la Révolution francaise*, (Paris 1848), i, 272−81.

77 FOP, pp. 266−7. The Petrashevtsy were, however, aware of the imperfect (i.e. paternalist) nature of Owen's experiments, see DP, ii, 309.

78 DP, i, 449.

79 DP, i, 78n.; ii, 361.

80 Beklemishev and Danilevskii described Fourier's theory of attractive labour in great detail (DP, ii, 301−9, 338−62; iii, 320).

81 DP, i, 72; TsGAOR, fond 1071, N. A. Speshnev, opis' 1, ed.khr. 33, 1. 2ob.

82 TsGVIA, delo 55, ch. 13, 11. 24−5; see Proudhon, 'Avertissement aux propriétaires', *Oeuvres*, ii, 22; Saltykov, i, 99.

83 See DP, i, 535−56; FOP, pp. 187, 238−9.

84 In Gatti de Gamond's final version of the phalanstery, the social product was to be 'divided equally among all the adult *sociètaires*, without distinction of rich and poor, without regard to more or less labour, to more or less talent' (Z. Gatti de Gamond, *Paupérisme et association*, Paris 1847, pp. 87−92). Whole sections of Dézamy's *Code de la communauté*, Paris 1842, are quotations from Fourier and Gatti de Gamond. On his intentions of mixing Fourierism and communism, see J. Maître ed., *Dictionnaire biographique du mouvement ouvrier francais*, ii, 85.

85 FOP, pp. 488, 491−2; DP, i, 324, 533−4; ii, 402, 433.

86 Saltykov, xvi, 40; Herzen, ii, 345; ix, 116.
87 Maikov, ii, 69−84; Miliutin, p. 343.
88 J. Mongin, 'Utopie', *Encyclopedie nouvelle*, vol. 8, pp. 575−8; Miliutin, pp. 343−50; (Jastrzębski), review of 'Opyt o narodnom bogatstve', p. 7.
89 Petrashevtsy, iii, 65.

VI — RUSSIAN SOLUTIONS

1 DP, i, 520; see Maikov, ii, 3.
2 Marquis de Custine, *Lettres de Russie. La Russie en 1839*, ed. P. Nora, Paris, Gallimard, 1975, p. 120; see TsGVIA, delo 55, ch. 34, 1. 41; DP, i, 70; Dostoevskii, 'Peterburgskaia letopis', *Sanktpeterburgskie vedomosti*, 1847, no. 121.
3 DP, iii, 303; ii, 41−2; FOP, p. 193; TsGAOR, fond 1071, opis' 1, ed. khr. 7, N. A. Speshnev, 'Zametki po voprosam istorii Evropy i Rossii', 1. 1.
4 DP, i, 236, 521, 532; iii, 57; Saltykov, i, 74.
5 DP, i, 552.
6 K. S. Aksakov, *Polnoe sobranie sochinenii*, Moscow 1861−80, i, 192.
7 (Jastrzębski), review of, 'O zemledelii v politiko-ekonomicheskom otnoshenii', pp. 92−3; review of, 'Opyt o narodnom bogatstve', pp. 3−4.
8 DP, i, 95; see ii, 182; iii, 418; TsGVIA, delo 55, ch. 13, 11. 31ob−35ob, on the future unification of nations.
9 'Vnutrennye izvestiia', *Otechestvennye zapiski*, 1848, no. 3−4, viii, 63; FOP, pp. 192−4; Maikov, ii, 251−2.
10 Maikov, ii, 3−49 (*Finskii vestnik*, 1845, no. 1, iv, 1−62), for his advocacy of nationality; Maikov, i, 53−4, 55−6, 60, 81−3, 165−6; 253−5 (his later position).
11 Belinskii, x, 23−9, 31−3; ix, 532.
12 For instance V. Sviatlovskii, 'Fur'erizm v Rossii. Petrashevtsy', *K istorii politiko-ekonomii i statistiki v Rossii*, St. Petersburg 1906, pp. 77−82.
13 Belinskii, x, 21; DP, i, 121.
14 DP, iii, 18, 348; i, 10, 159.
15 *Petrashevtsy*, iii, 91; DP, i, 311, 408, 149; KS, 4; TsGVIA, delo 55, ch. 1, 1. 11.
16 DP, i, 280; TsGVIA, delo 55, ch. 3, 1. 130; see Belinskii, x, 215−16.
17 TsGVIA, delo 55, ch. 3, 11. 91−2, 155; ch. 42, 1. 27; ch. 2, 1. 148ob; DP, iii, 417−19; ii, 89; i, 280; *Pis'ma V. A. Engel'sona*, p. 30 (30 November 1852).
18 DP, iii, 366; TsGVIA, delo 55, ch. 2, 1. 134ob.
19 DP, iii, 383, 385, 355; TsGVIA, delo 55, ch. 2, 1. 179; ch. 1, 1. 140ob.
20 DP, iii, 455−6; Poroshin, *O zemledelii*, pp. 67−75; FOP, p. 323; Balasoglo, *Ob izlozhenii nauk*, 11. 20ob, 1ob, 45; S. F. Durov, 'Publius Sirus', *Finskii vestnik*, 1847, no. 23, vi, 11−18 (Greece and Rome); DP, iii, 387, 391;

'Emerson', *Finskii vestnik*, 1847, no. 13, vi, 1–12 (France and America). As a result of the Petrashevtsy affair, restrictions were placed on the teaching of classics in schools.

21 DP, iii, 100–1.

22 DP, iii, 417–18, 99; TsGVIA, delo 55, ch. 42, 1. 27.

23 Bel'chikov, p. 101; DP, ii, 44; Chernyshevskii, i, 121 (18 September 1848).

24 DP, ii, 44, 45; see Chernyshevskii, i, 121; Herzen, ii, 39; I. A. Fedosov, 'Konstitutsional'nye proekty A. V. Berdaeva v 40kh godakh XIXv.', *Voprosy istorii*, 1955, no. 16, p. 87.

25 Bel'chikov, p. 101; DP, i, 27–8, 43, 46.

26 DP, ii, 318, 322. The Petrashevtsy tended to exaggerate their fondness for this aspect of Fourierism at their trial (DP, ii, 201, 372; iii, 177).

27 Maikov, ii, 60, 66–7; Miliutin, pp. 318–19; 'Proletariat i pauperizm', iv, 157.

28 Miliutin, pp. 265–6; Saint-Simon, 'De l'organisation sociale', *Oeuvres*, v, 131–2; Saltykov, i, 265–6.

29 Chernyshevskii, i, 355–6 (20 January 1850); DP, i, 290–1; Petrashevtsy, iii, 191–2; FOP, pp. 257–61; Engel'son, *Chto takoe gosudarstvo?*, pp. 15–17.

30 DP, i, 242, 250–3; iii, 235–6.

31 FOP, pp. 195–6; Chernyshevskii, i, 372 (15 May 1850); DP, iii, 235.

32 KS, 11; see K. N. Lebedev, 'Zapiski senatora', *Russkii arkhiv*, 1910, no. 9, p. 237.

33 DP, i, 105, 123, 249–50, 545; ii, 73; FOP, pp. 194, 354; no. 214, ch. 142, 1. 154ob; *Petrashevtsy*, iii, 191; Pekarskii, 'Studencheskie vospominaniia', p. 232; see E. Lacroix, *Mystères de Russie*, Paris 1844, pp. 214–15; Belinskii, x, 213.

34 DP, iii, 301, 271, 419; Delo 55, ch. 43, 1. 14; ch. 44, 1. 3; Pekarskii, op. cit.; V. N. Nazar'ev, 'Zhizn' i liudi', p. 719.

35 DP, i, 481, 546; ii, 96; FOP, p. 199.

36 DP, ii, 257–9; TsGVIA, delo 55, ch. 29, 1. 19; TsGAOR, no. 214, ch. 4, 1. 115ob; L'vov, *Zapiska o dele petrashevtsev*, p. 180; see *Petrashevtsy*, iii, 192.

37 TsGVIA, delo 55, ch. 47, 1. 7; DP, ii, 426. The reviews of legal literature in *Finskii vestnik* appear from their contents to have been written by one of the Petrashevtsy. Golovinskii, after Petrashevskii the leading legal expert in the circle, had connections with *Finskii vestnik* and first met Petrashevskii at a party given by its editor, Dershau (DP, iii, 218).

38 DP, iii, 321, 400, 402, 425; ii, 284; i, 449–50; FOP, p. 322.

39 DP, i, 27, 120; ii, 96; iii, 95–6, 209; FOP, pp. 261, 296; *Petrashevtsy*, iii, 193; TsGVIA, delo 55, ch. 29, 1. 6ob.

40 DP, iii, 425; (Golovinskii), review of 'O sushchestve nakazanii i o zavedeniiakh ispravitel'nykh, pp. 1–30; Pekarskii, 'Studencheskie vospominaniia', p. 220; see DP, i, 29, 35, 43; ii, 426.

41 DP, i, 146, 120, 555–6; TsGVIA, delo 55, ch. 47, 1. 7ob; Shtrandman,

'Sovremennye zametki', *Sovremennik*, 1847, no. 3, iv, 61−4; no. 9−10, iv, 248−58; FOP, p. 187; Makashin, *Saltykov-Shchedrin*, pp. 203−4.

42 TsGVIA, delo 55, ch. 37, 1. 27ob; TsGAOR, no. 214, ch. 4, 1. 115; Engel'son, *Petrashevtsy*, pp. 492−3; L'vov, *Zapiska*, p. 180; DP, i, 135, 140−1.

43 KS, 149; Dostoevskii, 'Peterburgskaia letopis', *Sankpeterburgskie vedomosti*, 1847, no. 93; see DP, i, 308; iii, 348; FOP, p. 261.

44 Bel'chikov, pp. 100−2; Dostoevskii, *Pis'ma*, i, 95 (17 September 1846); TsGVIA, delo 55, ch. 3, 1. 140ob; ch. 103; 1. 10; ch. 43; 1.4ob−5; ch. 37, 1. 10; ch. 38; 1. 1; FOP, pp. 292−9; see DP, i, 105; F. P. G. Guizot, *Des Moyens de gouvernement et de l'opposition, dans l'état actuel de la France*, Paris 1821.

45 See DP, ii, 48−9; iii, 542; *F. M. Dostoevskii, Stat'i i materlaly*, p. 250.

46 DP, iii, 451−3; i, 225; TsGVIA, delo 55, ch. 13, 1. 38ob; KS, 134; 'Chto takoe nos? ego prava i naznachenie', *Finskii vestnik*, 1847, no. 23, vi, 22−7; see no. 24, iv, 1−10; no. 13, vi, 1−12.

47 FOP, pp. 200−8; see also pp. 197, 229.

48 Belinskii, x, 213; DP, iii, 234−5.

49 R. Shtrandman, 'Sovremennye zametki', *Sovremennik*, 1847, no. 3, iv, 63; In the debate on kindness to animals, the liberal argument was put in V. S. Poroshin, 'Krylov', *Sanktpeterburgskie vedomosti*, 1847, no. 113−16; *Otechestvennye zapiski*, 1847, no. 8, viii, 7; no. 11, vii, 77; 1848, no. 1, v, 13; the radical in 'Sovremennye zametki', *Sovremennik*, 1848, no. 2, iv, 151−5; *Finskii vestnik*, 1847, no. 21, vi, 53−4; no. 22, vi, 25−60; no. 23, vi, 58; V. V. Tolbin, 'Skotoliubie', no. 24, iii, 1−7.

50 A. P. Zablotskii-Desiatovskii, *Prichina kolebanii tsen na khleb*, 1847 (see V. I. Semevskii, *Krest'ianskii vopros v Rossii*, St. Petersburg 1888, ii, 327−33); (Jastrzębski), review of 'Opyt o narodnom bogatstve', p. 3; Shtrandman, 'Sovremennye zametki', *Sovremennik*, 1847, no. 3, iv, 27−30; no. 6, iv, 61−3, 102−5; see DP, ii, 251; iii, 287. The Petrashevtsy also made thinly-veiled attacks on the Russian system of landholding by discussing Ireland, also a country of absentee landlords, harsh bailiffs and poverty-stricken peasants. Their chief source was Gustave de Beaumont's *l'Irlande sociale, politique et religieuse*, Paris 1839, also used by Marx (see Miliutin, pp. 248−54; (Jastrzębski), review of 'O zemledelii', p. 91; Poroshin, *O zemledelii*, pp. 9−12). The best and most detailed study was by N. M. Satin, Herzen's friend, 'Irlandiia', *Sovremennik*, 1847, no. 6, ii, 1−34.

51 DP, i, 466; ii, 235, 394; iii, 210.

52 TsGVIA, delo 55, ch. 101, 1. 18; Nazar'ev, 'Zhizn' i liudi', p. 719; Pekarskii, 'Studencheskie vospominaniia', p. 229.

53 TsGVIA, delo 55, ch. 13, 11. 45ob−46; Poroshin, *O zemledelii*, pp. 4−8, 37−9, 67−76.

54 Miliutin, pp. 240−7; (Jastrzębski), review of 'O zemledelii', pp. 77−8, 87−8;

Maikov, ii, 281–90; KS, 174. Poroshin partly justified rent, *O zemledelii*, pp. 32–5, 49–64.

55 TsGVIA, delo 55, ch. 47, 1. 61; DP, ii, 425–6.

56 DP, ii, 394; N. I. Veselovskii, *V. V. Grigor'ev*, St. Petersburg 1883, p. 9.

57 DP, ii, 252; Shtrandman, 'Sovremennye zametki', *Sovremennik*, 1847, no. 12, vi, 181–2.

58 TsGVIA, delo 55, ch. 37, 1. 3; DP, i, 163; iii, 197, 300 (Ushakov); DP, ii, 394–7 (Beklemishev); DP, i, 123; L'vov, *Zapiska*, p. 180; V. I. Semevskii, *M. V. Butashevich–Petrashevskii i petrashevtsy*, pp. 109–14 (Petrashevskii). See also *Finskii vestnik*, 1847, no. 18, vi, 12–30.

59 O. F. Miller, 'Materialy dlia zhizneopisaniia F. M. Dostoevskogo', *Biografiia, pis'ma i zametki iz zapisnoi knizhi F. M. Dostoevskogo*, St. Petersburg 1883, pp. 88–9; DP, iii, 261–2; TsGVIA, delo 55, ch. 43, 11. 13–13ob (letter of 15 December 1848).

60 *Sovremennik*, 1847, no. 7–8, iv, 139; TsGAOR, no. 214, ch. 141, 1. 288.

61 FOP, pp. 359–64; TsGVIA, delo 55, ch. 29, 1. 7.

62 A. S. Khomiakov, *Polnoe sobranie sochinenii*, Moscow 1914, iii, 71–7, (article *On Rural Conditions*, first published in *Moskvitianin*); (Jastrzębski), review of 'Opyt o narodnom bogatstve', p. 3; DP, ii, 209.

63 KS, 123; see also p. 143.

64 A. F. von Haxthausen, *Studien über die inneren Zustände, das Volksleben und insbesondere die ländlischen Einrichtungen Russlands*, Hannover, 1847, i, xi–xii.

65 V. V. Grigor'ev, 'Baron Haxthausen i ego puteshestvie po Rossii', *Finskii vestnik*, 1847, no. 22, iv, 1–16; (Jastrzębski), review of 'O zemledelii', (September 1846), pp. 92–3; of 'Opyt o narodnom bogatstve', (December 1847), pp. 3–4.

66 Miliukov, *Literaturnye vstrechi*, pp. 177–8; DP, iii, 19, 225, 250; i, 95, 514; TsGAOR, no. 214, ch. 3, 1. 142.

67 O. F. Miller, 'Materialy', p. 92; see Herzen, ix, 149–50.

68 Z. Gatti de Gamond, *Fourier et son système*, pp. 295–301. Her collaborator, the Pole, Jean Cyzinski, wrote a banned study of Russia, *La Russie pittoresque*, Paris, 1837.

69 DP, i, 30.

70 *Otechestvennye zapiski*, 1842, no. 20, vi, 44; see 1848, no. 3, vii, 102.

71 DP, i, 44–5, 183, 185, 175; ii, 320–2.

72 DP, i, 120, 157, 520; iii, 21, 115, 121, 141, 199; TsGAOR, no. 214, ch. 142, 1. 123.

73 DP, i, 40–2. 72–3.

74 S. D. Ianovski, 'Vospominaniia a Dostoevskom', *F. M. Dostoevskii v vospominaniiakh sovremennikov*, Moscow 1964, p. 161, 165; Dostoevskii, *Pis'ma*, i, 95, 112 (17 September, 26 November, 1846); O. F. Miller, 'Materialy', p. 70.

75 IRLI, fond 265, opis' 2, Arkhiv zhurnala russkoi stariny, no. 2010, (18
    January 1844, 13 May, 1846).
76 DP, iii, 256−9.
77 DP, iii, 171.
78 DP, ii, 340−50; iii, 513.
79 Semevskii, *M. V. Butashevich-Petrashevskii i petrashevtsy*, pp. 174−5;
    Leikina-Svirskaia, *Petrashevtsy*, p. 83. Leikina dismisses it as 'undoubtedly
    invented', but then one must remember that the whole purpose of her book
    is to show how un-utopian and un-Fourierist the Petrashevtsy were.
80 V. P. Zotov, 'Peterburg v sorokovykh godov', *Istoricheskii vestnik*, 1890,
    no. 6, pp. 541−3.

VII — PROPAGANDA AND LITERATURE

1   DP, iii, 408; TsGVIA, delo 55, ch. 44, 1. 13.
2   DP, iii, 103, 113−14.
3   DP, iii, 134 (Debu); Chernyshevskii, i, 178−346 (25 November 1848 to 28
    December 1849); TsGVIA, delo 55, ch. 2, 11. 39, 124, 148 (Shaposhnikov);
    149, 186, 205 (Lamartine Club); DP, ii, 241−2 (Kuz'min).
4   Belinskii, ix, 581 (letter to Botkin, 10−11 December 1840).
5   Belinskii, x, 217; see Herzen, vii, 99.
6   DP, i, 6; iii, 378.
7   BL, OIDR, ms. 822311, Pis'ma I. V. Pavlova k A. I. Malyshevu, summer
    1845; see also Makashin, *Saltykov-Shchedrin*, pp. 161−2.
8   DP, iii, 378, 382, 398−9.
9   M. I. Veniukov, *Iz vospominanii*, Amsterdam 1895, i, 103−5; TsGAOR,
    no. 214, ch. 16, 11. 1−2; J-F. L. Jastrzębski, 'Memuar petrashevtsa',
    Minuvshye gody, 1908, no. 1, p. 34.
10 TsGVIA, delo 55, ch. 50, 11. 3−60; DP, ii, 189; iii, 438−9.
11 DP, iii, 423.
12 F. F. Vigel', letter of 28 April 1849, *Russkaia starina*, 1871, no. 4, p. 679;
    M. I. Veniukov, op. cit., pp. 106−8; A. M. Miklashevskii, 'Vospominaniia',
    Russkaia starina, 1891, no. 1, pp. 116−17; 1892, no. 4, p. vii.
13 DP, i, 411.
14 Maikov, i, 2−3, 95−6; Belinskii, ix, 21; x, 5; ix, 535; Bel'chikov, pp. 84−5.
15 See T. I. Usakina, *Petrashevtsy i literaturno-obshchestvennoe dvizhenie 40kh
    godov XIXv*, Saratov, 1965, ch. 5.
16 Maikov, i, 21−3; see Feuerbach, 'Das Wesen des Christenthums', p. 29.
17 Maikov, i, 35−8; ii, 91; see Feuerbach, op. cit., p. 30; Chernyshevskii, ii, 47.
18 KS, 156−7; V. V. Tolbin, 'Khudozhestvennye vystavki v S-Peterburge',
    Finskii vestnik, 1847, no. 22, vi, 64; see also Maikov, i, 124; FOP, p. 132.
19 Maikov, i, 144, 45; DP, ii, 19; Chernyshevskii, ii, 81−2.

20 A. P. Miliukov, 'Tennyson i sovremennoe napravlenie poezii v Anglii', *Finskii vestnik*, 1847, no. 18, vi, 26–32; see Maikov, i, 39–40; Saltykov, 'Neskol'ko slov o chtenii roman', *Otechestvennye zapiski*, 1847, no. 3, vi, 40–1; Bel'chikov, p. 103.

21 Belinskii, x, 16–17.

22 Maikov, i, 99; (S. F. Durov), review of 'Stikhotvoreniia A. Pleshcheeva', *Finskii vestnik*, 1846, no. 12, v, 4. On Kol'tsov, see Maikov, i, 10–11; Chernyshevskii, ii, 10–11.

23 V. V. Tolbin, 'Khudozhestvennye vystavki v S-Peterburge', p. 67; DP, ii, 20; Ap. Grigor'ev, review of 'Peterburgskie vershiny, soch. N. la Butkova', *Finskii vestnik*, 1846, no. 7, v, 3; F. K. Dershau, *Finskii vestnik*, 1846, no. 9, v, 21–34; Maikov, i, 268; KS, 168.

24 Belinskii, *Izbrannye pis'ma*, Moscow 1955, pp. 369–70.

25 P. V. Annenkov, *Literaturnye vospominaniia*, Moscow 1960, p. 296; see A. Galakhov, *Otechestvennye zapiski*, 1848, no. 1, v, 12–13; I. S. Turgenev, *Sochineniia v 12 tomakh*, Moscow 1956, x, 286.

26 Maikov, i, 35; ii, 299.

27 Belinskii, x, 303–4, 326; xii, 467; Maikov, i, 190–1, 220–2.

28 DP, i, 126, 399; ii, 116, 118, 185–6; iii, 116, 244, 262, 412, 441–2; TsGVIA, delo 55, ch. 55, 1. 30; ch. 43, 11. 2–2ob. For evidence that Dostoevskii had read the socialists, se Semenov T'ian-Shanskii, *Memuary*, i, 202.

29 Bel'chikov, p. 106; M. G. Zeldovich, 'K kharakteristike literaturno-esteticheskikh vzgliadov M. V. Petrashevskogo', *Uchenye zapiski Kharkovskogo universiteta*, Kharkov 1956, no. 70, pp. 255–9. However, many other Soviet scholars say that Dostoevskii's position had 'nothing in common with the theory of "art for art's sake"', e.g. S. S. Derkach, in *Vestnik LGU*, 1957, no. 14, series 3, p. 88.

30 DP, iii, 441–2; ii, 185–6, 366; see Maikov, i, 230–2; ii, 299; Belinskii, viii, 167–87; x, 307, 109, 114; vi, 278–9.

31 Bel'chikov, pp. 107–8.

32 *Russkii invalid*, 1844, 24 December; See V. Zotov in *Istoricheskii vestnik*, 1888, no. 32, p. 445; on *Encyclopedie nouvelle*, *Pis'ma I. M. Debu*, ed. khr. 44, 1. 2ob.

33 A. V. Starchevskii, 'Vospominaniia starogo literatora', *Istoricheskii vestnik*, 1890, no. 9, p. 522; V. N. Maikov, review of 'Entsiklopedicheskii slovar' K. Kraia', *Sovremennik*, 1847, no. 4, iii, 1–2.

34 TsGVIA, delo 55, ch. 66, 1. 13; ch. 47, 11. 15–15ob; Belinskii, x, 60–2; see IRLI, Razriad 1, opis' 7, no. 118, 1. 78.

35 TsGVIA, delo 55, ch. 4, 1. 15.

36 Engel'son, *Petrashevtsy*, pp. 419–2.

37 TsGVIA, delo 55, ch. 2, 11. 148ob–149.

38 FOP, p. 354 (see N. V. Gogol, *Mertvye dushi*, ch. x); KS, i, 85; TsGAOR, fond lll otdelenie, Sekretnyi arkhiv, 1849, no. 99B.I., 11. 255ob–257;

I.P. Liprandi, 'Zapiska o dele petrashevtsev', *Poliarnaia zvezda*, 1872, no. 2, p. 255.

39 FOP, pp. 357–8.

40 See A.I. Malein and P.N. Berkov, 'Materialy dlia istorii Karmannogo slovaria inostrannykh slov', *Trudy Instituta knig, dokumenty i pis'ma*, iii, Leningrad 1934, pp. 54–5. Petrashevskii dedicated the book to the Grand Duke Mikhail, the Tsar's notoriously reactionary brother.

41 *Russkaia starina*, 1903, no. 8, p. 422; TsGAOR, 111 otdelenie, 1 eksp. 1849, no. 400, 11. 1–70. See DP, iii, 378; TsGVIA, delo 55, ch. 2, 11. 148ob–149; Moskovskii Otdel AN SSR, fond 489, no. 120; V.I. Semevskii, *M.V. Butashevich–Petrashevskii i petrashevtsy*, pp. 79–80.

42 V.V. Flerovskii, *Tri politicheskie sistemy*, St. Petersburg 1897, p. 10; TsGAOR, 111 otdelenie, 1 eksp, 1848, no. 400, 11. 1–70. Liprandi to Dubel't, 8 January 1856; F.M. Klacel, *Slovnik po ctenare novin, v nemz se vysvetluji slova ciziho puvodu*, Brno 1849.

43 DP, iii, 120. Speshnev and Danilevskii had a similar plan for popular encyclopedias (DP, iii, 288).

44 Balasoglo, *Ob izlozhenii nauk*, 11. 8, 14, 18, 24, 78, 99, 214, 174, 84–7ob.

45 *Stikhotvoreniia Veronova*, St.P. 1838. Some are in V.V. Zhdanov ed., *Poety–petrashevtsy*, Biblioteka poeta, malaia seriia, Leningrad 1950.

46 DP, ii, 76; see *Pamiatnik iskustv*, St. Petersburg 1840, no. 4; Belinskii, iv, 577–8.

47 DP, ii, 16–48, 188, 279 (see i, 555).

48 TsGIAL, fond 647, A.P. Balasoglo, opis 1, ed. khr. 9; TsGVIA, delo 55, ch. 59, 1. 5; ch. 103, 1. 5; DP, ii, 134.

49 TsGIAL, fond 647, A.P. Balasoglo, opis' 1, ed. khr. 6; Balasoglo, *Ob izlozhenii nauk*, 11. 174, 210–14; DP, ii, 91, 121.

50 A. Belosokolov (A.P. Balasoglo), *Bukva E. Rukovodstvo k upotrebleniiu etoi bukvi v pis'me*, St. Petersburg 1847, p. 10.

51 KS, 72; TsGVIA, delo 55, ch. 55, 1. 141; ch. 2, 1. 46ob; ch. 3, 1. 142ob; DP, i, 556; iii, 25, 441–2.

52 DP, i, 548; Makashin, *Saltykov–Shchedrin*, pp. 165–6.

53 TsGIAL, fond 777, Sanktpeterburgskii tsenzurnyi komitet, opis 1, no. 208520, 11. 1–1ob.

54 V.N. Maikov, 'Ot redaktsii Finskogo vestnika', *Finskii vestnik*, 1845, no. 1, Prilozhenie, pp. 1–8.

55 See V.M. Morozov, 'K voprosu ob ideino-obshchestvennoi pozitsii zhurnala ''Finskii vestnik''', *Uchenye zapiski Karelo-Finskogo universiteta*, 1955, no. 5, series 1.

56 BL, OIDP, Po-11 //9//40, Letter of V.V. Grigor'ev, 2 January 1848, 1. 2ob.

57 TsGVIA, delo 55, ch. 91, 11. 7–8; ch. 119, 1. 96; DP, iii, 261; V.V. Grigor'ev, *Zhizn' i trudy P.S. Savel'eva*, St. Petersburg 1861, pp. 85–6.

58 Belinskii, x, 33; DP, iii, 441; Saltykov, i, 240; T. I. Usakina, 'O literaturno-kriticheskoi deiatel'nosti molodogo Saltykova', p. 409.
59 Maikov, ii, 102–3.
60 See FOP, 271; DP, iii, 166 (Béranger); Pleshcheev's poem *Duma*, A. N. Pleshcheev, *Stikhotvoreniia*, Moscow 1975 ed., p. 27 (Lermontov).
61 Maikov, ii, 103–5.
62 Pleshcheev's poem *Son* begins by quoting Lamennais, *Paroles d'un croyant*, see Pleshcheev, *Stikhotvoreniia*, p. 46; F. R. de Lamennais, *Paroles d'un croyant*, p. 38.
63 Pleshcheev, *Stikhotvoreniia*, p. 56.
64 Ibid., pp. 56–7, 68, 46–7, 71, 29–30.
65 TsGAOR, fond 109, 111 otdelenie, 1 eksp. 1855, no. 269, no. 8.
66 A. P. Miliukov, *Ocherk istorii russkoi poezii*, 2nd ed., St. Petersburg 1858, p. 187n; see S. F. Durov in *Poetry-petrashevtsy*, p. 152; V. Considerant and Barbier in *Destinée sociale*, pp. 86, 105–6.
67 *Poetry-petrashevtsy*, pp. 144, 155, 74.
68 Ibid., pp. 121–9, 97–8, 249–50. On Balasoglo's poetry see DP, iii, 87–9, 141; on Ap. Maikov's involvement with the Petrashevtsy, TsGVIA, delo 55, ch. 92.
69 Belinskii, v, 602–03.
70 S. F. Durov, 'Khalatnik', pp. 189–235; 'Peterburgskii Van'ka', *Panteon*, 1848, no. 8–9, pp. 27–36; 'Luka Lukich', *Finskii vestnik*, 1845, no. 4, pp. 1–10; 'Tet'inka', *Panteon*, 1848, no. 2, pp. 148–72.
71 DP, iii, 439; GPB, Arkhiv Poniatovskogo, otchet za 1907, p. 158, (letter of Dershau's, 18/30 July 1848); Delo 55, ch. 91, 11. 7–9.
72 V. V. Tolbin, 'Loskutnitsy', *Finskii vestnik*, 1847, no. 19, iii, 1–5; 'Iaroslavtsy', ibid., 1847, no. 16, iii, 3–9; 'Markery i billiardnye igroki', ibid., 1847, no. 21, iii, 5–34; 'Borzopistsy', ibid., (1847), no. 22, iii, 2–12; 'Ulichnye muzykanty', *Panteon*, 1848, no. 7, pp. 2–11. His preference of the immoral poor to the rich is expressed with especial clarity in 'Markery i billiardnye igroki', pp. 33–4.
73 V. V. Tolbin, 'Skotoliuby', *Finskii vestnik*, 1847, no. 24, iii, 1–7; 'Mon Chers', ibid., 1847, no. 20, iii, 1–15; 'Vengertsy', (1846), no. 12, iii, 1–24.
74 A. I. Pal'm, 'Zhak Bichovkin', *Otechestvennye zapiski*, 1849, no. 3–4, i, 212–46; no. 5–6, i, 1–79; 'Shalost', *Finskii vestnik*, 1846, no. 9, i, 23–84; Pleshcheev, *Povesti i rasskazy*, pp. 105–80; Herzen, ix, 9–209.
75 Saltykov, i, 285–6, 182, 9.
76 Pleshcheev, *Povesti i rasskazy*, pp. 183–276; Dostoevskii, ii, 115–16.
77 Maikov, i, 207.
78 Maikov, ii, 258; i, 206–10; see also FOP, pp. 315, 20; A. Grigor'ev, review of, 'Brynskii les', *Finskii vestnik*, 1846, no. 9, v, 37.
79 Belinskii, x, 40–2; *Izbrannye pis'ma*, ii, 388.
80 Saltykov, i, 205; see Pleshcheev, *Povesti i rasskazy*, p. 107.

81 V. V. Tolbin, 'Chernyi den', *Finskii vestnik*, 1847, no. 23, ii, 117–36; Dostoevskii, i, 168.

82 V. V. Tolbin, 'Lubin'ka', *Severnoe obozrenie*, 1849, no. 1, ii, 350–64; 'Nochnye babochki', *Illiustratsiia*, 1847, no. 35, 20 September, pp. 165–6; no. 36, 27 September, pp. –181–83.

83 Saltykov, i, 80–2.

84 S. F. Durov, 'Chuzhoe ditia', *Finskii vestnik*, 1846, no. 10, ii, 13–38.

85 V. Drashusov, 'Dva slova o George Sand', *Moskovskoi gorodskoi listok*, 1847, no. 12, p. 45. All the stories listed were published in *Sovremennik*. 'Elevated moral purity' is Dostoevskii's phrase (*Diary of a Writer*, p. 347).

86 DP, iii, 45–8, 356. Most of the Petrashevtsy rejected Fourier's amorous theories, see DP, i, 82, 399; ii, 210, 318; TsGVIA, delo 55, ch. 37, 1. 8ob.

87 DP, iii, 19.

88 S. F. Durov, 'Roman v zapiskakh', *Illiustratsiia*, 1847, no. 41, pp. 260–7; 'Mat i doch', ibid., 1847, no. 87, pp. 33–8; 'Baryshny', ibid., 1847, no. 85, pp. 3–6; 'Prizrak', *Severnoe obozrenie*, 1848, no. 2, i, 25–38; 'Grustnaia povest' c veselym kontsom', *Biblioteka dlia chteniia*, 1848, no. 87, pp. 59–98.

89 *Poetry-petrashevtsy*, p. 137; see Dostoevskii, i, 221–22.

90 Tolbin, 'Nochnye babochki'; see DP, iii, 45–6, 112; Miliutin, 'Proletariat i pauperizm', iv, 25–6; Dostoevskii in *Netochka Nezvanova*, and *A Little Hero*. The fallen woman was a favourite theme in Natural School literature.

91 TsGVIA, delo 55, ch. 47, 1. 4ob; ch. 2, 1. 11ob; DP, iii, 203–4 (Durov); ii, 55, 71–3, 85, 119, 202; iii, 323.

92 Saltykov, i, 106, 227–30; DP, iii, 107.

93 TsGVIA, delo 55, ch. 3, 1. 146; DP, iii, 181; see DP, iii, 412–13.

94 TsGVIA, delo 55, ch. 2, 11. 46, 206ob–207; ch. 3, 1. 144ob. On her poetry, see Iulia Zhadovskaia, *Polnoe sobranie stikhotvorenii*, St. Petersburg 1885–6; Belinskii, x, 34–5; *Finskii vestnik*, 1846, no. 11, v, 23–5; Maikov, ii, 100–1.

VIII — REVOLUTIONARY CONSPIRACIES

1 The library contained almost all the classic historians of the first French Revolution — the conservative version by Thiers (1823–7), the liberal version by Michelet (1847) and the more revolutionary versions (banned in Russia) — Lamartine's strongly republican *Histoire des Girondins*, (1847), Esquiros's pro-Robespierrian *Histoire des Montagnards* (1847) and the first two volumes of Louis Blanc's socialist *Histoire de la Révolution francaise*, (1847).

2 FOP, p. 198; TsGVIA, delo 55, ch. 2, 11. 118ob–119.

3 KS, 141; FOP, pp. 152–3, 164; TsGVIA, delo 55, ch. 50, 11. 28–28ob, 32–3; see *Finskii vestnik*, 1847, no. 17, iv, 1–28 (Louis Blanc) and Belinskii, xii, 70–1.

4 A. Weill, 'La guerre des paysans', *La Phalange*, 1845, no. 1, pp. 105, 110, 303; no. 2; no. 3; 1846, p. 489; TsGVIA, delo 55, ch. 25, 'Krest'ianskaia voina iii. Pervoe vosstanie krest'ian gertsoga Ulrika', 11. 10–15; FOP, p. 228.

5 TsGAOR, fond 109, 111 otdelenie, 1 eksp. 1855, no. 269, ch. 9, 11. 160–160ob; DP, i, 448; iii, 141, 394–5; TsGVIA, delo 55, ch. 3, 1. 93ob.

6 *Finskii vestnik*, 1846, no. 12, v, 43–4; Saltykov, i, 230, 241–2; Perepiska Ia. K. Grota s P. A. Pletnevym, St. Petersburg 1896, iii, 209.

7 I. Golovine, *L'Europe revolutionnaire*, Paris 1849, p. i.

8 Saltykov, xiv, 113; M. K. Korbut, 'Kazan'skii gosudartvennyi universitet za 125 let', *Uchenye zapiski Kazan'skogo gos. universiteta*, Kazan 1930, vol. 5, p. 783; Miliukov, *Literaturnye vstrechi*, pp. 169–71.

9 *Vestnik Moskovskoi gorodskoi politsii*, 1848, no. 549; *Petrashevtsy*, iii, 49; M. A. Korf, 'Zapiski', *Russkaia starina*, 1900, March, pp. 559–65. Engel'son, *Petrashevtsy*, pp. 494–5; see A. Nifontov, *1848 god v Rossii*, Moscow-Leningrad 1931, pp. 105–9; *Sovremennik*, 1849, no. 1.

10 DP, ii, 163; *Petrashevtsy*, iii, 190 (at Petrashevskii's); DP, iii, 355, 357; TsGVIA, delo 55, ch. 2, 1. 123 (Shaposhnikov's); DP, ii, 51 (8 July 1848); i, 241 (Kuz'min).

11 TsGAOR, fond 109, 111 otdelenie, 1 eksp. 1849, opis' 12, no. 195, 11. 7–7ob; TsGVIA, delo 55, ch. 2, 1. 180ob; TsGAOR, no. 214, ch. 141, 1. 288.

12 *Petrashevtsy v vospominaniiakh sovremennikov*, Moscow–Leningrad 1926, p. 44; TsGVIA, delo 55, ch. 119; 1. 79; Chernyshevskii, i, 107–11 (6–8 September 1848).

13 F. Pyat, *La Presse*, 1848, 2 and 3 November; DP, iii, 276; i, 532.

14 Engel'son, *Petrashevtsy*, p. 495; DP, i, 217–18.

15 Herzen, x, 45; Pal'm, *Aleksei Slobodin*, p. 338; DP, iii, 430.

16 Speshnev, *Pis'ma k materi*, 9 August 1848; DP, ii, 209; see Chernyshevskii, i, 96, 115 (24 August and 12 December 1848).

17 Engel'son, *Petrashevtsy*, p. 495; DP, i, 95; Herzen, vi, 118–19; *Pis'ma V. A. Engel'sona*, no. 6 (30 November 1852).

18 *Petrashevtsy*, iii, 195; TsGVIA, delo 55, ch. 120, 1. 184ob; Chernyshevskii, i, 66, 121–2 (2 August, 18 September 1848); 357 (20 January 1850); see Ianovskii, 'Vospominaniia o Dostoevskom', p. 174.

19 See DP, ii, 321; iii, 63, 72–3, 177.

20 Bel'chikov, pp. 145–6.

21 DP, i, 33; ii, 329; iii, 142.

22 DP, ii, 88–90; Pleshcheev, *Stikhotvoreniia*, p. 71; see DP, iii, 108.

23 DP, i, 284–9.

24 TsGAOR, fond 109, 111 otdelenie, 1 eksp. 1849, delo 25.

25 A. S. Nifontov, *Rossiia v 1848g.*, Moscow 1949, p. 227; DP, iii, 263.

26 'Obozrenie khoda i deistvii kholernoi epidemii v Rossii v techenii 1848 goda', *Zhurnal Ministerstva vnutrennykh del*, 1849, no. 9, pp. 316–17; DP, ii, 51–2; A. V. Nikitenko, *Zapiski i dnevnik*, i, 312.

27 'Statiskiki pozharov v Rossii v 1848 god', *Zhurnal Ministerstva vnutrennykh del*, 1849, no. 7, pp. 7–44; DP, i, 465; iii, 347.

28 DP, i, 280.

29 See TsGAOR, fond 109, 111 otdelenie, 1 eksp. 1848, delo 51, ch. 3, 4, 5.

30 DP, iii, 258; i, 42, 202; TsGVIA, delo 55, ch. 2, 11. 130ob, 134; see DP, ii, 394.

31 DP, iii 431, 103; ii, 97; Chernyshevskii, i, 372–3 (15 May 1850); Saltykov, i, 253.

32 Chernyshevskii, i, 196 (11 December 1848); see TsGVIA, delo 55, ch. 2, 1. 131ob.

33 P. M. Kovalevskii, 'Itogi zhizni', *Vestnik Evropy*, 1883, no. 2, p. 567.

34 TsGVIA, delo 55, ch. 2, 11. 135, 180; DP, iii, 159, 431, 287; Chernyshevskii, i, 291.

35 DP, i, 42–3; iii, 386; TsGVIA, delo 55, ch. 2, 11. 146ob, 205ob, 206.

36 DP, iii, 409; TsGVIA, delo 55, ch. 3, 1. 111; ch. 2, 1. 147ob.

37 V. V. Tolbin, 'Zavoevanie Anglii normanami', *Finskii vestnik*, 1846, no. 12, ii, 1–71 (tr. from J. N. A. Thierry, *Histoire de la conquête de l'Angleterre par les Normands*, Paris 1825); FOP, pp. 291, 312–15; DP, i, 546; iii, 380, 386.

38 See V. A. D'iakov, 'Pol'skie konspiratory 1830–40kh godov v ikh sviazakh s Frantsii', sb. *Slaviane i Zapad*, Moscow 1975, pp. 234–46; 'Warszawska organizacja konspiracyjna 1848 roku', *Kwartalnik Historyczy*, 1976, no. 2; *Osvoboditel'noe dvizhenie v Rossii 1825–1861gg.*, Moscow 1979, p. 162.

39 DP, ii, 293, 296 (*Do Przyjacielow Moskali* in Polish); see also DP, ii, 264–7 i, 513; iii, 431, 159.

40 B. Ratch, *La question polonaise dans la Russie occidentale*, (Paris 1868), p. 103; *Vestnik zapadnoi rossii*, Vilnius 1864, vol. 11, no. 4; FOP, p. 492.

41 Makashin, *Saltykov–Shchedrin*, pp. 152, 450–53; see DP, iii, 399.

42 DP, i, 309–12; iii, 407; P. A. Zaionchkovskii, *Kirillo-mefiodicheskoe obshchestvo, Izbrannye obshchestvenno-politicheskie i filosofskie proizvedeniia ukrainskikh revoliutsionnykh demokratov XIXv.*, Moscow 1955, p. 86. According to Mombelli, 'With a rising in the Ukraine, the Don, long discontented, would be aroused. The Poles would seize the opportunity. Therefore the whole south and west of Russia would take up arms'.

43 DP, iii, 409.

44 DP, iii, 380, 383–5, 429; TsGVIA, delo 55, ch. 47, 1. 6ob; ch. 3, 1. 162ob.

45 DP, i, 462, 457–9, 547.

46 DP, ii, 104–5.

47 On this, see G. Sand, *Le Compagnon du Tour de France*, Paris 1885, 1st ed. 1840, pp. 5, 7.

48 *Petrashevtsy*, iii, 65–6; TsGAOR, no. 214, ch. 4, 1. 114. Speshnev was probably one of the Russians Engels saw at the communist clubs in Paris, see D. Riazanov, 'Karl Marx i Friedrich Engels v ikh perepiske, 1844–1882', *Sovremennyi mir*, St. Petersburg 1914, no. 5, p. 28.

49 Petrashevtsy, iii, 52. The candidate for affiliation to Blanqui's *Société des familles* was asked, 'When the signal for combat is given, will you be prepared to run, armed to the teeth, to fight for the cause of humanity? Have you weapons? ammunition?' (*Le Constitutionnel*, 1839, 14 May, quoted in P. Zaccone, *Histoire des sociétés secrètes, politiques et religieuses*, Paris 1847—9, iv, 241.

50 Speshnev, *Pis'ma k materi*, (Dresden 29/31, December 1845); *Petrashevtsy*, iii, 300.

51 Engel'son,*Petrashevtsy*, pp. 490—1. The library contained A. Blanc's *Histoire des conspirations et des exécutions politiques*, 1846 and P. Zaccone, op. cit., several accounts of Freemasonry, as well as Barruel's and Buonarotti's works.

52 DP, i, 538—9, 543, 546, 56—7; iii, 386—7, 399—400; TsGVIA, delo 55, ch. 55, 1. 43.

53 TsGVIA, delo 55, ch. 3, 11. 36ob—37, 46ob; ch. 2, 11. 130—1, 134—35ob.

54 TsGVIA, delo 55, ch. 3, 11. 36ob—37, 41; ch. 2, 11. 176, 123, 190ob; DP, iii, 354—5, 358, 366—7.

55 TsGVIA, delo 55, ch. 2, 1. 204; Engel'son, *Petrashevtsy*, p. 498.

56 TsGVIA, delo 55, ch. 2, 11. 36ob—38, 136ob; DP, iii, 23, 358 (Shaposhnikov); FOP, pp. 315—28; TsGVIA, delo 55, ch. 2, 11. 185—6 (oratory in general).

57 TsGVIA, delo 55, ch. 2, 11. 131, 147ob—148.

58 TsGVIA, delo 55, ch. 2, 11. 147ob, 149ob—151, 164ob, 178, 180; TsGAOR, no. 214, ch. 3, 1. 144ob; DP, iii, 349—50, 278—9.

59 DP, i, 96, 325, 351, 363, 446; *Petrashevtsy*, iii, 60.

60 DP, iii, 386; i, 462, 98—9. In fact, Chernosvitov had only seen Murav'ev once, for a few minutes (DP, i, 463).

61 DP, i, 105—6.

62 DP, i, 449; TsGVIA, delo 55, ch. 55, 1. 48.

63 DP, i, 446—7, 469—79, 100.

64 DP, i, 102, 488.

65 DP, i, 447—8, 467—8, 488—9, 450—5, 470, 96, 102.

66 Chernosvitov seems not to have been a revolutionary and to have treated these conversations as a game, see G. Chulkov, in *Katorga i ssylka*, 1930, no. 2.

67 DP, iii, 55, 199, 321, 324.

68 DP, i, 324—5, 447; iii, 33—4.

69 DP, i, 326; ii, 195—6, 183, 117, 186—7; iii, 29, 55, 272; V. I. Semevskii, *M. V. Butashevich-Petrashevskii i petrashevtsy*, p. 125; L'vov, *Zapiska*, p. 172.

70 DP, i, 326, 467; ii, 412; iii, 29.

71 DP, i, 524—40.

72 TsGVIA, delo 55, ch. 3, 11. 143ob—144; TsGAOR, Sekretnyi Arkhiv, 111 otdelenie, 1849, fond 109, opis 1, ed. khr. 67, 1. 20ob; DP, ii, 402, 415, 440.

73 DP, i, 112—13, 347, 349—51; see Bazot's *Manuel de Franc-Maçon*, 2nd ed., Paris 1812, in Petrashevskii's library.

74 DP, i, 421; L'vov, *Zapiska*, pp. 175–6; E. Sue, *Le Juif errant*, Paris 1844–5, ii, 266–8.
75 DP, i, 107, 347, 351, 359; *Petrashevtsy*, iii, 61; L'vov, *Zapiska*, pp. 175–6.
76 DP, i, 217, 364; *Petrashevtsy*, iii, 62.
77 DP, i, 365, 351–2, 358, 414, 422; iii, 81–2; l'Abbé Barruel, *Mémoires pour servir à l'histoire du Jacobinisme*, London 1797, i, pp. vii, xxi; iii, pp. 28–9. On the third proposal, see Barruel, iii, 116; on the fourth, P. Zaccone, *Histoire des sociétés secrètes*, iv, 244.
78 DP, i, 115, 108, 352–3, 360, 414, 418; *Petrashevtsy*, iii, 62; L'vov, *Zapiska*, pp. 175–6.
79 *Petrashevtsy*, iii, 63; DP, i, 366. Speshnev's opportunist theory is set out more fully in the discussion of the early Christians, Cabet and Dézamy in his *Philosophical Letters* (FOP, pp. 489–90).
80 DP, i, 107, 110, 351, 353–4, 422, 426; *Petrashevtsy*, iii, 63; L'vov, *Zapiska*, pp. 175–6.
81 DP, iii, 419; *Petrashevtsy*, iii, 191; TsGVIA, delo 55, ch. 43, 1. 4; ch. 3, 1. 121.
82 On this speech, see: DP, iii, 424–6, 220–1, 30, 197; ii, 203, 235, 220; i, 400, 409; TsGVIA, delo 55, ch. 47, 11. 7–7ob, 54; ch. 3, 11. 178, 426; ch. 35, 1. 1ob; ch. 55, 11. 3–4ob; L'vov, *Zapiska*, p. 172; P. A. Kuz'min, 'Zapiski', *Russkaia starina*, 1895, no. 2, p. 159; *Petrashevtsy*, iii, 58.
83 TsGVIA, delo 55, ch. 47, 1. 7; ch. 35, 1. 1ob; ch. 3, 11. 161, 159; DP, i, 229; iii, 426–7, 221; L'vov, *Zapiska*, pp. 173–4.
84 TsGVIA, delo 55, ch. 47, 1. 54; L'vov, *Zapiska*, p. 174.
85 DP, i, 299, 344; iii, 427, 221–2; *Petrashevtsy*, iii, 192–3; TsGVIA, delo 55, ch. 35, 1. 1ob; ch. 3, 1. 11; A. I. Pal'm, *Aleksei Slobodin*, p. 354; On Dostoevskii, see Semenov T'ian-Shanskii, *Memuary*, i, 204.
86 DP, i, 409, iii, 32, 272, 433–6.
87 DP, i, 388–9; iii, 60, 204, 272–6, 309. Herzen wrote *Moscow and Petersburg* in 1841, while in exile in Novogorod. His denial of any historical role to either gentry Moscow or bureaucratic St. Petersburg was so extreme that Belinskii felt obliged to protest, in *Petersburg and Moscow* (1844). It was a work of which, as Herzen said, 'the radical passages constitute the whole worth' and was widely circulated in manuscript form. (Herzen, ii, 33–42; Belinskii, viii, 385–413).
88 *Petrashevtsy*, iii, 53–7, 60; DP, ii, 324, 332; Semenov T'ian-Shanskii, *Memuary*, i, 198. For other discussion of a press among the Petrashevtsy, see TsGVIA, delo 55, ch. 119, 1. 197ob; Chernyshevskii, i, 372 (15 May 1850).
89 *Petrashevtsy*, iii, 64, 59; DP, iii, 115, 248, 272–8; L'vov, *Zapiska*, p. 174.
90 DP, i, 184–5, 372, 354–5, 432; iii, 200–1, 272, 326; TsGVIA, delo 55, ch. 59, 11. 9–11; ch. 93, 1. 6; ch. 95, 11. 8–9; Miliukov, *Literaturnye vstrechi* pp. 175–6.
91 O. F. Miller, 'Materialv', p. 85; G. Chul'kov, 'Dostoevskii i utopicheskii sotsializm', *Katorga i ssylka*, 1929, no. 3, p. 144; *Petrashevtsy*, iii, 59.

92 DP, ii, 273–74, 248; i, 254–55, 372, 376, 433–35.
93 TsGVIA, delo 55, ch. 93, 1. 6; DP, iii, 246.
94 *Petrashevtsy*, iii, 193–94; DP, iii, 202, 273, 249, 246; i, 424–5; TsGVIA, delo 55, ch. 101, 11. 15–17; ch. 120, 1. 132; ch. 59, 1. 11.
95 Bel'chikov, p. 141.
96 DP, i, 425–6; TsGVIA, delo 55, ch. 120, 11. 11–12.
97 DP, iii, 228, 249, 272–4; *Petrashevtsy*, iii, 194; TsGVIA, delo 55, ch. 120, 1. 132; ch. 101, 1. 26; J. Frank, *Dostoevsky, The Seeds of Revolt*, p. 278.
98 DP, i, 425; iii, 230; TsGVIA, delo 55, ch. 120, 1. 12.
99 DP, i, 426; iii, 201, 274.
100 TsGVIA, delo 55, ch. 120, 1. 145ob; DP, iii, 349, 369; *Petrashevtsy*, iii, 194–5; O. F. Miller, 'Materialy', p. 90.
101 A. S. Dolinin, *Dostoevskii. Stat'i i materialy*, i, 198 (letter of A. N. Maikov to P. S. Viskovatov, 1885); 'Rasskaz A. N. Maikova o F. M. Dostoevskom i petrashevtsakh', *Istoricheskii vestnik*, 1956, no. 3, pp. 224–5.
102 Ibid. A seal was put on the door and that was all. By removing the hinges, Mordvinov's family managed to get rid of the press without breaking the seal (*Petrashevtsy*, iii, 194–5; TsGVIA, delo 55, ch. 120, 1. 145ob).
103 Ianovskii, 'Vospominaniia o Dostoevskom', p. 174.
104 TsGVIA, delo 55, ch. 59, 1. 11ob; DP, iii, 273–4, 291, 294–5 (letters of 14 and 26 March), 2–8; E. M. Feoktistov, *Vospominaniia. Za kulisam politiki i literatury*, Leningrad 1929, p. 164; see K. N. Bestuzhev-Riumin, *Vospominaniia*, St. Petersburg 1900, p. 25.
105 Belinskii, x, 212–20; Herzen, ii, 33–42; vi, 19–39; I. S. Turgenev, *Polnoe sobranie sochinenii i pisem*, Moscow–Leningrad, 1960–8, ii, 122–84; DP, ii, 340–50, 384–94, 394–8.
106 Miliukov, *Literaturnye vstrechi*, pp. 182–3; TsGVIA, delo 55, ch. 101, 11. 7–10, 202, 126; ch. 119, 1. 129; DP, i, 425; iii, 201, 248, 275; E. M. Feoktistov, *Vospominaniia*, p. 164.
107 TsGAOR, fond 109, 111 otdelenie, 1 eksp. 1855, no. 269, no. 12, 11. 178–207 (quoted here, 11. 179–179ob, 189–90, 178–178ob; see Lamennais, *Paroles d'un croyant*, pp. 45–6, 41–3). The translation escaped notice in 1849 because Mordinov, though a member of Speshnev's conspiracy, was little implicated at the trial and soon released. It was seized when he was rearrested for conducting revolutionary propaganda in Tambov in 1855, but the secret police were unable to make head or tail of it. I. V. Porokh, author of *Istoriia v cheloveke. N. A. Mordvinov – deiatel' osvoboditel'nogo dvizheniia v Rossii 40–80gg. XIXv*, Saratov 1971, noticed it, but paid little attention to it. The only mention of it since then is in F. G. Nikitina, 'Petrashevtsy i Lamennais', *Dostoevskii. Materialy i issledovaniia*, Leningrad 1978, no. 3, pp. 256–7.
108 DP, iii, 233–7, 200, 226, 228, 245–6, 275–7; TsGVIA, delo 55, ch. 3, 1. 158ob; ch. 107, 1. 11; ch. 3, 1. 138.

109 FOP, pp. 637–42.
110 Dostoevskii, *Diary of a Writer*, pp. 311, 147; *Dostoevskki v izobrazhenii ego docheri L. Dostoevskoi*, Moscow–Petrograd 1922, p. 235; O. F. Miller, 'Materialy', p. 83.

IX — CONCLUSION

1 M. K. Lemke, *Nikolaevskie zhandarmy i literatura 1825–1855 godov*, 2nd ed., St. Petersburg 1909, p. 190.
2 Chernyshevskii, i, 274.
3 Ibid., ix, 334.
4 Ibid., ix, 75–80.
5 Ibid., i, 196; xi, 277–84; ix, 357–62; vii, 58–63. (The *obshchina* and the phalanstery are compared by M. N. Iurin in 'Spor ob obshchinnom vladenii zemli', *Athenei*, 1858, November–December).
6 Ibid., ii, 86.
7 Akhsharumov, *Iz moikh vospominanii*, p. 16.
8 N. P. Ogarev, 'Zapiska o tainom obshchestve', *Literaturnoe nasledstvo, Gertsen I*, M. 1941, no. 39–40, pp. 323–7.
9 DP, iii, 103.
10 See Akhsharumov, *Iz moikh vospominanii*, pp. 102–11 (this is the fullest account, but he gets some of the facts wrong); L'vov *Zapiska*, pp. 187–8; MA. Korf, 'Zapiski', *Russkaia starina*, 1900, no. 5, May, pp. 279–80; no. 214, ch. 142, 11. 368–9; Dostoevskii, viii, 56.
11 Gosudarstvennyi istoricheskii muzei, otdel pisem i istochnikov, fond 250, ed. khr. 1, 1. 8, Pis'mo Petrashevskogo k D. I. Zavalishinu, 1860. see FOP, pp. 465–71.
12 On the Petrashevtsy in Siberia, see V. I. Semevskii, 'M. V. Butashevich– Petrashevskii v Sibirii', *Golos minuvshego*, 1915, nos. 1, 3, 5.
13 TsGVIA, delo 55, ch. 145, 11. 23–28ob; M. I. Mikhailov, 'Zapiski', *Russkoe bogatstvo*, 1906, September, p. 5.
14 V. P. Demor, *M. V. Butashevich-Petrashevskii*, Petrograd 1920, pp. 20–32.
15 Dostoevskii later remarked that, in his opinion, 'Petrashevets' was an incorrect name, 'since a much larger number, compared with those who stood on the scaffold – who thought just as we Petrashevtsy did, have been left intact and undisturbed', *Diary of a Writer*, p. 147.
16 In his last work, he wrote of utopias, 'I believed and I believe now in their life giving force'. See Saltykov, xvii, 72; xvi, 400–1; 39–40.
17 On Speshnev's acquaintance with Chernyshevskii, see N. M. Chernyshevskaia, *Letopis' zhizni i deiatel'nosti N. G. Chernyshevskogo*, Moscow 1953, p. 82.

18 V.I. Semevskii, 'Durov', *Entsiklopedicheskii slovar Granat*, vol.19, pp. 169–70.

19 TsGAOR, fond 109, 111 otdelenie, 1 eksp. 1855, no.269; see I.V. Porokh, *Istoriia v cheloveke.*

20 T. Emmons, *The Russian Landed Gentry and the Peasant Emancipation of 1861*, Cambridge 1968, p.343; See TsGAOR, no.214, ch.144, 11. 122, 125–6.

21 TsGAOR, no.214, ch.30, O pomeshchike N.A. Speshneve, 1. 150, June 1862.

22 TsGIAL, Fond 1282, Kantselariia Ministerstva vnutrennykh del, no.226, 1. 25ob. In Kazan in 1864 Golovinskii had founded a society of fifty people who sat round a table covered with a red cloth and discussed the proposed legal reforms.

23 Engelson, *Chto takoe gosudarstvo?; Pis'ma V.A. Engel'sona*, pp.43, 33–6 (10 July 1854, 8 December 1852).

24 Herzen, x, 343–6; the material is published in Herzen, ed. Lemke, vi, 487–502.

25 I.V. Porokh, *Istoriia v cheloveke*, pp.48–9, 58–65.

26 N.Ia. Danilevskii, *Rossiia i Evropa*, 4th ed., St. Petersburg 1889, pp.538–9; see R.E. McMaster, *Danilevskii. A Russian Totalitarian Philosopher*, Cam. Mass. 1967, p.286.

27 E.g. Shigalev's socialist solution in *The Devils*; the Grand Inquisitor in *The Brothers Karamazov*, (Dostoevskii, x, 312; xiv, 235–7).

28 Dostoevskii, xiv, 214; vi, 54.

29 Some of the details of Stavrogin's life are Bakunin's, but Stavrogin's character is much closer to that of Speshnev, with whom Dostoevskii was closely involved at what turned out to be a catastrophic point in his career; see L. Grossman, 'Speshnev i Stavrogin', *Spor o Bakunine i Dostoevskom*, Leningrad 1976, pp.162–4.

30 See L. Grossman, *Dostoevsky, A Biography*, tr. M. Mackler, London 1974, pp.548–9, 586–7.

31 Dostoevskii, *Pis'ma*, iv, 17, 34; L. Grossman, op.cit., p.607.

32 Dostoevskii, *Diary of a Writer*, p.1029.

33 A.G. Dostoevskaia, quoted in O.F. Miller, 'Materialy', p.80.

SELECTED BIBLIOGRAPHY

This is a bibliography of Russian sources only. It includes the most important works by and about the Petrashevtsy, but is not an exhaustive compilation of materials on the subject. Extensive use has also been made of French sources in the research for this book, in particular the works of the French utopian socialists, above all the disciples of Charles Fourier.

ARCHIVAL SOURCES

Tsentral'nyi Gosudarstvennyi Voenno-Istoricheskii Arkhiv S.S.S.R., g. Moskva, (TsGVIA).
Fond 9, Glavnoe voenno-sudnoe upravlenie, opis' 28, 1849, No. 55, O zloumyshlennikakh Butasheviche-Petrashevskom, Speshneve i drugikh. (This is the major single source on the Petrashevtsy and has 136 parts, 25 of which have been published, some of these not fully).
Tsentral'nyi Gosudarstvennyi Arkhiv Oktiabr'skoi Revoliutsii, g. Moskva, (TsGAOR).
Fond 109, III otdelenie, I ekspeditsiia.
opis' 10
1844, No. 139, O nadzore za Petrashevskogo.
1846, No. 52, O besporiadkakh v Kazan'skom universitete.
—, No. 232, I. A. Romashkov, ch. I.
opis' 11
1847, No. 193, O propovediakh Nil'sena.
—, No. 194, O knigakh vozmutitel'nogo soderzhaniia v Odesse.
—, No. 285, O zapreshchennykh knigakh zakazannykh iz Leipziga.
—, No. 201, Russkoe geograficheskoe obshchestvo.
opis' 12
1849, No. 46, Ob arestantakh v Petropavlovskoi kreposti.
—, No. 55, Donos Politskogo na Gagarina i Belikovicha.
—, No. 90, O vospitannikakh Uchilishcha pravovedeniia Von-Stein i Depreradoviche.
—, No. 102, Poeziia.
—, No. 159, Ob Uchilishche pravovedeniia.

—, No. 195, O zapreshchenii prodavat' portrety Ledru-Rollina, Barbesa, Raspailia i drugikh revoliutsionerov.

—, No. 214, Po razyskaniiu Liprandi i doneseniiam Antonelli, o Butasheviche-Petrashevskom i ego sotovarishchakh.

—, No. 245, Ob osmotre knizhnykh lavok v gorodakh: Rige, Derpte i Moskve.

—, No. 263, O P. V. Verevkine.

—, No. 365, O zapreshchennykh knigakh, naidennykh u perepletchika Meiersona.

—, No. 400, Ob iz'yatii iz prodazhi Karmannogo slovaria inostrannykh slov.

—, No. 426, O postanovlenii novykh pravil k preduprezhdeniiu vvozu v Rossii u inostrannykh zapreshchennykh knig.

1855, No. 269, O predstavlennoi d'iakonom Alekseem Metropol'skim bezimiannoi zapiske vosmutitel'nogo soderzhaniia.

Fond 109, Sekretnyi arkhiv.

Novyi opis', razdelenie Revoliutsiia i obshchestvennoe dvizhenie v Rossii, 1826–80.

Nos. 64–74, O petrashevtsakh.

Fond 801, V. I. Semevskii. Materialy ego raboty.

Fond 1076, N. A. Speshnev.

Fond 95, A. F. Golitsyn.

Tsentral'nyi Gosudarstvennyi Istoricheskii Arkhiv, g. Leningrad, (TsGIAL).

Fond 1282, Kantseliariia Ministerstva vnutrennykh del, opis' 1.

No. 10, O zloumyshlennom obshchestve Butashevicha-Petrashevskogo.

No. 82, Po proshenii ssyl'nogo Butashevicha-Petrashevskogo.

No. 226, O V. A. Golovinskom i drugikh.

Fond 772, Glavnoe tsenzurnoe upravlenie.

opis' 1

Nos. 191, 2126, 2260, Ob inostrannykh knigakh.

opis' 4

Nos. 149247, 257, 400, 430, Ob inostrannykh knigakh.

Nos. 149286, 294, 305, 328, 346, 353, 354, 363, 367, 374, 389, 405, 409, 440, 466, Buturlinskii komitet.

Fond 647, A. P. Balasoglo.

Fond 673, I. P. Liprandi.

Fond 560, Tsentral'nyi Gosudarstvennyi Arkhiv narodnogo khoziaistva.

Fond 1280, Departament upravleniia komendanty Petropavlovskoi kreposti, opis' 123.

Fond 1286, Departament politsii ispolnitel'noi opis' 11.

Gosudarstvennaia Biblioteka S.S.S.R. imeni V. I. Lenina, g. Moskva, Otdel Rukopisei, (BL).

Fond OIDR, Obshchestvo istorii i drevnostei rukopisnykh.

No. 221, Doneseniia Antonelli k P. A. Perovskomu.

No. 225, I. P. Liprandi.

Fond V. A. Gol'tseva, Pis'ma D. D. Akhsharumova.

Fond F. M. Dostoevskogo.

Fond Kashkiny.

Fond 135, V. G. Korozhnyi, Pis'ma I. V. Pavlova k A. I. Malyshevu, 1845—9.

Fond M. P. Pogodina, P//9//, V. V. Grigor'ev.

Gosudarstvennaia Publichnaia Biblioteka imeni M. e. Saltykov-Shchedrina, g.
Leningrad, Otdel Rukopisei, (GPB).

Fond 4, Raznoiazychnye, Nos. 179, 833, O Petrashevtsakh.

Fond 237, N. Ia. Danilevskii.

Arkhiv K. A. Voenskogo, opis' 2, No. 299, O V. M. Petrashevskom.

Arkhiv Pomyalovskogo, O V. V. Tolbine.

Sobranie A. E. Burtseva.

Sobranie avtografov Gerbelia.

Bumagi K. K. Shil'dera.

Bumagi I. P. Liprandi.

Otdel Rukopisei Instituta Literatury A.N. S.S.S.R. (Pushkinskii Dom), g.
Leningrad, (IRLI).

Razriad I, opis' 5, No. 27, Pis'ma V. A. Engel'sona k A. I. Gertsenu.

—, opis' 17, A. N. Maikov.

—, opis' 22, S. F. Durov.

Bumagi Maikovy.

Fond 265, Arkhiv zhurnala Russkoi stariny, opis' 2, No. 2010, Pis'ma
       Petrashevskogo k neizvestnomu.

Fond 36, opis' 1, No. 41, Vospominaniia V. Burenia o Durove.

Fond 93, opis' 3, Nos. 420, 489, S. F. Durov.

Fond 181, opis' 1, No. 38, D. D. Akhsharumov.

Fond 274, M. I. Semevskii, opis' 1.

Fond 434, Arkhiv Mashkeva, O N. A. Mombelli.

Fond 528, V. I. Semevskii, opis' 1.

Fond 548, Zapisi V. P. Zotova.

Sobranie Modzhalevskogo, Pis'ma Kashkina.

Arkhiv F. A. Koni, Fond 134, opis' 5.

—, Fond 274, opis' 1, 5.

Moskovskoe Otdelenie Arkhiv A.N. S.S.S.R.

Fond 489, V. I. Semevskii.

Institut Istorii A.N. S.S.S.R., g. Leningrad, Otdel drevnykh rukopisei i aktov,
(LOII).

Pis'ma I. M. Debu.

Irkutsk Oblastnoi Arkhiv.

N. A. Speshnev, Pis'ma k materi, 1838—1882. Microfilm used by kind permission of E. Azhusoeva & I. Ulanovskaia.

PUBLISHED SOURCES

i — Primary sources

COLLECTIONS OF DOCUMENTS AND OTHER BASIC MATERIALS
RELATING TO THE PETRASHEVTSY

Delo petrashevtsev, ed. A.N. S.S.S.R., (3 vols., Moscow 1937, 1941, 1951).

Dostoevskii v protsesse petrashevtsev, ed. N.F. Bel'chikov, (Moscow 1936 and 1971).

V.A. Engel'son, 'Petrashevskii', in A.I. Herzen, *Polnoe sobranie sochinenii i pis'em*, ed. M.K. Lemke, (22 vols., Petrograd 1915–25), vol. vi.

Filosofskie i obshchestvenno-politicheskie proizvedeniia petrashevtsev, ed. V.E. Evgrafov, (Moscow 1953).

Karmannyi slovar' inostrannykh slov, voshedshikh v sostav russkogo iazika, ed. N.S. Kirillov, (2 vols., St. Petersburg 1845 and 1846).

F.N. L'vov, 'Zapiska o dele petrashevtsev', *Literaturnoe nasledstvo, Gertsen i Ogarev iii*, (Moscow 1956), vol. 63.

Petrashevtsy, Sbornik materialov, ed. P.E. Shchegolev, (3 vols., Moscow–Leningrad 1923–8).

Poety–petrashevtsy, ed. V.V. Zhdanov, (Biblioteka poeta, Leningrad 1940 and 1950).

Obshchestvo propaganda v 1849g., ed. E. Kasprovich, (Leipzig 1875).

Politicheskie protsessy nikolaevskoi epokhi, ed. V.M. Sablin, (Moscow 1907).

'Rasskaz A.N. Maikova o Dostoevskom i petrashevtsakh', two versions: ed. E. Pokrovskaia, in *Dostoevskii. Staat'i i materialy*, ed. A.S. Dolinin, (Moscow 1922); ed. N.M. Ovseiannkova, in *Istoricheskii arkhiv*, (1948), vol. 26.

NEWSPAPERS AND PERIODICALS OF THE 1840s AND 1850s

Biblioteka dlia chteniia.

Finsky vestnik.

Illiustratsiia.

Irkutskie gubernskie vedomosti.

Kolokol.

Literaturnaia gazeta.

Literaturnoe pribavlenie k Russkomu invalidu.

Moskovskii gorodskoi listok.

Moskvitianin.

Nevskii almanakh.

Otechestvennye zapiski.

Panteon, (Panteon i repertuar).

Poliarnaia zvezda.

Sanktpeterburgskie vedomosti.
Severnoe obozrenie.
Sovremennik.
Syn otechestva.
Vedomosti Sanktpeterburgskoi politsii.
Russkii invalid.
Zhurnal Ministerstva narodnogo prosveshchenniia.
Zhurnal Ministerstva vnutrennykh del.

MEMOIRS AND WRITINGS OF THE PETRASHEVTSY AND
THEIR CONTEMPORARIES

D. D. Akhsharumov, *Iz moikh vospominanii (1849–51g.)*, (St. Petersburg
　1905).
—, *Prostitutsiia i ee reglamentatsiia*, (Riga 1889).
—, *Zapiski petrashevtsa*, (Moscow–Leningrad 1930).
P. V. Annenkov, *Literaturnye vospominaniia*, (Moscow 1960).
P. V. Annenkov i ego druzh'ia, (St. Petersburg 1892).
K. K. Arsen'ev, *Nachertanie statistiki rossiiskogo gosudarstva*, (St. Petersburg
　1848).
—, *Statisticheskie svedeniia o Sankt-Peterburge*, (St. Petersburg 1836).
—, 'Vospominaniia ob Uchilishche pravovedeniia 1849–55gg.', *Russkaia
　Starina*, (1886), No. 4.
M. A. Bakunin, *Pis'ma k A. I. Gertsenu i N. P. Ogarevu*, ed. M. P. Dragomanov,
　(Geneva 1896).
A. P. Balasoglo (A. Belosokolov), *Bukva E. Rukovodstvo k upotrebleniiu etoi
　bukve v pis'me*, (St. Petersburg 1847).
—, *Oblomki. Chernovye zapiski morskogo soderzhaniia (1817–67)*, (Nikolaev
　1875).
—, 'Otklik petrashevtsa A. P. Balasoglo na smert' Pushkina', ed. A. A. Bem,
　Pushkinskii sbornik pami ati S. A. Vengerova IV, (Moscow 1972).
N. Barsukov, *Zhizn' i trudy M. P. Pogodina*, (22 vols., St. Petersburg 1888–
　1910), vol. x.
P. I. Beletskii, 'Pis'mo k P. S. Biliarskomu', *Pis'ma k akademiku P. S.
　Biliarskomu*, (Odessa 1907).
V. G. Belinskii, *Izbrannye pis'ma*, (2 vols., Moscow 1955).
—, *Polnoe sobranie sochinenii*, (13 vols., Moscow 1953–9).
V. G. Belinskii vospominaniiakh sovremennikov, ed. K. T. Tiun'kin, (Moscow
　1977).
N. A. Belogolovyi, *Vospominaniia i drugie stat'i*, (Moscow 1897).
E. A. Belov, 'Vospominaniai 1852–3', *N. G. Chernyshevskii v Saratove*, (Saratov
　1939).
V. V. Bervi (N. Flerovskii), 'Kratkaia avtobiografiia', *Russkaia mysl*, (1905),
　No. 5.

—, 'Vospominaniia. Tsarstvovanie Nikolaia Pervogo', *Golos minuvshego*, (1915), Nos. 3, 5.

—, *Tri politicheskie sistemy*, (St. Petersburg 1897).

E. A. Bestuzheva, *Vospominaniia Bestuzhevykh*, (Moscow 1951).

K. N. Bestuzhev-Riumin, *Vospominaniia*, (St. Petersburg 1900).

P. D. Boborykin, *Za polveka*, (Moscow–Leningrad 1929).

V. P. Botkin, *Sochineniia*, (3 vols., St. Peterburg 1890).

General Bronevskii, 'Zapiska o Litsee, (po povodu Delo Petrashevskogo)', ed. V. Vodovozov, *Glavnoe upravlenie arkhivnym delom. Sbornik materialov i statei*, series I, II, (Petrograd 1921).

N. Ia. Butkov, *Peterburgskie vershiny*, (St. Petersburg 184).

V. P. Bykova, *Zapiski staroi smolianki*, (St. Petersburg 1899).

P. Ia. Chaadaev, *Sochineniia*, (Moscow 1913–14).

N. G. Chernyshevskii, *Literaturnoe nasledie*, (Moscow–Leningrad 1930).

—, *Polnoe sobranie sochinenii*, (16 vols., Moscow 1939–50).

B. N. Chicherin, *Vospominaniia. Moskva v sorokovykh godakh*, (Moscow 1929).

A. Chulinkov, 'Peterburgskii universitet polveka nazad. Vospominaniai byvshego studenta', *Russkii arkhiv*, (1888), No. 9 (3).

A. A. Chumnikov, 'Iz zapisok', *Russkii arkhiv*, (1902), No. 10.

G. P. Danilevskii, *Sochineniia*, (St. Petersburg 1893).

N. Ia. Danilevskii, *Rossiia i Evropa*, (4th ed., St. Petersburg 1889).

N. A. Dobroliubov, *Sobranie sochinenii v trekh tomakh*, (Moscow 1950).

F. M. Dostoevskii, *Diary of a Writer*, tr. B. Brasol, (2nd ed., SantaBarbara 1979).

—, *Polnoe sobranie sochinenii*, (30 vols., Leningrad 1972–   ).

—, 'Peterburgskaia letopis'', *Sanktpeterburgskie vedomosti*, (1847), Nos. 81, 93, 104, 121, 133.

F. M. Dostoevskii v vospominaniaikh sovremennikov, ed. A. S. Dolinin, (Moscow 1964).

Dostoevskii v izobrazhenii ego docheri L. Dostoevski, (Moscow–Leningrad 1922).

V. Drashusov, 'Dva slova o George Sand', *Moskovskoi gorodskoi listok*, (1847), No. 12.

S. F. Durov, 'Baryshny', *Illiustratsiia*, (1847), No. 1.

—, 'Chuzhoe ditia', *Finskii vestnik*, (1846), No. 10.

—, 'Grustnaia povest' c veselym kontsom', *Biblioteka dlia chteniia*, (1848), No. 87.

—, 'Khalatnik', *Nevskii almanakh na 1847–8*, (St. Petersburg 1847).

—, 'Luka Lukich', *Finskii vestnik*, (1845), No. 4.

—, 'Mat i doch', *Illiustratsiia*, (1847), No. 3.

—, 'Neskol'ko slov o N. I. Khmel'nitskom', *Sochineniia N. I. Khmel'nitskogo*, (St. Petersburg 1849).

—, 'Peterburgskii vank'a', *Panteon i repertuar*, (1848), No. 8–9.

—, 'Prizrak', *Severnoe obozrenie*, (1848), No. 2.

—, 'Roman v zapiskakh', *Illiustratsiia*, (1847), No. 41.

—, 'Tantal', *Biblioteka dlia chteniia*, (1848), No. 89.

—, 'Tet'inka', *Panteon*, (1848), No. 2.

—, 'Sosed', *Finskii vestnik*, (1847), No. 24.

—, 'Strannik', ibid.

P. Efebovskii, 'Peterburgskie raznoshchiki', V. A. Sollugub, ed., *Vchera i segodnia. Literaturnyi sbornik*, (St. Petersburg 1846), vol. 2.

V. A. Engel'son, 'Chto takoe gosudarstvo?', *Poliarnaia zvezda*, (1855), No. 2.

—, 'Pis'ma k Gertsenu', *Vsemirnyi vestnik*, (1901), No. 1.

—, *Stat'i, proklamatsiia, pis'ma, Petrashevskii*, (Moscow 1934).

E. M. Feoktistov, *Vospominaniia. Zu kulisami politiki i literatury 1848–96*, (Leningrad 1929).

Fiziologiai Peterburga, ed. V. G. Belinskii and N. A. Nekrasov, (St. Petersburg 1845).

M. I. Glinka, *Zapiski i perepiska s rodnymi i druz'iami*, (St. Petersburg 1891).

N. V. Gogol, *Polnoe sobranie sochinenii*, (8 vols., Moscow 1913).

A. Ia. Golovachaeva-Panaeva, *Russkie pisateli i artisti*, (St. Petersburg 1890).

N. S. Golytsin, 'Ocherki i vospominaniia', *Russkaia starina*, (1890), No. 11.

E. Greben'ka, 'Sila Kondrat'ev', *Sovremennik*, (1848), No. 5.

A. A. Grigor'ev, 'Dva egoizma', *Panteon*, (1845), No. 121.

—, *Stikhotvoreniia*, (St. Petersburg 1915).

—, *Izbrannye proizvedeniia*, (Leningrad 1959).

V. V. Grigor'ev, *Zhizni i trudy P. S. Savel'eva*, (St. Petersburg 1861).

D. V. Grigorovich, *Literaturnye vospominaniia*, (Leningrad 1928).

Ia. K. Grot, *Perepiska s P. A. Pletnevym*, (3 vols., St. Petersburg 1896).

A. I. Herzen, *Polnoe sobranie sochinenii i pisem*, ed. M. K. Lemke, (22 vols., Petrograd 1915–25).

—, *Sobranie sochinenii v tridtsati tomakh*, ed. A.N. S.S.S.R., (Moscow 1954–66).

Izbrannye obshchestvenno-politicheskie i filosofskie proizvedeniia ukrainskikh revoliutsionnykh demokratov XIXv., ed. M. T. Novchuk and D. F. Ostrianin, (Moscow 1955).

N. N. Kashkin, *Rodoslovnye razvedki*, ed. B. L. Modzalevskii, (St. Petersburg 1913), vol. 2.

M. P. Khitrovo, 'Vospominaniia ob odnom iz petrashevtsev, N. A. Mombelli', *Russkaia mysl'*, (1907), No. 7.

Baron M. A. Korf, 'Iz zapisok', *Russkaia starina*, (1900), Nos. 3–6.

I. V. Kovalevskii, 'Itogi zhizni', *Vestnik Evropy*, (1883), Nos. 1–3.

P. A. Kuz'min, 'Zapiski Generala-Leitenanta P. A. Kuz'min, 1819–85', *Russkaia starina*, (1895), Nos. 2–4.

E. I. Lamanskii, 'Iz vospominanii', *Russkaia starina*, (1915), Nos. 1–3.

K. N. Lebedev, 'Zapiski senatora', *Russkii arkhiv*, (1910), No. 11.

I. P. Liprandi, 'Pis'mo k A. I. Gertsenu po povodu stat'i v Kolokole', A. I. Herzen, *Polnoe sobranie sochinenii i pisem*, ed. M. K. Lemke, vol. ix.

—, 'Zapiska o dele petrashevtsev', *Poliarnaia zvezda*, (1862), No. 7.

—, 'Zapiska o dele petrashevtsev', *Russkaia starina*, (1872), No. 7.

F. N. L'vov, 'Iz Irkutska', *Sovremennik*, (1861), No. 9.

—, 'Mestnoe obozrenie', *Amur*, (1860), No. 16.

—, 'Opiat' ob irkutskoi dueli', *Kolokol*, (1861), 15 July.

—, 'Peredovaia', *Irkutskie gubernskie vedomosti*, (1858), No. 2, (1859), No. 17.

—, 'Pis'ma k D. I. Zavalishinu 1860g.', *Sbornik starinnykh bumag khraniash-chikhsia v muzee imeni Shchukina*, (Moscow 1902) vol. x.

—, 'Zapiski odnogo otstavnogo kantselliarnogo sluzhitelia v poiskakh za promyshlennost'iu', *Sovremennik*, (1861), No. 3.

—, 'Vyderzhki iz vospominaniai ssyl'nogo-katorzhnogo', *Sovremennik*, (1861), No. 9, (1862), No. 1–2.

A. N. Maikov, *Polnoe sobranie sochinenii*, (4 vols., St. Petersburg 1914).

V. N. Maikov, *Kriticheskie opyty 1845–7*, (St. Petersburg 1891).

—, 'Ot redaktsii Finskogo vestnika', *Finskii vestnik*, (1845), No. 1.

—, *Sochineniia v dvukh tomakh*, (Kiev 1901).

M. Marks, 'M. V. Butashevich-Petrashevskii', *Russkaia starina*, (1889), No. 5.

M. K. Mart'ianov, 'V perelome veka', *Istoricheskii vestnik*, (1895), Nos. 10–11.

D. I. Meier, *O zhachenii praktiki i sisteme sovremennogo iuridicheskogo obrazovaniia*, (Kiev 1855).

N. A. Mel'gunov, 'Spor o blagotvoritel'nosti', *Sovremennik*, (1847), No. 5.

M. I. Mikhailov, *Zapiski 1861–2*, (Petrograd 1922).

—, 'Dnevnik', *Russkaia starina*, (1906), vol. 128.

A. M. Miklashevskii, 'Vospominaniia', *Russkaia starina*, (1891), No. 1, (1892), No. 4.

A. P. Miliukov, *Literaturnye vstrechi i znakomstva*, (St. Petersburg 1890).

—, *Ocherki istorii russkoi poezzi*, (St. Petersburg 1847).

V. A. Miliutin, *Izbrannye proizvedeniia*, (Moscow 1946).

—, 'Proletariat i pauperizm v Anglii i vo Frantsii', *Otechestvennye zapiski*, (1847), Nos. 1–4.

V. N. Nazar'ev, 'Zhizn' i liudi bylogo vremeni', *Istoricheskii vestnik*, (1890), December.

A. V. Nikitenko, *Zapiski i dnevnik*, (St. Petersburg 1904).

G. Novopolin, 'Petrashevtsy i ikh vremia v vospominaniaikh N. P. Balina', *Katorga i ssylka*, (1930), No. 2.

V. A. Obruchev, 'Obriad smertnoi kazni nad petrashevtsym', *Stoletie Voenno-ministerstva, xii. Glavnoe voenno-sudnoe upravlenie*, (St. Petersburg 1914), vol. 1.

N. P. Ogarev, *Izbrannye sotsial'no-politicheskie i filosofskie proizvedeniia*, ed. M. T. Iovchuk and N. G. Tarakanov, (Moscow 1952).

—, 'Zapiska o tainom obshchestve', *Literaturnoe nasledstvo, Gerzen I*, (Moscow 1941).

E. G. Osokin, 'O postepennom razvitii ekonomicheskikh idei v istorii', *Zhurnal Ministerstva narodnogo prosveshcheniia*, (1845), April.

—, *Polozheniia, izvlechennye iz 'Rassuzhdenie o bednosti i pauperizme' predstavlennogo dlia polucheniia stepeni magistra gos. pravy*, (Kazan 1846).

V. Ostrogorskii, *Iz istorii moego uchitel'stva*, (St. Petersburg 1895/1914).

A. I. Pal'm (P. Al'minskii), *Aleksei Slobodin*, (St. Petersburg 1873).

—, 'Delo o nadvornom sovetnike A. I. Pal'm', V. D. Stasovich, *Sochineniia*, (St. Petersburg 1889–90), vol. v.

—, 'Odin den' iz budnichnoi zhizni', *Moskovskoi gorodskoi listok*, (1847), Nos. 110, 113, 115–18.

—, 'Pis'mo k N. A. Nekrasovu', *Literaturnoe nasledstvo*, (Moscow 1949), Nos. 51–2.

—, 'Shalost'', Finskii vestnik, (1842), No. 9.

—, 'Zhak Bichovkin', *Otechestvennye zapiski*, (1849), Nos. 5–6.

I. I. Panaev, *Literaturnye vospominaniia*, (Leningrad 1950).

L. Pantaleev, *Iz vospominanii proshlogo*, (Moscow 1934).

T. P. Passek, *Iz dal'nykh let*, (St. Petersburg 1903).

V. S. Pecherin, *Zamogil'nye zapiski*, (Moscow 1932).

P. Pekarskii, 'Studencheskie vospominanii o D. I. Meiere', *Bratchina (Sbornik)*, (St. Petersburg 1859), vol. 1.

Peterburgskii sbornik, (St. Petersburg 1846).

A. V. (Petrashevskaia) Semevskaia, 'M. V. Petrashevskii v 1849 g.', *Russkaia starina*, (1901), No. 2.

M. V. Butashevich-Petrashevskii, 'Mestnoe obozrenie', *Amur*, (1860), Nos. 1–8.

—, 'Neskol'ko slov o Sibirii', *Irkutskie gubernskie vedomosti*, (1857), No. 9.

—, 'Peredovaia', ibid., (1858), No. 50.

—, 'Pis'ma iz ssylki 1856–64', *Zven'ia*, (1933), No. 11.

—, 'Pis'mo k N. S. Kirillovu. 10 May 1846', *Golos minuvshego*, (1914), No. 8.

—, 'Pis'mo k D. I. Zavalishinu', *Sbornik starinnykh bumag, kraniashchikhsia v muzee imeni Shchukina*, (Moscow 1902), vol. x.

—, 'Pros'ba Ministru vnutrennykh del', *Kolokol*, (1860), 9 May.

—, 'Proshenie v Senat, 28 July 1858', ibid., (1859), 1 October.

Petrashevtsy i ikh vremia, (St. Petersburg 1907).

Petrashevtsy v vospominaniiakh sovremennikov, ed. P. E. Shchegolev, (Moscow–Leningrad 1926).

Petrov, 'Vospominaniia uchastniki v dele M. V. Petrashevskogo', *Russkaia starina*, (1903), No. 4.

A. F. Pisemskii, 'Liudi sorokovykh godov', *Sobranie sochinenii*, (1911), vol. v.

A. N. Pleshcheev, 'Pis'ma k N. A. Dobroliubovu', *Russkaia mysl'*, (1913), No. 1.

—, 'Pis'ma k S. F. Durovu', *Pole Star*, (1861).

—, 'Pis'ma k N. A. Nekrasovu i N. G. Chernyshevskomu', *Literaturnoe nasledstvo*, (1949), Nos. 51–2.

—, A. N. Pleshcheev, *Povesti i rasskazi*, (St. Petersburg 1896–7).

—, *Stikhotvoreniia*, (St. Petersburg 1846).

—, *Stikhotvoreniia*, (Moscow 1975).

V. S. Poroshin, *Besedy diadia s plemiannikom o politicheskoi ekonomii*, (St. Petersburg 1842).

—, 'Cobden', *Sanktpeterburgskie vedomosti*, (1847), No. 21.

—, *Kriticheskie issledovaniia ob osnovaniiakh statistiki*, (St. Petersburg 1838).

—, 'O sredstve k opredeleniia klimata', *Zapiski russkogo geograficheskogo obshchestva*, (1847).

—, *O zemledelii v politiko-ekonomicheskom otnoshenii*, (St. Petersburg 1846).

—, 'Peterburg', *Sovremennik*, (1848), No. 1.

A. G. Rubinstein, 'Avtobiografiia', *Russkaia starina*, (1889), No. 11.

M. E. Saltykov-Shchedrin, *Sobranie sochinenii v dvadtsati tomakh*, (Moscow 1965—77).

—, Reviews of childrens' books in *Otechestvennye zapiski* not included in his collected works:

'Blagovospitannoe ditia', (1848), Nos. 1—2.

'Detskaia korzinochka', (1847), Nos. 1—2.

'Neskol'ko slov o chtenii roman', (1848), No. 3.

'G. A. Potemkin', (1848), Nos. 1—2.

'Robinson Crusoe', (1847), Nos. 1—2.

'Russkie skazki dlia detei', (1848), Nos. 1—2.

—, 'Zapiski chteniia M. E. Saltykova iz Cabanisa v sorokovykh godakh', ed. N. V. Iakovlev, *Izvestiia A. N. S. S. S. R.*, social sciences series, (1837), No. 4.

N. M. Satin, 'Irliandiia', *Sovremennik*, (1848), No. 11.

P. P. Semenov Tian'-Shanskii, *Memuary*, (Petrograd 1917), vol. 1.

N. V. Shelgunov, *Vospominaniia*, (Moscow—Petrograd 1923).

L. M. Shelgunova, *Iz dalekogo proshlogo*, (St. Petersburg 1901).

S. Shpitser, 'Novoe o dele petrashevtsev', *Katorgai ssylka*, (1926), Nos. 7—8.

R. R. Shtrandman, 'Sovremennye zametki (Sections on home news)', *Sovremennik*, (1847 and 1848).

A. D. Shumakher, 'Pozdnie vospominaniia o davno minuvskikh vremenakh', *Vestnik Evropy*, (1899), No. 3.

Sorokovye gody v memuarakh sovremennikov, (Moscow, 1959).

N. A. Speshnev, 'Irkutskaia starina', *Irkutskie gubernskie vedomosti*, (1857), Nos. 1—3, 16, 30.

—, 'Peredovaia', ibid., (1857), No. 11, (1858), No. 48, (1859), No. 3.

—, 'N. A. Speshnev o sebe samom', ed. B. Koz'min, *Katorga i ssylka*, (1930), No. 1.

A. V. Starchevskii, 'Vospominaniia starogo literatora', *Istoricheskii vestnik*, (1890), No. 9.

V. V. Stasov, 'Uchilishche pravovedeniia sorok let tomu nazad, 1836—42gg'., *Izbrannye sochineniia v trekh tomakh*, (Moscow 1952), vol. ii.

F. G. Tol', 'Iz zapisok moego soslannogo priiatelia', *Sovremennik*, (1863), No. 95.

—, 'Nasha detskaia literatura', (St. Petersburg 1862).

—, 'Nastol'nyi slovar' dlia spravok po vsem otrasliam znanii', (3 vols., St. Petersburg 1863—4).

—, 'O pervonachal'nom (elementarnom) obuchenii', *Russkoe slovo*, (1859), Nos. 7—8.

—, *Trud i Kapital*, (St. Petersburg 1861).

V. V. Tolbin, 'I. K. Aiviazovskii i ego proizvedeniia', *Biblioteka dlia chteniia*, (1855), vol. cxxxv.

—, 'Bobrovyi vorotnik', *Finskii Vestnik*, (1847), No. 23.

—, 'Borzopistsy', ibid.

—, 'Chernyi den' ', ibid.

—, 'O P. A. Fedotove', *Panteon*, (1854), No. 1.

—, 'Ispanskaia zhivopis' ', *Panteon*, (1853), No. 1.

—, 'Khudozhestvennye vystavki v S-Peterburge', *Finskii Vestnik*, (1847), No. 22.

—, 'Krovavaia bania', ibid., (1846), No. 12.

—, 'Loskutnitsy', ibid., (1847), No. 19.

—, 'Liubin'ka', *Severnoe obozrenie*, (1848), No. 3.

—, 'Markery i billiardnye igroki', *Finskii Vestnik*, (1847), No. 21.

—, 'Mon Chers', ibid., (1847), No. 20.

—, 'Nochnye babochki', *Illiustratsiia*, (1847), Nos. 35—6.

—, 'Nian'ki bylogo i nastoiashchego vremeni', *Severnoe obozrenie*, (1848), No. 1.

—, 'Perepetuia Petrovna', *Finskii Vestnik*, (1847), No. 24.

—, 'Rubensova golovka', *Panteon*, (1853), No. 12.

—, 'Ulichnye muzikanty', *Panteon*, (1848), No. 7.

—, 'Var'enka Doleva', *Panteon*, (1855), Nos. 2, 12.

—, 'Vengertsy', *Finskii Vestnik*, (1846), No. 12.

—, 'Iaroslavtsy', ibid., (1847), No. 16.

—, 'Zavoevanie Anglii normanami', ibid., (1846), No. 12.

—, 'Zhizn' Schillera v Vienna', *Severnoe obozrenie*, (1848), No. 3.

N. Tsylov, *Atlas 13 chasti S-Peterburga*, (Moscow 1849).

N. A. Tuchkova-Ogareva, *Vospominaniia*, (Moscow 1959).

I. S. Turgenev, *Khronika russkogo. Dnevnik*, (Moscow—Leningrad 1964).

—, *Polnoe sobranie sochinenii i pis'em*, (15 vols., Moscow—Leningrad 1960—8).

A. M. Unkovskii, 'Zapiski', *Russkaia mysl'*, (1906), No. 6.

F. N. Ustrialov, 'Universitetskie vospominaniia', *Istoricheskii vestnik*, (1884), No. 16.

Sbornik. Vchera i segodnia, ed. P. A. Sollugub, (St. Petersburg 1846).

I. I. Vedediktov, 'Za shest'desiat'let', *Russkaia starina*, (1905), No. 10.

M. I. Veniukov, *Iz vospominaniia*, (Amsterdam 1895), vol. 1.

K. S. Veselovskii, 'Statistiki nedvizhimykh imushchestv v Sankt-Peterburge', *Zapiski Russkogo geograficheskogo obshchestva*, (1849), Nos. 3—4.

—, 'Vospominaniia o nekotorykh litseiskikh tovarishchakh', *Russkaia starina*, (1900), Nos. 7–9.

N. I. Veselovskii, *V. V. Grigor'ev po ego pis'mam i trudam, 1816–81*, (St. Petersburg 1883).

I. I. Vvedenskii, 'Donos F. F. Vigelia na nego', *Russkaia starina*, (1871), No. 4.

A. N. Iakhontov, 'Vospominaniia tsarskosel'skogo litseista', *Russkaia starina*, (1888), No. 10.

S. Ianovskii, 'Vospominaniia o Dostoevskom', *Russkii vestnik*, (1885), No. 4.

J.-F. L. Jastrzębski, 'Memuar petrashevtsa', *Minuvshie gody*, (1908), No. 1.

—, 'Biografiia Sir Robert Peel', *Finskii Vestnik*, (1846), No. 11.

—, review of, 'Ob istochnikakh i upotreblenii statisticheskikh svedenii, soch. D. P. Zhuravskogo', ibid., (1847), No. 1.

—, review of, 'Ob otmenenii khlebnykh zakonov v Anglii, soch. N. Ia. Linovskogo', ibid., (1846), No. 11.

—, review of, 'Opyt o narodnom bogatstve, soch. A. I. Butovskogo', ibid., (1847), No. 12.

—, review of, 'O zemledelii v politiko-ekonomicheskom otnoshenii, soch. V. S. Poroshina', ibid., (1846), No. 11.

—, review of, 'Zapiski russkogo geograficheskogo obshchestva', ibid., (1846), No. 12.

M. Iur'in, 'Spor ob obshchinnom vladenii zemli', *Atenei*, (Moscow 1858), No. 44.

A. P. Zablotskii-Desiatovskii, *Prichina kolebanii tsen na khleb*, (St. Petersburg), (1847).

D. I. Zavalishin, *Zapiski dekabrista*, (St. Petersburg 1906).

Iu. Zhadovskaia, *Polnoe sobranie stikhotvorenii*, (St. Petersburg 1885–6).

L. Zhemchuzhnikov, 'Moi vospominaniia', *Vestnik Evropy*, (1900), No. 12.

D. P. Zhuravskii, *Ob istochnikakh i upotreblenii statisticheskikh svedenii*, (Kiev, 1846).

V. P. Zotov, 'Peterburg v sorokovykh godakh', *Istoricheskii vestnik*, (1890), Nos. 5–6.

ii—Secondary sources

A. Ia. Aizenshtok, 'T. G. Shevchenko i petrashevets A. V. Khanykov', *Uchenye zapiski Leningradskogo gosudarstvennogo pedagogicheskogo instituta imeni Gertsena*, (1948), vol. 67.

M. A. Akhmedova, 'Pleshcheev i pisateli-petrashevtsy (sorokovye gody),' *Uchenye zapiski Azerbaidzhanskogo pedagogicheskogo instituta iazykov imeni M. F. Akhunova*, (1967), series xii, No. 4.

I. Aleshintsev, *Istoriia gimnazicheskogo obrazovaniia v Rossii XVIII i XIXv.*, (St. Petersburg 1912).

M. Alexander, *Der Petrachevskij – Prozess. Eine 'Verschwörung der Ideen' und ihre Verfolgung in Russland von Niklaus I*, (1979).

A. M. Ardavatskaia, 'Petrashevtsy o revoliutsionnom perevorote', *Nauchnyi ezhegodnik za 1955*, (Saratov 1958).

V. Aref'ev, 'M. V. Butashevich-Petrashevskii v Sibirii', *Russkaia starina*, (1902), No. 1.

K. K. Arsen'ev, 'Valerian Maikov', *Vestnik Evropy*, (1886), No. 4.

M. Balabanov, *Ocherk istorii revoliutsionnogo dvizheniia v Rossii*, (Leningrad 1929).

N. P. Balina, 'Petrashevtsy i ikh vremia', *Katorga i ssylka*, (1930), No. 2.

F. M. Bartholemew, *The Petrashevskii Circle*, (Phd. Thesis, Princeton 1969). This is derivative and uses no archival material.

V. Basakov, *Sotsiologicheskie vozzreniia V. G. Belinskogo*, (Moscow 1948).

V. Baturinskii, 'Gertsen, ego druzh'ia i znakomye', *Vsemirnyi vestnik*, (1904), No. 7.

N. F. Bel'chikov, 'F. M. Dostoevskii – chlen tainogo obshchestva', *Krasnyi arkhiv*, (1927), No. 2.

N. Belozerskii, 'Ot Peterburga do Nerchinska', *Russkaia mysl'*, (1902), No. 12.

I. Berlin, *Russian Thinkers*, (Harmondsworth 1978).

G. Beshkin, *Idei Fourier u Petrashevskogo i petrashevtsev*, (Moscow–Petrograd 1923).

A. V. Bezbrodnyi, 'K biografiia Butashevicha-Petrashevskogo', *Istoricheskii vestnik*, (1901), No. 1.

P. A. Bibikov, *Kriticheskie etiudi*, (St. Petersburg 1865).

I. G. Bliamin, 'Ekonomicheskie vozzreniye V. A. Miliutina', V. A. Miliutin, *Izbrannye proizvedeniia*, (Moscow 1946).

—, 'Ocherki ekonomicheskoi mysli v Rossii v pervoi polovine XIX veka', *Istoriia russkoi ekonomicheskoi mysly*, (Moscow–Leningrad 1940).

—, 'Russkii fourierizm sorokovykh godov XIX v.', *Izvestiia A.N. S.S.S.R.*, social sciences series, (1938), No. 2.

Iu. Bocherov, 'Moskovskie otkliki na delo petrashevtsev', *Katorga i ssylka*, (1924), No. 6.

V. V. Bogatov, *Osnovnye cherty mirovozzreniai vydaiushchikhsia predstavitelei dvizheniia petrashevtsev*, (Moscow 1958).

T. A. Bogdanovich, *Pervy revoliutsionnyi kruzhok nikolaevskoi epokhi. Petrashevtsy*, (Petrograd 1917).

H. E. Bowman, *Vissarion Belinsky: A Study in the Origins of Social Criticism in Russia*, (Cambridge Mass. 1954).

E. G. Bushkanets and G. I. Vul'fson, 'Iz istorii obshchestvenno-politicheskoi mysli v Kazan'skom universitete v pervoi polovine XIXv.', *Uchenye zapiski Kazan'skogo gosudarstvennogo universiteta*, (1956), vol. 116, No. 5.

M. Cadot, *La Russie dans la vie intellectuelle francaise, (1839–56)*, (Paris 1967).

E. H. Carr, *The Romantic Exiles*, (Harmondsworth 1968/33).

N. M. Chernyshevskaia, *Letopis' zhizni i deyatel'nosti N. G. Chernyshevskogo*, (Moscow 1953).

G. Chulkov, 'Dostoevskii i utopicheskii sotsializm', *Katorga i ssylka*, (1929) No. 2.

—, 'Rafail Chernosvitov', ibid., (1930), No. 2.

—, 'Sluchainyi gost' na vechera Petrashevskogo. N. A. Serebriakov', ibid., (1930), No. 2.

—, 'Uchitel' Beletskii i provokator Antonelli', ibid., (1932), No. 10.

A. G. Dement'ev, *Ocherki po istorii russkoi zhurnalistiki 1840–1850 gg.*, ((Moscow–Leningrad 1951).

V. P. Demor, *M. V. Petrashevskii (Butashevich). Biograficheskii ocherk*, (Petrograd 1920).

S. S. Derkach, 'O literaturno-esteticheskikh vzglyadath petrashevtsev', *Vestnik LGU*, (1957), No. 14.

Deiateli revoliutsionnogo dvizheniai v Rossii. Bio-bibliograficheskii slovar', (Moscow 1927), vol. 1.

A. S. Dubnov, *Ekonomicheskie vzgliady V. A. Miliutina*, (Moscow 1958).

A. V. Dulov, *Obshchestvenno-politicheskaia deiatel'nost' i evoliutsiia vzgliadov petrashevtsev v Sibirii*, (Irkutsk 1965).

A. S. Dolinin, 'Dostoevskii sredi petrashevtsev', *Zven'ia*, (1936), No. 6.

Dostoevskii Stat'i i materialy, ed. A. S. Dolinin, (Moscow 1922).

I. Ia. D'iakov, *Mirovozzrenie Belinskogo*, (Amur 1962).

V. A. D'iakov, *Osvoboditel'noe dvizhenie v Rossii 1825–1861gg.*, (Moscow 1979).

—, 'Pol'skie konspiratory 1830–40kh godov v ikh sviazakh s Frantsii', *Sbornik. Slaviane i Zapad*, (Moscow 1975).

—, 'Warszawska organizacja konspiracyjna 1848 roku', *Kwartalik Historyczy*, (1976), No. 2.

Dzhanshiev, *A. M. Unkovskii i osvobozhdeniia krest'ian*, (Moscow 1894).

V. M. Eikhenbaum, 'Tolstoi i petrashevtsy', *Russkaia literatura*, (1959), No. 4.

A. A. Ekimov, 'Iz istorii razvitiia krupnoi mashinoi industrii v Peterburge v doreformennom periode (1800–60)', *Vestnik LGU*, (1954), series I, No. 3.

Ia. El'sberg, *A. I. Gertsen*, (3 vols., Moscow 1948).

T. Emmons, *The Russian Landed Gentry and the Peasant Emancipation of 1861*, (Cambridge/Stanford 1968).

Epokha Nikolai Pervogo, ed. M. O. Gersbenzon, (Moscow 1910).

V. Evgen'ev, 'Redaktsiia Sovremennika v 1866 g.', *Golos minuvshego*, (1905), Nos. 1, 31.

V. E. Evgen'ev-Maksimov, *Sovremennik v 1840–1850gg.*, (Leningrad 1934).

V. E. Evgrafov, 'Filosofskie i sotsiologicheskie vozzreniia petrashevtsev', *Istoriia Filosofii*, (Moscow 1957), vol. ii.

—, 'Petrashevtsy', *Istoriia filosofii v S.S.S.R.*, (Moscow 1968), vol. ii.

—, 'Vstupitel'naia stat'ia', *Filosofskie i obshchestvenno-politicheskie proizvedeniai a petrashevtsev*, (Moscow 1953).

I. A. Fedosov, 'Konstitutsional'nye proekty A. V. Berdaeva v sorokovykh godak' XIXv.', *Vopros istorii*, (1955), No. 16.

—, *Revoliutsionnoe dvizhenie v Rossii v vtoroi chetverti XIXv.*, (Moscow 1958).

V. A. Fedorov, *Krest'ianskoe dvizhenie v tsentral'noi Rossii 1800–1860gg.*, (Moscow 1980).

J. Frank, *Dostoevsky. The Seeds of Revolt (1821–49)*, (Princeton 1976).

B. Frommett, *Sotsialisticheskie i kooperativnye idealy petrashevtsev v sorokovykh godakh*, (Petrograd 1918).

G. G. Frumenkov, 'Pol'skii vopros vo vzgliadakh petrashevtsev', *Nauchnye doklady vyshei shkoly. Istoricheskie nauki*, (1958), No. 3.

G. Galagan, 'L. Tol'stoi i petrashevtsy', *Russkaia literatura*, (1965), No. 4.

Iu. I. Gerasimov, 'Krest'ianskoe dvizhenie v Rossii 1848–9gg.', *Istoricheskie zapiski*, (1955), No. 50.

M. Gernet, *Istoriia tsarskoi tyurmy*, (Moscow 1951), vol. ii.

J. Golovin, *Der russische Nihilismus*, (Leipzig 1883).

M. Gor'kii, O petrashevtsakh, I. Turgeneve, F. Dostoevskom, L. Tol'stoi', *Literaturnaia kritike*, (1936), No. 6.

V. Gor'ev, 'Rol' Proudhona v istorii russkogo melkoburguaznogo sotsializma', *Krasnaia nov'*, (1935), No. 1.

Gosudarstvennye sovet 1801–1901 gg., (St. Petersburg 1902).

A. I. Gozulov, *Istoriia otechestvennoi statistiki*, (Moscow 1967).

V. V. Grigor'ev, *Imperatorskii S. Peterburgskii universitet v techenie pervykh 50 let*, (St. Petersburg 1870).

M. Grigor'ian, 'Fourierism v Rossii', *Front nauki i tekhniki*, (1938–9), No. 3.

L. P. Grossman, *Dostoevsky. A Biography*, tr. M. Mackler, (Moscow 1965/ London 1974).

—, *Molodoi Dostoevskii 1821–50*, (Moscow 1928).

—, *Put' Dostoevskogo*, (Moscow 1928).

—, 'Speshnev i Stavrogin', *Spor o Bakunine i Dostoevskom*, (Leningrad 1926).

P. Gusev, 'I. I. Vvedenskii v 1849g.', *Russkaia starina*, (1879), No. 8.

E. Haumant, *La culture francaise en Russie (1700–1900)*, (Paris 1910).

V. E. Illeritskii, *Revolutsionnaia istoricheskaia mysl' v Rossii*, (Moscow 1974).

Istoricheskie svedeniia o tsenzure v Rossii, (St. Petersburg 1862).

Istoriia sotsialisticheskogo uchenii. Pamiati akademiku V. P. Volginu, (Moscow 1964).

V. I. Ivanov-Razumnik, *Istoriia russko-obshchestvennoi mysli*, (St. Petersburg 1906), vol. 1.

P. Ia. Kann, *Petrashevtsy*, (Leningrad 1968).

E. I. Kann-Novikova, *M. I. Glinka. Novye materialy i dokumenty*, (Moscow 1955).

F. I. Kaplan, 'Russian Fourierism of the 1840s: A contrast to Herzen's Westernism', *American Slavic and East European Review*, (1958), vol. xvii, April.

E. Karpevich, *Russkie chinovniki v byvshie i nastoiashchee vremia*, (St. Petersburg 1897).

S. M. Kasovich, 'K voprosu o kruzhkakh, blizkikh k Petrashevskomu', *Uchenye zapiski Saratovskogo gos. universiteta imeni N. G. Chernyshevskogo*, Philiological series, (1959), vol. 67.

V. Ia. Kirpotin, *Ideinye predshestvenniki marksizma-leninizma v Rossii*, (Moscow 1950).

—, *Molodoi Dostoevskii*, (Moscow 1947).

—, *M. E. Saltykov-Shchedrin*, (Moscow 1939).

E. G. Kislitsina, 'M. E. Saltykov-Shchedrin i Saint-Simon', *Izvestiia A. N. S.S.S.R.*, (1937), social sciences series, No. 4.

D. F. Kobeko, *Imperatorskii tsarskosel'skii litsei. Nastavniki i pitomtsi*, (St. Petersburg 1911).

B. L. Komarovich, 'Idei frantsuzskikh sotsial'nykh utopy v mirovozzreniiakh Belinskogo', N. K. Pisanov ed., *Venok Belinskomu. Sbornik*, (Moscow 1924).

—, 'Yunost' Dostoevskogo', *Byloe*, (1924), No. 23.

M. K. Korbut, 'Kazanskii gos. universiteta imeni V. I. Ul'ianov-Lenina za 125 let', *Uchenye zapiski Kazanskogo gos. universiteta*, (1930), No. 5.

A. Kornilov, *Krest'ianskaya reforma v Kaluzhskoi gubernii*, (St. Petersburg 1904).

M. Kovalevskii, 'A. I. Gertsen i zapadnye sotsialisty', *Vestnik Evropy*, (1912), No. 61.

V. P. Koz'min, *Literatura i istoriia. Sbornik statei*, (Moscow 1959).

Krest'ianskoe dvizhenie 1827—69gg., (Moscow 1931), part i.

V. I. Kuleshov, *Literaturnye sviazi Rossii i zapadnoi Evropy v XIX v., (pervaia polovina)*, (Moscow 1965).

—, *"Otechestvennye zapiski" i literatura sorokovykh godov XIX v.*, (Moscow 1958).

R. Labry, *Herzen et Proudhon*, (Paris 1928).

P. Lacroix, *Histoire de la vie et du règne de Nicholas I*, (8 vols., Paris 1864—9).

E. Lampert, *Sons against Fathers*, (Oxford 1965).

—, *Studies in Rebellion*, (London 1957).

V. R. Leikina, *Petrashevtsy. S biografii, al'fabitom petrashevtsev*, (Moscow 1924).

——-Svirskaia, 'Ateizm petrashevtsev', *Voprosy istorii, religii i ateizma*, (Leningrad 1955), No. 3.

—, 'Formirovanie raznochinnoi intelligentsii v Rossii v sorokovykh godakh XIXv.,' *Istoriia S.S.S.R.*, (1958), No. 1.

—, 'O kharaktere kruzhkov petrashevtsev', *Voprosy istorii*, (1956), No. 4.

—, *Petrashevtsy i obshchestvennoe dvizhenie sorokovykh godov XIXv.*, Unpublished doctoral dissertation, (Moscow 1956). (Very dogmatic).

—, *Petrashevtsy*, (Moscow 1965).

—, 'Revoliutsionnaia praktika petrashevtsev', *Istoricheskie zapiski*, (1954), No. 47.

M. K. Lemke, *Nikolaevskie zhandarmy i literatura 1826—1855 gg.*, (St. Petersburg 1908).

W. Bruce Lincoln, *Nicholas I. Emperor and Autocrat of All the Russias*, (London 1978).

R. I. Liashchenko, *Istoriia narodnogo khoziaistva S.S.S.R.*, (Moscow 1956).

E. Liatskii, 'N. G. Chernyshevskii i Ch. Fourier', *Sovremennyi mir*, (1909), No. 11.

—, 'N. G. Chernyshevskii v 1848–50gg.,' Ibid., (1912), No. 3.

—, 'N. G. Chernyshevskii i I. I. Vvedenskii, Ibid., (1910), No. 6.

A. Liubavskii, *Russkie ugolovnye protsessy*, (St. Petersburg 1867), vol. ii.

R. E. MacMaster, *Danilevsky. A Russian Totalitarian Philosopher*, (Cambridge Mass. 1967).

S. A. Makashin, 'Literaturnye vzaimootnosheniia Rossii i Frantsii XVIII–XIXvv.,' *Literaturnoe nasledstvo*, (Moscow 1937), vol. 29–30.

—, *M. E. Saltykov-Shchedrin. Biografiia*, (Moscow 1951).

A. I. Malein & P. N. Berkov, 'Materialy dlia istorii karmannogo slovaria inostrannykh slov', *Trudy Instituta kniga, dokumenty i pis'ma*, (Leningrad 1934), vol. iii.

M. Malia, *Alexander Herzen and the Birth of Russian Socialism*, (Cambridge Mass. 1961).

Iu. Mann, 'Valerian Maikov', *Voprosy literatury*, (1963), No. 11.

V. S. Martynovskaia, 'Sotsial'no-ekonomicheskoie vozzreniai petrashevtsev', *Istoriia russkoi ekonomicheskoi mysli*, (Moscow 1958).

T. G. Masaryk, *The Spirit of Russia*, (London 1919).

N. K. Mikhailovskii, 'Proudhon i Belinskii', *Sochineniia*, (St. Petersburg 1897), vol. iii.

O. F. Miller, 'Materialy dlia zhizneopisanii a F. M. Dostoevskogo', *Biografiia, pis'ma i zametki iz zapisnoi knizhi F. M. Dostoevskogo*, (St. Petersburg 1883).

P. N. Miliukov, *Iz istorii russkoi intelligentsii*, (St. Petersburg 1903).

N. V. Minaeva, *Petrashevtsy i idei utopicheskogo sotsializma*, (Unpublished candidat dissertation, Moscow Pedagogical Institute 1957). The only Soviet dissertation on the Petrashevtsy besides Leikina's to use any archival sources.

N. I. Mordovchenko, 'Belinskii v bor'be za natural'noi shkoloi', *Literaturnoe nasledstvo*, (Moscow 1948), No. 55.

V. M. Morozov, ' "Finskii vestnik" v bor'be protiv literaturno-obshchestvennoi reaktsii', *Uchenye zapiski Petrazavodskog gos. universiteta*, series historical and philiological sciences, (1956), 1 (6).

—, 'K voprosu ob ideino-obshchestvennoi pozitsii zhurnala "Finskii vestnik"', *Uchenye zapiski Karelo-Finskgo universiteta*, (1955), series 1, No. 5.

—, *Russkii progressivny zhurnal 'Finskii vestnik'*, (Unpublished candidat dissertation, Leningrad University 1961). Very diffuse.

V. Nechaeva, 'Petrashevtsy i T. G. Shevchenko', *Zapiski Otdel Rukopisei Biblioteka Lenina*, (1939), No. 5.

A. Nifontov, *1848 god v Rossii*, (Moscow–Leningrad 1931 & 1949).

A. Nifontov, 'Rossiia i revoliutsiia 1848 goda', ed. F. M. Potemkin & A. I. Molok, *Revoliutsiia 1848–9g.*, (Moscow 1952).

F. G. Nikitina, 'Ateizm petrashevtsev', *Materializm i religii*, (Moscow 1958).

—, Mirovozzreniia M. V. Butashevicha-Petrashevskogo', (Unpublished candidat dissertation Moscow University 1951).

—, 'Obshchestvenno-politicheskie i filosofskie vzgliady M. V. Butashevicha-Petrashevskogo', *Iz istorii russkoi filosofii*, (Moscow 1952).

—, 'Petrashevtsy i Lamennais', *Dostoevskii. Materialy i issledovaniia*, (Leningrad 1978).

Iu. G. Oksman, 'Mery nikolaevskogo tsenzura protiv fourierisma i kommunizma', *Golos minuvshego*, (1917), Nos. 5–6.

—, 'Pis'mo Belinskogo k Gogole kak istoricheskii dokument', *Uchenye zapiski gos. Saratovskogo universiteta*, (1952), vol. xxxi.

O. V. Orlik, *Iz istorii sotsialisticheskikh ucheny*, (Moscow 1964).

—, *Peredovaia Rossiia i revoliutsionnaia Frantsiia*, (Moscow 1973).

I. M. Ostroglazov, 'Knizhnye redkosti', *Russkii arkhiv*, (1891), No. iii.

K. A. Pazhitnov, *Fourierizm v Rossii v kontse sorokovykh godov. Petrashevtsy*, (Petrograd 1917).

—, *Istoriia kooperativnoi mysli*, (Petrograd 1918).

—, *Polozhenie rabochego klassa v Rossii*, (Leningrad 1925).

—, *Razvitie sotsialisticheskikh idei v Rossii*, (Petrograd 1924).

A. Pankratov, 'Poslednyi petrashevets. (N. S. Kashkin)', *Russkoe slovo*, (1910), No. .

A. Piper, *Mirovozzrenie Gertsena*, (Moscow–Leningrad 1935).

R. Pipes ed., *The Russian Intelligentsia*, (New York 1961).

G. V. Plekhanov, 'V. G. Belinskii i V. N. Maikov', *Sochineniia*, (Moscow 1926), vol. x.

M. N. Pokrovskii, *Ocherki istorii russkoi kul'tury*, (Petrograd 1923).

—, *Ocherki istorii russkoi revoliutsionnogo dvizheniia*, (Moscow 192).

P. Pokrovskii, 'Iz ideinoi istorii russkogo sotsializma sorokovykh godov', *Russkoe bogatstvo*, (1909), No. 2.

M. Poliakov, *Belinskii*, (Moscow 1960).

I. V. Porokh, *Istoriia v cheloveke. N. A. Mordvinov – deiatel' obshchestvennogo dvizheniia v Rossii 40–80 godov XIXv.*, (Saratov 1971).

A. Presnov, 'Frantsuzskaia burzhuaznaia revoliutsiia i russkaia obshchestvennai mysl'', *Istoricheskii zhurnal*, (1939), No. 7.

V. Prokofiev, *Petrashevskii*, (Moscow 1962).

L. S. Pustil'nik, *Poet-petrashevets A. N. Pleshcheev*, (Moscow 1975).

A. N. Pypin, *Kharakteristiki literaturnykh mnenyi ot dvatsatikh do piat'desyatikh godov*, (St. Petersburg 1890).

—, *Moi zametki*, (Moscow 1910).

—, 'Valerian Maikov', *Vestnik Evropy*, (1892), No. 2.

Rabochee dvizhenie v Rossii v XIXv., (Moscow 1951), vol. i.

L. Raiskii, *Sotsial'nye vozzreniia petrashevtsev*, (Leningrad 1927).

B. Ratch, *La question polonaise dans la Russie occidentale*, (Paris 1868).

N. V. Riasanovsky, 'Fourierism in Russia: An Estimate of the Petrashevtsy', *American Slavic and East European Review*, (1953), xii, October.

Ia. I. Rostovtsev, *Nastavlenie voenno-uchebbykh zavdenii*, (St. Petersburg 1907).

N. A. Rozhkov, 'Ekonomicheskoe polozhenie Rossii v pervoi polovine XIXv.,' *Sbornik. Istoriia Rossii v XIXv.*, (St. Petersburg 1907).

E. L. Rudnitskaia, *Ogarev v russkom revoliutsionnom dvizhenii*, (Moscow 1969).

N. S. Rusanov, 'Iz ideinoi istorii russkogo sotsializma sorokovykh godov', *Russkoe bogatstvo*, (1909), No. 2.

D. Riazanov, 'Karl Marx i Friedrich Engels v ikh perepiske 1844–82gg.', *Sovremenny mir*, (1914), No. 5.

—, *Karl Marx i russkie liudi sorokovykh godov*, (Moscow 1919).

P. N. Sakhulin, *Russkaia literatura i sotsializm*, (Moscow 1924).

Th. Schiemann, *Geschichte Russlands unter Kaiser Nikolaus I*, (4 vols., Berlin 1908/19).

P. P. Semenov T'ian-Shanskii, *Istoriia poluvekovoi deiatel'nosti imperatorskogo russkogo geograficheskogo obshchestva, 1845–1895*, (St. Petersburg 1896), vol. i.

V. I. Semevskii, 'Akhsharumov', *Vestnik Evropy, (1910), Nos. 11–12.*

—, *'Beklemishev', ibid., (1916), No. 11.*

—, *M. V. Butashevich-Petrashevskii i petrashevtsy*, (Moscow 1922).

—, 'M. V. Butachevich-Petrashevskii v Sibirii', *Golos minuvshego*, (1915), Nos. 1, 3, 5.

—, 'Iz istorii obshchestvennykh idei v Rossii v kontse sorokovykh godakh', *Sbornik. Na slavnom puti*, (St. Petersburg 1901).

—, *Krepostnoe pravo i krest'ianskaia reforma v proizvedeniiakh M. E. Saltykova*, (Petrograd 1917).

V. I. Semevskii, *Krest'ianskii vopros v Rossii v xviii i pervoi polovine xix veka*, (St. Petersburg 1888).

—, 'Kruzhkok Kashkina', *Golos minuvshego*, (1916), Nos. 2–4.

—, 'Petrashevtsy. Beklemishev i Timkovskii', *Vestnik Evropy*, (1916), No. 11.

—, 'Petrashevtsy. Durov, Pal'm, Dostoevskii i Pleshcheev', *Golos minuvshego*, (1915), Nos. 11–12.

—, 'Petrashevtsy i krest'ianskii vopros', *Sbornik. Velikie reformy*, (Moscow 1911).

—, 'Petrashevtsy. Studenty Tolstov i G. M. Danilevskii, meshchanin P. G. Shaposhnikov, literatory Katenev i B. I. Utin', *Golos minuvshego*, (1916), Nos. 11–12.

—, 'Propaganda petrashevtsev v uchebnykh zavedeniiakh,' *Golos minuvshego*, (1917), No. 2.

—, 'Saint-Simonism i fourierism v Rossii v tsarstvovanii Nikolaia Pervogo', *Kniga dlia chteniia po istorii novogo vremeni*, (St. Petersburg 1914), vol. iv.

—, 'Saltykov – petrashevets', *Russkoe bogatstvo*, (1917), No. 1.

—, 'Sledstvie i sud po delu petrashevtsev', *Russkie zapiski*, (1916), Nos. 9–11.

—, 'Vliianie fourierisma v Rossii', *Entsiklopediia Brockhausen*, vol. 36, (1902).

Semevskii also wrote articles on Durov, Fourier, Golovinskii, Grigor'ev, Kashkin, Speshnev and Tol' for *Entsikopediia Granat*.

D. Shcheglov, *Istoriia sotsial'nykh sistem*, (St. Petersburg 1889), vol. ii.

S. P. Shevyrev, *Istoriia imperatorskogo Moskovskogo universiteta*, (Moscow 1855).

N. K. Shil'der, *Imperator Nikolai Pervyi: Ego zhizh' i tsarstvovanie*, (St. Petersburg 1903).

A. A. Shilov, 'Revoliutsiia 1848 g. i ozhidanie ee v Rossii', *Golos minuvshego*, (1918), Nos. 4–6.

S. Shpitser, 'Novoe o dele petrashevtsev', *Katorga i ssylka*, (1926), Nos. 7–8.

A. Skabichevskii, *Ocherki istorii russkoi tsenzura*, (St. Petersburg 1892).

—, 'Sorok let russkoi kritiki', *Sochineniia*, (St. Petersburg 1890), vol. i.

W. Sliwowska, 'Mikolaj Spieszniow', *Slavia Orientalis*, (1958), No. 1.

—, *Sprawa pietraszewcow*, (Warsaw 1964).

M. Sokolovskii 'Delo petrashevtsev kak epizod v istorii obshchestvennogo dvizheniia v Rossii', *Russkaia starina*, (1905), No. 11.

M. Sosnovskii, 'D. D. Akhsharumov', *Russkoe bogatstvo*, (1913), No. 2.

G. Souvrine, *Le Fouriérisme en Russie*, (Paris 1936).

P. S. Squire, *The Third Department. The Establishment and Practices of the Political Police in the Russia of Nicholas I*, (Cambridge 1968).

Iu. M. Steklov, *M. A. Bakunin. Ego zhizn' i deiatel'nost' (1814–1876)*, (Moscow 1926).

—, *N. G. Chernyshevskii. Ego zhizn' i deiatel'nost'*, (St. Petersburg 1909).

V. Svyatlovskii, 'Fourierism v Rossii', *K istorii politicheskoi ekonomii i statistiki v Rossii*, (St. Petersburg 1906).

S. Tkhorzhevskii, *Iskatel' istin, A. P. Balasoglo*, (Leningrad 1974).

—, *Zhizn' i razdum'ia Aleksandra Pal'ma*, (Leningrad 1971).

S. Tokarev, *Krepostnye kartofel'nye bunty*, (Kirov 1939).

N. Troian, 'Filosofskie vozzreniia petrashevtsev', *Pod znamenem marksizma*, (1943), No. 11.

'Tsenzura v tsarstvovanii Nikolaia Pervogo', *Russkaia starina*, (1903), No. 8.

T. I. Usakina, 'Chernyshevskii i Val. Maikov', *Sbornik. N. G. Chernyshevskii. Stat'i i issledovaniia i materialy*, (Saratov 1962), vol. iii.

—, 'O literaturno-kriticheskoi deiatel'nosti molodogo Saltykova', *Literaturnoe nasledstvo*, (Moscow 1959), vol. 67.

—, *Petrashevtsy i literaturno-obshchestvennoe dvizhenie sorokovykh godov XIXv.*, (Saratov 1965).

—, 'M. E. Saltykov – kritik Proudhona', *Iz istorii obshchestvennoi mysli i obshchestvennogo dvizheniia v Rossii*, (Saratov 1964).

S. V. Utechin. *Russian Political Thought. A Concise History*, (London 1964).

S. A. Vengerov, *Istoriia noveishei russkoi literatury*, (St. Petersburg 1885), vol. .

F. Venturi, *Il populismo russo*, (Turin 1952).

—, *Les intellectuels, le peuple et la révolution. Histoire du populisme russe au XIX siècle*, (French tr., Paris 1972). The best and most up-to-date version.

—, *Roots of Revolution*, (English tr., London 1960).

Ch. Vetrinskii, 'D.D. Akhsharumov', *Vestnik Evropy*, (1910), No.5.

—, *T.I. Granovskii i ego vremia*, (Moscow 1912).

—, *V sorokovykh godakh*, (Moscow 1899).

Z. V. Vlasova, 'Pisatel'-petrashevets S.F. Durov', *Vestnik LGU*, (1959), No.8.

—, 'Pisatel'-poet V.V. Tolbin, posle 1849g.', *Vestnik LGU*, (1962), No.2.

—, *Proza petrashevtsev (S.F. Durov, V.V. Tolbin)*, (Unpublished candidat dissertation, Leningrad University 1964).

V.P. Volgin, 'Sotsializm Gertsena', *Ocherki istorii sotsialisticheskikh idei pervaia polovina XIXv.*, (Moscow 1976).

A. Voronov, *Istoriko-statisticheskoe obozrenie uchebnykh zavedenii S.-Peterburgskogo uchebnogo okruga s 1829 po 1853 godu*, (St. Petersburg 1854).

A. Walicki, *A History of Russian Thought. From the Enlightenment to Marxism*, tr. H. Andrews-Rusiecka, (Oxford 1980).

—, *The Slavophile Controversy*, tr. H. Andrews-Rusiecka, (Oxford 1975).

D. Iazykov, *Obzor zhizni i trudov russkikh pisatelei*, (Moscow 1915).

M.L. Iudin, 'K biografiia Pleshcheeva', *Istoricheskii vestnik*, (1905), No.10.

N.P. Zagoskin ed., *Biograficheskii slovar' professorov i prepodavatelei imperatorskogo Kazanskogo universiteta*, (Kazan 1904).

P.A. Zaionchkovskii, *Kirillo-mefodievskii obshchestvo*, (Moscow 1959).

D. Zaslavskii, 'K voprosu o politicheskoi zaveshchanii Belinskogo', *Literaturnoe nasledstvo, Belinskii i*, (Moscow 1948), vol.55.

M.G. Zeldovich, 'K kharakteristike literaturno-esteticheskikh vzgliadov M. V. Petrashevskogo', *Uchenye zapiski Kharkovskogo universiteta*, (1956), vol.70.

V.V. Zhdanov, 'Poeziia v kruzhke petrashevtsev', *Poety-petrashevtsy*, (Leningrad 1940 & 1950).

P.L. Zheglov, 'Literaturnye vzgliady petrashevtsev', *Uchenye zapiski LGU*, series philological sciences, (1939), No.4.

I.I. Zil'berfarb, 'Idei Fourier v Rossii v 30−40kh godah XIXv.', *Istoricheskie zapiski*, (1948), vol.27.

—, *Sotsial'naia filosofiia Ch. Fouriera i ego mesto i istorii sotsialisticheskoi mysli pervoi pologiny XIXv.*, (Moscow 1964).

N.A. Zinevich, *F.G. Tol' (1823−67). Ocherk zhizni i deiatel'nosti*, (Moscow 1964).

V.P. Zotov, 'Nashi entsiklopedicheskie slovari', *Istoricheskii vestnik*, (1888), No.5.

TRANSLITERATION SCHEMA

Russian Alphabet — Library of Congress transliteration

А	— A	Р	— R
Б	— B	С	— S
В	— V	Т	— T
Г	— G	У	— U
Д	— D	Х	— KH
Е	— IE	Ц	— TS
Ж	— Z	Ч	— CH
И Й	— I	Ш	— SH
К	— K	Щ	— SHCH
Л	— L	Ю	— IU
М	— M	Ы	— Y
Н	— N	Э	— E
О	— O	Я	— IA
П	— P	Ь	— '

INDEX OF NAMES